HIGHER EDUCATION

in the

REVOLUTIONARY DECADES

edited by

LEWIS B. MAYHEW

Professor of Education
Stanford University

LB2321
.M46

95195

McCutchan Publishing Corporation
2526 Grove Street
Berkeley, California 94704

Library of Congress Catalog Card Number 67-20868

Printed in the United States of America

Contents

INTRODUCTION

The period since World War II is one of the most revolutionary in history. Compared to the development of modern weapons, the revolt of colonial peoples, the discovery of new sources of energy, and the development of new systems of transportation, the discoveries of fire and steam power and the inventions of gunpowder and printing seem like halting first steps.

Higher education is part of this revolutionary development, yet is expected to respond to it as an external agent. The purpose of these essays is to indicate the nature of the revolution, how higher education has already changed, the problems which remain to be solved, and something of the future; they are presented in the hope that they will provoke thought and perhaps suggest ways by which higher education can successfully adapt.

Any anthology reflects the editor's point of view. Several selections deal with the affluent society, for I believe that it represents a fundamental shift of life style. Other essays deal with the dilemma of the American Negro, both as an example of the world-wide revolt of have-not peoples and as an example of how the United States is affected by its most urgent domestic problem.

I have chosen not to include all areas of change in American society; I believe, however, that those I have selected are the key areas from which others are derived.

LEWIS B. MAYHEW

Stanford, California

SECTION I

American Higher Education and Social Change

LEWIS B. MAYHEW
Stanford University

Higher education, like other social institutions, performs services which the supporting society requires, and its success and viability are determined by how well it performs and by how responsive it is to changing social demands. Medieval universities were established to provide the leadership necessary to the church which had fallen heir to the Roman Empire. Additionally, they provided the trained assistance needed by the secular states which were emerging from the divisive feudal system, for strong monarchy could be realized only when the power of feudal lords was replaced by more centralized government. Such government required trained professionals. The founders of American colonial colleges, such as Harvard and William and Mary, recognized that the colonies could not long depend for leadership on those educated in England. These colleges were intended to produce religious and secular leaders who could fuse the twin intellectual traditions of the Reformation and the Renaissance into an ethos to sustain an English Puritan culture in the New World.

When an institution is unresponsive to the fundamental demands and needs of its society, it loses its vitality and becomes irrelevant. This happened to the American college chiefly because of its preoccupation with a classical curriculum and continued until a more relevant curriculum was developed. Similarly, in France the Napoleonic centralization of life left the provincial universities without the resources to be of vital service to their regions; eventually the concept of university itself was equated with bureaucracy.

The interpretation of higher education as primarily an institution in the service of society is not unanimously accepted. Robert M. Hutchins remarks that

The fundamental objection to the current general attitude toward

3

the purposes of the university in America is that it takes the society as given, with all its folly and pretentiousness, and asks the university to supply some of the facilities, most of the hands, a lot of the energy and all of the ideas that will enable the society to achieve its mistaken goals.[1]

He believes that the university should lead society and not merely adapt, and so it could if that particular mandate were ever really given to higher education. American educational leadership has never been in the vanguard in developing social thought. Colleges and universities have generally not taken positions as institutions, on the grounds that they should be neutral forums. And presidents and professors have apparently seen their roles as providers of the education, research, and service which Americans want.

Since World War II the society has made heavy demands for service on higher education. As colleges and universities have attempted to respond, they have experienced serious dislocations and obstacles. The proof of their adaptability and creativity is that many of the critical challenges have been met and the institution has not only survived, but prospered. But perhaps higher education has succeeded too well; many now regard it as a panacea for all of society's ills.

When Ronald Thompson published his *Impending Tidal Wave of Students*, predicting between six and seven million students wishing a college education by 1970, he addressed an unprepared profession.[2] No college or university had a long-term plan. Most colleges had provided for the enrollment of veterans after World War II by augmenting limited space with temporary facilities. Moreover, colleges did not exist in some rapidly-developing regions of the country. Even in states such as Ohio, where there were several colleges, the available space was inadequate if Thompson's predictions were accurate. Many colleges continue to be overcrowded, and some institutions are still without plans for the future. However, the significant fact is that higher education has been able to accept almost six million students. Further, through such devices as state master plans, it appears likely that many more students can be accommodated.

The level of training of faculty is a critical condition of the accommodation. In the American system in the twentieth century, the Ph.D. has been considered the ideal preparation for college teachers. However,

---

[1] Robert M. Hutchins, *The University of Utopia* (Chicago: University of Chicago Press, 1964).

[2] Ronald Thompson, *Impending Tidal Wave of Students* (Washington: American Council on Education, 1954).

faced with unprecedented demands for collegiate instruction, a choice had to be made between rejecting many applicants for college and diluting the quality of instructional staff. We elected the latter. Thus, during the late 1950's the proportion of new college faculty members possessing the doctorate dropped from approximately thirty-five percent to below twenty-five percent.

The question then became whether the level of quality could be regained. Graduate schools answered by enlarging their capacities and producing more Ph.D.'s. In the opinion of Allan Cartter,[3] although there will be a shortage of professors in some fields for several years, by the early 1970's the supply of college teachers will be adequate. Indeed, Cartter can even visualize an oversupply by the early 1980's, especially if the number of graduate schools increases. Not all observers are as sanguine about an early solution to the shortage of college teachers. However, higher education has come closer to responding to the challenge of numbers than most theorists believed possible.

The large increase in the number of college teachers is due, at least in part, to higher salaries. For generations American college faculties, by accepting marginal salaries, in effect subsidized students. By the early 1950's, in a period of general affluence, faculty salaries had lagged seriously behind both professional and nonprofessional incomes, so that by 1956, in terms of 1939 dollars, faculty purchasing power had actually declined.

At that point, stimulated by a White House Conference on Education beyond High School, the American Association of University Professors, and college administrators, higher education began a program of salary increases with a goal of doubling salaries between 1958 and 1970. The most recently published averages indicate that if present trends continue the goal will have been reached, with faculty salaries finally becoming competitive with other professions.

Such a change could come about only because new methods of financing were developed. Rising personal incomes permitted both public and private institutions to increase tuition charges which, combined with increases in enrollment, provided a large share of the resources needed to increase faculty salaries. Of course faculty salaries were only part of the general financial crisis facing higher education and were not the only neglected area. Rising costs and necessary expansion required development of other sources of income. And they were developed. By 1958 corporate contributions had reached $98 million.

----

[3] Unpublished paper delivered at the annual conference, American Council on Education, 1966.

Alumni giving has also increased as have legislative appropriations for tax-supported schools. For example, in the southern region from 1959 to 1966 state appropriations for higher education more than doubled.

However, all of this support was not enough, and the resources of the Federal government were called upon. The college housing program, the National Defense Education Act, the provision for construction of educational facilities, and the education acts of 1965 brought Federal funds in sufficient volume to improve the financial condition of most colleges and universities.

Acceptance of large-scale Federal aid became palatable when several misapprehensions concerning the proper role of government in education were allayed. For example, the fear has persisted that Federal aid would breach the wall between church and state; especially in the South there has been the fear that Federal aid would end race segregation in education; and less specifically there has been general uneasiness that Federal aid would mean Federal control, and education has long prized local control and institutional autonomy.

Now to varying degrees these issues have been resolved. Supreme Court decisions, Federal legislation, the successes of the civil rights movement, and a gradual moderating of southern opinion have ended segregation as a theoretical ideal. Thus most southern institutions now can accept Federal funds because to do so imposes no greater integration than already exists. By differentiating between higher and lower education, between religious and secular education, and by concentrating on aid to students or specific programs, formulas have been developed for assistance to church-related institutions. Congress and the Federal government have exercised self-restraint, and there are few examples of Federal regulation of higher education as a requirement for Federal funds. Undoubtedly Federal financing is a powerful influence on educational policy but outright control does not exist.

The changes in higher education have not been limited to fiscal matters. In the 1950's college students were properly described as silent and apathetic. Colleges and universities apparently were little concerned with student values and attitudes. In the words of one scholar,[4] students entered college self-centered, unmoved by social problems, and divinely self-satisfied—and they graduated the same way. Now a fundamental shift has taken place. Students are involved in protest, work in altruistic causes, such as the Peace Corps and VISTA, and are deeply troubled about our malfunctioning society. The conclusion is inescapable that much student activism stems from influence of professors who

---

[4] Philip Jacob, *Changing Values in College* (New York: Harper and Brothers, 1956).

have sought to end student apathy. In a very real sense higher education has responded to the charge of noninvolvement.

And it has similarly responded to the charge of not providing a sufficiently rigorous education, especially in the areas of science, mathematics, and engineering. After World War II we took for granted our pre-eminence in science and technology, but Soviet achievements in atomic power and space exploration rudely jolted our tranquility. As a result, the whole educational system, including especially college-preparatory curriculums, was tightened and accelerated. The demands on college students became so intense that there is now some feeling that academic pressures have taken the joy out of learning. And the declining numbers of new enrollments in engineering and the physical sciences were reversed to the extent that in 1965 over 37 per cent of the winners of National Merit Scholarships entered these fields.

Where higher education was once regarded as something of a finishing school for the children of the middle- and well-to-do classes, it is now an essential for an ever-larger percentage of the college-age group. Professors and administrators are highly regarded and in demand by the industrial and political centers of national power. Higher education has become a vital national resource and there is every reason to hope that its prodigious financial needs will be met.

American higher education now finds itself at a high point in its development. It is affluent, well regarded, and perhaps overly self-satisfied. James A. Perkins[5] may represent a general sentiment when he says that

> The university has become one of the great institutions of the modern world. In the United States it is central in the conduct of our national life. It is the most sophisticated agency we have for advancing scholarship and research. It is crucial in the transmittal of knowledge from one generation to the next. And it is increasingly vital in the application of knowledge to the problems of modern society.

Whether such high esteem will continue depends on the response to challenges which have arisen even while colleges and universities were achieving eminence. One of the challenges is the question of educational relevance. Unfortunately, logical development of subjects, based on continuing research, has replaced the student as the central concern. Undergraduate courses in chemistry, physics, psychology, and even in literature are considered primarily as the first disciplinary steps necessary to prepare future scholars and researchers. Such courses

---

[5] James A. Perkins, *The University in Transition* (Princeton: Princeton University Press, 1966).

make no attempt to accommodate the problems and tensions which students experience. For instance, too often a course in history is only a device for expounding the professor's theory of history instead of a chance to help students see life from a historical perspective. Students question the relevance of their educational experience. They are perplexed by a democracy which tolerates a caste system and by the apparent gap between ideal and performance. They live in an age of affluence and find that it has not produced satisfied people. And they want their college courses to relate to these concerns. When the institution fails to provide the appropriate curricular structures, they turn to the utopians for guidance and to each other for instruction. The free university and the experimental college are students' attempts to remedy irrelevant curriculums.

Historically, colleges and universities have been class-related institutions. Family socioeconomic level, race, and geographic location of the home are reasonable predictors of academic success. But higher education can no longer afford the luxury of exclusivity, for it is the principal device by which an open society can be maintained. Colleges and universities have been slow in responding to the need for making their services available to the disadvantaged. It is true that most northern institutions indicate they would like to recruit more Negro students, but only if they possess the necessary skills and aptitudes needed to survive the academic program. Public junior colleges say they want to serve all of the people, but insist that low-income Negro students enter and participate on exactly the same terms as do white students from middle-class homes. Knowing that it costs at least $1500 a year for a student to attend a tuition-free institution and that many Negro family incomes are less than twice that amount, colleges still insist that Negroes are welcome. Higher education must make large and relevant provisions to meet these urgent needs if it is to remain a vital social agency.

These demands are made by a society which has been cut loose from its past. The medieval university spoke out of a well-accepted theology as did the colonial colleges. Thus character development was a major responsibility of education; many early American college presidents believed that moral training was considerably more important than intellectual growth. And that training was generally accepted by students for it was an accurate reflection of early American life. Now, however, the conditions of life and society have changed drastically. The bomb and the real possibility of genocide have brought into question long-established moral principles. Refined methods of contraception have removed fear of pregnancy as a sanction to enforce sexual continence. Cybernation throws the work ethic into doubt. Knowledge of the genetic code and the possibility of scientific creation of life challenge the teachings of orthodox religions. And contemporary religious writings raise questions whether orthodoxy has any real contemporary meaning. All of us, students most particularly and perhaps most vociferously, are seeking new standards by which we can live. And higher education is one of the institutions being severely strained for answers,

As American higher education has accommodated the many demands for its services, it has become much larger and more specialized. And both size and specialization have brought problems. For example, the administrative machinery designed for a small student body cannot accommodate a large one. States seek to allocate resources to a complex system of higher education as they once did to small independent institutions. Social regulations derived from a small, homogeneous student body are applied to large, cosmopolitan campuses. Facilities appropriate for a small, rural college are transplanted without change to an urban setting. Admission procedures which falter in dealing with a million freshmen must surely fail when five million seek admission by the mid-1970's.

The point has been made that in the past higher education responded to society's need for trained workers. And contemporary higher education has the same end. But the nature of work is changing as is the demand for workers. Educated adults are not prepared for the unprecedented leisure which the future promises. Their sense of identity has come from their work, their ethical values are related to work, and their education has been largely motivated by work expectations. The essential feelings of worth and identity which work once provided will in the future have to be gained by creative use of leisure.

It is anticipated that, by the 1980's, over eighty per cent of college-age youth will be involved in some form of higher education. Clearly, not all will want or need the same kind of institution. To insure the best possible match of student and institution, without jeopardizing the individual's freedom of choice, is the dilemma which confronts educational planners.

A related phenomenon is the problem of maintaining a sufficiently diverse system of higher education to serve our pluralistic society. And this diversity has been provided by public and private institutions—large and small, secular and religious, single- or multipurpose. Now, however, several countertendencies have begun to operate. One is the propensity of all institutions to become complex and multipurpose. Thus teachers' colleges and technical institutes become universities, liberal arts colleges begin to offer graduate work, and junior colleges want to evolve into four-year institutions. State master plans for higher education seek to maintain the needed diversity. For example, the California legislature had defined exclusive jurisdictions for junior colleges, state colleges, and the state university. At its inception the plan was considered a model for emulation, but the junior and state colleges now criticize the plan for defining their roles too narrowly. Perhaps master plans are no panacea either.

Until the late 1950's private institutions educated the majority of college students; since then public colleges and universities have assumed the major share, and the trend is continuing at the rate of two per cent per year. By the mid-1970's private education will probably enroll a maximum of twenty per cent of all students. Public schools, because they are tax-supported, are politically sensitive. With so much of the nation's education dependent on public schools, the potential dangers of political influence will be intensified.

We have briefly described several of the challenges which confront higher education in America in the revolutionary decades. In order to understand the revolution, it is necessary to examine in greater detail the more explosive of the issues and the various responses, effective and ineffective, which higher education is making to them. The bulk of this book will present elaborations of such matters.

THE REVOLUTIONS

World War II exerted intense pressures on American society, and higher education has been greatly affected. The year 1945 may well be regarded by future historians as a major turning point. Before that year changes had been generally evolutionary; now we are in the midst of many revolutions. In the essays which follow, the effects of those revolutions on higher education are explored.

The Dependence Effect

JOHN KENNETH GALBRAITH

The notion that wants do not become less urgent the more amply the individual is supplied is broadly repugnant to common sense. It is something to be believed only by those who wish to believe. Yet the conventional wisdom must be tackled on its own terrain. Intertemporal comparisons of an individual's state of mind do rest on doubtful grounds. Who can say for sure that the deprivation which afflicts him with hunger is more painful than the deprivation which afflicts him with envy of his neighbor's new car? In the time that has passed since he was poor his soul may have become subject to a new and deeper searing. And where a society is concerned, comparisons between marginal satisfactions when it is poor and those when it is affluent will involve not only the same individual at different times but different individuals at different times. The scholar who wishes to believe that with increasing affluence there is no reduction in the urgency of desires and goods is not without points for debate. However plausible the case against him, it cannot be proven. In the defense of the conventional wisdom this amounts almost to invulnerability.

However, there is a flaw in the case. If the individual's wants are to be urgent they must be original with himself. They cannot be urgent if they must be contrived for him. And above all they must not be contrived by the process of production by which they are satisfied. For this means that the whole case for the urgency of production, based on the urgency of wants, falls to the ground. One cannot defend production as satisfying wants if that production creates the wants.

Were it so that a man on arising each morning was assailed by demons which instilled in him a passion sometimes for silk shirts, some-

From *The Affluent Society* by J. K. Galbraith, (Boston: Houghton Mifflin Co., 1958), pgs 152–160. Reprinted by permission of Houghton Mifflin Co.

times for kitchenware, sometimes for chamber pots, and sometimes for orange squash, there would be every reason to applaud the effort to find the goods, however odd, that quenched this flame. But should it be that his passion was the result of his first having cultivated the demons, and should it also be that his effort to allay it stirred the demons to ever greater and greater effort, there would be question as to how rational was his solution. Unless restrained by conventional attitudes, he might wonder if the solution lay with more goods or fewer demons.

So it is that if production creates the wants it seeks to satisfy, or if the wants emerge *pari passu* with the production, then the urgency of the wants can no longer be used to defend the urgency of the production. Production only fills a void that it has itself created.

II

The point is so central that it must be pressed. Consumer wants can have bizarre, frivolous, or even immoral origins, and an admirable case can still be made for a society that seeks to satisfy them. But the case cannot stand if it is the process of satisfying wants that creates the wants. For then the individual who urges the importance of production to satisfy these wants is precisely in the position of the onlooker who applauds the efforts of the squirrel to keep abreast of the wheel that is propelled by his own efforts.

That wants are, in fact, the fruit of production will now be denied by few serious scholars. And a considerable number of economists, though not always in full knowledge of the implications, have conceded the point. In the observation cited at the end of the preceding chapter Keynes noted that needs of "the second class," i.e., those that are the result of efforts to keep abreast or ahead of one's fellow being "may indeed be insatiable; for the higher the general level the higher still are they."[1] And emulation has always played a considerable role in the views of other economists of want creation. One man's consumption becomes his neighbor's wish. This already means that the process by which wants are satisfied is also the process by which wants are created. The more wants that are satisfied the more new ones are born.

However, the argument has been carried farther. A leading modern theorist of consumer behavior, Professor Duesenberry, has stated explicitly that "ours is a society in which one of the principal social goals is a higher standard of living.... [This] has great significance for the theory of consumption ... the desire to get superior goods

---

[1] *Op. cit.*

takes on a life of its own. It provides a drive to higher expenditure which may even be stronger than that arising out of the needs which are supposed to be satisfied by that expenditure."[2] The implications of this view are impressive. The notion of independently established need now sinks into the background. Because the society sets great store by ability to produce a high living standard, it evaluates people by the products they possess. The urge to consume is fathered by the value system which emphasizes the ability of the society to produce. The more that is produced the more that must be owned in order to maintain the appropriate prestige. The latter is an important point, for, without going as far as Duesenberry in reducing goods to the role of symbols of prestige in the affluent society, it is plain that his argument fully implies that the production of goods creates the wants that the goods are presumed to satisfy.

III

The even more direct link between production and wants is provided by the institutions of modern advertising and salesmanship. These cannot be reconciled with the notion of independently determined desires, for their central function is to create desires—to bring into being wants that previously did not exist.[3] This is accomplished by the producer of the goods or at his behest. A broad empirical relationship exists between what is spent on production of consumers' goods and what is spent in synthesizing the desires for that production. A new consumer product must be introduced with a suitable advertising campaign to arouse an interest in it. The path for an expansion of output must be paved by a suitable expansion in the advertising budget. Outlays for the manufacturing of a product are not more important in the strategy of modern business enterprise than outlays for the manufacturing of demand for the product. None of this is novel. All would be regarded as elementary by the most retarded student in the nation's

---

[2] James S. Duesenberry, *Income, Saving and the Theory of Consumer Behavior* (Cambridge, Mass.: Harvard University Press, 1949), p. 28.

[3] Advertising is not a simple phenomenon. It is also important in competitive strategy and want creation is, ordinarily, a complementary result of efforts to shift the demand curve of the individual firm at the expense of others or (less importantly, I think) to change its shape by increasing the degree of product differentiation. Some of the failure of economists to identify advertising with want creation may be attributed to the undue attention that its use in purely competitive strategy has attracted. It should be noted, however, that the competitive manipulation of consumer desire is only possible, at least on any appreciable scale, when such need is not strongly felt.

most primitive school of business administration. The cost of this want formation is formidable. In 1956 total advertising expenditure—though, as noted, not all of it may be assigned to the synthesis of wants —amounted to about ten billion dollars. For some years it had been increasing at a rate in excess of a billion dollars a year. Obviously, such outlays must be integrated with the theory of consumer demand. They are too big to be ignored.

But such integration means recognizing that wants are dependent on production. It accords to the producer the function both of making the goods and of making the desires for them. It recognizes that production, not only passively through emulation, but actively through advertising and related activities, creates the wants it seeks to satisfy.

The businessman and the lay reader will be puzzled over the emphasis which I give to a seemingly obvious point. The point is indeed obvious. But it is one which, to a singular degree, economists have resisted. They have sensed, as the layman does not, the damage to established ideas which lurks in these relationships. As a result, incredibly, they have closed their eyes (and ears) to the most obtrusive of all economic phenomena, namely modern want creation.

This is not to say that the evidence affirming the dependence of wants on advertising has been entirely ignored. It is one reason why advertising has so long been regarded with such uneasiness by economists. Here is something which cannot be accommodated easily to existing theory. More pervious scholars have speculated on the urgency of desires which are so obviously the fruit of such expensively contrived campaigns for popular attention. Is a new breakfast cereal or detergent so much wanted if so much must be spent to compel in the consumer the sense of want? But there has been little tendency to go on to examine the implications of this for the theory of consumer demand and even less for the importance of production and productive efficiency. These have remained sacrosanct. More often the uneasiness has been manifested in a general disapproval of advertising and advertising men, leading to the occasional suggestion that they shouldn't exist. Such suggestions have usually been ill received.

And so the notion of independently determined wants still survives. In the face of all the forces of modern salesmanship it still rules, almost undefiled, in the textbooks. And it still remains the economist's mission—and on few matters is the pedagogy so firm—to seek unquestioningly the means for filling these wants. This being so, production remains of prime urgency. We have here, perhaps, the ultimate triumph of the conventional wisdom in its resistance to the evidence of the eyes. To equal it one must imagine a humanitarian who was long ago persuaded of the grievous shortage of hospital facilities in the town. He continues to importune the passers-by for money for more beds and refuses to notice that the town doctor is deftly knocking over pedestrians with his car to keep up the occupancy.

And in unraveling the complex we should always be careful not to overlook the obvious. The fact that wants can be synthesized by advertising, catalyzed by salesmanship, and shaped by the discreet manipulations of the persuaders shows that they are not very urgent. A man who is hungry need never be told of his need for food. If he is inspired by his appetite, he is immune to the influence of Messrs. Batten, Barton, Durstine & Osborn. The latter are effective only with those who are so far removed from physical want that they do not already know what they want. In this state alone men are open to persuasion.

IV

The general conclusion of these pages is of such importance for this essay that it had perhaps best be put with some formality. As a society becomes increasingly affluent, wants are increasingly created by the process by which they are satisfied. This may operate passively. Increases in consumption, the counterpart of increases in production, act by suggestion or emulation to create wants. Or producers may proceed actively to create wants through advertising and salesmanship. Wants thus come to depend on output. In technical terms it can no longer be assumed that welfare is greater at an all-round higher level of production than at a lower one. It may be the same. The higher level of production has, merely, a higher level of want creation necessitating a higher level of want satisfaction. There will be frequent occasion to refer to the way wants depend on the process by which they are satisfied. It will be convenient to call it the Dependence Effect.

We may now contemplate briefly the conclusions to which this analysis has brought us.

Plainly the theory of consumer demand is a peculiarly treacherous friend of the present goals of economics. At first glance it seems to defend the continuing urgency of production and our preoccupation with it as a goal. The economist does not enter into the dubious moral arguments about the importance or virtue of the wants to be satisfied. He doesn't pretend to compare mental states of the same or different people at different times and to suggest that one is less urgent than another. The desire is there. That for him is sufficient. He sets about in a workmanlike way to satisfy desire, and accordingly he sets the proper store by the production that does. Like woman's his work is never done.

But this rationalization, handsomely though it seems to serve, turns destructively on those who advance it once it is conceded that wants are themselves both passively and deliberately the fruits of the process by which they are satisfied. Then the production of goods satisfies the wants that the consumption of these goods creates or that the producers of goods synthesize. Production induces more wants and the need for more production. So far, in a major *tour de force*, the implications have been ignored. But this obviously is a perilous solution. It cannot long survive discussion.

Among the many models of the good society no one has urged the squirrel wheel. Moreover, as we shall see presently, the wheel is not one that revolves with perfect smoothness. Aside from its dubious cultural charm, there are serious structural weaknesses which may one day embarrass us. For the moment, however, it is sufficient to reflect on the difficult terrain which we are traversing. . . . [We have seen] how deeply we were committed to production for reasons of economic security. Not the goods but the employment provided by their production was the thing by which we set ultimate store. Now we find our concern for goods further undermined. It does not arise in spontaneous consumer need. Rather, the dependence effect means that it grows out of the process of production itself. If production is to increase, the wants must be effectively contrived. In the absence of the contrivance the increase would not occur. This is not true of all goods, but that it is true of a substantial part is sufficient. It means that since the demand for this part would not exist, were it not contrived, its utility or urgency, ex contrivance, is zero. If we regard this production as marginal, we may say that the marginal utility of present aggregate output, ex advertising and salesmanship, is zero. Clearly the attitudes and values which make production the central achievement of our society have some exceptionally twisted roots.

Perhaps the thing most evident of all is how new and varied become the problems we must ponder when we break the nexus with the work of Ricardo and face the economics of affluence of the world in which we live. It is easy to see why the conventional wisdom resists so stoutly such change. It is a far, far better thing to have a firm anchor in nonsense than to put out on the troubled seas of thought.

The Invisible Wall

KENNETH B. CLARK

"Ghetto" was the name for the Jewish quarter in sixteenth-century Venice. Later, it came to mean any section of a city to which Jews were confined. America has contributed to the concept of the ghetto the restriction of persons to a special area and the limiting of their freedom of choice on the basis of skin color. The dark ghetto's invisible walls have been erected by the white society, by those who have power, both to confine those who have *no* power and to perpetuate their powerlessness. The dark ghettos are social, political, educational, and—above all—economic colonies. Their inhabitants are subject peoples, victims of the greed, cruelty, insensitivity, guilt, and fear of their masters.

The objective dimensions of the American urban ghettos are overcrowded and deteriorated housing, high infant mortality, crime, and disease. The subjective dimensions are resentment, hostility, despair, apathy, self-depreciation, and its ironic companion, compensatory grandiose behavior.

The ghetto is ferment, paradox, conflict, and dilemma. Yet within its pervasive pathology exists a surprising human resilience. The ghetto is hope, it is despair, it is churches and bars. It is aspiration for change, and it is apathy. It is vibrancy, it is stagnation. It is courage, and it is defeatism. It is cooperation and concern, and it is suspicion, competitiveness, and rejection. It is the surge toward assimilation, and it is alienation and withdrawal within the protective walls of the ghetto.

The pathologies of the ghetto community perpetuate themselves through cumulative ugliness, deterioration, and isolation and strengthen the Negro's sense of worthlessness, giving testimony to his impotence. Yet the ghetto is not totally isolated. The mass media—radio, television, moving pictures, magazines, and the press—penetrate, indeed, invade the ghetto in continuous and inevitable communication, largely one-way, and project the values and aspirations, the manners and the style of the larger white-dominated society. Those who are required to live in congested and rat-infested homes are aware that others are not so dehumanized. Young people in the ghetto are aware that other young people have been taught to read, that they have been prepared for college, and can compete successfully for white-collar, managerial, and executive jobs. Whatever accommodations they themselves must make to the negative realities which dominate their own lives, they know consciously or unconsciously that their fate is not the common fate of mankind. They tend to regard their predicament as a consequence of personal disability or as an inherent and imposed powerlessness which all Negroes share.

The privileged white community is at great pains to blind itself to conditions of the ghetto, but the residents of the ghetto are not themselves blind to life as it is outside of the ghetto. They observe that others enjoy a better life, and this knowledge brings a conglomerate of hostility, despair, and hope. If the ghetto could be contained totally, the chances of social revolt would be decreased, if not eliminated, but it cannot be contained and the outside world intrudes. The Negro lives in part in the world of television and motion pictures, bombarded by the myths of the American middle class, often believing as literal truth their pictures of luxury and happiness, and yet at the same time confronted by a harsh world of reality where the dreams do not come true or change into nightmares. The discrepancy between the reality and the dream burns into their consciousness. The oppressed can never be sure whether their failures reflect personal inferiority or the fact of color. This persistent and agonizing conflict dominates their lives.

The young people in Harlem, in the Negro ghettos of Chicago, Washington, Cleveland, Detroit, Los Angeles, and other cities, who persist, in spite of obstacles, in seeking an education, who insist upon going to night school and then the day session of a municipal college, whose parents, friends, or teachers encourage and support them demonstrate that a positive resolution of the ghetto's nuclear conflict is possible. But many resolve the conflict negatively—in either a passive or defiant way. Those within the ghetto who are defeated—those who accept the "evidence" of their personal inferiority and impotence, those who express a pervasive sense of personal failure through stagnation and despair, who drop out of school, who depend on marijuana and narcotics—demonstrate a passively negative and self-destructive solution.

The overt delinquent, the acting-out rebel, on the other hand, seeks his salvation in defiant, aggressive, and in the end self-destructive forms. Because the larger society has clearly rejected him, he rejects—or appears to reject—the values, the aspirations, and techniques of that society. His conscious or unconscious argument is that he cannot hope to win meaningful self-esteem through the avenues ordinarily available to more privileged individuals. These avenues have been blocked for him through inadequate education, through job discrimination, and through a system of social and political power which is not responsive to his needs. When a warlord of one of the last of Harlem's active fighting gangs was asked why he did not "go downtown and get a job," he laughed and replied:

> Oh come on. Get off that crap. I make $40 or $50 a day selling marijuana. You want me to go down to the garment district and push one of those trucks through the street and at the end of the week take home $40 or $50 if I'm lucky? They don't have animals doing what you want me to do. There would be some society to protect animals if anybody had them pushing them damn trucks around. I'm better than an animal, but nobody protects me. Go away, mister. I got to look out for myself.

Such rebels are scornful of what they consider the hypocrisy and the dishonesty of the larger society. They point to corruption and criminal behavior among respected middle-class whites. Almost every delinquent or marginal adolescent in a Negro urban ghetto claims to know where and how the corrupt policeman accepts graft from the numbers runners and the pimps and the prostitutes. The close association, collaboration, and at times identity, of criminals and the police is the pattern of day-to-day life in the ghetto as these young people come to know and accept it. Not only do they not respect the police, but they see the police as part of their own total predicament.

Large numbers of other ghetto youth, however, are caught in the paradox of the ghetto unable to resolve their personal conflicts either in positive and socially acceptable forms of adjustment or in direct and assertive antisocial behavior. They are aware of the values and standards of the larger society, but they know that they are not personally equipped to meet its demands. They have neither succumbed totally to pathology nor have they been able to emerge from it. As adults they live out lives they feel helpless to change, in a kind of unstable equilibrium, aware of their plight and yet accepting it. They are the ones who listen to Malcolm X but do not join; who vote Democratic if they bother to register but recognize at the same time that City Hall will do little for them. They are momentarily stimulated by the verbal militance of certain Negro newspaper editors and soapbox orators; they gain vicarious satisfaction through temporary identification with the flamboyance and antiwhite verbal extremisms of charismatic Negro politicians. They send their children to bad public schools reluctantly because they do not have the money for private schools. They are the great potential who could engage in constructive social action or who could become the pawns of the demagogues. They have no inner-determined direction. Whoever develops any movement toward power in the ghetto finally does so through winning the allegiance of this group—the largest in the ghetto—not of the semicriminal and certainly not of the elite and comfortable.

The ferment within Negro communities throughout the nation—hitherto more obvious in certain Southern communities, but beginning to express itself with increasing intensity and even spasmodic ferocity in such Northern urban communities as Chicago, Boston, Philadelphia, Rochester, and New York—suggests that the past cycle, in which personal and community powerlessness reinforces each other, is being supplanted by a more forceful pattern of personal and community action. This is proof that the reservoir of energy was there, ready to be stirred by hope, for effective or even sporadic protest could never have emerged out of total stagnation.

Although the civil rights movement gives Negroes more leverage, enabling many to channel their energies into constructive protest, there is a possibility that these energies could also be diluted into meaningless catharsis. Demonstrations that do not lead to results may become only one more safety valve—as the church has long been for Negroes—releasing Negro energies without the transformation of society, without any actual change in their relative status.

If mobilized community power and protest do succeed in winning concrete positive changes, Negro self-confidence and pride will grow, and a new cycle of greater personal and community effectiveness should emerge. But it would not be realistic for the white community to expect protest to subside in the face of gains, for the closer the Negro community gets to the attainment of its goals—the removal of the causes and effects of racial exploitation and powerlessness—the more impatient will Negroes become for total equality. In the complex turbulence of the Negro ghetto, and consistent with the affirmative dynamics of the civil rights thrust, success feeds hope and provides the strength and the motivation for further activity. This, in turn, makes existing barriers even more intolerable. Accelerated impatience and the lowering of the threshold of frustration toward remaining inequities, paradoxically increase the chances of racial tensions and ferment and conflict. Failure would reinforce the sense of stagnation and despair and establish as fact the sense of personal and group powerlessness. A truly hopeless group makes no demands and certainly does not insist upon stark social confrontations.

The summer of 1964 brought violent protests to the ghettos of America's cities, not in mobilization of effective power, but as an outpouring of unplanned revolt. The revolts in Harlem were not led by a mob, for a mob is an uncontrolled social force bent on irrational destruction. The revolts in Harlem were, rather, a weird social defiance. Those involved in them were, in general, not the lowest class of Harlem residents—not primarily looters and semicriminals—but marginal Negroes who were upwardly mobile, demanding a higher status than their families had. This was not a race riot in the sense that mobs of whites were assaulting mobs of Negroes or vice versa, yet the fact of race was pervasive. The 1964 Harlem riot was indeed in many respects more frightening than a race riot and the participants' deliberate mockery more threatening than a mob. Small groups of young people seemed to take delight in taunting the police, whose white faces were accentuated by their white helmets: "Here's a nigger, kill me." Even those Negroes who threw bottles and bricks from the roofs were not in the grip of a wild abandon, but seemed deliberately to be prodding the police to behave openly as the barbarians that the Negroes felt they actually were. You cannot hear conversations of a mob, but during the disturbance in Harlem, groups of young people discussed their plans: "I'll go home and come back tomorrow. Whitey will still be here." "I don't want to be killed tonight; tomorrow will be all right." There was an eerie, surrealistic quality, a silence within the din, punctuated by gunfire and sporadic shattering of glass, a calm within the chaos, a deliberateness within the hysteria. The Negro seemed to feel nothing could happen to him that had not happened already; he behaved as if he had nothing to lose. His was an oddly controlled rage that seemed to say, during those days of social despair, "We have had enough. The only weapon you have is bullets. The only thing you can do is to kill us." Paradoxically, his apparent lawlessness was a protest against lawlessness directed against *him*. His acts were a desperate assertion of his desire to be treated as a man. He was affirmative up to the point of inviting death; he insisted upon being visible and understood. If this was the only way to relate to society at large, he would die rather than be ignored.

At times of overt social unrest, many white persons who claim to be in favor of civil rights and assert that they are "friends" of the Negro will admonish the Negro not to engage in disruptive and lawless demonstrations lest he incite racism and reverse the progress made in his behalf. These often well-meaning requests may reflect the unconscious condescension of benign prejudices. They demonstrate mistaken assumptions concerning the nature and dynamics of Negro protest. It is argued, for example, that Negroes should "choose" only those techniques, tactics, and demonstrations which do not inconvenience the dominant white society; the oppressed are urged to be concerned about the comfort and sensitivities of those they regard as their oppressors. The implication is that if they do not, middle-class whites will use their own power to retaliate against all Negroes. Negroes are increasingly reminded of the sting of the "white backlash." Many middle-class Negroes as well as whites accept these arguments and behave accordingly. Yet the threat is not new. The struggle of those with power to deny power to those who have none is age-old, and accommodation and appeasement have not resolved it. The "white backlash" is a new name for an old phenomenon, white resistance to the acceptance of the Negro as a human being. As the Negro demands such status—as he develops more and more effective techniques to obtain it, and as these techniques come closer to success—the resistance to his demands rises in intensity and alarm. The forms it takes vary from the overt and barbaric murders and bombings to the more subtle innuendo of irritation and disparagement.

Many whites also assume that a governing group of Negro leaders chooses tactics for the Negro masses. Yet leaders of the stature and responsibility of Roy Wilkins and Whitney M. Young, Jr., James Farmer or Martin Luther King cannot impose tactics upon the masses of marginal Negroes, who are not disciplined members of any group. And the masses of Negroes do not "choose" tactics at all. They respond to the pressures of their lives and react spontaneously to incidents which trigger explosions or demonstrations. When a bewildered white liberal asks why, in the face of the passage of the Civil Rights Bill of 1964, "they" still revolt—and not in the dignified, respectable nonviolent way of the earlier student sitins—he betrays his own alienation from the Negroes whose cause he espouses. The Civil Rights Act was so long coming it served merely to remind many Negroes of their continued rejected and second-class status. Even well-meaning whites continue to see and talk of negroes as "they," clearly differentiated from "we," the "outgroup" from the "ingroup." As long as this alienation remains, the masses of whites will be irritated and inconvenienced by any meaningful activity by Negroes to change their status. No real revolt can be convenient for the privileged; no real revolt can be contained within comfortable bounds or be made respectable.

In the face of the growing unrest, careful, thoughtful, and realistic planning becomes starkly imperative. Some whites would react to renewed protest by warning Negroes not to go too far too fast, not to alienate the white liberals who have, even if often timidly, supported them. To others, less well-intentioned, Negro unrest is but confirmation of their own prejudice: Negroes are, after all, behaving as the uncivilized do. But unrest *is* a characteristic of civilization, and to fight against oppression—even unwisely—is a sign that men have begun to hope. As studies on social disasters have demonstrated, people who feel there is no escape submit to their fate; it is those who see an exit sign and an open door who struggle to reach it.

Furthermore, energies devoted to a struggle for constructive social change are clearly not simultaneously available for antisocial and self-destructive patterns of behavior. In those communities such as Montgomery, Alabama, where Negroes mobilized themselves for sustained protest against prevailing racial injustice, *the incidence of antisocial behavior and delinquency decreased almost to a vanishing point during the period of protest.*

The Negro cannot any longer feel, if he ever did, that he should have to prove himself "worthy" in order to gain his full freedom— the rights guaranteed to all other American citizens, including those most recently naturalized. The Negro cannot be asked to prove that he "deserves" the rights and responsibilities of democracy, nor can he be told that others must first be persuaded "in heart and mind" to accept him. Such tests and trials by fire are not applied to others. To impose them on the Negro is racist condescension. It is to assume that the Negro is a special type of human being who must pass a special test before admission to a tenuous status worthy of governmental protection. It is to place upon the Negro a peculiar burden reflecting and exploiting his powerlessness, and it is, paradoxically, to deny him the essential human rights of frailty and imperfection. The experience of inferior racial status has not transformed the Negro into a super human being. To demand that he demonstrate virtues not ordinarily found in more privileged people, before he may enjoy the benefits of democracy, is not only irrational and inconsistent but gratuitously cruel. And above all it is evidence that the invisible wall is opaque from outside in.

No one ought to expect the transition from a system of injustice to a system of social justice to occur without personal and social trauma for the Negro as well as the white. The intensification of conflict and resistance inherent in the immediacy of the Negro's demands, and the dramatic methods which he is now using to attain his goals, understandably obscure some of the more profound human problems involved in progressing from a racially segregated to a nonsegregated society. But, when the cries of anguish of the segregationists have subsided, as they will eventually, the Negro will be confronted with his own inner anxieties, conflicts, and challenges as he dares to move into a society of open competition. It will then be clear that though the problems of adjusting to change are difficult for whites, in even more insidious ways they are quite painful for Negroes. The invisible walls of a segregated society are not only damaging but protective in a debilitating way   There is considerable psychological safety in the ghetto; there one lives among one's own and does not risk rejection among strangers. One first becomes aware of the psychological damage of such "safety" when the walls of the ghetto are breached and the Negro ventures out into the repressive, frightening white world. Some Negroes prefer to stay in the ghetto, particularly those who have developed seemingly effective defenses to protect themselves against hurt, those who fear for their children, and those who have profited from the less competitive segregated society. Other Negroes, particularly the young, are militant in their efforts to crash the remaining barriers of race. But even among this group it is not always easy to tell who is totally committed and willing to assume the risks and who is only talking militance. Most Negroes take the first steps into an integrated society tentatively and torn with conflict. To be the first Negro who is offered a job in a company brings a sense of triumph but also the dread of failure. To be the "show" Negro, the symbol of a new-found policy of racial democracy in an educational institution, private industry, or governmental agency, imposes demands for personal restraint, balance, and stability of character rare among any group of mere human beings. For a Negro to be offered friendship and to find himself unable to accept it fully, to find that he is himself in the grip of hitherto unrealized racial prejudice—or, more precisely racial anger—is to look into the hidden recesses of his own mind. A person—or a race—who has been forced to be ashamed of his identity cannot easily accept himself simply as a human being and surrender either the supportive group identification or hostility toward those who have rejected him.

The newly emerging Negro—the assertive, militant, defiant, self-affirming Negro seeking his identity—will probably at first seem a caricature, a person who wears the mask of race with its fixed artificial expression. No more than the white bigot who succumbs to his passion of hatred and fear, or the white "liberal" who struggles to reconcile his affirmation of racial justice with his visceral racism, has the Negro escaped domination of his own individuality by the role of race. Only when the need to play such a role is no longer urgent will the individual Negro and white feel free to be merely themselves, without defenses.

Section II-3

The Acceleration of History

GERARD PIEL

Consider the fallacies that underlie a superstition embraced with reverence and conviction throughout all ranks in our society. This is the proposition that learning is divided into two separate provinces: the scientific and the humane. The falsehood here can be surfaced by stating explicitly what is implied: that truth can be sought in the absence of concern for value and value cherished without courage to face the truth. This invitation to irresponsibility has sterilized scholarship on both sides of the nonexistent line between the sciences and humanities and deprived society of the leadership and wisdom it desperately needs.

I do not propose to trace now the historical antecedents of this subversive doctrine. Suffice to say it is of recent origin and so perhaps more easily cured. Coming the longer way around I would like to review the historical evidence against it, evidence that compels us to the opposite conclusion.

Henry Adams is one of the few historians who ever undertook to explore the relations between science and the history of society. Looking back over the tumult of modern history, he plotted the rising curves of the rate of scientific discovery, of coal output, of steam power, of the transition from mechanical to electrical power. Any schoolboy, he said, could plot such curves and see that "arithmetical ratios were useless"; the curves followed "the old familiar law of squares": that is, they rose more sharply as they ascended from the time base line. The logarithmic scale of the time base line of Adams' chart gives equal space to the last millennium and to the preceding 10,000 years. It thus not only serves geometrical convenience but also reflects the compression of the past in our memory.

From *Current Issues in Higher Education*, Association for Higher Education, 1964, pg. 22–32. Reprinted by permission of the Association for Higher Education.

"The acceleration of the seventeenth century," Adams observed, "was rapid, and that of the eighteenth was startling. The acceleration even became measurable, for it took the form of utilizing heat as force, through the steam engine, and this addition of power was measurable in the coal output." Acceleration was the law of history.

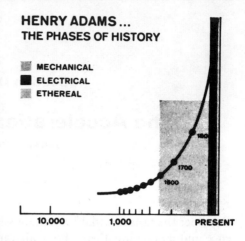

HENRY ADAMS...
THE PHASES OF HISTORY

▨ MECHANICAL
■ ELECTRICAL
▨ ETHEREAL

From his acquaintance with the historic work of his contemporary Josiah Willard Gibbs—the great American mathematical physicist—Adams was prepared to recognize that such changes in quantity amounted to changes in quality: changes in "phase" according to the terminology of Gibbs. The history of thought was in passage through three phases, each with a duration in years that was the inverse square of the duration of the preceding phase. "Supposing the Mechanical Phase to have lasted 300 years—from 1600 to 1900—the next or Electric Phase would have a life of . . . about seventeen years and a half, when—that is, in 1917—it would pass into another or Ethereal Phase, which, for half a century, science has been promising, and which would last only . . . about four years, and bring Thought to the limit of its possibilities in the year 1921. It may well be! Nothing whatever is beyond the range of possibility; but even if the life of the previous phase, 1600–1900, were extended another hundred years, the difference to the last term of the series would be negligible. In that case, the Ethereal Phase would last till about 2025."

By Adams' calculations our lives are on probation: we are living in the grace period between 1921 and 2025. Adams despaired of our capacity to withstand the overriding force of acceleration. In 1905, he declared,

> Yet it is quite sure, according to my score of ratios and curves, that, at the accelerated rate of progression since 1600, it will not need another century or half century to turn thought upside down. Law, in that case, would disappear as theory of *a priori* principle and give place to force. Morality would become police. Explosives would reach cosmic violence. Disintegration would overcome integration.

Most of us are less well-prepared than Adams to explore the relevance of science to history. Yet we may charge to his personal circumstances the despair to which he came at the end of his exploration; for he had come as well to the end of life. I am not here to urge his despair upon you.

On the contrary, it is my thesis that the dilemma of our age—the catatonic indecision of men and nations in their present perilous confrontation with the choice of life or death—follows directly from the general failure to understand that science is relevant to history. That failure is compounded by another: the failure to comprehend the lesson that is pointed by the relevance of science to history.

I shall state the lesson in didactic terms in the hope to state it plainly: science is the ultimate source of value in the life of mankind.

Man's ascending mastery over the forces of nature has progressively transformed not only the relationship of man to nature, but the relationship of man to man. From age to age, discovery and invention have opened new scope and possibility to human life. With each new possibility has come the necessity to choose. In the succession of choices, the moral and the social order—men's ideas of good and evil and the institutions that embody them—have evolved. The now steeply accelerating advance of science allows no time for evolution. We are compelled to an immediate re-examination and deliberate overhaul of the values and institutions that we have carried into the present from the swiftly receding past.

Let us spread out the pattern of events and see how it sustains this thesis. I have projected Henry Adams' curve backward to the classical period, 2,000 years ago, and forward 50 years to the present. A wealth of statistical data supports the ascent of the curve to twice the height of which Adams charted it at the turn of the century. Every index, from the consumption of energy *per caput* to the volume of scientific publication, has more than doubled in this period in the United States. Since few statistical series reach beyond 150 to 200 years into the past, the projection of the curve back behind 1600 must be regarded as largely symbolic. The projection is documented, however, by a number of crucial indexes, especially if one may reverse the rule of phase and count changes in quality as accumulations in quantity.

Consider, for example, the shrinking time intervals shown here from the discovery of one primary force of nature to the next. At the outset there had to be the notion of a natural or inanimate force, as distinguished from the animistic *genius* of the place, thing, or process; this elementary idea was first propounded in the science of the Greeks two millennia ago. Then, 300 years ago, came the Galilean-Newtonian great world system ordered by the force of gravity. Next, only 100 years ago, came the Franklin-Faraday-Maxwell discovery of the electromagnetic force. Now, only 50 years ago, Einstein, Planck, Rutherford, and Bohr uncovered the most energetic of the forces, that which binds the nucleus of the atom. Last, at this very moment, physics is comprehending the presence of the fourth primary force of the universe: the so-called weak force observed in the decay of elementary particles.

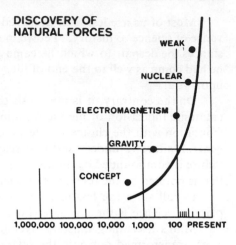

DISCOVERY OF NATURAL FORCES

Consider the successive isolations of the ninety-two elements into which matter is chemically differentiated. Perhaps as many as a half-dozen elements—carbon, copper, gold, silver, iron—had come into use in more or less pure form at the dawn of recorded history 10,000 years ago. The number rose abruptly to twenty with the beginning of modern chemistry 200 years ago. By the time Mendeleyev laid out the table of elements, a century ago, the number of elements isolated had more than doubled again to sixty-odd. Today physics has carried the series out beyond the bounty of nature, adding ten so-called synthetic elements to the table—and the curve might be extended indefinitely by grafting on the lengthening table of fundamental particles.

Consider still another curve—that plotted by the mastery of the major sources of inanimate power. The starting point carries our projection back behind the beginning of history to at least 50,000 years ago when man discovered the first uses of fire. With his own vital energy amplified by fire, man must already, in that remote time, be reckoned as a geologic force. He used fire not only to warm his body and to cook his food, but more significantly to burn forests and extend the grasslands over which he could hunt more safely and productively. The next point on the curve marks the harnessing of water power in the Bronze Age, 5,000 years ago. It was only 800 years ago that man began to make comparable use of the wind; the invention of the windmill in twelfth century Europe was something of a technological revolution, spreading in a century from Normandy to the Black Sea. The industrial revolution itself began, of course, with the harnessing of steam, 200 years ago. Direct or internal combustion—which generates as much mechanical and electrical enery as steam in contemporary technology—dates back only a century. And now the first nuclear reactors are delivering electricity to the power networks of the world.

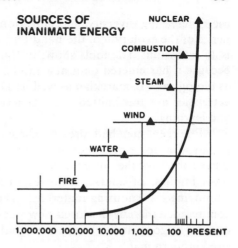

The pattern of events shows history on a course of accelerating accelaration. The major developments in man's accumulative experience have occurred within the most recent times, and these developments occur at shorter time-intervals into the very present. This chart does not, of course, begin to tell the full story of history. Plotting only the accumulative elements of human experience, it excludes the rest—the glory and tragedy, the shame and honor, the bestial and the humane—and so, by some lights, it excludes all that gives meaning to history. Yet the exponential curve of science, I believe, plots the mainstream of history insofar as history has not merely repeated itself. This assertion is confirmed when we place the brief period of recorded time in the perspective of man's longer past.

The starting point of the plot of history may now be established as far back as 1.7 million years before the present and proportionately closer to the time baseline. As a site reliably dated to that distant time, on a buried lake shore in the Rift country of Africa, anthropologists have recently unearthed an assemblage of stone tools. With these tools they found fragments of the bones of the hands that had made them. The hands are not human hands—not our hands. They are the hands of a primate who still used them at times for walking. In the old taxonomy of primates it was supposed that man had made the first tools; tool-making was the status symbol of membership in our species. Now, it would appear, tools made man. Certainly, tool-making conferred a competitive advantage on the maker of better tools. But the meaning of this phase of history goes deeper. The truth is, man made himself.

The record as to bones of hands and skulls is scanty. There is an abundance, however, of the fossils of behavior—the stone tools. In their increasing diversity, specialization and refinement, they give evidence of the evolution of the hand and of the brain, of which the hand is an extension. The tools show, in time, that evolution has quickened because it has entered on a new mode. It has become cultural as well as biological—Lamarckian as well as Darwinian in that acquired characteristics are transmitted from generation to generation by teaching and learning.

Emergent man had already discovered in his own head the notion of purpose, for which men have since sought validation in so many other corners of the universe. The increasing specialization of the stone tools implies, of course, a corresponding elaboration of technology employing less enduring materials. The mastery of new environments commanded thereby disclosed new possibilities and new ways of life—one might go so far as to say new goals and values—to the men who sired modern man.

As long as 50,000 years ago, the diversity of hunting and food-gathering technologies enabled man to make himself at home in every environment on earth. Some primitive cultures have persisted even into modern times on the Arctic shores of the northern continents, in the interior of the southern continents, and on oceanic islands in the Pacific. These peoples have taught us to use the term primitive with respect. There is no human language that is primitive; each has a grammar as well as a vocabulary. The aesthetics of these cultures is the more compelling because it so directly articulates the experience of life. Typically, their social order is the extended family, and the code of law and custom submerges the individual in the common identity and destiny of the group.

Imperceptibly, over tens of thousands of years, as certain of these peoples came into possession of more intimate understanding of their environments, they found a more secure way of life, as herdsmen and cultivators of the soil. By 10,000 years ago they had domesticated all of the plants and animals now grown on the world's farms. There could be no doubt about the progressive nature of this development. It multiplied by 100 the potential size of the population that could be sustained on the land. As history was soon to show, the labor of four families in the field could now support a fifth family in the city.

The transition of agricultural civilization was made in the same 2,000–3,000-year period in Asia Minor, in the valley of the Nile, in the Indus Valley in India, and in China; the transition was made more recently in pre-Columbian America but in entire independence of events in the Old World. Wherever this revolution occurred, it gave rise to essentially the same social and economic institutions. The function of these institutions was to secure the inequitable distribution of the product of the soil. Law and custom speedily legitimized the necessary measures of coercion. But the primary compulsion, as we can now see, was supplied by the slant of the curve of discovery and invention. Over millennia or centuries, progress was substantial; in the lifetime of a man, however, it brought no appreciable increase in the product of his labor. Population tended always to increase faster than production, maintaining a constant equilibrium of scarcity. Bertrand de Jouvenel has described the situation with precision:

> As long as there is a fairly constant limit to production *per caput*, one man can gain wealth only by making use of another man's labor; only a few members of society can gain wealth, therefore, and at the expense of the rest. All ancient civilizations rested upon the inexplicit premise that the productivity of labor is constant.

The inexplicit premise of scarcity is stated plainly enough in the plan of the ancient cities. Invariably it shows the palace, the temple, and the garrison within the ruin of the walls and, outside, the traces in the soil of the hovels of the slaves. Thus four-fifths of the population was made to render up the surplus necessary to sustain one-fifth in the new enterprises of high civilization.

Because history is written by its beneficiaries, history has little to say about the eighty percent of the population who were excluded from history. It has even less to say about the underlying inequity of the social and economic institutions—whether slavery, serfdom, taxes, rent, or interest—that laid the burden of history on their backs. Laws were passed to regulate the treatment of slaves and serfs, but the gross immorality of these institutions was never called in question until modern times—not until, that is, the inexplicit premise of scarcity itself had been overturned.

It is easy now to mark the turning point of history. But even in the seventeenth century people sensed the acceleration of thought. Without doubt, the most revolutionary idea in the life of man was the concept of inertia advanced in 1638 by Galileo—then already past the age of seventy and writing in secret under house arrest for the lesser heresy of advocating the Copernican revolution. Galileo's great insight comprehended at once the swinging of a pendulum and the motion of the planets on their orbits. The idea of inertia not only changed men's view of nature; it placed a primary force of nature in their hands. Within a few generations they were setting much else besides pendulums in motion.

The surplus gathered in by the institutions of scarcity found a new historic function. It became the wealth of nations to be invested in the increase of capacity to produce wealth. Though hindsight encourages us to place emphasis on the acceleration of the rate of discovery and invention in this period, we must not fail to credit the role of the institutions of political economy. In 1802, looking in satisfaction on the ascendance of Britain, then in the vanguard of the industrial revolution, Sir Humphry Davy astutely observed: "The unequal division of property and of labour, the difference of rank and condition amongst mankind, are the sources of power in civilized life, its moving causes, and even its very soul."

Today, after two centuries of industrial revolution, we have come to speak of two kinds of nations: developed and underdeveloped, or, in plainer language, rich and poor. The poor nations—of Latin America, Africa, and Asia—embrace two-thirds of the world's population. There is nothing novel about their condition. The poor have always been with us; always, that is, since agricultural civilization secured its foundations in the inequitable distribution of capacity. The unprecedented historical novelty is the rich nation. Within the past century some twenty nations have made the transition from agricultural to industrial civilization. The heady experience of increasing personal well-being entrains substantially their entire populations.

In our own country we observe the contemporary climax of the industrial revolution. Our standard of living serves as the usual index of our revolutionary leadership. The income *per caput* of the American people has, in fact, multiplied twelve times in the past 200 years. At the same time of the French and Indian War, frontier America was an underdeveloped country with average individual income of $100. Today, at $1,200 (1929 dollars) per annum, personal expenditure exceeds that of

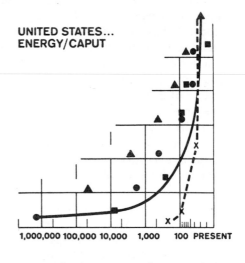

UNITED STATES...
ENERGY/CAPUT

1,000,000 100,000 10,000 1,000 100 PRESENT

the average inhabitant of the poor countries by twenty times, and that of other denizens of industrial civilization by at least three times. But the American celebration is dampened somewhat by evidence that at least a quarter, and perhaps a third, of our families live under the poverty line, and there is cause for downright alarm when we learn from the 1960 census that the middle income groups have been shrinking upward from the bottom, losing increasing numbers to the sink below the poverty line.

No, it is not our success as consumers but rather as producers that gives us our special place in history. America's capacity to produce has long since been freed from the limitations of mere human capacity. The output of mechanical energy, rising in accordance with the law of squares, first exceeded the output of biological energy in the American economy just about a century ago, at the time of the Emancipation Proclamation. By 1930, central power stations were furnishing each American man, woman, and child with 750 kilowatt-hours of electricity per year, that is, with energy equivalent to the labor of three human slaves each. By 1940, the figure had increased to 1,000 kilowatt-hours; in the next decade it doubled to 2,000 kilowatt-hours. In 1960, the power grids were delivering 5,000 kilowatt-hours *per caput*, the electrical equivalent of thirty-two man-years of labor for each of us.

The energy index is significant, for it bears directly on the changing role of human beings and the nature of the work they do in our industrial society. At the turn of the century three-quarters of our labor force were engaged as "producers of goods." The plurality of farmers, farm hands, and unskilled labor among these producers indicates that human muscle still had a role in the production function. These were the men who put in "an honest day's work." By comparison, the "providers of services" could scarcely be called workers at all!

Today less than half the labor force is employed in the production of goods. Farmers, farm hands, and unskilled laborers are vanishing from the scene; human muscle has long since been displaced by electrical energy. The "operative"—the most numerous producer of goods —is a human nervous system interposed in feed-back loops that have not yet been completely closed by electronics. But even this kind of work is losing its role in production. During the last sixteen years, the blue collar workers in manufacturing (principally "operatives") declined from 12.8 to 12 million. Yet the index of industrial production increased by eighty-six percent. The resolution of this paradox has already been suggested by the exponential increase in the output of kilowatt-hours; the paradox is resolved by the knowledge that the number of scientists and engineers in our economy has doubled in this same period—from 750,000 to 1.5 million.

It is plain that we have already drastically revised our notion of what constitutes work. More than half of our labor force is engaged in new kinds of nonproductive work as "providers of services." In this company of providers of services "nonproductive" is, of course, a

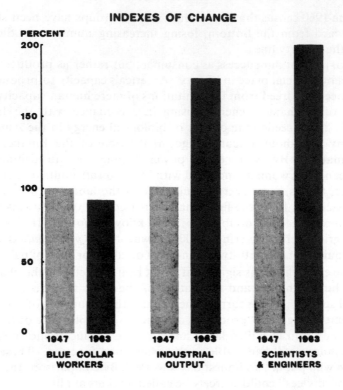

INDEXES OF CHANGE

PERCENT

fighting word. Each of us will argue that the terms "productive" and "work" must be given broader moral construction and technically more sophisticated meaning. To begin with, we can show that the providers of services include the scientists and engineers who have so vastly amplified the output of our producers of goods.

It is plain, nonetheless, that the expansion of employment in trade and distribution and in services has served an economic function that transcends the distribution and servicing of goods. In a word, such employment had provided employment. As the accelerating advance of technology has displaced people from productive work, strictly defined, the concurrent transformation of our values has qualified a rising percentage of our population—now well over half—as consumers of abundance.

Inevitably such profound transformation in the work and values of our citizenry must be reflected in corresponding changes in our institutions. Again, the turn of the century provides the bench mark to measure how far these changes have run. In 1900, America still ap-

proximated its image of itself as a nation of people engaged in "the pursuit of happiness"; that is, occupied in employment for private interests, their own or their employers'. The minimal place of government was reflected in the negligible percentage of the adult population
(just over three percent) that was employed in the public sector. Then
as now, the forty percent of the adult population "not employed" included the unemployed, the busy housewife, the elderly retired, and the
more fortunate young whose entrance into the labor market was postponed by the prolonging of their education.

Today, however, we behold a drastic change in the occupational
status of the sixty percent of the adult population that is employed.
Only forty percent find their jobs in the private sector. A full twenty
percent—one-third of the working population—are employed in the
public sector. Thus, with the decline of employment in productive
work, expansion of the public sector has provided a rising percentage
of the new jobs that have kept a constant sixty percent of the adult
population employed.

The public sector generates about half of its twenty-three or
twenty-four million jobs directly, that is, on its own payroll, and about
half through its expenditures in the private sector. This blurring of the
old clear-cut boundary between the public and the private sector is itself a reflection of the institutional transformations under way in our
land. But even deeper changes are implied here. By definition, the
functions and enterprises embodied in these jobs are undertaken in the
public interest. Principal among them today is national defense which
accounts for seven million jobs, in and out of uniform and on both
sides of the blurred boundary between the public and the private
sectors. The next largest public enterprise is education; closely allied
to it is the most rapidly expanding public enterprise, the research and
development activities of the federal government, which employ two-
thirds of the nation's scientists and engineers. The rest of the endless
catalog of public services ranges equally over the spectrum from the
traditional to the novel, the large to the small, the essential to the
dubious, from public health to space exploration, from agricultural
extension to highway building. Each has its constituency in the elec-
torate to back its claim upon the national, state, and local budget;
altogether they provoke universal resistance to the increasing tax they
lay on personal incomes. Yet, however well or ill these jobs serve their
explicit ends, they fulfill a vital economic function: that of certifying
their holders with pay checks to enter the market as consumers of the
abundance that flows from twentieth century technology.

The sensitivity of the economic ties that bind the public and the private sectors is dramatized presently by the faltering of the largest public enterprise. It turns out that national defense is not an endless frontier. Even in advance of disarmament, the miniaturization and automatization of violence have halted the expansion of this enterprise and started the contraction of its payroll. The immediate consequences are already felt acutely in certain communities; the prospective repercussions are arousing wide concern. While our air marshals extol the virtues of the manned bomber, our Senators man the defenses of our local navy yards, and military contractors turn uncertainly to thoughts of reconversion, the most reassuring word is the official declaration that our country has acquired "a backlog of demand for public services comparable in many ways to the backlog of demand for consumer durable goods and housing and producers' plant and equipment at the end of World War II."

Let us now summarize the evidence. No rate of expansion in the output (Gross National Product) of our economy can overtake the rate at which human beings are being displaced from the productive process. There are signs that people can be and are being displaced even faster from such nonproductive (still strictly defined) functions as clerking and selling. Work that can be done by machines is either too dull, repetitive, demanding, dangerous, or degrading for human beings; it is better done by machines. The liberation of people from such servitude should set them free for the exercise of their more recognizably human capacities. Among these are learning, teaching, research, social and public service, the crafts, arts, and letters. Characteristically these activities engage people in interaction with people rather than with things. Admittedly nonproductive, such activities are highly rewarding to the individuals so engaged and redound richly to the wealth of the nation. Our country has not only been employing its citizens in these activities in increasing numbers but educating them for these activities in still more rapidly increasing numbers. Employment in the public sector has been rising at more than twice the rate in the private sector; enrollment in higher education has been swelling even ahead of the bulge of the baby boom.

Here, then, in the long and short perspective of this survey are the signs that history in America has entered on a new phase. In the America of the not so distant future we may expect to see wiser use of our capacity to generate abundance: the deployment of that capacity to the cherishing of our natural resources, to the building of more spacious cities, to attaining a happier accommodation of Americans to their bountiful environment, and so to the evocation and fulfillment of individual human endowment.

Inevitably the transition to this latest phase of human evolution, which I have called the humane phase, must bring our values and our institutions into disarray and even into crisis. The acceleration of history has brought the old regime of scarcity to a sudden end in our time. Industrial technology, fructified by the increase in human understanding, has repealed the iron law that says one man's well-being can be increased only at the expense of his brother's. In its place we are training new institutions and values to respond to the new dispensation of abundance. We are learning that, in our day, the well-being of each man can increase only with increase in the well-being of all men. The ancient habit of truth-seeking has disclosed the noblest and most generous aims to human life and placed in our hands the means to accomplish those ends here on earth.

Section II-4

Consumers of Abundance

GERARD PIEL

The advance of science has for many years been undermining the two pillars of our economy—property and work. Each at length has fallen from its place. Property is no longer the primary source of economic power, and ownership no longer establishes the significant, functioning connection between people and the things they consume. Work occupies fewer hours and years in the lives of everyone; what work there is grows less like work every year, and the less the people work, the more their product grows. In the place of work and property, illusions and old habits and compulsions now support the social edifice. Public understanding must eventually overtake this transformation in the relationship of modern man to his physical environment. Fundamental changes in the social order—in man's relationship to man—are therefore in prospect and are already in process.

It is difficult and perhaps dangerous to forecast where these changes may lead. Full employment, for example, now seems to be not only an unattainable but an outmoded objective of economic policy. What takes the place of wages in a workless society? If such a question must be asked, then others follow. Does profit remain a useful standard of accounting in a propertyless society? But these questions are not only too big; they are premature. Before they can even be asked, the scientific revolution that occasions them must be more closely examined.

As the withering of these institutions from the life of society suggests, property and work are artifacts of civilization. In the kinship economies of pre-agricultural societies they have no place whatever or appear only in the faintest analogues. The wampum hoard that confers prestige in one culture becomes the potlatch of another. Hunting and food-gathering are not work, but adventure, assertion of manhood, magic, and craft.

From *Science in the Cause of Man* by Gerard Piel, 1961. Reprinted by permission of Alfred A. Knopf, Inc.

Property and work make their appearance with the agricultural revolution. They are devices for gathering and impounding the surplus that four families at work upon the land can now produce to support a fifth family off the land. Property is the institution by which the church, the state, and their individual agents assert their control over the land as one of the two primary factors of production. Work is the institution by which they assert their control over the other primary factor of production—the energy of human muscle. The word "work" signifies toil and at the same time the product of toil; it is the measure ("according to his works") of the portion of the product that may be allocated to the unpropertied worker. The two institutions together furnished the rationale for the compulsions necessary to assure the removal of the surplus from the land. Thanks to these arrangements, even fairly primitive agricultural technologies were capable of supporting substantial urban civilizations, as in Mexico.

In the feudal societies identified with agricultural technology, land was the only economically significant property. It was typically inalienable, except by order of the suzerain; it was cherished and maintained from generation to generation, physically occupied by its possessors, who enjoyed all the rights of usufruct as well as the power to exploit. In medieval Europe the land so completely dominated economic life that the taking of interest was synonymous with usury, a crime as well as a sin. It took a religious revolution to establish the practice of selling things for more than they cost and to secure propriety for profit in the worldly virtue of thrift.

Profit, thrift, and the accumulation of capital brought an entirely new kind of property into ascendance in economic affairs. This was the machine. At first the machine had the same immemorial look of permanence as the land. It embodied a high ratio of brute material to design and was built for depreciation over at least one generation of ownership. Through such time periods, ownership of the machine carried the same stability of power and place as ownership of the mine or plantation.

It was not long, however, before the ratio of design to material in the machine began to rise and then reverse. As the machine became ever less substantial, its lifetime grew shorter. Today the economically significant industrial property is not the machine, but the design, and not so much the design as the capacity to innovate design in process and product. This is scarcely property at all, but is rather a capacity inhering in an organization. To have that capacity encumbered by gigantic plant can be hazardous. This is what the steel industry has found in the present technological free-for-all that has brought steel into competition with materials—glass, ceramics, reconstructed wood, plastics, and exotic new metals—that no self-respecting steelmaker ever heard of fifteen years ago. The most profitable manufacturing enterprises are those that show a shrinking ratio of plant to output and a rising ratio of instrumentation to plant. Not only the plant but the product and the very industry in which the company is engaged may be subject to obsolescence. The decisive factor of production is research and development.

As the nature of property, in the sense of the thing that is owned, has changed, so has the nature of the social institution of property. Property was subverted by another social institution, the corporation. With ownership represented by stock certificates, the proprietor ceased to occupy the premises. The right of property vested in the stockholder, as A. A. Berle, Jr., and Gardiner C. Means made clear more than a generation ago in *The Modern Corporation and Private Property,* was reduced to the right to vote for the directors of the corporation (if the stockholder bothers to return the proxy statement) and to a claim on earnings (if the directors declare them out in dividends on his class of stock). Even these vestiges of power are delegated today to a third party for the increasing percentage of the voting equities in American industrial enterprise that is held by insurance companies, pension funds, and mutual investment companies.

The puissance in research and development that determines the fortunes of a corporate enterprise is commonly valued at one dollar on the balance sheet. This accounting fiction hypothecates the talents of the men who make up the organization, and the common-stock certificate is a thrice-removed share in that hypothecation. Under the circumstances, it is hard to see how the stockholder could be vested with a larger claim. The instrumentalities of ownership have become as insubstantial as the decisive factor of production itself.

Against this statement of the terms on which the present owners of the American industrial system hold their property, it may be argued that the really giant new fortunes are being made in the old-fashioned kind of property; that is, land and the mineral riches underneath it. But even the discovery of mineral resources has moved into the realm of invention. It is *par excellence* a yield on instrumentation, implemented by an equally intangible talent for politics. As a result, most of the prospecting is carried on by large corporations, and ownership stands at the same remove as in other activities of the industrial system.

With the emergence of two to five corporations in control of assets and sales in all but a few realms of industrial activity, economic power has become highly concentrated in our society. But it is no longer at-

tached to property. The power is vested in self-perpetuating manage-
ments. How they derive their legitimacy is a question that troubles a
great many people, including those who exercise the power as well as
those who are critical of the power-holders.

Edward S. Mason, of the Harvard economics faculty, has astutely
asked what difference, if any, this transfer of power has made. It is true
that the profit margin—the yield to ownership—remains the ruling
discipline of corporate management. And it is also true that operation
under this discipline chronically fails to realize the full potential of
industrial technology. That failure is the measure of the present
business recession: with the gross national product holding steady at
an all-time high, fully one third of the steel plant and comparable percentages of capacity in other industries lie idle. As the self-appointed
management contemplates the troubling question of the legitimacy of
its power, it must also face increasingly insistent questions about its
stewardship of power.

The same transformation of the nature of property is to be seen
again in the relationship of the owner to property as usufruct. There
are more home-owners today in the United States than ever before in
this century, more than 60 per cent of the occupiers of dwelling places
compared with less than 50 per cent in 1900. But whereas 30 per cent of
the homes were mortgaged to 40 per cent of their aggregate value in
1900, more than 60 per cent are mortgaged to more than half their aggregate value today. The builders and bankers of the new suburbs
will tell you that the ownership of one out of six homes there turns
over every year. Plainly, the so-called home-owner is buying not a
home but a housing service, much as he buys transportation, not a car,
from the auto industry. His equity in these two utilities rarely controls
before he turns in the old house or car for the new model. By the same
token, the total installment debt represents, from one year to the next,
by far the major property interest in all of the other consumer durable
goods in use in the country. The householder is correct in regarding
these transactions as the purchase of a service rather than property.
For the objects themselves are self-consuming, designed for depreciation to desuetude in 1,000 hours of service.

In sum, the typical American consumer owns no property in the
classical meaning of the term. Out of current income he pays for services currently rendered. Through income set aside in social security
taxes and in pension and insurance funds, he reserves a claim on services to be rendered in the future.

Mention of the social security now provided for the overwhelming
number of United States citizens brings this discussion to the topic of

work. Social security is one of the devices evolved in the recent history of our industrial economy to help solve the problem of "distribution." This, as is well known, is the last frontier of economics. Viewed from the vantage of the economy as a whole, it is the problem of finding people qualified to consume the increasing abundance of goods produced by a declining number of workers. From the point of view of the individual citizen, it is the problem of finding work in a shrinking labor market in order to qualify as a consumer of that abundance. Thus, as we shall see, the primary function of work in our economy today is to secure not the production but the distribution of goods. This is clearly a different situation from that which prevailed in the valleys of the Tigris and Euphrates 7,000 years ago, when the surplus had to be extracted from scarcity by coercion.

Modern industrial technology produces a vast material surplus of goods, many times greater than the need of the workers engaged in producing it. That surplus goes begging for consumers because technology has subverted the social institution of work. The subversion of work began, of course, with the displacement of the biologically generated energy of human muscle by the mechanically generated energy of steam engines. The reciprocal steam engine gave way after little more than half a century to the steam turbine, the generator of electrical energy in the huge quantities that are measured in kilowatts. Studies conducted many years ago, when muscles were yielding a day's work to steam, showed that one man can put out about 48 kilowatt-hours in useful work in a year. On that basis, the 750 billion kilowatt-hours of electricity generated in the United States puts the equivalent of eighty-five slaves at the disposal of each man, woman, and child in the population.

But this is an old story. The new story is the disemployment of the human nervous system. In industrial production the function of the human worker has been to set the tool, start up the machine, supervise its performance, correct its error, and keep its parts in working order. The machine has been doing all the work, including work that exceeds human physical capacity. But, for lack of a nervous system, it has had to depend upon human beings to regulate its operations.

The robot, or artificial nervous system, is the steam engine of the present phase of the industrial revolution. Unlike the steam engine, it does not announce its presence by huffing and puffing, and it has no easily recognized anatomical structure. But it does have a single underlying principle, which is as clear-cut and universal as the idea of converting heat into mechanical energy. This essential idea is known to engineers as feedback.

Feedback is the principle that underlies all self-regulating systems, including living organisms. The nearest and simplest example of feedback in action is the household thermostat: A mechanical sense organ absorbs a little of the heat generated by the household heating plant and thereby makes a measurement of its output. This small fraction of the output is fed back in the form of a signal to correct the input of fuel to the heating unit. By this feeding-back of output to input, the household heating plant is made to regulate itself.

Now, the principle of converting heat to mechanical energy is embodied in about half a dozen economically important heat engines—including the steam turbine, the internal combustion engine, the gas turbine, and the rocket engine. The feedback control systems in our economy, on the other hand, appear in a host of species and varieties—electrical, electronic, pneumatic, hydraulic, mechanical—and in such diversity of design and appearance that they have only the essential feedback principle in common.

An accurate census of these robots has not been made. But the evidence is strong that they now outnumber the human workers employed in industry. Our entire energy economy—from the steam plant out across the high-tension lines to the rotating machinery of industry—is now subject to automatic control. The new technology of atomic energy is critically dependent upon automatic control; dozens of feedback circuits in the depths of a nuclear reactor control the dreadful flux of atomic particles in which no living things could survive. Our petroleum refineries and almost all of our chemical process plants are today so highly robotized that their entire operations are controlled by one or two human operators stationed at the central push-button control panel.

It is only a few steps from here to the fully automatic factory. In the petroleum industry, such a factory would make use of an instrument—such as the nuclear resonance spectrometer, which has only recently graduated from the laboratory—to analyze the output stream of a refinery. The spectrometer would feed back its reading to a mechanical computer, one of the "giant brain" variety. These machines are already equal to doing the work of the human operator at the control panel; they need merely to be equipped with instructions covering all possible contingencies in the operation of the plant. Comparing the spectrometer report on the output of the refinery with the instructions stored in its memory, the computer would check and correct the performance of the robot valves at all points on the process stream. In fact, the first full-scale refineries incorporating the principal elements of the self-regulating robot factory are now "on stream."

Obviously, the purpose in designing the automatic petroleum refinery is not to replace the one or two human operators who still remain on the payroll. This was the naïve idea of a Middle Eastern petroleum prince for whom an American oil company was building a refinery not long ago. Out of consideration for the underemployed *fellaheen* who were to squat in the sand outside the refinery fence, he asked whether jobs might not be created by disengaging the robots from the valves. The engineers took him seriously enough to reexamine the entire control system. They had to conclude that no team of human beings could be trained and coordinated to do its work.

So, also, the dial telephone, with the ramifications of direct long-distance and direct inward dialing, is designed not to save the wages of human female telephone operators, but to make the operation of the modern telephone system possible. The heart of that system is not the dial on the telephone but a computer in the central station known in the telephone company as the "line marker." Its self-regulating internal circuitry is so complex that its designers cannot tell at any given moment just which elements in it are performing the work at hand. The American Telephone and Telegraph Company estimates that, at the present rate of traffic, it would have to employ all of the women in the labor force, plus 20 per cent more, to do the work of its line markers. The task of coordinating the output of that many human nervous systems in a single telephone system is quite impracticable.

To engage the robot in functions of this kind takes some doing. The control system must be furnished with receptor organs, like the spectrometer or the dial on the telephone, to supply it with inputs from the world outside. And it must be linked with the world on its output side by means of effector organs, the hands that carry out its instructions. These may take the form of the electrical and pneumatic motors that drive the valves on a refinery or the relays that close connections in the telephone system.

Since the computer's function is to handle information, the easiest way to hook it up to the world outside it is by typewriter. Equipped with typewriters, it becomes a white-collar worker.

Thus far the impact of the automatic control revolution upon the industrial payroll has been felt most acutely by the production worker. Until about twenty-five years ago, the ranks of skilled and semi-skilled factory hands were the growing element in the labor force, absorbing the inward migration from farm to city. In the last ten years, however, as the index of manufacturing output has climbed from 75 to 110, the number of production workers has hovered around 12,000,000. It is evident that the number is now due to decline. In the electrical industry, for example, production employment shrank by 10 per cent in the six-year period from 1953 to 1959; during that same period production in this industry increased by 20 per cent. Even more striking records have been made by the larger units of the industry. In three years, from 1956 to 1959, the General Electric Company increased its output by 8 per cent and at the same time reduced its production payroll by 25 per cent. Its non-production workers now outnumber those on the factory payroll proper. Corresponding trends are to be observed in other industries. After the last retooling, the auto industry produced more units than ever before, and yet the auto cities of Michigan were rated as distress unemployment areas throughout the year of peak production. Projection of these trends into the future shows factory workers becoming as scarce as farmers toward the end of the century.

Vocal union organizations imbued with the Luddite spirit have made the public uncomfortably aware of these developments in recent years. Less is heard of what must be the already considerable impact of the white-collar computer. This movement has only just begun. Since typewriters furnish all the necessary linkage, it is clear that the liberation of white-collar workers from their routine tasks is due to proceed at a much faster rate. Again it should be emphasized that the object is not labor-saving alone. With a computer to do the job, all the many records kept by a corporation become a deck of punched cards or a length of magnetic tape that serves as the single record for every function from inventory control to the computing of a salesman's bonus. Herbert A. Simon, of the Carnegie Institute of Technology, has pointed out that the computer so programed is not merely a clerk but stands ready to assume a large portion of the functions of middle and top management. As a decision-maker, the computer can subject much larger masses of data to more sophisticated analysis in much shorter periods of time. Not only does it know the theory of linear programing better than most of our highest-paid executives; it can also learn from experience to improve its performance in the managerial function.

From decade to decade, the American economy has adjusted to the subversion of the social institution of work with flexibility and something of the same inventiveness with which it has absorbed the consequences of the subversion of property. One man-hour of work today produces what it took three man-hours to produce sixty years ago. This means that we could be producing the same national product as in 1900 with one third of the 1900 labor force. That would leave 58,000,000 members of the present labor force unemployed. But, of course, the American people have elected to apply their rising productivity to the production of a much larger volume of goods, about six times as much as in 1900. A major part of this vast increase in output is represented by products not dreamed of in 1900. In other words, the workers disemployed by rising productivity in the old industries have been absorbed in new ones to produce an expanding variety of goods or in entirely new functions created by the flow of abundance.

They could be producing goods in even greater volume if not variety today, but they have chosen to take a substantial portion of the gain in leisure. With the work week shortened from around sixty hours to forty hours, the much larger 1960 labor force is putting in a total number of man-hours that is only 40 per cent larger than that worked by the 1900 labor force. If the sixty-hour work week still prevailed, only 40,000,000 workers would be needed to produce the 1961 national product and some 27,000,000 workers would be unemployed.

This invention—the spreading of the same amount of work over the larger labor force by giving everyone less work to do—constitutes only one of the measures so far evolved to handle the problem of distribution. Moreover, it should be distinguished from the desperate share-the-work measures taken in the Great Depression, because it does not involve sharing the wage.

On the contrary, the portion of the national income going to the labor factor—that is, compensation of employees as against profit, interest, rent, and so on—has risen slowly from 53 to 73 per cent since 1900. Some substantial portion of this shift must be attributed to the decline in the number of proprietors, large and small, especially in agriculture. That the shift also reflects a gain on the problem of distribution becomes clear, however, when it is considered in connection with the way the total income is shared among the income groups. Since 1929 the share of the national income going to the most fortunate fifth of the nation's families has shrunk from 55 to 45 per cent. Almost the entire 10 per cent subtracted from the income of the top fifth has gone to the three middle fifths, improving their relative position by about 25 per cent.

This redistribution of purchasing power is another important factor in reducing the amount of work people do in the course of their lives. It makes it possible for young people to postpone their entrance into the labor market through high-school and even college age, and it takes workers out of the labor market by voluntary retirement at the other end of their careers.

But the shortening of the work week and the working life still leaves untold the real story of how work has been spread in order to secure the spread of purchasing power. If work is defined with any sort of strictness to mean productive work—that is, the extraction of raw materials and the making of consumable goods from them (farming, mining, manufacturing, building, and transportation)—then less than half of the labor force, only 25,000,000 people, are really at work.

The distribution of the abundance they produce is secured in large part by employing people in the task of distribution. This is not to say that the distributors do not serve a valid economic function. But selling and distribution costs commonly mark up the manufacturing cost of durable goods by 250 per cent. The major portion of the profit on the sales price therefore comes from the distribution process. Since gimmickry is thus made to grow by what it feeds upon, the distribution system pays a premium on waste. Its principal economic justification is that it does provide "work" and so increases the number of consumers.

To the 12,000,000 employed in distribution should be added another 12,000,000 who qualify as consumers by virtue of their employment in financial, clerical, and service functions—necessary but again not productive work even as it is formally defined in our national bookkeeping. Another large group of consumers are qualified by their enrollment on government payrolls. Certain members of the community will stoutly deny that these people ever do a day's work. Not counting the armed forces, their number now exceeds 5,500,000. If the figure looks too big, it is because we usually forget local and state governments in these calculations. The figure comes back into scale when we recognize that $132,000,000,000, nearly 30 per cent of the gross national product, turned over in government budgets in 1959. Those expenditures not only set up 5,500,000 consumers for the goods made by those more productively employed; the money also made substantial direct purchases of goods and so generated millions of the jobs in the production sector.

Our roll-call ends with the approximately 2,000,000 household employees and the 2,000,000 or more who are employed in teaching or self-employed in the learned professions. Those whom we have here classified as nonproductive workers constituted only 30 per cent of the labor force of 1900; they make up 60 per cent of it today. Compared with the day's work that confronts most of mankind every morning, most American citizens are not engaged in work at all.

Thus, up to the present, the American society has managed to handle the subversion of the institution of work without undue stress upon the system of distribution that has carried over from the days of scarcity. Work, the illusion of work, and pleasant substitutes for work furnish an expanding population with the purchasing power to consume an even more rapidly expanding volume of production. For most of the past twenty years employment has been "full."

It now appears, however, that the advance of technology has begun to outstrip our capacity for social invention. Before the second World War, in the flux of technological change and the oscillations of the business cycle, the system chronically fell 5 or 10 per cent below full employment and fell as far as 25 per cent below in 1933. It is instructive to compare this experience with the present. During the past several years, despite a steady rise in gross national product, unemployment has been rising. Each wavelet in the now well-damped business cycle has left a larger number of workers high and dry on the beach. Unemployment now approaches 6,000,000, or nearly 10 per cent of the labor force. But this figure seriously understates the gap between the jobs available in the production and distribution of goods in the economy and the number of people who need employment in order to be able to purchase their share of those goods.

That gap has been filled for the past fifteen years by the war economy that has grown up alongside the consumer economy in our country. The rolls of the employed include today the 2,500,000 in the armed forces; they are certainly not employed in the production and distribution of goods. To their numbers should be added the 1,000,000 civilian employees of the Department of Defense, whose principal employment is that of housekeeping and procurement for those in uniform. Finally, we must add the 2,500,000 workers in industry engaged in filling the procurement orders of the military. The total of those unemployed or employed outside the civilian economy thus comes to 12,000,000, close to 20 per cent of the labor force, only 5 per cent below the unemployment peak of 1933—and this at a time when the gross national product has reached an all-time high.

Wassily Leontief, of Harvard University, has recently adapted his "input-output" technique to permit detailed analysis of the prospective economic consequences of disarmament. Study of his tables indicates that even if the gross national product is maintained at peak levels through the transition period following an agreement to disarm, the civilian economy would very likely fall short of re-employing all of those who would be disemployed by the cut in military expenditure. The same study indicates that by 1965 technological disemployment will, in any case, eliminate about one fifth of the jobs in industry now generated by the procurement of arms (unless progress in the technology of armament continues to generate new starts on new weapons systems). In other industries, in the same period, technological progress promises to reduce employment by an average of close to 10 per cent.

The evidence that full employment is no longer an attainable objective seems to be growing. Of course, the arms budget can be arbitrarily increased, and the size of the armed forces along with it, to offset technological disemployment in the armament industries. But no one really wants to contemplate an indefinite continuation of the arms race. Alternatively, or concurrently, some of the slack can be taken up by a thirty-hour work week, a measure advocated by both presidential candidates as long ago as 1956. After that, the work week could be reduced to twenty-five, then twenty hours—and the inefficiencies inherent in such a short work week would help to create more jobs. At that point the nation will have come really close to being a workless society.

No reasonably predictable rate of growth in the productive sectors of the economy seems equal to overtaking the current rate of technological disemployment. Every step of progress in automatic control reduces the capital investment as well as the employment per unit of output. As the cost of investment goes down, the rate of technological progress must increase and with it disemployment. Even an expanding economy must employ progressively fewer workers in its productive sectors. At some point the terminus of full investment will be reached; even at the present level of opulence, the consumer economy shows signs of surfeit. There is, of course, a vast untapped market in the income groups at bottom third of the economic pyramid. But how are their wants to be implemented with purchasing power when that bottom third already counts the disemployed among its members?

In the long run, larger questions must be asked and answered. If a fraction of the labor force is capable of supplying an abundance of everything the population needs and wants, then why should the rest of the population have to work for a living? Preposterous alternatives come forward: give-away programs on television suggest that television might be employed to give the abundance away instead of trying to sell it. If production cannot be maintained at a profit under such circumstances, then why should a profit be made? Some other standard of accounting might serve even better to reduce waste and inefficiency.

These questions are put in a deliberately extreme form. They suggest the kind of overturn in the values of our society which is already quaking the ground beneath our feet. The virtues of hard work and profit are rooted in scarcity. They have no relevance to the economics or the sociology of abundance.

Any hard work that a machine can do is better done by a machine; "hard" these days means mostly boring and repetitive, whether in the factory or in the office. But the instinct for workmanship, the need to feel needed, the will to achieve, are deeply felt in every human heart. They are not universally fulfilled by the kind of employment most people find. Full employment in the kind of employment that is commonly available, whether blue-collar or white-collar, has been plainly outmoded by technology. The liberation of people from tasks unworthy of human capacity should free that capacity for a host of activities now neglected in our civilization: teaching and learning, fundamental scientific investigation, the performing arts and the graphic arts, letters, the crafts, politics, and social service. Character- istically these activities involve the interaction of people with people rather than with things. They are admittedly not productive activities; nor are they profitable in the strict sense. But they are highly reward- ing to the individuals involved and add greatly to the wealth of the nation. There is no question that our population numbers increasing millions of people qualified for such functions; our institutions of higher learning will have an enrollment of 6,000,000 before the decade is out. The nation's principal economic problem has become that of certifying its citizens as consumers of the abundance available to sus- tain them in tasks worthy of their time.

What disturbs the scarcity economist, of course, is that such certi- fication is likely to be provided by the public payroll. It must be recog- nized, however, that these activities—along with urban rapid transit, the enhancement and conservation of natural resources, public works, the best kind of medicine, the operation of museums, and so on—have never been or can no longer be conducted at a profit. Most of these activities and institutions are now short-changed. With abundance to support the expanding portion of the population engaged in them, we may anticipate that they will assume a higher priority in our civiliza- tion.

In any event, so long as the institutions of work and property preside over our economic activities, it is clear that the distribution of material goods will be achieved as it has been in the past, by expan- sion of the "nonproductive" payroll in both the public and the private sectors of the economy. The "peace corps" and the revival of the con- servation corps proposed by the Kennedy administration are the latest steps in this direction. There is plenty of need, if not demand, for labor of this kind. A really adequate program of assistance to the under-de- veloped countries might engage large numbers of disemployed factory workers in teaching their skills to people now entering on their industrial revolution. For some time to come we can be sure, the real work that remains to be done in the world will stave off the specter of universal leisure.

As for profit, considerations other than profit are already being pressed upon the great corporations by society through governmental regulatory agencies. The self-perpetuating management is understandably wary of such invasion of its prerogatives. In the present ascendance of its reputation, however, it should be more concerned about its performance than its prerogatives. What is most to be asked of the corporate enterprise system is the vigorous promotion of technological progress. This, in fact, is the primary purpose served by profit in the industrial system today; as a kind of involuntary savings, extracted beforehand from the thriftless consumer, retained corporate earnings have furnished the principal capital for industrial expansion throughout the past fifty years. In the future, the "economic republic" of A. A. Berle envisions the insistent intrusion of the public interest in the councils of the private governments that operate our economy, especially when it comes to the deployment of investment funds.

Our society is probably closer to being propertyless than workless today. But the rate of technological progress is speeding up. It appears now to be moving faster than even the responsive and resilient American social order can evolve. Some of the changes may have to come in quantum jumps. For these we need economic and political leadership whose perception and judgment are not compromised in any fashion by commitments to the past.

Section II-5

No Life Untouched

By the end of the century computers will affect every field in innumerable ways; some specific predictions.

By DAVID SARNOFF

In our increasingly complex world, information is becoming the basic building block of society. However, at a time when the acquisition of new scientific information alone is approaching a rate of 250 million pages annually, the tide of knowledge is overwhelming the human capability for dealing with it. So man must turn to a machine if he hopes to contain the tide and channel it to beneficial ends.

The electronic computer, handling millions of facts with the swiftness of light, has given contemporary meaning to Aristotle's vision of the liberating possibilities of machines: "When looms weave by themselves, man's slavery will end." By transforming the way in which he gathers, stores, retrieves, and uses information, this versatile instrument is helping man to overcome his mental and physical limitations. It is vastly widening his intellectual horizon, enabling him better to comprehend his universe, and providing the means to master that portion of it lying within his reach.

Although we are barely in the second decade of electronic data processing, the outlines of its influence on our culture are beginning to emerge. Far from depersonalizing the individual and dehumanizing his society, the computer promises a degree of personalized service never before available to mankind.

By the end of the century, for the equivalent of a few dollars a month, the individual will have a vast complex of computer services at his command. Information utilities will make computing power avail-

From *Saturday Review*, July 23, 1966. Reprinted by permission of David Sarnoff and the *Saturday Review*.

able, like electricity, to thousands of users simultaneously. The computer in the home will be joined to a national and global computer system that provides services ranging from banking and travel facilities to library research and medical care. High-speed communications devices, linked to satellites in space, will transmit data to and from virtually any point on earth with the ease of a dial system. Students, businessmen, scientists, government officials, and housewives will converse with computers as readily as they now talk by telephone.

In the health field, computers will be employed to maintain a complete medical profile on every person in the country from the hour of birth. The record will be constantly updated by a regional computer for immediate access by doctors or hospital personnel. The computer also will maintain files on every known ailment, its symptoms, diagnosis, and treatment. A doctor will communicate a patient's symptoms to the computer center and within seconds receive suggestions for treatment based both on the symptoms and the patient's history.

Computers will handle the nation's fiscal transactions from a central credit information exchange, to which all banks, business enterprises, and individuals will be connected. Purchases will be made, funds invested, and loans issued by transfers of credit within the computer without a dollar or penny physically exchanging hands. Even the soil will be computerized. The long-range outlook for agriculture includes new sensing devices that will be placed on larger farms, feeding information to the computer on soil moisture, temperature, weather outlook, and other details. The computer will calculate the best crops to plant, the best seeding times, the amount of fertilizer, and even the correct harvesting time for maximum yield.

Some of the most profound changes wrought by the computer will be in education. Here, the machine will do more than assist students to solve problems and to locate up-to-date information: It will fundamentally improve and enrich the entire learning process. The student's educational experience will be analyzed by the computer from the primary grades through university. Computer-based teaching machines, programmed and operated by teachers thoroughly trained in electronic data processing techniques, will instruct students at the rate best suited to each individual. The concept of mass education will give way to the concept of personal tutoring, with the teacher and the computer working as a team. Computers will bring many new learning dimensions to the classroom. For example, they will simulate nuclear reactors and other complex, dangerous, or remote systems, enabling students to learn through a form of experience what could formerly be taught only in theory.

The computer's participation in the field of learning will continue long after the end of formal education. The government estimates that 50 per cent of the jobs to be held ten years from now do not even exist today. With this tremendous rate of occupational obsolescence, future generations of Americans may pursue two or three careers during their lifetimes. The home computer will aid in developing career mobility by providing continuing self-instruction.

Just as it is recasting the educational process, the computer is also fundamentally changing the production and distribution of the printed word. Five centuries ago, Gutenberg broke words into individual letters. Electronic composition now breaks the letters into tiny patterns of dots that are stored in the computer's memory. Any character can be called up by the computer, written on the face of a cathode ray tube, and reproduced on film or paper in thousandths of a second. Nothing moves except the electrons.

When the electronic computer first appeared in composition rooms and printing shops several years ago, its job was to hyphenate words and justify text. But the computer, working at speeds of thousands of words a minute, was driving mechanical typesetting devices capable of setting only a few words per minute. Now, the development of computerized composition makes it possible to set text at hundreds of lines per minute. Photographs and drawings will be set the same way. Since the printed picture is itself a dot structure, the computer can electronically scan any photograph or drawing, reduce it to dots and store it, then retrieve it and beam it on a cathode ray tube for immediate reproduction.

In the future, electronics will develop processes that will make it possible to go from final copy and illustrations to printing in one integrated electronic process. One result will be that newspapers, in the foreseeable future, will no longer be printed in a single location. Instead, they will be transmitted through computers in complete page form to regional electronic printing centers that will turn out special editions for the areas they govern. Local news and advertising will be inserted on the spot. Eventually, the newspaper can be reproduced in the home through a small copying device functioning as part of a home communications center.

Basic changes also will come to other areas of the printed word. For example, of the more than one billion books published every year, almost half are textbooks. The growth of knowledge and the factor of obsolescence mean that these texts must be supplemented by a professor's mimeographed notes. Today, these notes have a small distribution of only a few hundred copies. Computers will make it possible to catalogue this information and thus broaden its availability.

At the turn of the century, most large universities will not only have electronic composition systems that allow them to reprint original research, theses, or course notes upon demand; they will also have a computerized information retrieval library. This process of information retrieval can be duplicated in almost any other field. The scientist will have the latest technical papers culled by the computer and reproduced in the laboratory or home. The computer will bring to the attorney all the pertinent laws, decisions, and precedents on any case that concerns him. The business executive need not rush to the office every morning; most of the information he will need to conduct his business will be run off for him at home, and he will have two-way national and global closed-circuit television, via satellites, for meetings and conferences.

Some of these developments are probabilities, some of them are certainties, and all of them are or soon will be within the capabilities of the computer art. But one fact is absolute: the incredible growth of the computer in numbers, power and availability.

In just ten years, the typical electronic data processor has become ten times smaller, 100 times faster and 1,000 times less expensive to operate. These trends will continue, and our national computing power, which is doubling every year, will soon be sufficient to make the computer a genuinely universal tool.

In 1956, there were fewer than 1,000 computers in the United States. Today, there are 30,000, or more than $11 billion worth; and by 1976 the machine population may reach 100,000. And these figures will, of course, be greatly increased through the growth of data processing in other nations.

A decade ago, our machines were capable of 12 billion computations per hour; today, they can do more than 20 trillion, and by 1976—a decade from now—they will attain 400 trillion—or about two billion computations per hour for every man, woman and child. Quite evidently, the threshold of the computer age has barely been crossed.

Nevertheless, for all its potential to stretch the mind a thousand-fold, it is perhaps necessary to point out that the computer is still a thing—that it cannot see, feel, or act unless first acted upon. Its value depends upon man's ability to use it with purpose and intelligence. If his postulates are wrong, the computerized future can only be a massive enlargement of human error.

Ramsay MacDonald once warned against "an attempt to clothe unreality in the garb of mathematical reality." Computers echo this warning. For they cannot usurp man's unique ability to blend intuition with fact, to feel as well as to think. In the end, this remains the basis of human progress.

The task ahead will be to assign to the machine those things which it can best do, and reserve for man those things which he must provide and control. It is my conviction that society will adjust itself to the computer and work in harmony with it for the genuine betterment of life.

Section II-6

The New World Coming

Tomorrow's computers will revolutionize business, education, communications, science—in ways only dimly foreseen.

By JOHN DIEBOLD

It is an extraordinary era in which we live. It is altogether new. The world has seen nothing like it before. I will not pretend, no one can pretend, to discern the end; but everybody knows that the age is remarkable for scientific research into the heavens, the earth, what is beneath the earth; and perhaps more remarkable still is the application of this scientific research to the pursuit of life. The ancients saw nothing like it. The moderns have seen nothing like it until the present generation ... The progress of the age has almost outstripped human belief.

Those words were not spoken today—though I choose them to set today in perspective—but were used in 1847 by Daniel Webster when he opened a new stretch of railroad track in New Hampshire. A greater parallel exists between that era and our own than we normally realize. In that earlier era, science first began to be applied on a wide scale and out of that process came an entirely new society—an industrial society. Out of it, too, came problems, many of which still plague us. When we look back at that great technological upheaval, the real significance of those then-wondrous machines is the human and social change that accompanied their industrial use.

Just as yesterday's innovations proved to be moments in history— way stations leading to newer technology—so today the conception of the computer which we have learned to accept is becoming a thing of the past. Up-to-date systems are no longer glassed-in, carefully iso-

---

From *Saturday Review,* July 23, 1966. Reprinted by permission of John Diebold and the *Saturday Review.*

lated accounting machines. Instead they perform an almost limitless variety of functions, and vary with individual requirements.

For example, the newest computer systems may appear as input/ output units in individual desks; small television-like screens with keyboards and copying devices. When you ask a question you see the answer almost simultaneously on the screen. If you want a copy of the answer, you can make it immediately. The heart of the system is a switching center rather like the telephone system. Computers, storage elements of many varieties, and many other devices used as part of the system are accessible as you need them, connected through the switching center to the terminal unit at your fingertips. Thousands of people may use such systems at the same time, and each need know no more about the operation of the system than the average person knows about the telephone. In the next decade the typical computer system is going to be of this kind.

Another radical change stemming from these new computer systems involves the relationship between man and machine. One no longer need carry data down to a computer center, or go through a laborious process of getting it into the machine and then waiting for results. Each technological development is moving us toward an easier, more productive relationship between man and machine. Already, for example, a computer can transpose a rough design into exact specifications. If an engineer makes a free-hand drawing of a bridge on such a system's television-like screen, the computer will convert the drawing into exact engineering specifications, will calculate and display materials and stress, and show the design in whole, in part, or in any perspective, in immediate response to the engineer's requirements.

Looking ahead, we see important changes in technology such as chemical memories; fluid and pneumatic systems that have instantaneous response; ability to store images, graphs, drawings and photographs, and to transmit them around the world. All these will be important elements of future computer systems. Graphic elements and the ability to communicate with TV screens are already becoming influential in progress being made in computer design. Yesterday these elements were undreamed of.

Work is being done on language translation by machine. Some document-translation is already on a regular production basis—in fact, people are now attempting to digest articles by machine. This work is still in its beginning stages and there are many problems to be overcome. But the history of this technology is that what seems impossible today becomes an accepted part of our lives tomorrow.

Development of voice recognition by computer, while rife with problems, also is yielding results.   Despite all the difficulties, voice-recognition equipment can be purchased today.   No serious forecast about computer systems in the 1970s can omit voice recognition systems with several-thousand-word vocabularies.   If this sounds unpromising, remember that only a few years ago people used to have two- and three-day meetings to discuss the problem of keeping records on magnetic tape.   How naïve that seems to us now.   Today, we already have machines that learn (they are called heuristic machines), that devise their own route to a goal or solution; machines that recognize patterns; and machines that can devise their own strategies—for example, winning at games with the men who design them.

Adding tremendous impetus to the technological explosion is the fact that, as computer capabilities are increasing, costs are decreasing. Between 1963 and 1972—a single decade—there will be a decrease of 85 per cent in the cost of completing a typical data-processing job. During this period, the cost of storage by magnetic tape will go down by 97 per cent; the cost of image storage by 96 per cent; and communication line costs, because of increased speeds of transmission, will decrease by 50 per cent.   These changes in economics will mean that we will be able to do more with information technology than we now can even imagine.

Let me turn to the problems of putting these machines to work.

Nowhere is the turn toward technology more obvious than in the *way* we manage.   When we first started to apply computers to business operations in 1954, we went through a very difficult experimentation period and were faced with the most puzzling kinds of problems.   We have largely emerged from that period, however, and today we are using computers in business for almost everything conceivable—and much that was not just a few years ago.   Senior management has begun to realize that the application of this technology is too important to leave to technicians, and that dramatic things can be accomplished if people who know the objectives of a business will take the responsibility of putting these new capabilities to work.   When this happens, you find remarkable achievements.

But along with this progress have come new questions and problems.   There are, for instance, union negotiation questions.   Throughout the country, a number of owners of newspapers have been willing to stake the very existence of their enterprises on the right to install a computer to prepare punch-tape to drive linecasting machines.   Just over the horizon, it is clear that this entire process will be bypassed.   Is it worth risking an enterprise on a process that is disappearing?

There are many similar questions.   What kind of men, for example, should be trained as managers in the new technological environment? How do we create an atmosphere that is conducive to creative people— for more and more of our businesses must be staffed by highly educated and creative personnel? These are only a few of the problems we face.

Most important are the human aspects. They are related to every problem we have in this field: questions of fear and uneasiness when faced with technological changes; questions of education; questions of identification with an enterprise, with a profession.

But along with the question of how we manage are questions concerning what we manage—of new areas of business opportunity. Here, I will speak of four main new entrepreneurial opportunities. The first is the obvious one that has already taken form—the industry that supplies the systems and the equipment. It is already a multi-billion dollar industry, and this is only the beginning.

The second example, as yet nonexistent but about to bloom as an important basic industry, is the data utility field. This is analogous in some ways to the electrical utility industry: It is cheaper for many people to use a central utility than for each individual to have his own generator. The same economic reasoning applies to the data utility industry, where many people can use a machine simultaneously. The technology of real-time processing, time-sharing, and communication will allow this to happen. Small and medium-sized businesses—and for some purposes large businesses—will just plug in for data processing as we now do for electricity.

The third example is the one now being called the inquiry industry —in some ways, the publishing field of the future. This will allow the sale of proprietary data over a communications system in answer to a query placed by the customer. The possibilities are unlimited; practically any information can be provided. We have already started to see the purchase of publishing firms by electronic companies, and this is just the beginning. There will be major changes in ownership in this area in the near future as businesses begin to position themselves to offer such services.

The fourth example is an industry of computer-based educational systems. As technology allows a dynamic or "alive" relationship between a student and a machine system that answers questions as they are posed and discerns gaps in a student's basic grasp of a subject, the much-heralded but until now disappointing teaching machines (better, I think, called learning machines) will begin to mean something. Such systems are already at work in some industrial situations—IBM's Maintenance Training being a good example. Other precursors can be seen in mentally handicapped children's use of computer-driven type-writers to help them overcome some of their handicaps.

If there is one salient fact about information technology, it is that it is going to produce enormous social change. As the quality of life is changed, as the rate of learning, information, travel, and communications all change, we will see a major change in living patterns, in hopes and desires. In short, a complete new environment will exist.

Section II-7

Mechanisms of Population Control*

HUDSON HOAGLAND**

It is impossible for the thoughtful man to excape a certain ambivalence of response to the social impact of most great scientific discoveries. The unlocking of nuclear energy promises enormous potential benefits as a source of industrial power and as a servant of the medical sciences. But the rapid multiplication of nuclear bombs in the arsenals of growing numbers of nation states, uncontrolled by enforceable world law, may render man an extinct species. All organisms must adapt to the environments or perish. After Hiroshima, the notable change in our environment is that it now contains nuclear weapons, which have made obsolete not only traditional views of national sovereignty but traditional concepts of how the security of nations can be protected. The hope for man is that he can change his ways of thinking to cope with this new environment before it destroys him.

There are of course many other examples of antithetical applications of science. The automobile and the airplane are of great convenience in transportation, but the automobile kills 40,000 Americans a year, and the airplane overhead may be an enemy bomber. The knife is a tool that can be used as well for murder as for surgery, and most drugs of value in medicine are harmful and even lethal when used inappropriately.

---

*This is an expansion of a shorter paper by the author entitled "Cybernetics of Population Control," presented at a seminar in May, 1963, on Human Fertility and Population Problems, held at the American Academy of Arts and Sciences. The original paper was published in March, 1964, in the *Proceedings* of this seminar (Schenkman Publishing Company, Cambridge, Mass.).

**From *Daedalus*, American Academy of Arts and Sciences, Harvard University, Summer, 1964.

It is especially ironic that the humane practices of medicine and public health, dedicated to reducing physical suffering and prolonging healthful lives, should be the primary cause of a major social disease. This disease is the unprecedented increase in the world population, especially in economically underdeveloped countries least able to afford the increased burden. Prior to World War II, during nearly 100 years following Pasteur and the development of bacteriology and immunology, the European population growth rate accelerated as a result of the conquest of infectious diseases and the improvement in public health measures, which reduced death rates. Since World War II western medicine has administered its sophisticated techniques in underdeveloped countries. Medical missionaries, using relatively inexpensive insecticides, antibiotics, inoculations, and vaccinations applied to masses of people, have drastically reduced the death rate, leaving the birth rate, always large, either unchanged or somewhat increased as a result of improvements in health and longevity. This beneficent process has greatly increased populations in the poverty-stricken countries of Asia, the Near East, Africa, and Latin America, which now contain, according to Kingsley Davis, 69 per cent of the world's adults and, through marked decreases in infant mortality, 80 per cent of its children.[1]

In most of the underdeveloped countries, the death rate has dropped at a record rate. Davis has pointed out that on the island of Mauritius in the Indian Ocean, within an 8-year period after the war, life expectancy increased from 31 to 51 years, a gain that took Sweden 130 years to achieve. In Taiwan, within two decades, the life expectancy increased from 43 to 63 years. This 20-year gain in life expectancy took 80 years to effectuate in the white population of the United States. These figures are typical of what has happened in most underdeveloped countries. In many countries the population is increasing at the rate of over 3 per cent per year, which will result in a doubling in 23 years. The world population as a whole is increasing at 2 per cent per year, a rate at which it will double in about 35 years. Oncoming generations of poverty-stricken, economically unproductive young people will increase the birth rate further as they come of age. Already this generation in some places is hungrier and more illiterate than that of its parents, and has fewer job opportunities. This is bad news in those countries with rising expectations, which now contain two-thirds of the world's people, such as China, India, Pakistan, the United Arab Republic, and various Latin American countries, where the average per capita income is less than $100 per year. The increasing numbers of the unproductive make increasingly difficult the accumulation of developmental capital, since most local produce must be consumed to maintain the growing population.

There are only two solutions to the disease of overpopulation. One is to increase death rates, and the other is to decrease birth rates. So far we have manipulated death control by decreasing death rates and so increasing the population. No one that I know of advocates reversing this process, although a nuclear war would certainly do so, and such a war is made increasingly likely by run-away populations. The alternative solution is birth control and family limitation on a rational basis. Man is the only animal that can deliberately direct and control his own evolution. It will be interesting to see which of these two variables, death or birth, he will manipulate. It must be one or the other, since a 2 per cent growth rate will result in one square yard of land area per person 600 years hence, an obvious absurdity.

We may learn something relevant to our problem from a consideration of how animals regulate and control their population problems. Many organisms possess remarkable methods of population control as contrasted with the conscious devices available to man.

In multiplying cultures of micro-organisms the growth rate accelerates exponentially; but as toxic metabolic products, such as acids or alcohol, accumulate, the rate declines and the curve describing numbers of organisms as a function of time ultimately flattens off. These S-shaped growth curves for bacteria and yeasts have been described by equations aimed at elucidating the dynamics of such population growths. Human populations, when relatively isolated by geography, social habits, and cultural factors, also display S-shaped growth curves; in other words, they reach asymptotic levels as a result of Malthusian brakes such as infectious diseases, war and famine, or, more hopefully, by migration or by rational family planning and birth control. The motivation for family planning has historically been a desire for better economic and educational advantages for small families desirous of upward social mobility. It is this factor that is primarily responsible for the small present growth rates of about a half of one per cent in most advanced industrial nations of Europe, rather than the Malthusian factors active in more primitive societies.

There are many studies on the regulation of insect populations. It has been shown that the fruit fly, *Drosophila*, above certain population densities decreases its egg laying, and to an amount proportional to the density. Many investigations have been made of flour beetles. Below a fixed number of grams of flour per beetle, cannibalism occurs in some species, egg production drops off, and in one species crowding results in females puncturing and destroying some of the eggs they have produced.   Frequency of copulation also declines with crowding.   There are some species of flour beetles with glands that produce a gas, the release of which is increased with crowding.   This gas is lethal to larvae and acts as an antaphrodisiac at high densities of population.   Flour contaminated with beetle excrement inhibits egg production of one species of beetle investigated, and the mixing of this contaminated flour with fresh flour decreases the rate of population growth, which is entirely reversible in the presence of fresh flour In these cases, the food supply is ample.

Among populations of mammals other than man, it was long thought that food and predators were the controlling factors in limiting populations of hares, lemmings and other rodents as well as of deer, caribou, and other forms.   The predators might be lynxes, wolves, foxes, and birds of prey, or micro-organisms producing epidemic diseases.   It was thought, for example, that the four-year cycles of build-up and decline of lemming populations terminating in their suicidal migrations were due to an increase in predators accompanying population growth, which ultimately caused the panic and decline. But the migrations and deaths appear now not to be caused by the predators.   Rather, the predators appear to multiply in response to the multiplying prey.   Similarly, for well over a century various observers have reported repetitive wide cyclic variations in the number of fox and lynx pelts taken by trappers in our northern woods.   These predators increase in number following cyclic increases in their prey. Lionesses have been reported to bear larger litters, two to four cubs, in environs of plentiful game. When game is scarce, there are only one or two cubs per litter.   While the lemming cycles have not been studied as systematically as those of some other species, it seems likely that these four-year fluctuations in population densities are determined by factors now known to regulate population cycles in other mammalian species, and I should now like to say something about these factors.

In past years the snowshoe hare population of Minnesota has been studied extensively.   These populations rise and fall through cycles of several years' duration.   There is a period of build-up, followed by a dying off.   Why do these marked oscillations in numbers of hares occur?   It was observed that when the animals died off there was usually plenty of food—they had not starved.   There were no evidences of an excessive number of predators.   Furthermore, the bodies showed no sign that any specific epidemic had killed them.   To quote from a 1939 study of the dead animals: "This syndrome was characterized primarily by fatty degeneration and atrophy of the liver with a coincident striking decrease in liver glycogen and a hypoglycemia preceding death.

Petechial or ecchmotic brain hemorrhages, and congestion and hemorrhage of the adrenals, thyroid, and kidneys were frequent findings in a smaller number of animals. The hares characteristically died in convulsive seizures with sudden onset, running movements, hindleg extension, retraction of the head and neck, and sudden leaps with clonic seizures upon alighting. Other animals were typically lethargic or comatose."[2] The adrenals were hypertrophied in some cases and atrophied in other. Signs of liver disease, hypertension, atherosclerosis and adrenal deterioration were typical of what one finds following Hans Selye's acute syndrome resulting from overactivity of the pituitary-adrenal axis.

Since effects of social stress have been found to limit populations of birds and mammals, a brief discussion of its operation is in order. Elsewhere I have defined stress as follows:[3] Any external situation threatening the organism may function as a stress. Situations calling for flight or fight, with their concomitant psychological and physiological expressions of fear and anger, are stressful. Especially in man the processes of inhibiting fight or flight may themselves result in stressful anxiety states. Psychological stress may result from the intensification of our instinctual drives and of the control of these drives to meet the demands of society. Such stresses may be chronic and produce far-reaching disturbances of a psychosomatic nature, including neuroses, in susceptible individuals. The balancing of one's needs and satisfaction in terms of learned inhibitions and prohibitions occasions stresses of this sort. The same stress situation may have quite different significance, psychologically, for different organisms in terms of their life histories and past conditionings, and therefore attempts to objectify and standardize such stresses meet with difficulty.

The physiologist has a variety of measures of how stress may disturb the body's regulation of the internal fluid environment of its tissues. The maintenance of constancy in this internal environment of blood and lymph is of great importance for proper functioning of the body. Blood and urinary measurements of certain endocrine systems brought into play by stress are particularly useful response indices, and have been used extensively in our laboratories as well as elsewhere. The quantitative analyses of adrenalin, secreted primarily by the medulla of the adrenal gland, and noradrenalin, a neurohumor primarily released at certain synapses and nerve endings of the autonomic nervous system, reflect defense responses especially to acute stress. Blood and urine measurements of the steroid hormones from the adrenal cortex and their metabolites have been used more widely than any other indices in recent years in studies of stress responses in mammals, including man. The adrenal cortex is activated by the pituitary adrenocorticotrophic hormone (ACTH), which, in turn, is released in increased amounts by action of the hypothalamus following bodily damage or threats. The adrenocortical hormones have ubiquitous actions on many tissues involved in response to stress and the maintenance of homeostasis.

Hans Selye has developed the concept of the general adaptation syndrome, which he defines as the characteristic emergency reaction or general stress responses of an animal, developing through three stages: (1) the alarm reaction, in which adaptation is attempted; (2) the stage of resistance, in which adaptation is optimal; and (3) the stage of exhaustion, in which adaptation fails. These various phases of the general adaptation syndrome may be studied in terms of the type of changes in constituents of body fluids, especially those involving activity of the adrenal cortex. In animals, the studies may include determinations, before and after stress, of adrenal size, adrenal ascorbic acid, and adrenal cholesterol as indices of adrenocortical function. Selye has concluded that many diseases are primarily a result of failure of the bodily mechanisms for adaptation to meet chronic stress situations adequately. He considers that disturbed patterns of endocrine secretion following the prolonged application of stressors may result in various chronic diseases and he thus speaks of the diseases of adaptation resulting from prolonged stress.[4]

Prolonged stressor actions may produce anxiety and chronic behavioral disturbances in man and in experimental animals. The role of life stresses as contributory agents to hypertension, arthritis, ulcers, skin disorders, asthma, and other allergic manifestations has been investigated by many biochemical, physiological, psychological, and psychiatric procedures. Experimentally induced states in animals, closely resembling the neuroses and psychosomatic disturbances seen in man, have been regularly brought about by frustrating conditioned reflex techniques, in themselves mild procedures but productive of highly abnormal and crippling behavior when carried on at regular intervals over periods of time. Life stressors producing neurotic behavior in man are very varied and may be difficult to define or to measure. In the biosciences, stresses for the most part are not directly identifiable, but are measured by the strains they produce as reflected in the above indices, especially those reflecting activity of the adrenal cortex.

In studies of rodents it has been found that, after the severe stress of winter crowding in burrows, there was much fighting among the males, sex drives were at a low ebb, the young were often eaten, and the females produced premature births. Susceptibility to nonspecific infections was also found, another by-product of excessive production of adrenal corticoids. After the numbers of such a colony are depleted through the effects of the stress syndrome, the colony then tends to build up again, going through repeated cycles of growth and decline.

There are many other examples. About forty years ago, a pair of deer was put on a small island of about 150 acres in Chesapeake Bay. The deer were kept well supplied with food. The colony grew until it reached a density of about one deer per acre. Then the animals began to die off, and this in spite of adequate food and care. When these dead animals were examined, marked evidence was found that the adrenal stress syndrome had been in operation. Studies made of the crowding of animals in the Philadelphia Zoo disclosed that in some species there was a ten-fold increase in atherosclerosis under conditions of severe crowding, as well as many other symptoms characteristic of stress. John Christian of the Naval Medical Research Institute made population studies in relation to the crowding of mice. In his 1950 paper in the *Journal of Mammalogy* entitled "The Adreno-pituitary System and Population Cycles in Mammals," he wrote in part: "We now have a working hypothesis for the die-off terminating a cycle. Exhaustion of the adreno-pituitary systems resulting from increased stresses inherent in a high population, especially in winter, plus the late winter demands of the reproductive system, due to increased light or other factors, precipitates population-wide death with the symptoms of adrenal insufficiency and hypoglycemic convulsions."[5]

John Calhoun at the National Institutes of Health has studied effects of crowding on rats, and I should like to describe his work in some detail. He investigated colonies of rats kept in pens at critical levels of crowding, and under these circumstances observed high infant mortality, high abortion rates, failures of mothers to build nests. The young were often scattered about and eaten. When the rats were examined, there was also evidence of the stress syndrome, and Calhoun has spoken, most appropriately, of what he calls "pathological togetherness." He has reviewed this work in an article entitled "Population Density and Social Pathology," published in the *Scientific American,* in February, 1962.

Calhoun confined wild Norway rats in a one-quarter-acre enclosure with plenty of food and water. At the end of 27 months the population stabilized itself at 150 adults. From the very low adult mortality rate in uncrowded conditions, one would have expected a population of 5000, not 150 rats. But infant mortality was extremely high. The stress from social interaction disrupted maternal behavior so that only a few of the young survived. Calhoun later studied groups of domesticated white rats confined indoors in observation rooms under better controlled conditions. Six different populations were examined. Each group was allowed to increase to twice the number that his earlier experience indicated could occupy the allotted space with only moderate stress. Pathological behavior was most marked in the females: pregnancies were often not full term; there were many abortions and many maternal deaths; the mothers often could not nurse or care for their young. Among the males there was much sexual deviation, homosexual behavior and cannibalism, and abnormal behavior ranging from frenetic overactivity to pathological withdrawal, in which some males emerged from their nests only to eat and drink. Patterns of social behavior were thus badly deranged at twice normal crowding.

The experiments took place in four interconnecting pens, each 6 × 6 feet in area. Each was a complete dwelling unit, with a drinking fountain, a food hopper, and an elevated artificial burrow, which was reached by a winding ramp that held five nest boxes. One of these storied rat apartment houses was located in each of the four pens. There was comfortable space in the colony for 12 adult rats in each pen, the size of group in which rats were normally found to thrive. The setup should thus have been able to support 48 rats comfortably without overcrowding. At the stabilized number of 80 to 100, double the comfortable population, which they were allowed to reach by breeding, an equal distribution of the animals would have found 20 to 25 adults in each pen, but the animals did not dispose themselves in this way.

Biasing factors were introduced in the following fashion. Ramps were arranged enabling the animals to get from one pen to another and so traverse the entire four pens in the room. However, the two end pens, numbers 1 and 4, each had only one ramp connecting them with pens 2 and 3 respectively, while the middle pens had two ramps each, one ramp connecting in each direction. The rats had to make a complete traverse of the pens to go from one of the end pens to the other. This arrangement of ramps immediately weighted the probabilities in favor of a higher density in the two middle pens, since pens 2 and 3 could be reached by two ramps, whereas pens 1 and 4 by only one ramp each. With the passage of time strange aspects of the behavior of the group skewed the distribution in an unexpected way. As a result there developed an unexpected arrangement of the sex ratios of the animals in the various pens. The females distributed themselves about equally in the four pens, but the male population was concentrated almost overwhelmingly in the middle pens, the reason for this being the status struggle which takes place among the males. Shortly after six months of age each male enters into a round robin of fights that eventually fixes his position in the social hierarchy. These fights took place in all of the pens, both the middle and the end pens; but in the end pens, during the period when the social hierarchy was being established, it became possible for a single dominant male to take over the area as his territory.

Calhoun describes how this came about. The subordinate males in all pens adopted the habit of arising early in order to be able to eat and drink in peace. Rats generally eat in the course of their normal wanderings, and the subordinate residents of the end pens, having been defeated by the dominant males there, were likely to feed in one of the middle pens, where they as yet had not had to fight for status. When, after feeding, they wanted to return to their original quarters, they met with difficulty. By this time the dominant male in the end pen would have awakened and would engage the subordinates in fights as they tried to come down the single ramp to the pen. For a while the subordinate would continue his efforts to return to his home pen, but after a succession of defeats he would become so conditioned that he would not even make the attempt. In essence, Calhoun points out that the dominant male established his domination in the end pens and his control over a harem of females, not by driving the other males out, but by preventing their return over the one lead ramp. While the dominant male in an end pen slept a good part of the time, he made his sleeping quarters at the base of the ramp. He was therefore on perpetual guard, awakening as soon as another male appeared at the head of the ramp. He usually had only to open his eyes for the invader to wheel around and return to the adjoining pen. Since there were two ramps for pens 2 and 3, no one male could thus dominate both means of access. The dominant males in pens 1 or 4 would sleep calmly through all the comings and goings of his harem, seemingly not even hearing them. His behavior during his waking hours reflected his dominant status. He would move about in a casual and deliberate fashion, occasionally inspecting the burrow and nests of his harem. But he rarely entered a burrow, as did some other males in the middle pens merely to ferret out the females. A territorial male might tolerate other males in his domain provided they were phlegmatic and made themselves scarce. Most of the time these subordinate males hid in the burrows with the adult females, and only came out onto the floor to eat and drink; they never tried to engage in sex activity with the females.

In the end pens, where population density was thus kept low, the mortality rate among infants and females was also low. Of the various social environments that developed during the course of the experiments, the breed pens—as the two end pens were called—were the only healthy ones, at least in terms of group survival. The harem females generally made good mothers and protected their pups from harm. In the middle pens the pregnancy rates of the females were the same as those in the end pens, but a very much lower percentage of their pregnancies terminated in live births. In one series of experiments 99 per cent of the young born in pens 2 and 3 perished before weaning, and in others of the six experiments somewhere between 80 and 95 per cent perished.

The females that lived in the densely populated middle pens became progressively less adapted to building adequate nests, and eventually stopped building them at all. Normally rats of both sexes build nests, the females doing so most vigorously around the time of parturition. It is an undertaking that involves repeated periods of sustained activity, with the searching out of appropriate materials, such as strips of paper, and transporting the strips to a nest, which they arrange in cup-like form. In the crowded middle pens, however, the ability of the females to persist in this activity was greatly impaired. The females began merely to pile the strips in heaps, sometimes trampling them into a pad that showed little sign of cup formation. Later they brought fewer and fewer strips to the nesting site, and in the midst of transporting a bit of material often dropped it and engaged in some other activity occasioned by contact and interaction with other rats met on the way. In the extreme disruption of their behavior during the later months of the population's history, they built no nests at all, but would bear their litters on the sawdust in the burrow box. The females also lost the ability to transport their litters from one place to another, a task they would normally accomplish with skill. If they did try to move a litter, they would drop individuals and scatter them about on the floor. The infants thus abandoned throughout the pens were seldom nursed. They would die where they were dropped and be eaten by the adults. In the middle pens, when a female came into heat, she would be relentlessly pursued by all of the males until she was exhausted, with the result that, within a relatively short time, 25 per cent of the females in the crowded pens died; in contrast, only 15 per cent of the adult males died over the same period in the middle pens. In the end brood pens, however, this sort of thing did not happen. The females there would retire to bear their young in nests they made in a normal fashion, and were protected from the excessive attention of other males by the territorial male.

In the middle pens, a great deal of fighting among the males went on, with now one and now another assuming the dominant position. After a while, most of the males in the middle pens gave up the struggle and simply retired, making themselves as scarce as possible and spending a lot of their time sleeping. In contrast, in pens 1 and 4 one male predominated and peace reigned. These dominant males took care of the females and of the juveniles, never bothering them in any way.

Among the sub-dominant males there was much abnormal behavior. For instance, there was a group of homosexuals. They were really pan-sexual animals, and apparently could not discriminate between sex partners. They made sexual advances indiscriminately to males, juveniles, and females that were not in oestrus. Frequently attacked by their more dominant associates, they very rarely contended for status.

Another type of male emerged in the crowded pens. This was essentially a very passive type, that moved a good deal like a somnambulist, ignoring the other rats of both sexes, and ignored by all of them. Even when the females were in oestrus, these passive animals made no advances to them, and only very rarely did other males approach them for any kind of play. They appeared to be healthy, attractive and sleek, but they were simply zombies in their conduct as far as the other rats were concerned.

The strangest of all of the abnormal male types described by Calhoun were what he called the probers. These animals, which always lived in the middle pens, took no part at all in the status struggle. Nevertheless, they were the most active of all the males in the experimental population, and persisted in their activities in spite of attacks by the dominant animals. In addition to being hyperactive, the probers were hypersexual, and in time many of them became cannibalistic. They constantly chased females about, entering their nests, having intercourse with them in the nest, a thing that normal rats would never do. These probers conducted their pursuits of oestrus females in a very abnormal manner, abandoning all courtship ritual, which is characteristic of mating rats.

In these experiments by John Calhoun we see the development of serious pathology directly attributable to overcrowding at only twice the number of rats per unit area normally required for a healthy society. It is tempting to draw a comparison of city slums with the crowded middle pens and of prosperous suburbs with the orderly end pens, far-fetched though it may be.

We are, however, justified in asking to what extent the stress syndrome may be a limiting factor in reducing the growth rate of human populations. As far as I know, there are no adequate data on which to base an answer. Studies from a number of laboratories, including our own, have demonstrated that the pituitary adrenal system responds under stress in a way similar to that of other mammals. There is direct evidence that inmates of concentration camps experienced acute forms of the stress syndrome that may have accounted for many deaths. Concentration camps would be more appropriate sources of comparison to highly congested animal populations than city slums, since in crowded cities even the very poor do have some mobility. They can escape from their immediate congestion onto the streets and associate with other members of the population. The high incidence of street gangs and juvenile delinquency is especially characteristic of overcrowded city areas and constitutes a form of social pathology. Several studies have also indicated a higher incidence of schizophrenia and of other psychotic and neurotic behavior in congested urban areas than in more spacious surroundings, but other factors may be involved here. The increased incidence of atherosclerosis and other cardiovascular pathology associated with urban living and its competitive stresses may also be enhanced by crowding, although direct evidence for this effect of population density is lacking. In underdeveloped countries with high birth rates and recently lowered death rates, resulting in population growth rates of 2 to 4 per cent per year, any possible decrease occasioned by the stress syndrome would be obliterated through the action of medical and public health measures that are enhancing life expectancies and would mask any small reduction in life expectancies resulting from stress.

There is a large literature on the social behavior of animals in relation to population density. Of especial importance is a book by V. C. Wynne-Edwards entitled *Animal Dispersion in Relation to Social Behavior*,[6] some of whose conclusions I should like to summarize.

In nature, when food supplies are fortuitously removed or fail to materialize, a local overpopulation emergency results; among highly mobile flying animals, such as insects and birds, this can be immediately relieved by emigration. The social hierarchy and code of behavior to which the animal subscribes act as devices to force out whatever surplus of animals exists. The exiles may be condemned to perish, or under other circumstances, they may set up new communities in other localities. In the cold boreal and arctic regions, most of the erupting species are birds. Many birds are adapted to exploit intermittent or undependable crops of food, and are to a large extent nomadic in their search for regions where supplies are temporarily plentiful. Two distinct biological functions appear to be served by emigration. One is that of a safety valve to give immediate relief to overpopulation; the other is a pioneering function to expand and replenish the range of the species as a whole, and provide for gene exchange. Emigration of the safety valve kind is associated with stress and with quickly deteriorating economic conditions (locusts). On the other hand, providing pioneers can be afforded only when conditions are good. In more variable environments, both functions tend to become important and to be exercised on a large scale. The individuals expelled are in either case usually the junior fraction of the hierarchy.

In this connection I am reminded of human colonizing activities— the Greek city states that sent young people off to colonize the Mediterranean area, Italy, Sicily, and Africa, and the lands around the Aegean and the Black Sea. It was the younger sons of British families and the emigrants of Portugal, Spain, and France who established colonies in the western hemisphere, thereby relieving population pressures at home. Like many animal colonies, Australia was originally colonized by a group very low in the British pecking order, namely, prisoners. Ireland is an especially interesting case. In 1670 Ireland had a population of approximately a million people. By 1845 this had increased to eight million. The Irish were heavily dependent upon one crop, the potato, which was grown on small plots sufficient to feed a family. Over a period of six years (1848–1854), a blight destroyed the potato crop. Nearly a million persons starved and another million emigrated. Agriculture reforms were introduced, the small plots being consolidated for purposes of diverse crop farming, and ultimogeniture was established. But the population continued to fall, until it is now about four million, only half of what it was before the potato famine. The reasons for this decline were continued emigration, and a social change characterized by very late marriages, or often no marriage at all. The pattern is for the youngest son to maintain the farm, care for his parents, and usually not marry while they are alive. The result is that population growth in Ireland is low despite the influence of the Catholic Church.

To revert to animal societies, Wynne-Edwards points out that the same general social machinery that controls safety valve emigrations is involved in regulating such seasonal redispersions of animals as the annual two-way migrations of birds. Among other investigations of mortality promoted by stress, the white stork has been intensively studied. Nestling mortality is often very heavy under crowded conditions; individual chicks may be deliberately killed and sometimes eaten by one of their parents, usually the father. This is most likely to happen where the parents are beginners or young adults, and presumably of lower status in the pecking hierarchy. The killing off of the young in prolific breeding conditions is characteristic of a great many birds that have been investigated, as well as of many mammals, and is a direct result of social stress. Both the killing of the young and cannibalism are known to occur quite widely in mammals: for instance, in rodents, lions, and also in primitive man. Cases of cannibalism are found in fish, spider crabs, spiders, and fractricide in insect larvae of various types. *In all cases experimentally investigated, the mortality is found to be density dependent and to cease below a certain critical population density.*

Mortality from predation, which has also been examined, appears to be density dependent to the extent that the prey cooperates by making its surplus members especially vulnerable to predators. As mentioned earlier, the density elements in predation seem to arise first on the side of the prey and not on that of the predators. Because of lowered resistance to infective agents following prolonged stress, disease as a form of predation may effectively reduce excessive population. In this case a surplus of individuals predisposed to injury by their dominant fellows naturally experiences a variable amount of uncontrolled mortality, which tends to fall most heavily on the young, as yet unprotected by acquired immunity from bacterial and viral infections. Social stress can lead to casualties at all ages, both through direct and mortal combat and through stress-induced disease. The victim of severe stress is likely to develop physiological disorders affecting many organs, especially the lymphatic apparatus, and including the spleen and thymus, the nervous system, circulatory, digestive and generative organs, the endocrine glands. As we have seen, the effect of stress is especially notable in the adrenal cortex, which serves an intermediary role between the stressor and the organs responding to adrenal cortical hormones. Social stress is sometimes partly physical, as when the exercise of peck-order rights leads to the infliction of wounds, or the withholding of food and shelter. But, as Wynne-Edwards points out, it may also be largely mental, as in man, who in his more unsophisticated states may die from the conviction that he has been bewitched. Instances are known of birds, mammals, and amphibians similarly dying from non-specific injuries apparently induced by social stress.

And now, what about man? What can we do about the world population explosion? We can, of course, do nothing and wait for the stress syndrome or for some new virus to do its work. We can leave our destruction to some trigger-happy dictator with a suitable stock pile of nuclear weapons, or, finally, we can decide on an optimal population for the world and, by education and such social pressure as tax bonuses for small families, try to see that it is not exceeded.

Psychological prejudice, indifference, and downright hostility are the major blocks to planned population limitation. We know many methods of birth control: coitus interruptus, jellies, douches, diaphragms, condums, surgical procedures, and "the pill," and ongoing research will give us more and better methods, but none is of value if people refuse its use. Among the very poor and illiterate, cost and the difficulties of use of contraceptives demand massive government aid, financial, social and educational. Prudery and politics, myth, superstition and tradition have so far rendered birth control ineffective in the very countries most in need of it.

There are certain factors that specifically inhibit human population growth. One of these is a rise in the social, economic, and educational level of the people. Thus birth rates in the United States, with the exception of the postwar baby boom, have, in general, fluctuated inversely with economic conditions. Davis has pointed out that in all of the industrialized countries of Europe economic growth always outpaces population growth, thus repeatedly demonstrating that population pressure on the means of subsistence does not operate to lower populations as has often been thought. Other things being equal, the richer the nation the slower the population growth, an observation sharply divergent from the claim that the population explosion is good for business. The decline in birth rates attendant on opulence results from a desire for upward social mobility on the part of parents, who know that their incomes will go further to advance the welfare of a small family and will make possible a better education for a few children and higher standard of living for themselves than for a big family. Within a single country and at a given time, one can see this principle in operation. Thus, in northern industrial Italy, the birth rate is low compared to that in the poor agricultural regions of the south, and this despite the influence of the Catholic Church and cash bonuses paid by the Italian government to encourage large families.

Decrease in birth rates with opulence has led some to the erroneous conclusion that an increase in food supplies decreases birth rates. It has therefore been argued that all we need to do to control the population explosion is to feed people well, as if there were an inverse correlation between food intake and fertility. As a matter of fact, the opposite appears to be the case. We have already pointed out that predatory animals increase in numbers and may have larger litters in the presence of ample prey. This fact has been established for a number of species, although its basis is obscure. A parallel situation also appears to exist for man. William Langer has presented an interesting and well documented discussion of what he calls "Europe's Initial Population Explosion."[7] Before the mid-eighteenth century Europe's population increases were slow and spasmodic. He points out that a population of 140 million in 1750 rose to 188 million in 1800 and to 266 million by 1850. A careful consideration of death rates demonstrates that they did not decrease significantly over this period. The increase appears to be due to fertility increases, and the question is why?

Langer points out that historically it has been established that there are correlations between harvest conditions and marriage and birth rates. In Sweden, where careful statistics go back to the seventeenth century, the annual excess of births over deaths in the eighteenth century was only 2 per thousand after a poor crop, but 6.5 after an average harvest, and 8.4 after a bumper crop. As late as the mid-nineteenth century high wheat prices resulting from scarcity were reflected in low marriage rates and to some extent in low birth rates.

Langer attributes the European population increase between 1750 and 1850 to the introduction of potato culture. The potato, introduced from South America via Spain in the late sixteenth century, within a hundred years had spread widely over Europe. It furnished a food yield per acre of two to four times that of grain, and an acre of even poor soil could feed a large family. Langer points out that under the feudal system the seigneur frequently denied marriage to able young people he had selected for special service, and guild masters also blocked or delayed marriages of apprentices and artisans. Thus during the seventeenth and early eighteenth centuries marriages were late and few compared to a later period after the old regime had broken down, with a resulting increase in marriages and birth rates.

Potato cultivation contributed to the decline of great feudal estates. It facilitated early marriages and made possible the nourishment of larger families. Thus in Ireland, with no industrial revolution and no war and no change in patterns of famine or disease and despite terrible poverty, the population increased from 3,200,000 in 1754 to 8,174,000 in 1846, just before the potato famine, the disastrous consequences of which we have seen. These figures do not include some 1,500,000 who migrated before the famine.

Thus both human and animal populations tend to increase with increasing food supplies, other things being equal. On the other hand, human populations decrease their growth rates with opulence, for in the opulent society economic and social advantages other than food make for small families and usually constitute more effective agents for reducing birth rates than improved food supplies are in increasing them.

Grenville Clark has argued that the population explosion probably cannot be controlled until the world has accepted universal and complete disarmament under world law, and devotes a substantial part of the 120 billion dollars now being spent on weaponry to raising the living standards of have-not peoples. He bases his view on the often demonstrated fact that birth control procedures are used extensively only by literate and prosperous people with hope and ambition for bettering their own lots and those of their children. The take-off point for family planning and limitation required a critical level of education and prosperity not now found in the very poor countries.

The completely gloomy view would be that if we do not manage to disarm within a decade or two we may solve the population problem by nuclear extermination. In any case, the two major problems of our time—nuclear war and the population explosion—are closely linked together. The physical sciences and the medical sciences have given mankind these two world-wide challenges never dreamed of by previous generations. Only by fundamental changes in our ways of thinking can they be solved.

REFERENCES

1. Kingsley Davis, "Population," *Scientific American,* 209:3 (September, 1963), 62–71.
2. This quotation is from an unusually interesting review by Edward S. Deevey, *American Scientist,* 48 (September, 1960), 415–430. He does not, however, cite the original paper containing this quotation.
3. Hudson Hoagland, "Stress," *McGraw-Hill Encyclopedia of Science and Technology* (New York: McGraw-Hill, 1960), pp. 180–182.
4. H. Selye, *The Physiology of Stress and Pathology of Exposure to Stress* (Montreal: Acta, Inc., 1950); *Fifth Annual Report on Stress* (New York: MD Publications, 1956); "Stress and Mental Illness," *Lancet,* 275 (1958), 205–208.
5. John J. Christian, "The Adreno-pituitary System and Population Cycles in Mammals," *Journal of Mammalogy* 31:3 (1950), 247–259.
6. V. C. Wynne-Edwards, *Animal Dispersion in Relation to Social Behavior* (New York: Hafner Press, 1962).
7. William L. Langer, "Europe's Initial Population Explosion," *American Historical Review,* LXIX, 1 (October, 1963) 1–7.

Section II-8

International Security— The Military Aspect

I. FRAMEWORK OF THE STUDY

The world is living through a period of swift and far-reaching up-heavals. Standards and institutions that have remained unchanged for centuries are breaking down. Millions who have hitherto passively endured their place in life are clamoring for a new and more worthy existence. Western Europe, the fountainhead of our civilization, has lost its position of dominance in world affairs. Across the great land mass of Eurasia and on the continent of Africa, new nations are rising in the place of colonial empires.

Mankind is yearning to realise its aspirations in peace. But it is faced by two somber threats: the Communist thrust to achieve world domination that seeks to exploit all dissatisfactions and to magnify all tensions; and the new weapons technology capable of obliterating civilization.

The United States has thus been placed in a fateful position. Our whole tradition impels us to desire peace. Relatively invulnerable behind two great oceans, we have until the end of World War II asked little of the world save to be free to work out our destiny undisturbed. But we have been forced to realize that our security is inextricably bound up with the safety of the rest of the free world and that freedom everywhere depends on our strength and resolution. Force alone will not supply the answer to the hopes of humanity. Yet our strength, effectively mobilized, can help bring about a framework of security in which these aspirations may be realized in freedom and without fear.

Looking at the world from the perspective of our past isolation and recent nuclear supremacy, perhaps the most difficult thing for us is to accept the reality of our peril. Other more exposed nations have had to learn to live over a period of centuries with the awareness that their existence might be imperiled by foreign attack. It is a new experience for Americans.

A new technology of unprecedented power and destructiveness has placed *all* nations of the world in dire peril. The largest "conventional" bomb of World War II—the famous blockbuster—had an explosive power of 20 tons of TNT. The first atomic bomb had an explosive power equivalent to 20 thousand tons of TNT, a thousandfold increase. Today, weapons with an explosive equivalent of 20 million tons (20 megatons) have been tested, and there is no theoretical upper limit: it is possible to construct weapons of almost any explosive power.

As the weapons have become more powerful, their speed of delivery has grown ever faster. Soon* missiles will be able to travel intercontinental distances and wipe out whole cities in one blow. A blow on fifty of our most important metropolitan areas would bring under attack 55 per cent of our population and 75 per cent of our industry. Moreover, if the fireball of a nuclear weapon touches the ground, it sucks up particles of earth and buildings and deposits them downwind as radioactive material. The area of this "fallout" would depend on meteorological conditions, but it could cover an area of 10 thousand square miles, or the size of the state of New Jersey. A successful attack on fifty of our most important urban centers would produce at least 10–15 million dead and 15–20 million injured from blast and heat and another 25–35 million casualties from "fallout" or a total of 60–65 million dead and injured.

What gives this weapons technology its ominous quality is that it is in the hands of a Communist movement which has proclaimed for over a generation now—the last time in the Moscow declaration of all Communist states on November 16, 1957—the irreconcilability of its system with that of the free world. Of course "peaceful coexistence" has reappeared periodically as a Soviet slogan. But, as used in Soviet propaganda, it has in the past been primarily a device to disarm intended victims. After World War II, it did not stand in the way of Soviet domination of the satellite orbit and the breaking of the most solemn wartime pledges regarding respect for freedom and independence of Eastern Europe. It did not stop the Berlin blockade, the Greek civil war, and the Korean aggression. After the Geneva "summit" conference, "peaceful coexistence" did not restrain the Soviet Union

*Written in January 1958.

from fomenting a crisis in the Middle East or from brutally suppressing the Hungarian revolution. In 1957 it did not keep the Soviet Union from threatening nuclear attacks on Norway, Denmark, and Turkey. Both their doctrine and their internal dynamism will impel the Soviet Union and Communist China to try to encourage every dissatisfaction and to fill every vacuum. Should we ever allow the U.S.S.R. and Communist China to attain strategic superiority, we can be certain that subsequent events will be brutal. And the power of these states, particularly of the U.S.S.R., has been growing both absolutely and relative to the United States until today it constitutes a grave threat.

The willingness and ability to resist aggression is the best guarantee for peace. Until there occurs a change in Soviet attitudes, everything depends on the steadfastness of the United States and other free nations and on the willingness to act resolutely in the face of continuing peril and ambiguous challenges.

II. THE NATURE OF OUR STRATEGIC PROBLEM

Ever since our unilateral disarmament at the end of World War II failed to produce the peace we desired so earnestly, the United States has been forced to engage in a military effort unprecedented in our history in peacetime. Even so, it has still proved inadequate to the challenge we confront. The sporadic nature of our effort has been caused by many factors, including the nature of our historical experience. Tradition impels us to believe that peace is the normal relation among states. As a result, we have conceived it to be the task of our military policy to assemble overwhelming power to "punish" the disturber of the peace—the aggressor. Also, aggression is best understood when it is an unambiguous and clear act. Because, in the past, many other states were threatened before the danger to our security became explicit, we have been able to count on other countries to hold a forward line while we rallied our physical, moral, and psychological resources. Thus, our remoteness from the other major centers of world affairs has enabled us hitherto to rely on relatively small forces-in-being and to mobilize our resources only *after* a war had started.

Many of these ideas have been overthrown by technological developments since World War II and by the emergence of the United States in the forefront of world affairs. Soviet policy has coupled an attempt to develop overwhelming power with a strategy of deliberate ambiguity. The ambiguity resides in advancing by steps so small that the risks of resisting any given advance always seem out of proportion to the objective, or masking the aggression so that the Soviet move ap-

peals to what the free world considers as "legitimate" methods of political warfare. As a consequence, the recognition of aggression has
often proved as difficult as finding the means to resist it. A symptom of
the difficulty is that a United Nations committee charged with the task
of defining aggression felt itself forced to abandon the effort.

At the same time that the forms of aggression have multiplied and
become more ambiguous, we have lost the safety indicators of a more
secure past. We can no longer think of our military effort as designed
for a conflict that we enter only after other nations have run the initial
risks, as was the case with our participation in World Wars I and II.
Since no other nation any longer has the strength to resist alone, the
safety of the non-Communist world will depend on our ability, psychological and military, to engage our forces promptly and decisively in
case of aggression.

The importance of forces-in-being is magnified by the changed significance of industrial potential. As long as the destructiveness of
weapons was relatively limited as compared to the complexity of their
means of manufacture, victory in war could be achieved only through a
quantity of equipment too large to stockpile before the outbreak of
hostilities. Massive production of armament during the course of a war
was thus a vital element of national strength, and an attack on production facilities was a highly effective strategy. But with the rapid and
overwhelming destructiveness of modern technology, each major power
will, in the absence of a massive and reliable defense, be able to disrupt
the production facilities of its opponents with relatively few weapons
in a matter of hours. Industrial strength is therefore a military asset
only to the extent that it can provide armaments before the outbreak of
war.

Thus our military problem, with which this particular panel is
exclusively concerned, has four aspects:

1. We require a growing industrial, technological, and scientific
base in order to achieve a state of continual readiness for the long haul.
Without an adequate industrial plant, we will not be able to produce
the ever-increasing variety of weapons required for our protection.
Without an expanding pool of scientific talent and a steadily rising level
of scientific activity, we shall not be able to maintain our security in a
situation where the real armaments race is in the laboratories.

2. Scientific development by itself is ineffective strategically, however, if it cannot be translated rapidly into operational weapons. Great
importance therefore attaches to two kinds of lead time: first, the in-
terval between the drawing board and operational weapon; and second,
the rapidity with which weapons are manufactured. A lag in either
category is certain to create a strategic weakness.

3. At the same time, long-range programs and balance cannot become ends in themselves. However powerful we may be potentially, our strategic effectiveness in any given crisis depends on our active forces supplemented by any quickly mobilizable reserve capabilities. Given the power and destructiveness of modern weapons, we cannot count on an extended period of mobilization prior to the outbreak of hostilities.

4. But however vast our over-all strength, it may still be ineffective in meeting certain challenges if it cannot be applied with discrimination. With the development of the Soviet nuclear stockpile and the means to deliver it, we can no longer rely on our capability to deliver crushing retaliation on the Soviet homeland as the deterrent to *all* types of aggression. For with the growth of the Soviet capability to inflict a massive blow on the United States, there exists the great danger that the Soviet Union will seek to use its nuclear striking force as a shield behind which to expand by more limited means. Thus the adequacy of our military establishment will be determined by its ability to discharge two distinct though related tasks: one, to discourage an all-out attack through the existence of a powerful, instantly ready retaliatory force, and, two, to react effectively to limited aggression through the ability to make our response fit the challenge.

These four factors—the importance of a growing industrial base, the crucial role of lead times, the increasing significance of forces-in-being, and the necessity of a versatile military establishment—impose on policy makers an unparalleled problem of choice. It is further complicated by the explosive rapidity with which technology is developing. Almost up to the outbreak of World War II, a weapons system would be good for nearly a generation; the equipment of U.S. ground forces, for example, changed very little between 1919 and 1940. Today a weapons system begins to be obsolescent when it has barely gone into production. The B-17 "Flying Fortress" remained in operational use for eight years; the B-36 intercontinental bomber was obsolescent in less than five years; and the B-52 jet bomber is beginning to be outdated even before all wings of our Strategic Air Command are fully equipped with it.

Moreover, all weapons are becoming increasingly costly. A new submarine costs ten times as much as its World War II counterpart. A B-52 wing is four times as expensive as the B-36 wing it replaces. Each new weapon system costs more than double its predecessor, which it replaces at shorter and shorter intervals.

This technological race places an extraordinary premium on the ability to assess developing trends correctly, to make and back decisions firmly, and to be prepared to change plans when necessary. It also places the side that is on the defensive at special disadvantage. The aggressor need prepare only for the war he proposes to fight. But the side that is militarily on the defensive must gear its planning and procurement to the possibility of an attack at any moment. We must therefore take care to see that no important strategic weakness exists at any given point of time.

The basic problem of American strategy then is the ability to make effective choices. This will depend on the courage and sense of purpose of our leadership, the effectiveness of the organization of our government, and the spirit of our people.

III. DEVELOPING POWER TRENDS

The outstanding characteristic of the strategic situation is a military technology in a state of spectacular change. Starting with World War II scientific research has produced military equipment and new patterns of military operations at an ever-accelerating pace. Four trends appear to be of particular significance.

1. Weapons technology will become increasingly complex with a corresponding increase in the difficulty of choosing the most effective combination of weapons. The atomic bomb of 1945 has been outmoded by a broad range of highly developed weapons both large and small. The original nuclear weapons required a large aircraft and crew. Equally powerful warheads have been reduced in size and simplified to the point where it will soon be possible to employ them effectively in antiaircraft rockets. And with the increasing capacity for the production of fissionable materials, nuclear and thermonuclear weapons have become available in very large quantities.

The outlook is even more portentous than the achievements of the recent past. Aircraft will be capable of cruising at several times the speed of sound, of bombing from altitudes of a dozen miles and more, and of carrying air-launched missiles so that they need not pass directly over heavily defended target areas. New high-energy fuels will give them greatly increased range and performance.

Within a very short time, a major role in both offense and defense will be played by missiles. It will be possible to produce missiles of almost any desired range, from very short distances analogous to traditional artillery to intercontinental ranges of five thousand miles or more. Because these weapons require less extensive installations than airplanes, it will be possible to disperse and protect them more easily, and they will therefore be less vulnerable to surprise attack.

Earth satellites are a special adaptation of missiles that explore a new frontier in outer space and that will have important military applications.

Submarines, already extremely powerful weapons, will be even more important as nuclear propulsion comes to play an ever greater role. They can imperil our harbors and our sea communications with friendly nations. As a platform for missiles they can pose a constant threat of a sudden, devastating blow from unpredictable directions.

These are not dreams of the far distant future. Many of these weapons are in existence now; even the most remote among them is attainable within the time frame of this report by both the United States and the Soviet Union. Many of them will be in the hands of several nations.

2. The rate of technological change will increasingly complicate the tasks of the defense relative to the offense. Both offense and defense will improve—and improve enormously. However, foreseeable new offensive weapons such as intercontinental ballistic missiles—sudden in action, massively destructive, difficult to destroy either before launching or in flight—will greatly aggravate the problems of strategic defense and enormously increase its costs.

3. The U.S.S.R. will continue to gain in over-all military strength greatly aided by Communist China and some of its other allies. Although the rate of growth of these countries may slow down, the economic superiority of the West will become less and less significant militarily at our present levels of effort. By sacrificing the civilian sector of its economy, the Soviet Union has caught up with the United States in major fields of technology. In certain areas assigned high priority by the Kremlin, the Soviet Union has surpassed us qualitatively as well as quantitatively. Unless we greatly increase the pace and level of our military effort, the Soviet Union will achieve superiority in other fields as well.

4. The concept of "scarcity" in nuclear weapons will disappear from the calculations of the United States, the U.S.S.R., and to a lesser extent Great Britain. The United States, the U.S.S.R., and Great Britain will continue to increase the number and variety of their atomic weapons. Other countries will in due course have their own atomic arms, if on a more limited scale.

Section III

NEW PURPOSES AND MISSIONS

Before World War II higher education had three missions—teaching, research, and public service—and interpreted them narrowly to a small and privileged segment of the population. If the curriculum did not speak to the students' basic psychological needs, the lack was of small concern, because they generally came from backgrounds which compensated for weaknesses in the educational establishment. Higher education made little impact on either the lives of students or society generally.

Since 1945, however, colleges and universities have been forced to rethink their purposes and to expand their missions. Higher education has become necessary both for developing individuals and for developing nations. Institutions are asked to provide leadership for all sectors of society. And the quality of higher education is of vital concern. Several authors have been selected to examine these changes.

Section III-1

The Objective

Freedom has many facets. It includes the freedom to think and speak, to choose and influence one's government, to worship as one pleases, to earn and own property and decide its disposition, to go unmolested while observing the laws. It is usually guaranteed or at least expressed by legal provisions.

But for the individual, freedom cannot be achieved by legal provisions alone. It is, in the deepest sense, a personal quality, a quality which can be approached but never fully achieved.

The man who is really free is capable of basing his choices and actions on understandings which he himself achieves and on values which he embraces for himself. He is aware of the bases on which he accepts propositions as true. He understands the values by which he lives, the assumptions on which they rest, and the consequences to which they lead. He recognizes that others have different values. He is aware of irrational forces, of the power of emotions and environment, over himself and over others. He is capable of analyzing situations in which he finds himself and of developing rational solutions to the problems before him.

A man is free, then, in the degree to which he has a rational grasp of himself, his surroundings, and the relations between himself and his surroundings. The main restrictions to freedom are prejudice and ignorance. It is in this sense that a person without some degree of intellectual sophistication, though he may be free to think, speak, and act as he pleases, is not free.

The rational dimension has always been an integral part of the ideal of freedom. But today, as life and the knowledge of life grow in

From *Universal Opportunity for Education Beyond the High School,* Education Policies Commission of the National Education Association, pgs 1–6. Reprinted by permission of the Educational Policies Commission.

97

complexity, the ideal is increasingly a practical necessity for both individual and society. The ability to keep a job in a rapidly developing technology or to make the decisions required of responsible citizenship and parenthood increasingly requires an advanced command of rational processes. Through the free use of these processes, man is growing rapidly in his understanding and control of the world. Although the rational powers provide the means to destroy as well as to create, to enslave as well as to liberate, they have proved to be man's most potent resource.

Thus, there are both idealistic and practical reasons for ensuring that all persons have an opportunity to achieve the mental development which will free their minds. But a man's mind is only potentially his own. Freedom is not an automatic achievement. It exists only for the individual who, by his own efforts, makes it real. For most people the society must stimulate and assist those efforts. Its primary agent is the school. The school at each level must help each person to realize his potential for freedom by developing his rational powers.

But much of the mental development that freedom requires is beyond the maturity attained by most adolescents. For the adolescent, unchallenged assumptions and blind loyalties frequently serve as anchors in an uncertain, changing world. As one's life enlarges from the boundaries of family and school, as his responsibilities increase and his body changes, he needs a new basis for relating securely to the world and for preserving the sense of importance which he may no longer feel as an individual. Loyalty to a group of friends and to their ways gives him that basis. Thus much of his conformity and many of his biases are developed to meet real needs and, as their preservation in many adults would indicate, are difficult to abandon.

As the student rises above the insecurities of early growth and adolescence, he should be more able to look clearly at himself and the world. With new confidence in his own powers, he no longer needs to rely so heavily on traditions or groups. Genuine independence, based on knowledge of self and the world rather than on unreasoned conformity or blind rebellion, now becomes possible. Conscious freedom is within his grasp.

It is within his grasp, but he may fail to reach for it. Progress toward freedom is difficult at best, even for those who choose to seek it. But many persons do not so choose; at this point of great promise in their lives, they cease significant progress toward freedom. Significant growth toward awareness of self and the world is time consuming and essentially introspective. It presupposes considerable learning and reflection. It can therefore be halted if one fails to find the intellectual stimulus which further progress requires or if other goals, such as earning a living, pre-empt the field.

Intellectual resources are plentiful in much of the United States. Virtually every community has museums, libraries, and programs of adult education through which motivated students can make progress in the rational dimensions. But most young people are unlikely to pursue, on their own, a serious, consistent development of their ability to think. They need an environment specifically designed to foster that pursuit—the environment of formal education. Here they can develop a critical understanding of the attitudes and beliefs which have guided them and of the sources of bias, distortion, and rigidity. Here an important element in their daily lives is association with persons whose lives are dedicated to the increase of understanding. Here progress toward understanding can be the major criterion of success, and the primary tool is an open and ranging mind.

Not all that goes by the name *education,* of course, is a contribution to freedom. Education can be so conducted as to cause people to adhere to a given point of view, to prevent them from questioning certain tenets or certain leaders, to make them unthinking but useful servants to the state, or otherwise to enslave them. Or, less perniciously, in institutions not intent on fostering any given dogma, education may still make little contribution to the student's freedom and even less to his desire for such freedom.

As a result the world has ample evidence of highly educated persons who have been flagrantly unreasonable and unthinking either in general or in particular fields and circumstances. There is equally ample evidence that education can move people toward freedom and that, indeed, the movement of a person toward freedom necessarily consists of educational experiences to which one is subjected in the ordinary course of life or in a specially provided environment. But the ordinary course of life cannot be relied upon to promote the ability to think well any more than the ability to read well. A specific environment is therefore preferable. That environment is usually called a college.

It follows that, if the goal of freedom, as it has been defined here, is valid for every American citizen, the American ideal of universal education through the secondary school is inadequate.

The goal of universal secondary education is now more than two thirds of the way toward achievement in the United States. But education beyond the high school is still considered to be selective. The public has traditionally assumed a responsibility for making further education available to those best able to profit from college education

as it is traditionally conceived. On occasion the nation has actively induced individuals in certain categories to seek more education, as in
the college programs of the armed services in or after both world wars.
Widespread public respect for higher education has influenced an increasing number of people to go to college. But the nation as a whole
has never accepted the idea of universal opportunity as applying to
education beyond the high school. It is time to do so.

This is not to say that all types of higher education should become
universal. Selectivity will obviously be maintained in professional and
technological education and in private colleges. But forms of further
education which contribute to the freeing of the mind must somehow
be opened to all.

Unless opportunity for education beyond the high school can be
made available to all, while at the same time increasing the effectiveness
of the elementary and secondary schools, then the American promise of
individual dignity and freedom cannot be extended to all. Increasingly
those persons who establish for themselves a life of independent dignity
are those whose minds have been developed by such education. In the
future, the important question needs to be not "Who deserves to be admitted?" but "Whom can the society, in conscience and self-interest,
exclude?"

A person cannot justly be excluded from further education unless
his deficiencies are so severe that even the most flexible and dedicated
institution could contribute little to his mental development. There is
reason to expect that most persons capable of completing the studies of
an American high school are also capable of further growth toward a
free mind. It is true that many pupils fail to complete high school and
that many others seem unpromising candidates for further learning.
The fault may lie with the pupil, the school, the family, or all of them.
But the nation seems increasingly determined to raise the level of real
opportunity for all. As measures are taken to this end and as research
and experience improve the quality of education, the percentage of the
population completing high school and capable of significant further
intellectual development should continue to rise.

The additional time required for such learning cannot be stated
precisely or uniformly for all. The time required will certainly vary
as schools and society change. But current educational practices provide some guidelines. Many four-year colleges today devote the first
two years of their program to general education, with specialized
education initiated in the third year. Junior colleges offer two years of
general education to students who then leave school or turn to special-

ized study. In this two-year period, many students advance significantly toward awareness of self and the world.

Obviously, the level of personal development here described is not completely achieved at the end of two years of college—or at any other time. However, it does not seem possible under present conditions to promote self-sustaining progress toward this goal for most people in less than two years beyond the high school.

Therefore, the nation's goal of universal educational opportunity must be expanded to include at least two further years of education, open to any high school graduate, and designed to move each student toward intellectual freedom.

Section III-2

American Colleges:
A Proposal for Reform

RUSSELL KIRK

The sound statesman, as Edmund Burke once said, combines a disposition to preserve with an ability to reform. So, I hope, does the better educator. American colleges are worth preserving; but they can be preserved, in our time of flux, only if they are reformed. I propose to suggest here the lineaments of a conservative reform. Perhaps I should call it a restoration, rather than a reform; for what I have in mind is a return to the original purposes and functions of American colleges.

Prudent change is the means for conserving the continuity of any institution. Whether that prudent change ought to be "forward" in a bold new direction, or "backward," to a restoration of old essentials neglected, depends upon particular circumstances and the temper of the age. In general, our age seems to require a reform that is reactionary, rather than innovating; for while there is slight risk that our generation may cease suddenly to invent new things, there is grave risk that our generation may break the contract of eternal society, forgetting that we are wise in our generation only because our modern intellectual edifices rest upon ancient foundations, the moral and intellectual achievements of our ancestors.

So I am proposing a prudent restoration of the ends and means of higher education in American colleges—a reactionary reform, if you will. I feel that American colleges must retrace their steps, or perish. The possibility of extinction is not remote. Various persons predict, some with regret, some with a tone resembling elation, that one fourth or more of our liberal arts colleges may cease to be within a decade. I think that some of these estimates are high; but undeniably a great

From *The Intemperate Professor and Other Cultural Splenetics*, by Russell Kirk. Reprinted by permission of Russell Kirk, 1965, pp. 42–58.

many of the several hundred old-fashioned American colleges are experiencing hard sledding, and every year that passes is marked by the disappearance of a number of colleges. I mean, of course, those characteristically American foundations we call liberal arts colleges, not our universities or technical institutes or agricultural colleges or teachers' colleges. No state-supported educational establishments are going by the board; on the contrary, nearly all of them are unhealthily swollen in enrollments and lavishly supported by state funds. Nor are many of our older private universities in straitened circumstances, though some are feeling the pinch—Johns Hopkins and Stanford among them— and even Harvard and Chicago complain that their endowments are inadequate for meeting present necessities. I am concerned here with America's especial contribution to higher education, the college of liberal arts and sciences, governed by a private board of trustees, ordinarily limited in enrollment to a few hundred students, and concerned with the schooling of undergraduates in the traditional intellectual disciplines which train the liberal understanding and prepare young people for the life of reason. And those colleges, most of them, have fallen upon evil days.

This situation is sufficiently paradoxical for no other nation spends so much upon higher education, per head of population, as does America; and never before has so large a proportion of the population of any country attended colleges and universities. The state-supported institutions are swamped by "the rising tide" of enrollments; and, for that matter, many of the liberal arts colleges enroll twice as many students as they did before the war. Yet in a time when the desire for a college degree, as social distinction and as means to economic advantage, is more general than ever before, the majority of private colleges find themselves lacking in funds and lacking in able students. Whatever is the matter?

A part of the difficulty is financial. The general inflation which this country has experienced since 1940 has cut in half the purchasing power of college revenues derived from fixed endowments, except when those endowments have been invested in enterprises whose profits have risen proportionately. At the same time, income taxes and inheritance taxes have considerably diminished gifts and legacies to colleges, except so far as partial exemption from taxation has encouraged some new beneficiaries to contribute to charitable and educational causes. But the millionaire patron of the college now is a very rare bird. I shall not advance any simple, direct remedy for this condition, except to suggest that if the colleges really were considered important by the public, sufficient money would be forthcoming somehow.

Another cause of the difficulty is the ascendancy of state-supported institutions. Formerly private colleges constituted the great majority in our roster of educational institutions; now slightly less than half the total number of college students in the country is enrolled in private colleges. In one or two states, there are no private colleges at all; in the growing industrial state of Michigan, only about 18 percent of the students are enrolled in private institutions of higher learning. As it has grown progressively more difficult for private colleges to obtain sufficient funds, it has grown progressively less difficult for state-supported institutions to obtain legislative appropriations. Thus the state institutions are able to afford the expensive buildings, the high salaries, the athletic fields and stadiums and swimming pools, the student-union buildings, the public relations departments, the recruitment campaigns, the triumphant football teams, and the name-band dances, which are the outward—but only the outward—signs of an educational institution which, the public thinks, is going places. Most private colleges simply are unable to compete in any appreciable degree with these trappings. Again, I do not intend here to suggest any simple solution for this particular difficulty; I venture only to murmur that to hold its own against these material attractions, the liberal arts college must offer something different in kind.

Now a third cause of the colleges' plight, and that cause much more pernicious than the previous two reasons for their distress, is the private colleges' failure to fulfill their own original purposes, to adhere to their own established methods, and to provide an education different in kind from that offered by the state-supported institutions. I do not mean that all the liberal arts colleges have been false to their traditions. At Haverford, Williams, Washington and Lee, Kenyon, the University of the South, Reed, Wesleyan, Mount Holyoke, and perhaps a score of other famous colleges, you will find the old curriculum and the old standards, at least, still rather closely adhered to, whatever may be said concerning fidelity to the moral and social principles of the founders of some of these institutions. Such colleges still respect the works of the mind and still produce a number of graduates who are genuinely educated persons. They are likely to endure, whatever happens to the bulk of the colleges in this country, because for the most part they fulfill their old function and are respected and supported accordingly. (Though even some of these feel the ground trembling underfoot.) But most colleges are now in a precarious situation because they do not profess anything not professed by the state-supported institutions, and because they do not provide any advantages to faculty, students, and the public which are not more than offset by the advantages of their rivals in the realm of higher education. Their failure, in short, is a punishment for a dereliction in duty.

A representative of a charitable foundation, accustomed to visiting a great many college campuses in the course of a year, recently observed to me that any college which believes in anything still is in a state comparatively healthy—and sometimes thriving—no matter how sound or how silly its belief may be. If that college clearly has faith in orthodox Christianity, or in militant atheism, or in old-fangled *laissez faire,* or in revisionist socialism, or in some ancient discipline of the mind, or in some startling intellectual departure, then that college does not lack for a vigorous faculty, or a lively student body, or a generous group of patrons. Commitment to principle brings success as a by-product. And my own desultory visits to some scores of campuses tend to confirm the argument of this foundation representative.

But most colleges are terrified of commitment to principle; indeed, they are opposed to principles on principle. Their trustees and presidents and faculty members tend to think of doubt as a good in itself, of ambivalence as identical with the liberal understanding, and of faith as bigotry. Thus they are left only with quantitative standards, or, at best, a vague aestheticism, for their rudder in this sea of troubles.

The state-supported institutions always can trounce the private colleges where quantitative standards are concerned; while as for aestheticism, art itself is froth when divorced from purposes and norms. If the colleges will not commit themselves to any principles, it is scarcely surprising that the public will not commit its education to the colleges. Weigh an institution with no standards and no stadium against an institution with no standards and a great massive stadium; well, it is no wonder that the balance swings to the state-supported institutions. Men of considerable intelligence and large means sometimes ask me why they should send their sons to small colleges, as against state universities, when the colleges no longer seem to stand for anything in particular; officers of charitable foundations sometimes ask me why they should expend funds upon small colleges with no particular reason for existence, when the famous professors and the great laboratories are at Behemoth University. And though I am a humble friend to the liberal arts colleges, I am unable to advance any very weighty argument in their favor, granted the dereliction from duty upon which I have touched.

But a very powerful defense of the liberal arts colleges can be made, if these colleges return to the performance of their old duties; and if, indeed, they resume their original functions, they will not require much apology from their well-wishers. For I think that the particular conditions of our century and our society demand now, more than ever before, a restoration of liberal learning. The hour is favorable to the colleges, if only the people who control college policy can perceive their present opportunity.

Although the American college derived its purposes and disciplines from a very old European scheme of education and was particularly influenced in its beginnings by the colleges of Oxford and Cambridge, it became, as it developed, a unique institution. Small, often secluded, and primarily a foundation for teaching rather than for the maintenance of finished scholars, it soon influenced the whole tone and temper of American life: the direct effect of Harvard and Yale in New England, or William and Mary in Virginia, upon the life of the mind and the conduct of society can scarcely be paralleled in any country or era. When the university, well into the nineteenth century, began to develop in the United States, it took the German system for its model; and until quite recent years, at least, the university in America has not affected the life and leadership of the nation so profoundly as has the college. If the liberal arts college ceases to be, the root of much in American culture will have been destroyed.

Now the aim of the old-fangled college education was ethical, the development of moral understanding and humane leadership; but the method was intellectual, the training of mind and conscience through well-defined literary disciplines. A college was an establishment for the study of literature: it is nearly that simple. Through an apprehension of great literature young men were expected to fit themselves for leadership in the churches, in politics, in law, in the principal positions of community responsibility. This was what the late Gordon Chalmers (after Sir Thomas Elyot) called "the education of governors." Whatever the faults of this system, it did produce a body of high-principled and literate men to be the leaders of the American democracy. They learned to govern themselves and to serve the republic, through strict attention to great literature: the poetry, philosophy, and history of Greece and Rome, especially; the Bible, with Hebrew history; something of modern thought and languages; and something of the literature of science. The subjects of study were few, and the course of study was uniform. The intention of the college was not to confer a vague smattering of every branch of knowledge upon its students, but rather to teach them the fundamental disciplines of logical thought, provide them with a taste and critical faculty for independent reading, and then send them into the world with a cast of character and mind fitted for ethical and intellectual leadership. If these young men remembered no more from college than something of Biblical history and precepts from Cicero and episodes from Plutarch—and some young men retained a great deal besides—still that knowledge prepared them better for life, the life of their age or of ours, than does the cafeteria-curriculum of many universities and colleges nowadays, whose graduates may read not a single important book after they have got their diplomas.

If an institution of higher learning could confer upon its students the sort of liberal education described by Newman, many of the problems of modern society might be solved in short order. But to expect such a general achievement is to set our sights impossibly high, in this day and age. We shall be fortunate if we manage to restore in our time a standard of achievement roughly equivalent to that attained by the old-fangled American college, which at its best fell considerably short of Newman's ideal. I am not arguing for a reform which promises to give us a nation of scholars and gentlemen, but only for a reform which may leaven the lump of modern American society with a sprinkling of men and women who know what it is to be truly human, who have some taste for contemplation, who take long views, and who have a sense of moral responsibility and intellectual order. That goal, though difficult to reach, is not beyond our powers.

Most surviving American colleges fail to achieve this fairly modest goal because they try to be all things to all men. They promise what they cannot perform, and never could perform. They promise to teach adjustment to the group, sociability, trades, salesmanship, business acumen, and the art of worldly wisdom. They ape the functions of the universities and the technical schools. With murmured apology and shame-facedness they consign their old disciplines to a dusty corner of the curriculum—when they do not abolish the classics, polite letters, languages, moral philosophy, and speculative science altogether. Business science, communications skill, journalism, and pre-medicine usurp the arts which teach us what it is to be a man. Most of the colleges have abandoned their ethical end and forgotten their intellectual means. The wonder is not that the colleges are in difficulties, but that they survive at all. For when function ceases, form atrophies.

Certain things a good college can do very well. It can give the student the tools for educating himself throughout his life. It can present to him certain general principles for the governance of personality and community. It can help him to see what makes life worth living. It can teach him basic disciplines which will be of infinite value to him in professional specialization at a university, or in his subsequent apprenticeship to any commercial or industrial occupation. And certain things no honest college can pretend to do at all. It cannot teach him directly how to win friends and influence people. It cannot make him a successful captain of industry, or an engineer, or a specialized scientist. It cannot guarantee him worldly prosperity. It cannot simply enroll him in a "survey course in world culture" and pour wisdom into him, as milk is poured into a bottle.

Now it is quite possible that a person who has been immersed in the pseudo-schooling and vocational courses of a corrupted college may enjoy a considerable measure of practical success, and at the same time be an intelligent and honest man. Two friends of mine, who attended the same college as I did, there majored in journalism. One can no more really learn the trade of journalism in college than one can really learn the craft of whaling from reading *Moby Dick*. One may acquire in college, indeed, a knowledge of what current events mean from courses in history. But "majoring in journalism" has nothing to do with this. My two friends, despite their college curriculum, read good books and fill responsible positions: one is chief project engineer of an important automobile factory, and the other is chief underwriter of a state workmen's compensation fund. They redeemed themselves from the faults of their formal education, and, for that matter, learned a good deal during their college years—but not from the vocational training they had fondly embraced. My moral, of course, is this: the good to be got from college is what the late Albert Jay Nock called the "useless knowledge" absorbed there—a body of knowledge commonly forgotten in detail, but infinitely valuable as discipline and residue. The useful knowledge, the practical instruction, is obsolete almost before the student enters the practical world. A college is wasting its students' time and its own resources when it pretends to teach what can really be taught only in workaday life, in the graduate school, or in the trade school.

What the college really ought to do, and we can do, was expressed succinctly by Irving Babbitt in a book published half a century ago, *Literature and the American College*. (The study of literature, I repeat, is the primary instrument of college education; and when British universities consider introducing a new course of study, they still put to themselves this essential question, "To what body of literature does the proposed course of study refer?") Babbitt, then, was not writing merely of courses in the poetry of Keats and Shelley when he gave his enduring little book its title. He wrote:

> "The best of the small colleges will render a service to American education if they decide to make a sturdy defense of the humane tradition instead of trying to rival the great universities in displaying a full line of educational novelties. In the latter case, they may become third-rate and badly equipped scientific schools, and so reenact the fable of the frog that tried to swell itself to the size of an ox. ... Even though the whole world seem bent on living the quantitative life, the college

should remember that its business is to make of its graduates men of quality in the real and not the conventional meaning of the term. In this way it will do its share toward creating that aristocracy of character and intelligence which is needed in a community like ours to take the place of an aristocracy of birth, and to counteract the tendency toward an aristocracy of money."

Throughout the past fifty years, the average American college has disregarded Babbitt's admonition, pleading that the college must give the public what the public demanded. But now the time is upon us when the college can and must return to the principles which Babbitt himself so well exemplified. The great state-supported institutions have so thoroughly yielded to the presumed "public demand" for specialization, vocationalism, and intellectual egalitarianism that even the most complaisant liberal arts college can no longer successfully compete with its vast subsidized rivals for the favors of the students who desire, or think they desire, a shallow veneer of "culture," a trade-school discipline with a college diploma, and four years of idleness. If the private college competes with the state-supported institution along such lines, the private college will succeed in enrolling only those students who fail to meet even the lax academic requirements of the state-supported institutions. And no one is going to be much interested in keeping alive a college which has become not much better than an intellectual bargain-basement stuffed with rejects from the upper floors.

The public demand now seems to be shifting from an emphasis upon narrow vocational schooling and "training for success" to a desire—as yet somewhat vaguely expressed—for liberal knowledge and cultivation of general aptitudes. In industry, in business, and in governmental service there has been felt a pressing need for men and women who know something of human nature, of history, of imaginative literature, of science in its larger meanings. The unpleasant necessity encountered by many industries for wholly retraining college graduates who had majored in chemical engineering, public relations, personnel management, or business administration has had something to do with this change of temper. The chief engineer of a great manufacturing company not long ago remarked to a friend of mine that he had found only one engineer under his jurisdiction, in all his years with the company, who both "knew, and knew how to write about it"—and that man he had imported from England. Even in the age of automation—or, perhaps, especially in the age of automation—the young person really prepared for life and work is the person who has been schooled in the humane disciplines.

With reference to this age of automation, Mr. Peter Drucker wrote once that our colleges ought not to feel that they now need to lower standards in order to attract students and thus survive. For as things are going, we shall have many more prospective college students than can possibly be enrolled anywhere. It is the college which can boast of its high standards, its exclusiveness, that will attract the better students and the benefactions of industry, the foundations, and the private patron. The college can survive not by imitating the mass-education methods of Brummagem University, but by offering a discipline of intellect, ethical in purpose, which mass education neglects. A return to original function, in short, is becoming the first law of self-preservation for the private college.

So I venture here to set down, tentatively, some general rules by which the prudent college might be guided in its work of conservative reform. To undertake them would require some courage of the people responsible for a college's policies; and the success of such a reform would be dependent, in part, upon what Professor Arthur Bestor calls "the restoration of learning" in our primary and secondary schools and upon certain readjustments in the graduate schools of our universities. But one had to begin somewhere; the American college cannot afford much longer to drift with the current of events; and out of urgent necessity, if from no higher motive, the college policy-makers may begin to reexamine the ends and means of a college education.

1. The college should reaffirm that the end of a liberal education is an ethical consciousness, through which the student is brought to an apprehension of the enduring truths which govern our being, the principles of self-control, and the dignity of man.

2. The college should make it clear that this ethical end is sought through an intellectual discipline, exacting in its character, which regards "useless knowledge" as infinitely more valuable than simple utilitarian skills.

3. The college should return to a concise curriculum emphasizing classical literature, languages, moral philosophy, history, and pure sciences, logic, rhetoric, and religious knowledge.

4. The college should set its face against amorphous "survey courses," "general education," and similar substitutes for real intellectual discipline: such a smattering of an inchoate mass of fact produces only the little learning which is a dangerous thing.

5. The college should turn away from vocationalism, resigning to trade schools and industrial "in-service" training programs what the college never was meant to undertake.

6. The college should abandon its attempt to encroach upon the specialized and professional studies which are the proper province of the graduate schools of universities.

7. The college should say less about "socialization" and "person-

ality-building" and more about the improvement of the human reason, for the human reason's own sake.

8. The smaller college should give up as lost endeavor its aspiration to attract those students who desire the "extra-curricular activities" of Behemoth University, and offer instead its own natural advantages of personal relationships, smallness of scale, and respect for individuality.

9. The college should not content ifself with enrolling those students who cannot obtain admittance to a great university or state college; on the contrary, it should begin to set its standards higher than those of Behemoth University.

10. The college should endeavor deliberately to keep its student body within reasonable limits, its humane scale being one of its principal natural advantages over Behemoth University.

11. The college should emancipate itself from quasi-commercialized programs of athletics, an expensive and often anti-intellectual pastime in which it cannot compete successfully with Behemoth University.

12. The college should reduce to a minimum the elective feature in its curriculum; for one of the college's principal virtues is its recognition of order and hierarchy in the higher learning, and the undergraduate ordinarily is not yet capable of judging with discretion what his course of studies ought to be.

13. The college should recall the importance of furnishing society with a body of tolerably well-educated persons whose function it is to provide right reason and conscience in the commonwealth.

14. The college should inculcate in its students a sense of diffuse gratitude toward the generations that have preceded us in time, and a sense of obligation toward the generations yet to be born; it should remind the rising generation that we are part of a great continuity and essence, and that we moderns are only dwarfs mounted upon the shoulders of giants. For this consciousness lies at the heart of a liberal education.

Section III-3

The Dynamics of University Growth

JAMES A. PERKINS

The university has become one of the great institutions of the modern world. In the United States it is central in the conduct of our national life. It is the most sophisticated agency we have for advancing knowledge through scholarship and research. It is crucial in the transmittal of knowledge from one generation to the next. And it is increasingly vital in the application of knowledge to the problems of modern society. Sir Eric Ashby quotes from a statement published by the University of Witwatersrand that makes the point with precision: "'Every civilized society tends to develop institutions which will enable it to acquire, digest, and advance knowledge relevant to the tasks which, it is thought, will confront it in the future. Of these institutions, the university is the most important.'"

At the same time, the modern university is, in one of those strange paradoxes of human affairs, dangerously close to becoming the victim of its own success. At a time when there is the greatest clamor among students for admission to the university, there is the greatest dissatisfaction with conditions of student life and studies. At a time when the professions are seeking a broader and more creative role in society, professional education is involving increased attention to the traditional disciplines. At a time when research is richly supported—and respected—it is being described as the academic Trojan horse whose personnel have all but captured the city of the intellect. And at a time when faculty members are in greatest demand for service around the world, there are intimations that their efforts to save the world will cost us our university soul.

How has this paradox come about? What forces are at work?

From *The University in Transition*, by J. A. Perkins, Princeton University Press, 1966. Reprinted by permission of the Princeton University Press.

How have they affected the external relations and the internal operations of the university? Can we resist a tendency to internal disorder? Is the university's autonomy and integrity inevitably compromised by its growing involvement with society and by the increasing necessity for state, regional, and national planning?

In the course of these lectures we shall explore some approaches to these questions, and some tentative answers. And although you may occasionally detect what might appear to be the corruption of a former Princeton graduate student and faculty member by recent experiences as an administrator, I would suggest that there may be offsetting advantages. While I have surrounded myself with the aura of scholarship, and I intend, as a scholar should, to keep as close a grip as possible on the difference between what is and what ought to be, the discussion of the university has now come to the point where theory and doctrine must encounter the practical problems of management and direction. We shall be interested in theory here, but we shall also examine some of the administrative challenges that are being posed in the modern university. We must, after all, find a way to run this extraordinary institution.

Perhaps we should remind ourselves, at the outset, that the university has an ancient and noble ancestry. Its earliest forebears include the Academy of Socrates and the Library of Alexandria, and it shows a line of descent in the Western world that traces the course of civilization. But irrespective of their names, ages, styles, and locations, universities are all what the great German philosopher Karl Jaspers so aptly describes as "the corporate realization of man's basic determination to know." It is here, with knowledge and with man's determination to acquire it, that we must begin. And, as is frequently the case, we must begin with those outsized men, the Greek philosophers of the fifth century B.C., who rise like the columns of their temples out of the plains of early history. For it was these audacious men who dared to suggest that those *determined* to know also had the *capacity* to know; that man, individual man, could by the exercise of his own mind discover truth—not all truth, perhaps, but much truth—about his natural world, his society, and himself.

Others had demonstrated that the realities of the natural world could be grasped better through observation than incantation. The Babylonians believed that to read the mysteries of the world and the universe it was better to observe the trails of stars than the entrails of sheep. But the Greeks did more, far more: they made essential connections among three powerful ideas—that reason could be applied to the results of observation, that knowledge so obtained had a validity apart from things observed, and that this knowledge could be applied to the whole range of human experience.

It would be difficult to overestimate the importance of this Greek affirmation of rational man and the nature of knowledge. Though the world had to wait many centuries for reason to win its major victories, the effects of this affirmation on Western civilization have been decisive. The idea that knowledge could be acquired through logical reasoning laid the groundwork for the whole modern structure which we have built for its pursuit and acquisition. And it gave man a totally different idea of himself which has affected his thought and his action ever since.

But the acquisition of knowledge through the exercise of reason is only part of the story. Knowledge acquired must be transmitted, or it dies. Knowledge acquired and transmitted must be used, or it becomes sterile and inert. Even more, the chemistry of knowledge is such that the very process of transmission, together with the discipline of application, stimulates and guides those who work at the frontiers of knowledge.

Knowledge is, therefore, in many respects a living thing—it grows, it changes, and various of its parts are replaced as they become obsolete. But the dynamic nature of knowledge is traceable to this interplay and tension connected with its acquisition, transmission, and application. It is this interaction that creates needs for new knowledge, that brings inaccurate teaching to account, that shows the world what could be rather than what is. Taken separately the three aspects of knowledge lead nowhere; together they can and have produced an explosion that has changed the world.

Communication has always been the companion of learning. Socrates had a habit of buttonholing people in the street and surrounding himself with students. In fact, the Socratic dialogue was a learning as well as a teaching process. Anaxagoras, a name that has bobbed up in recent literature, survives as an experimental and theoretical scientist because he was a teacher. Most scholars would toss in their sleep if they thought the new trails they had found would not be used. We would surely light fewer candles if we did not believe that they would illuminate the way for others.

But if transmission is important to the survival of knowledge, it is equally important for the discipline it imposes on those who seek knowledge. Edward Purcell, the Nobel Laureate, recently said that he had learned more about physics working on the new physics course for secondary schools than in any equivalent three-month period in his life. Most teachers have found that explanation is necessary for the academic soul, and most teachers have also found that the process of explanation frequently proves that mental slips are showing. Many times we listen to ourselves with a critical second ear, knowing our lecture is full of holes, both in fact and logic. When we are not called to account, our relief is always tinged with disappointment that our audience was caught napping.

With regard to the third characteristic of knowledge—its application or its use to man—much nonsense has been written about the difference between the proof of knowledge and the utility of knowledge. Certainly proof and utility are different ideas and involve different values. But just as certainly, proof without concern for the application of proof leads straight to the barren discussions of medieval scholasticism, while proof based on utility alone makes generalization impossible and thus leads to the destruction of knowledge itself. The two ideas of proof and utility are different but dependent, and their interaction lies at the very center of the enlightenment and progress of mankind. "This intimate union of theory and practice aids both," says Whitehead. "The intellect does not work well in a vacuum."

I have dwelt on the close connections of acquisition, transmission, and application of knowledge at some length because we cannot understand the modern university unless we understand these three aspects of knowledge. This is so because the three aspects of knowledge have their institutional reflections in the three missions of the university: the acquisition of knowledge is the mission of research; the transmission of knowledge is the mission of teaching; and the application of knowledge is the mission of public service.

It could be expected to follow that the three missions of the university are as organically related as are the three aspects of knowledge. I most profoundly believe that this is so. I also believe that these three missions not only describe the functions of the modern university— they also provide it with its enormous powers and its enormous problems.

But before we are ready to grapple more intimately with powers and problems, let us place the three great missions of the university in historical perspective. Perhaps this will help to illuminate the unique nature of the institution as we know it in modern America.

It is important to note that the three aspects of knowledge have not always been given equal emphasis. On the contrary, one aspect or another has customarily been emphasized throughout history at the expense of the other two. And this emphasis has largely been determined, at any given time, by the level of intellectual sophistication and the nature of the social environment that prevailed. Traditional societies were and are, naturally enough, bound to be preoccupied with traditional knowledge, and that kind of knowledge is a weak elixir for the rejuvenation of that kind of society. For such a society, the idea of university-based research is almost meaningless, possibly irrelevant, and certainly dangerous.

Thus the concern for knowledge was for centuries restricted to a concern for what *was* rather than what *could be*—to a transmission of old knowledge rather than a search for the new. And at the center of the wheel of history was the fact that the rulers of traditional societies, both clerical and civil, were not hospitable to the idea that truth could be discovered without the intervention of those specially trained in the mysteries. The authoritarian structure of the Middle Ages had to be dissolved by the Renaissance, the Reformation, the rise of the middle classes, and the revolution of scientific technology before change could become a desirable goal rather than a danger to be avoided. When the traditional crust was broken and man's curiosity and aspirations could assert themselves, the search for new knowledge was on. The universities became ready to produce it, and society prepared itself to receive it and use it. But not immediately, and not everywhere.

The German universities, in the third decade of the nineteenth century, were the first to raise the banner of research as a central mission— if not the central mission—of the university. The combination of the industrial revolution in the cities and the nationalistic fervor among the intellectual classes brought new intellectual life to the German university. Within two decades this combination had transformed both the theory and the practice of higher education.

But the flowering of the German university took place in a shady garden without appropriate drainage or fertilizer. The process was confined to an elite—around five per cent of the age group, at its maximum—and as a result the trained manpower needed to fuel German growth simply was not forthcoming. Even more important was the disjunction between the German university and German society, a disjunction that arose out of the monarchic, aristocratic, and essentially antidemocratic nature of the German ruling classes. The university could expect support as long as it did not meddle in affairs outside its walls. Conversely, there was little incentive for the research scholar to establish relations with public and private authorities. Thus the promotion of basic research became the true mission of the university, and both the university and German society were content.

But the price was high, both for higher education in Germany and for the social structure of the country. Neither its government nor its business leaders had the benefit of the humanizing influence that close contacts with the university might have provided. And the university was denied the stimulating feedback that would have come if it had been free to adapt both its academic doctrine and its organization to the requirements of a modernizing country. As a result, the missions of instruction and public service were neglected. The price of this neglect has been paid by each generation and is now a towering social and political problem for the managers of modern Germany.

In England the pattern was quite different. In Oxford and Cambridge, those two great bellwethers of English higher education, the resident undergraduate colleges were, and still are, the controlling elements. They have the money and the administrative muscle, so while collegiate functions could prosper, university interests were bound to be undernourished. Thus these two most ancient and most distinguished universities have become the measuring rods for excellence in undergraduate instruction.

But this decentralized and undergraduate-oriented environment was not very hospitable to research and graduate study, and even less so to interaction with English society. Without the continuous yeasty influence of new knowledge and the rude intrusion of new requirements, undergraduate education might be gracious but not necessarily stimulating; sometimes it may even be irrelevant. The promotion of research, advanced studies, and public enterprise—all of them university-wide responsibilities—has languished. Who was there to promote them against the collegiate inertia? A recent Cambridge University self-study reinforced this point when it stated: "The crux of any reorganization seems to us to be the provision of more personal direction of the University's affairs. A great University cannot work efficiently unless several senior men devote virtually the whole of their time to transforming policy decisions into action; bringing business to a head; reflecting on how one decision interacts with other decisions, negotiating both inside and outside the University; and doing a vast mount of informal consultation which cuts across committees."

These and similar considerations have produced a series of reports from Crowther, Robbins, and others; but real change will come hard. Until change comes at all, Great Britain will be without the benefit of that dynamo of the modern world—the modern university.

The moral is that the university in Germany and the university in England have both suffered because they have overemphasized one of the three missions, and the resulting biases are now frozen in the organizational concrete of the German institute and the English college. Now that German, and particularly English, social and economic development both demand and need a new and more rounded orientation in higher education, the universities face a major upheaval if they are to respond. The two experiences testify further that the acquisition, transmission, and application of knowledge are organically connected. Institutional policies and arrangements that grossly neglect one function in favor of the others build a low ceiling indeed on the institution's future growth and vitality.

The third and relatively underdeveloped characteristic of knowledge—its application to the world supporting the university—was clearly foreshadowed by Franklin and Jefferson, those farsighted products of eighteenth-century enlightenment. Both were early champions of the university's responsibility to include practical studies for the new age then struggling in early adolescence.

They dreamed of an open society, free of both ecclesiastical and civil control, with little to fear from the uninhibited search for truth or from experiments in the application of truth. The idea that a university should be useful required a society that would put it to use. It was the great genius of Franklin and Jefferson that they saw both developments as interrelated and important.

But they were prophets ahead of their time. Universities in name remained colleges in fact. All of higher education was in the doldrums until the Civil War released the industrial energies that had been growing beneath the surface of an agricultural society. The grip of classical traditions was broken, and the dreams of Jefferson and Franklin were enacted into law in the Morrill Land Grant Act of 1862.

And then everything began to blossom at once. American universities became the heirs of the British tradition of undergraduate instruction and the German concern for graduate education and research, and joined both to the new mission to be "in the nation's service." For the first time in history, the three aspects of knowledge were reflected in the three modern missions of the university. The results were both revolutionary and explosive. They changed the whole relationship between the university and society. And in the process, they produced a new idea of the university.

The first area to feel the impact of the new idea of the university was agriculture—not unnaturally, since the need to apply technology to agriculture was one of the driving requirements behind the Land Grant Act. From this concern for agricultural technology emerged the powerful partnership including the private sector, the government, and the university. Here the university combined with county, state, and federal agencies and private associations to produce a unique transmission belt by which ideas for the application of technology to the production and distribution of food could be translated into action. The same groups have worked out a balance of relationships that have led to the rapid reduction of farm workers and farmed land while food production has soared. It is reasonably safe to say that modern industrial development is almost impossible unless the farming population can be reduced and those freed from the farm made available for industrial and service industries. Today less than eight per cent of the working population is involved in the production of food. But this eight per cent produces more food and better food than did four times its number just a few generations ago.

The cyclical processes continue unabated. Research continues to pour from our universities and is rapidly translated into hardier grains, healthier animals, and more scientifically oriented farmers. And these farmers and their agents present the universities with ever new requirements for new ideas. This dynamic revolution has surely resulted from the functioning of the three related missions of the university—a process which has transformed the agricultural community and is operating at an ever-increased tempo. As the number of farmers and farms decrease, the pressure to apply more and more advanced technology continues to mount. The miraculous results of this whole process may be the only hope for millions of hungry persons in the world.

Of course, this dynamic interchange has not been confined to agriculture. In lesser or greater degree, it can be found in other fields of knowledge and in areas of public need. Engineering education was to industry what agricultural education was to the farm. And scientific research was behind both. Studies in public administration have introduced new criteria of excellence into the management of public business, which in turn has increased the demands on schools (like this great one at Princeton). As these demands are met with new ideas and better trained graduates, government sights will be further raised to produce new requirements for the School of Public and International Affairs.

The worlds of literature and the arts have also felt the invigorating effect of an interchange between the scholar and the writer, the musicologist and the musician, and the school of drama and the theater. Indeed, this interchange has proceeded to the point where there is now a most interesting debate in progress as to the proper role of the university in the arts.

Thus, there is practically no field that has not grown and prospered from the dynamic interrelations that now exist within the university, on the one hand, and between the university and public and private agencies on the other. The university and the other institutions of society—including the corporation, the farm, the cultural center, and the government agency—have now been joined together by a new kind of blood stream, made up of the ideas, the trained intelligence, and the manpower which provide the driving energy for our society. And the university is the great pumping heart that keeps this system fresh, invigorated, and in motion.

As this stream has run from the university to the corporation and the government bureau and back again, it has transformed both government and industry: the ideas and manpower of the university have helped turn government to an increasing preoccupation with public welfare, and they have helped give the profit-making corporation a far larger public orientation than it has ever had before. We should note again that this mixture of private pursuit and public purpose is hardly conceivable without the universities as partners, and this partnership would be impotent if the university had not come to embrace its complementary missions which have enabled it to digest new ideas, train new students, and participate in new applications.

The interplay of forces that the modern university has thus triggered has transformed our whole society—and the university with it. Our university is the engine of change and is transformed by it. For this story of success is also a story of the dangers of success: the functions of the university must now be performed amid the pressures of exceedingly rapid growth. Let us see what this has meant.

The first and most obvious manifestation of this growth has been the enormously increased load on instruction—an increase which has been both quantitative and qualitative. The college-age population has steadily risen, with a noticeably large jump after World War II for reasons that would be described by the building experts as deferred maintenance. At the same time, the percentage of those who wish to enter the university has expanded even faster. These two factors, powerful enough by themselves, have been joined by a third—a social philosophy which suggests that everyone should go beyond secondary education if he wishes, and should be financed if he hasn't the funds. As a result, we have almost five and one-half million students in our system of higher education each year, and we are adding four hundred thousand more—the equivalent of almost one hundred new Princetons—annually!

On the qualitative side, secondary education has improved dramatically, particularly since our rude awakening by Sputnik in 1957. As a result, the responsibilities for general education have slowly been assumed by the high school and the preparatory school. In the university, general instruction has given way to far more sophisticated work in the first two years. When the change in content and method has been too slow, the very good student has joined the ranks of the discontented. We shall deal with some of the reasons for student discontent more fully later.

Both pressures have come at a time when the pool of faculty talent has been reduced by the low birth rates of the depression and when that pool has also been tapped for the skills and talents needed by government, industry, and a variety of important services. Small wonder that undergraduate education has suffered in the university.

Meanwhile, scholarship and research, both basic and applied, have come to feel the great internal pressure of unleashed curiosity and the external demands of national interest. Periods of dramatic change stimulate the minds of everyone, and the pulse of this interest can be felt by scholars in every field of knowledge. Just list the summer activities of any faculty, and you will be astonished to discover that its members have scattered to the corners of the earth—not to escape, but to learn. And on their return, like bees from honey flights, the entire university hive is the beneficiary.

Still another factor adding to the university's growth has been the rising national interest in university research, strongly backed by federal dollars. The impact of all this on the university has been well documented by the Carnegie and Brookings studies and has been vividly described by Clark Kerr under the heading, "The Federal Grant University."

The results of this federal interest, I might add, have been soundly flailed in recent months by almost every critic in search of a subject. The problems created for the university are real enough. Instruction has frequently taken second priority; buildings, even when paid for by the government, involve increased operating costs; overhead returns are rarely adequate; and most colleges of arts and sciences feel, with some justice, that government rewards to the sciences tend to widen still further the breach between C. P. Snow's two worlds.

But the positive benefits of federal involvement cannot be ignored. The stimulation of scientific effort has brought new standards of excellence and new dimensions of service to most universities. Without any question, the natural sciences and engineering have made quantum jumps in their sophistication, and their fields are some of the most exciting in the curriculum. Moreover, federal support is now broadening to include the social sciences, and the new Humanities Foundation will include the arts. So universities will continue to receive the country's attention and the country's support.

Finally, the pressures of external demand have been felt directly by university staffs themselves. Once at work on a project initiated and often largely financed from the outside, faculty members find it an easy step to move from the university into government bureaus and industrial establishments, some to proffer their advice and counsel, others to stay for good. But wherever their activities lead them, the involvement of faculty members in specific projects with outside agencies is likely to do two things: first, to bring more new projects to the university; and, second, to lead to increasingly complex, if not disorderly, administrative relationships both within the university itself and between the university and other agencies.

Meanwhile, the spiral continues. Growth begets more growth, and specialization more specialization. Discovery leads only to more questions, which require new ideas and more specialized training, which—in turn—produce more discoveries. As the relations between the university and other institutions of society proliferate, it will become a major task of the universities to draw the lines between their legitimate and illegitimate functions and to see clearly where their mission begins and ends. No wonder that the despairing trustee and administrator have frequently shared the longing of the bewildered student and critic for a return to some academic Walden.

But the pressures and demands will continue from the outside, too. More and more young people will want the education that opens doors to the good life; there will be more and more problems to be attacked— moral, aesthetic, scientific, economic, social, and political; and there will be more and more demands for an imaginative application of knowledge around the world. The university—as the most sophisticated and, let us hope, independent agency now at work advancing, transmitting, and applying knowledge— has come too far to retreat before what may be its finest hour.

Yet the crucial questions remain: What will be the effects of this vast growth? In what direction is the university heading? Perhaps even more to the point, can the university keep pace with the modern world, let alone bear the torch that lights the way?

We may be able to respond to these questions by the end of these lectures. But there can be no denying the deep concern of all those who see the future as an extension of the recent past. Already too large in many cases, how can our universities absorb twice as many students in the next decade? Already extended by the demands and excitement of research, how can they survive the inevitably increased demands that come from the dynamic interchange we have just described? Already under pressure for services that take the university to every corner of the earth, how can they reply to the insistent demands of the new nations?

Various experts have predicted the future of the university by making projections of the recent past. The results are frightening. They are also not necessarily reliable. But they can stimulate us by picturing a future we must do our best to avoid.

The first of these projections was made famous by George Beadle, President of the University of Chicago. It is called the Brontosaurus projection, and it suggests that growth is out of hand. With a body growth curve far exceeding a mind growth curve, the university is doomed to repeat the sad history of the prehistoric monsters which are presumed to have emitted great noise but few constructive comments.

Then there is the Caretaker's Daughter projection. You will remember the old song that runs something like, "Who takes care of the caretaker's daughter when the caretaker's busy taking care?" With faculty in orbit, students out looking for their lost identities, and administrators out setting off dynamite under foundation vaults—who is taking care? Who says no to large-scale research enterprises? And on what theory? Who is in charge?

Next there is the Kent projection. This projection receives its title from a lady in Kent made famous in a limerick generally attributed to Don K. Price (and made still more famous by Clark Kerr):

> There was a young lady from Kent
> Who said that she knew what it meant
>   When men took her to dine
>   Gave her cocktails and wine
> She knew what it meant—but she went.

The Kent projection suggests that the university will become increasingly an agent rather than a principal—an agent whose facilities are available and whose activities will be determined more and more by the requirements of the state. In this image, the university would become an institution always for hire, and increasingly for hire for the short-run rather than for the long-run needs of society.

Finally, there is Kerr's Constructive Chaos projection. Here the arresting point is made that institutional integrity may be a danger rather than an asset. It may stifle creativity rather than protect it. It can limit freedom as well as extol it. It can be parochial, inward looking, reflective on past glories rather than preoccupied with the future. It can be resistant to change in the name of preserving institutional balance.

Therefore, the Kerr theory holds that university response to government blandishment for scientific research is a good thing—it has brought progress through constructive imbalance. Administrative neutrality has brought academic freedom through independence and mobility. And institutional decision-making decentralized down to the individual professor has made change possible with the fewest university convulsions. In short, institutional administrative integrity may be too high a price to pay if it comes at the expense of change and the restlessness that rapid change requires.

From our four projections we can find the four most common fears about the future of the university. The fear of uncontrolled growth—the Brontosaurus projection. The fear of loss of direction—the Caretaker's Daughter projection. The fear of loss of principle—the Lady from Kent. And finally, the fear that the university will be too rigid in an era of rapid change.

In fact, they boil down to two primary concerns. The first has to do with the external relations of the university—that it may lose its identity. The second has to do with the internal cohesion of the university—that it may lose its capacity to manage its own affairs. And since these two concerns reflect the deepest fears and deepest aspirations of mankind, we may well believe we are at the heart of the fears and aspirations of mankind's great intellectual institution.

So we shall continue our discourse next by an examination of the internal problem, and then we shall look at the external problem. We may even discover how these two concerns connect.

The Rise of Graduate Education

EVERETT WALTERS

EARLY CRITICISMS OF THE DOCTORATE

"The rage" after degrees, especially the Ph.D., was not welcomed on all sides. Professor James M. Taylor of Vassar College in 1894 typically expressed fear of domination by the Ph.D., specifying that too much emphasis on specialization might well bring about neglect of broad scholarship. He would redefine the master's degree and have it the degree for scholarship and learning.[1] President A. Lawrence Lowell of Harvard decried the conferring of advanced degrees, holding that results speak louder than degrees for original thinkers; he believed that graduate degrees were attracting a dangerous "mediocrity" which would later seriously affect school and college teaching.[2] Dean Andrew West of Princeton in 1912 questioned, "Why is the degree made the be-all and the end-all? It is beginning to be known like a 'union card' for labor."[3] Many condemned the failure of the Ph.D. as preparation for college teaching, a criticism that has been voiced with recurring regularity since 1900.

William James in 1903 took the new degree to task most savagely and urbanely in his famous essay, "The Ph.D. Octopus." Worried lest the degree damage the true spirit of learning, he joked at titles and degrees on pages of college catalogues which created an impression of "A terribly distinguished crowd,—their titles shine like stars in the firmament: Ph.D.'s, S.D.'s, Litt.D.'s, bespangle the page as it they were sprinkled over it from a pepper caster." America, he feared, was drifting into a situation "in which no man of science or letters will be accounted respectable unless some kind of badge or diploma is stamped upon him, and in which mere personality will be a mark of outcast estate." A degree such as the Ph.D., he charged, stifles freedom of

From *Graduate Education Today,* 1965, The American Council on Education, Washington, D. C., Reprinted by permission of the American Council on Education, pp. 17–28.

127

interest, does not guarantee success as a teacher, promotes academic snobbery, and above all is a sham.[4]

Edwin E. Slosson echoed James's criticism of the booming popularity of the Ph.D. In 1909-10 for *The Independent* he wrote a series of articles on American universities; in his conclusion he declared that the Ph.D. was being imperiled by its popularity, that its financial value was becoming too great, and that too many people now came to measure an institution's stature by the Ph.D.'s on its faculty roster. He also questioned the meaning of the "original contribution" as applied to the dissertation. Two remedies he suggested to strengthen the degree were the requirement of publication of the dissertation to ensure its high standards, and an examination of Ph.D. candidates to determine their general breadth of learning.[5]

EXPANSION OF GRADUATE EDUCATION, 1900-1940

From 1900 to 1940 graduate education, like higher education in general, grew in phenomenal proportions. The growth rate in higher education from 1900 to 1920 outdistanced the growth in the total population; from 1920 to 1940 the rise was even more pronounced. Graduate student enrollments soared, as did the numbers of master's and doctor's degrees conferred. Graduate school enrollments doubled approximately in each decade: 5,831 in 1900, 9,370 in 1910, 15,612 in 1920, 47,255 in 1930, and 106,119 in 1940. Earned doctorates increased from 382 in 1900 to 615 in 1920, and to 3,290 in 1940; master's went from 1,583 in 1900 to 4,279 in 1920, and to 26,731 in 1940. During these decades the number of institutions conferring the doctorate also increased, but at a modest rate.

The reasons for the growth of graduate education lay in the ever-increasing demand for persons with advanced degrees; primarily, the demand stemmed from the belief that college teachers should have advanced degrees, preferably the doctorate. Fewer and fewer institutions were willing to accept teachers holding only bachelor's degrees and former ministers with or without a degree. Increasingly, regional educational associations and national educational groups, as well as the public at large, came to use the number of doctors on faculty rosters as an important measure of collegiate standards. The doctorate became the union card of the college teacher and the mark of academic respectability. Similarly, schoolteachers and administrators began to recognize the importance of graduate education, primarily that leading to the master's degree. In many school systems the possession of this degree meant an automatic, although not necessarily substantial, salary increase. A few persons with master's and doctorates found their way into government agencies, publishing, industry, and research.* In a way, the growth of graduate study reflected the maturing of the nation: the rise in its cultural level, the desire for education for democracy, and belief in the American dream. These were stimulated by the prosperity of the pre-World War I years and the 1920's. The Great Depression of the 1930's did not in any way diminish the general growth since many young people, unable to find jobs after graduation from college, enrolled in graduate schools.

This general growth, beginning roughly in the 1890's, was accompanied by the creation, within the traditional colleges of arts and sciences, of new fields of academic interest and of new departments of specialization in these fields.

One vigorous newcomer was education, whose purpose was the preparation of schoolteachers and of teachers to teach in the normal schools. Although most schoolteachers attended normal schools (many became state teachers colleges and, more recently, state universities), a considerable number of prospective schoolteachers attended universities that had developed departments of pedagogy, or departments of education, or schools or colleges of education. At the University of Chicago in the 1890's, the philosopher John Dewey, working from within the Department of Philosophy, developed a new Department of Pedagogy and an elementary school. In many institutions, especially the large state universities of the Mid-west and the West, the schools of education admitted students as freshmen and offered four years of undergraduate work leading to a bachelor's degree and a teaching certificate. During the early years of this development, the teachers were drawn from the traditional fields of the arts and sciences. Soon after the turn of the century graduate work was offered in education itself, which had attained the status of a "professional" field. At most institutions graduate study was simply added onto the undergraduate program, and the same faculty members taught both groups; then and now two exceptions were Columbia's Teachers College and Harvard's Graduate School of Education, which offer only graduate work and have separate faculties. The school at Harvard led the way with a new degree, the Doctor of Education (Ed.D.) in 1922, and—with varying success—the degree has been widely adopted. From the beginning the

*A typical exception was in chemistry. At Wisconsin from 1899 to 1919 only eight doctors in chemistry entered industry; from 1919 to 1928, of the 109 doctors in chemistry, 56 went into industry. (American Association of University Professors *Bulletin*, XIV, 621.)

Ed.D. was sharply criticized, especially by professors in the traditional colleges of arts and sciences, who ridiculed it as a second-class degree. Yet its defenders—and there were many—retorted that the degree was a realistic recognition of the profession of Education (it was generally capitalized) and that calling a doctorate a Doctor of Philosophy did not necessarily make it a good degree. At some institutions the degree was administered by the school of education; at others, by the graduate school.

Between 1900 and 1940 somewhat similar developments took place in agriculture, business education, engineering, and other fields. Undergraduate work in these fields was expanded into graduate study, usually at a high level of application. In agriculture, for example, the Ph.D. was offered in agronomy, animal husbandry, and horticulture. In business, the emphasis was on "administration," marketing, or finance, and the Ph.D. and, more recently, the Doctor of Business Administration (D.B.A.) were awarded. The prestigious Harvard Graduate School of Business Administration, founded in 1908, flirted briefly with the Doctor of Commercial Science in the 1930's and 1940's but then cast its lot with the D.B.A. In engineering, the Ph.D. and the Doctor of Science degrees were awarded at a few institutions. And in other fields doctoral work was offered as in social work, pharmacy, library science, home economics, and public health. Occasionally "named" doctorates were devised, the most unusual of which are the Doctor of Physical Education and the Doctor of Nursing. Not to be outdone, the professional schools, medicine, veterinary medicine, theology, and law, joined the new trend and offered the doctorate, although in the case of law only a few schools offered work leading to advanced degrees.

Paralleling the developments in doctoral work was the expansion of master's study. In addition to the traditional M.A. and M.S. were the Master of Education (a great favorite with schoolteachers across the country) and a host of so-called professional master's, of which the following are most widely recognized: Master of Social Work (M.S.W.), Master of Business Administration (M.B.A.), Master of Public Health (M.P.H.), and Master of City Planning (M.C.P.).

Criticism of both the scope and quality of graduate work was persistently voiced during the 1920's and 1930's.[6] Like all other levels of education, it was continually censured from within and without. At meetings of the A.A.U. the question of the preparation of college teachers disturbed both university presidents and graduate deans. Was the Ph.D. a degree for college teachers or for researchers, or could it serve for both, were questions discussed at virtually every meeting. The

Association of American Colleges in the mid-1920's also examined the products of the graduate schools, since its members were the chief employers. In general, the findings of the association's committees were tepid. A study, prepared for the A.A.C. by President Raymond Hughes of Miami University in 1934, was based on estimates made by specialists in the various fields. In graduate departments of the arts and sciences about 20 percent were rated "distinguished," about 35 percent as "adequate," and about 45 percent as "inadequate."[7] The large number of students seeking graduate degrees continued to bother educational leaders as well as educational associations. A committee of the North Central Association in 1926 issued a typical word of warning:

> the crowding of the graduate schools has been so great as to raise some question as to the quality of work done and the value of the degree. Certainly in some way the young, ambitious teacher should be protected as far as possible from spending his time and money in acquiring a graduate degree which will not be regarded favorably by his colleagues.[8]

Undoubtedly the warning was directed primarily to students in education, but it could have been applied in other fields as well. A survey of the speeches of educational leaders and of association committees published during the 1920's reveals an uneasy concern with the quality of graduate study, closely linked with the belief that many of the M.A.'s and Ph.D.'s would be unable to secure employment.

THE NEW ROLE OF SCIENCE, 1940-1965

World War II brought significant changes to higher education, as it did to almost every other facet of American life. Perhaps most important were the exalted role of research, especially in the sciences, and the effects of a soaring growth of population. During the war, research in every field of science (and in some social sciences) developed phenomenally: great contributions were made to basic science, and applications of basic concepts were extensively explored. Universities carried on much of this research, particularly in atomic energy, communications, control systems, and propulsion. Although the amount of Federal funds spent on university research during this period has not been estimated, the total probably reached well over $500 million.

After the war the research-oriented universities continued to obtain Federal funds for research: they had become intimately bound up in the country's realization that science is a major national resource and that research is a vital element in national security. The haunting fear of a third world war was subtly dominant. The universities were regarded as essential contributors to the national security because (1) they engaged in basic research for the discovery of new knowledge and also pursued extensive programs of applied research, and (2) they educated and trained young persons who would become the scientists of the future.

Federally sponsored research at the universities was chiefly under the aegis of the Department of Defense, the Atomic Energy Commission, the Department of Health, Education, and Welfare, the National Science Foundation, the Federal Aviation Administration, and the National Aeronautics and Space Administration. Through these agencies, money was provided for research to be performed primarily by university personnel—teachers and graduate students alike—in university buildings. In a few instances universities set up separate research centers, for example, the Los Alamos Scientific Laboratory in New Mexico, managed by the University of California.

The National Science Foundation, founded in 1950 to "promote the progress of science," in the main supported basic scientific research at the universities and also encouraged other Federal agencies to do the same. After the war, Federal support at universities was aimed primarily at strengthening the military establishment, although this emphasis declined in the late fifties. By 1960 an increasing proportion of Federal funds was stemming from the National Science Foundation, the Department of Health, Education, and Welfare, and the National Aeronautics and Space Administration.

In the fall of 1957, the research efforts of the nation were sharply jolted when the U.S.S.R. launched Sputnik I into celestial orbit. The American people were astounded to learn that Russia had achieved a major scientific feat and that the United States could no longer claim superiority in science. Within the space of a few years Russia's ability to produce nuclear weapons and to launch man-made satellites, some of them carrying human beings, seemed to prove that she had overtaken the United States and had, indeed, surpassed our scientific achievements. By the opening of the 1960's Russian scientific prowess had enabled her to threaten world security and to create an international tension that was made the worse by fear of atomic bombing and the horrors of fallout.

Immediately in the United States, the Federally supported research programs at the universities and colleges were re-examined and new efforts undertaken. Congress voted huge sums of money to strengthen lagging Federal programs, and the role of scientific research was even further enhanced.

Concurrent with the increase in research for national security was the growth of research in industry. The applications of scientific knowledge, especially in the chemical and electronics industries, became one of the dramatic developments on the postwar economic scene.

The effects on graduate education were spectacular. First of all, there was a vast demand for research itself, from government and from private industry. Graduate faculty and students were caught up in this demand, for primarily they were responsible for research at the universities. Faculty members, especially, bore heavy responsibilities as both principal researchers on contracts and grants and teachers of the new generation of scientists. If this were not enough, they were expected to battle such problems as indirect costs, classified versus non-classified research, the suitability of sponsored research (government and industrial) for master's theses and doctoral dissertations, the development of proposals and negotiation of contracts for research, and housekeeping related to purchasing and facilities. Second, the demand for master's and for doctor's, especially the latter, increased apace. The need for teachers (discussed below) was growing critically at the same time that highly trained employees were being recruited by Federal agencies and laboratories, independent research establishments (many with lucrative government research contracts), private companies bent on expanding their range of products, and local governmental agencies. Most of the new employers sought Ph.D.'s or holders of other doctorates in the sciences, mathematics, and engineering, and increasingly they looked for doctors in the applied fields of psychology, sociology, agriculture, economics, and business. Thus, it has been reported that one of the giant computer companies would willingly employ the entire crop of Ph.D.'s in mathematics; that the Federal Government has employed almost as many Ph.D.'s as the ten leading universities; and that doctoral candidates in psychology, especially those clinically oriented, were spoken for long before they received their degrees. And the nation's deep commitments to international peace and aid to developing countries have produced a sharp demand for political scientists, sociologists, historians, economists, and agriculturalists.

NEW DEMAND FOR COLLEGE TEACHERS, 1955-65

The nation's population explosion and the increasing proportion of teen-agers seeking college educations, similarly created a major problem for graduate education. The tidal wave of college students predicted for the late 1950's, the 1960's, and the 1970's foretold serious shortages inasmuch as the graduate schools would be expected to pre- pare the teachers for these students. The annual production of Ph.D.'s could not possibly satisfy this need and the needs of government and industry as well. The situation in the physical sciences, mathematics, and engineering appeared to be particularly critical; that in the humani- ties, social sciences, and other fields was only somewhat less serious. The impending shortage of college teachers, first predicted by the Presi- dent's Commission on Higher Education in 1948, became increasingly acute in the late 1950's and early 1960's.

In an effort to help the graduate schools face their heavy respon- sibilities, financial support was given by the Federal Government, by industry, and by the great foundations. The contribution of the Fed- eral Government has been the heaviest. The National Science Founda- tion has financed, in addition to its research grants, several large grad- uate fellowship programs, a retooling program for college science teachers, and a system for granting assistance for graduate faculty members and graduate students. Three titles of the National Defense Education Act of 1958 (whose enactment was inspired by Sputnik) have materially assisted graduate students: title II established a repayable loan program; title IV created a substantial three-year fellowship pro- gram designed to help college graduates become college teachers and to expand doctoral programs; and title VI set up a program to assist in the teaching of modern foreign languages. In the health sciences, the National Institutes of Health have established extensive fellowship and training grants programs. To stimulate the training of research scien- tists for the nation's space effort, the National Aeronautics and Space Administration has granted large sums of money to the nation's leading universities for graduate fellowships and research assistance. Increas- ingly, other Federal agencies have developed programs for assisting graduate education. Indeed, the magnitude of this assistance, when added to the funds for sponsored research and facilities construction, has caused many observers to question the dependence of higher educa- tion on Federal support.

Industry, which profited so handsomely from university research, has contributed through such means as fellowship programs, unre- stricted research grants, and lecture funds. The benefits. from these have been impressive. Oustanding assistance has been given by the Ford Foundation grant to the Woodrow Wilson National Fellowship program, which annually finances about one thousand prospective college teachers through their first year of graduate study; important too has been the foundation's assistance in foreign studies programs and in business administration.   The Carnegie, Lilly, and Danforth Foundations, among others, have given impressive support through study grants and fellowships.

Thus after the turn of mid-century, the strenuous demands placed upon the established graduate pattern of education renewed the questioning about graduate study and the traditional degree requirements. This round of criticism, however, was voiced more widely than in earlier years.   Now graduate education was of national interest; the American people were worried about the impending shortage of college teachers and of scientists.   Research seemed to have become the hope of the future: research, they believed, would bring about a better world, certainly a safer one, and one with better health benefits and even greater material prosperity.

The public press reported fully the annual meetings of the associations for higher education, which usually had one or more sessions related to graduate education.   It also recorded the increasingly frequent comments of congressmen and local political leaders who sensed the future role of higher education in American life.   The *New York Times*, always alert to the temper of the times, saw the newsworthiness of the Association of Graduate Schools committee report which criticized existing doctoral programs and reprinted it only a few weeks after the launching of Sputnik I.   Less spectacular were the many other national and regional conferences on the preparation of college teachers and the educational associations' reports on the training of college teachers.   All implied the failure of the nation's graduate schools adequately to train future college teachers.

Not only were the graduate schools criticized for their failure to prepare college teachers, but also for continuing such "outdated" requirements as the foreign language requirement (at most institutions, French and German, although some graduate schools had relaxed this traditional requirement to permit the substitution of statistics or another tool subject), the year's residence requirement, and the dissertation as a contribution to knowledge.   The most significant of these criticisms have been described above.

Despite these criticisms, the prestige of the Ph.D. has been steadily enhanced—for those who possess it and for those who strive to acquire it.   In the prestige-conscious society of the 1960's, the Ph.D. is highly desirable.   It has become fashionable to introduce a Ph.D.-holder as "Doctor," not the "Mr." or "Professor" common in earlier times.

GRADUATE SCHOOL ORGANIZATION

One result of the growing stature of graduate education—and the criticisms—was the organization of graduate schools into associations and conferences. This typical American reaction to problems of a complex nature ("let's see what the other fellow is doing") brought about the formation of regional organizations of graduate schools, most of which were not members of the Association of Graduate Schools* or the Division of Graduate Work of the (then) Association of Land-Grant Colleges and Universities. Among these postwar regional groups were the New England Conference on Graduate Education, the Midwest Conference on Graduate Study and Research, the Conference of Deans of Southern Graduate Schools, the Western Association of Graduate Schools, and the Graduate Deans of the Slope Institutions of the Pacific. In some regions there were other informal groups. These conferences and associations held annual meetings; those with formal meetings published proceedings or minutes; following the custom of the A.A.U.-A.G.S. *Journal of Proceedings*, which has been published since 1900. A natural result of the duplication of effort by these organizations—some graduate deans attend at least four meetings annually—was the creation of a national organization to represent all graduate education. In 1960, the A.G.S., stimulated by its own limitations, especially its inability to speak as a national representative of graduate education before congressional committees, fathered a new organization, the Council of Graduate Schools of the United States. The growing fear that regional educational associations would begin to accredit was another important factor in founding the council.

In many ways the formation of the C.O.G.S. marked the coming of age of graduate education in the United States. One hundred years after the awarding of the first Ph.D.'s, the leaders in graduate education had come to feel sufficient unity and security to form a national organization, with an office in Washington and a full-time president. Such a development would not have been possible at an earlier time. As this essay has shown, the growth of graduate education has been slow, marked with uncertainty of direction and purpose, always with financial dependence and administrative subordination. University presidents and educational leaders all too often neglected it, indeed frequently denounced its growth in public. But post-World War II

---

*In 1948 the graduate deans established the Association of Graduate Schools in the American Association of Universities. In effect, then, the Association of American Universities became the organization of university presidents and the Association of Graduate Schools became an organization of graduate deans.

developments, especially the meteoric rise of science, drastically changed the scene and brought about recognition of graduate education and its role in higher education and in the nation's economic, cultural, and scientific growth. Significantly, the council was made possible by the representatives of the prestige graduate schools, who saw the new status of graduate study and its need for full national recognition. By 1964 the council, representing more than two hundred institutions, had become the spokesman for graduate education before Congress, the foundations, and the American people. Although only a few years old, it does represent a century of graduate education.

REFERENCES

1. James M. Taylor, "Graduate Work in the College," *Educational Review*, June 1894, p. 72.
2. A. Lawrence Lowell, *At War With Academic Tradition in America* (Cambridge, Mass.: Harvard University Press, 1934), pp. 337–43.
3. Quoted in Bernard Berelson, *Graduate Education in the United States* (New York: McGraw-Hill Book Co., 1960), p. 19.
4. William James, *Memories and Studies* (New York: Longmans, Green & Co., 1911), pp. 332–34.
5. Edwin E. Slosson, *Great American Universities* (New York: Macmillan Co., 1910), pp. 490–96.
6. Berelson, *Graduate Education*, pp. 27–32.
7. Raymond Hughes, *A Study of American Graduate Schools Conferring the Doctorate, 1937–38 to 1941–42* (Ames, Iowa: 1946).
8. Committee on Graduate Degrees, North Central Association, *North Central Quarterly*, I (1927), 216.

The University in World Affairs: An Introduction
WILLIAM W. MARVEL

No one has yet fully tabulated the many roles universities play in twentieth century society—and it is unlikely that anyone ever will. There are too many; the roster grows too rapidly; and, perhaps above all, variations from one country to another greatly complicate the task. But even a full catalog would reveal little we do not already know: it would simply support our recognition of the university as one of the most adaptable and evolutionary institutions of man's invention. There is pure fascination in the thought that a modern complexity such as Berkeley can trace its lineage back almost a thousand years to the medieval establishments at Bologna and Salamanca. And there is even greater fascination in contemplating the growth which this extended family system will experience, in every corner of the world, in the remaining years of this century.

Small wonder, therefore, that the university is the object of such world-wide attention, curiosity and affection. It has become a first necessity of every newly-independent country, frequently ranking ahead of a national airline as a prestige symbol. In many parts of Latin America, the perception of the university is changing: the old complacency with an assemblage of faculties of medicine, pharmacy and law—the ancient mechanisms whereby society's elites perpetuated themselves—is giving way to the search for modernity, quality and inclusiveness. Rebounding from the scourges of Nazism, Fascism and war, the universities of Western Europe have shown remarkable recuperative power. No longer content with the ivory tower, high abstraction, and all that the classical tradition implied, they are increasingly concerned with empiricism, the social sciences, and a linking up with contemporary problems.

From *The University Looks Abroad: Approaches to World Affairs in Six American Universities* by Allan A. Michie, ed., *Education and World Affairs,* 1966. Reprinted by permission of *Education and World Affairs.*

Who can.doubt that in the Soviet Union the universities have been major change agents in the maturation of that country as a great power, or in the "mellowing" of its role in world politics? Indeed, the first moves in the post-Stalin era to open up more normal intercourse with the West were in the field of educational and scientific exchanges, and therefore focused on the universities. The United Kingdom in the last few years has been going through an experience which in its case is unique: an intensive re-examination of the relevance and adequacy of its higher educational system. That country is now adding new universities and modifying its traditional approach in ways that would have been unimaginable a decade ago. The list could be expanded: in Japan, Australia, Egypt, India, and certainly not least Communist China (about which we in the United States know so little) universities have come to bulk large in the calculations of national leadership.

Thus, the concerted attention we in the United States have given our colleges and universities in the last fifteen or twenty years is not a peculiarly American phenomenon. The growth and change of our higher educational system, the extent to which our universities have become the object of inquiry, review and commentary, and the democratization of access to higher education—in all these things the differences that mark American developments are those of degree. We are part of a great world-wide effort of reshaping the university and strengthening its bonds with society—a movement largely stimulated by developments in the United States.

One tendency to be seen in this simultaneous, universal concern with education and especially with institutions of higher learning is the evolution of universities toward more common patterns. They are becoming increasingly similar, one to another, around the world. The point should not be exaggerated: there is little danger that universities are moving so fast in this direction that soon we shall have carbon-copy institutions around the earth. National, historical, and cultural traditions, fortunately, will never cease to exert their shaping influence, to impart a certain personality and idiosyncrasy to the institutions of a particular country or region. We can be thankful for the strength of those traditions, for who would welcome a world of homogenized universities, lacking the color and flavor which diversity and variation assure?

But, nevertheless, the trend is present. In many Latin American countries, for example, major efforts are being made to staff higher education with full-time teaching scholars, tending to bring those universities into line with the prevailing pattern in the United States and Western Europe. The increasingly prominent role of our own federal government in financing higher education makes our system more nearly comparable to the relationship of government to higher education found in other parts of the world.

Then there is the closing of the gap between science and non-science within higher education. This is far from being a massive trend, but on the other hand there can scarcely be a university leader who is not concerned about making scientists more humanistic, and assuring that humanists, social scientists and others are conversant with the purposes and methods of science. So the scientific and technological institutions will become more like general universities, while attention to science and engineering will be an increasingly strong requirement for any general university that aspires to first rank.

Even in the service role of the university, which is so distinctive a part of the American pattern, we observe a gradual involvement of European institutions of higher learning. There is not a headlong rush, but there is a trend toward adding service to the traditional European university purposes of research and teaching.

It is probably inevitable that the world's universities should be moving down different but converging roads in matters of purpose, orientation, structure, and staffing. They are, after all, being acted on by roughly the same constellation of forces: mounting costs of education, hence the need for huge financial investment; spiraling demands for university services, imposed by national societies in all stages of development; recognition of high-talent manpower (the "product" of universities) as a country's most precious and critical resource; the race to keep up with the advancing frontiers of scientific knowledge; and the sharp upward trend in the numbers of those seeking admission to universities, as the commitment to equality of educational opportunity becomes a nearly universal phenomenon. When an African vice-chancellor, a Latin American rector, and a United States university president meet, it is obvious why they so quickly find themselves on the same wave length!

From the standpoint of the pages which follow, it is the *result* of this process that interests us. One meaning of this growing alikeness of universities, rooted as they are in distinct cultural traditions and separated by thousands of miles of ocean and desert, is the strengthening of the *international intellectual community*. Essentially, that community exists among men of learning, who seek after new knowledge, who are at home in the realm of ideas—and who feel the responsibility to transmit their learning, knowledge and ideas to their own contemporaries and to the generations that follow. It is to be found among men who are drawn together by bonds of common interest and pursuit, who communicate across national boundaries and language barriers.

In theory, such a community might exist without universities, but the possibility is remote. The university is in fact the institutional form of this intellectual community. It is in the university itself, and in the things that university people do, that one senses and feels the existence of this community. Therefore, the more agreement exists among universities around the world on fundamental matters of purpose, role, structure and functioning, the more readily can scholars move about in the world of universities and the more easily are their ideas disseminated. Thus is the international intellectual community translated from concept to reality.

In the widest sense, it is with the membership of American colleges and universities in the intellectual community of the world that the present volume is concerned. In putting it this way, we include virtually every institution of higher learning in the United States, for surely this is not a case where some are members and others are not. Participation is a matter of degree; simply to *be* a college or university makes some extent of membership almost unavoidable. Even the most modest institution will have courses in European history, world literature and a few foreign languages. To move from there to the massive involvement in the outer world found at the universities examined in the following pages, is to travel far. But there is no predetermined point on the journey where the threshold is crossed and the candidate suddenly becomes eligible for membership in the world intellectual community. That membership, one might say, is inherent in the fact of being an institution of higher learning.

If this great intellectual community has therefore been present to some degree for as long as we have had universities in the world, it follows that most of the things now being done by U.S. institutions in the area of international affairs are not basically new activities. There are new forms, more sophisticated rationales, more elaborate machinery, and an enormous increase in the scale of activity, but the fundamental processes are the same. It all still has to do with learning and teaching and exchanging ideas across national boundaries. It is essential to keep this in mind when considering the proud chapter in the history of higher education now being written by American universities as they assume growing responsibilities in world affairs. To forget this thread of continuity with the past is to see present efforts as a vast disruptive and diversionary influence. To remember it is to recognize in what we are now doing the very essence of the university tradition.

In our approach to the international involvement of universities, we crossed an important watershed in the United States around 1960. Behind us were two decades of growing activity by American higher

education on the world affairs front. Early in the 1940's our universities were drawn into support of the national war effort, mounting a vast
array of training programs to produce the kind of quickly trained manpower demanded by the worst conflagration the world had ever seen.
But the beginnings of what a decade later would become a massive development in American higher education occurred during the peacetime years of the late 1940's. We had learned a bitter lesson during the
war concerning our national ignorance of peoples, cultures, and
languages outside the Western European tradition. Taking that lesson
to heart, leaders in some of the universities and the foundations collab-
orated on the first area study programs, which focused on the Soviet
Union and Asia.

Before 1950, therefore, the seeds of many of the important developments over the next fifteen years had been sown in the terrain of
American academia. The fifties were a period of sprouting and growth
on many different sectors of the front. This was the decade of the
Fulbright program and the start of university contracts for institution-
building abroad on the part of the foreign aid agency (first the Foreign
Operations Administration and then the International Cooperation
Administration). Area and language centers expanded in number and
grew in strength on the campuses of the nation. Concerted research
efforts in many aspects of international affairs were undertaken at the
larger universities. The comparative study of political systems underwent refurbishing and reinvigoration, largely through the impetus of
the group of dedicated scholars who made up the Comparative Politics
Committee of the Social Science Research Council.

This was also the decade of the foreign student, as men and women
came to the colleges and universities of America in ever-growing numbers, and as our own young people at both the graduate and undergraduate levels went abroad to pursue their studies as "foreigners" in
the universities of other lands. During the latter half of that decade
the Iron Curtain was first breached by a new program of academic and
scholarly exchanges with the Soviet Union.

It was a period of experimentation and innovation in many distinct
parts of the world affairs front of higher education. Programs were
launched in several key universities for the development of materials
and the training of teachers looking toward the growth of international
and non-Western studies among undergraduates, as a part of liberal
arts education. Attempts to correct America's weaknesses in foreign
languages, especially in the little-studied or "exotic" languages, got well
under way in the '50's. The Council on Higher Education in the American Republics (CHEAR) was founded as a new arrangement for reg-

ular exchanges on common problems of higher education among North American and Latin American university leaders. The ferment and new approaches of the 1950's were a fitting prelude to the even more significant changes that were to occur in the early 1960's.

The fact that the United States entered a new period of development about 1960 is revealed by several new trends that set in as the decade opened. For the first time *the whole university* came into focus as the major actor on the stage of international education. Up until then, although nearly everything that went on in that field was obviously related to the universities and colleges, we were not yet at the point of considering these diverse activities within the context of the university as a total, integral institution. One reason for tying this new conception to the year 1960 is the publication by the Ford Foundation in the last month of that year of the report of the Committee on the University and World Affairs, usually referred to as the Morrill Committee report. On the committee were assembled a distinguished group of men from the universities, foundations, business and government. Their report was a systematic attempt to clarify the international role of American universities and suggest ways that our institutions of higher learning might perform more effectively in the realm of world affairs. The Morrill Committee report has other significances, but the point here is that it took *the university as its focal point*, relating to it such constituent parts of the full picture as foreign students, language studies, education for technical assistance, and world affairs in liberal education.

The 1960's were to see two kinds of developments closely related to this focus on the whole university. First, there emerged a new concern with how universities should approach the problem of integrating and relating in a meaningful fashion their far-ranging international interests. On one campus after another, faculty and administration began to question how the institution should organize itself internally in order to carry its growing responsibilities on the international front and to derive from those activities the maximum possible educational benefit. Secondly, a strong trend developed toward new arrangements for interinstitutional cooperation, the working out of various patterns among colleges and universities that would permit greater division of labor, economy of effort, and the maximization of results. Major moves were made by some of the largest universities, for example, Illinois, Indiana, Wisconsin and Michigan State in the Midwest Universities Consortium for International Activities; and nine major American institutions in a consortium to assist the development of a new technological university in Kanpur, India. At the same time, some of the smaller colleges were coming together into new associations so as to achieve through common action a level of participation in world affairs that would be far beyond the reach of a single small institution acting on its own. The Associated Colleges of the Midwest, the Great Lakes College Association and the regional association of colleges based on the University of Pittsburgh—all were formed at least partly with an eye to the possibilities of educational enrichment that would stem from an active role on the international front.

The other reason for thinking of 1960 as a watershed was the shifts that occurred in the pattern of financial support for college and university programs in world affairs. The United States government came prominently into the picture under Title VI of the National Defense Education Act which, although adopted earlier, did not become a major influence in the academic world until the early 1960's. So the responsibilities which had been largely borne by the private foundations during the '40's and '50's were to be shared, on an increasing scale, by the federal government. And at about the same time, the Ford Foundation, the major private source of support for university activities in the international area, adopted a new approach. Ford began a series of grants which provided to selected institutions large-scale, long-term, all-university wide support for their international programs. Based on careful planning and the development of an integrated approach by the institution itself, these new grants further emphasized the total university as the framework for the participation of American higher education in world affairs.

Finally, 1960 represents a time of transition because our basic interpretation of foreign aid, and especially our understanding of the role of educational assistance within it, took on a new sophistication with the passage of the International Development and Security Act of 1961. Contracting with universities for the conduct of programs abroad began, of course, during the 1950's. But it was only after the opening of the new decade that the role of education and manpower planning in national development came to be generally appreciated within the foreign aid agency, then renamed the Agency for International Development (AID). Although this new understanding was not translated into action as rapidly as many observers wished, nevertheless it gradually brought significant changes—in the formulation of programs, in the evaluation of accomplishments, in the relationship of research to other aspects of foreign assistance, and in felt need within AID for a close partnership with the university community.

We are now five years past the watershed of 1960. The major, almost glacial resistances to constructive university involvements in world affairs have receded. These last five years have been a time of

inquiry and searching for new answers, of continuing efforts to make
our national performance more effective. One needs no crystal ball to
foresee that further progress and further refinements in our approach
lie ahead in the second half of this decade. We are still in an era of
re-thinking, re-assessment and re-formulation, within the government,
within the foundations, and within the universities themselves. The
Office of Education has recently been reorganized, among other
reasons, to enable it more effectively to discharge its proper responsibilities in the area of world affairs. The McGovern Bill now pending in
Congress would close some of the significant gaps in federal support,
by providing funds for universities to strengthen their resources for the
training of young people to work abroad in the technical assistance
field. AID continues to reach out in search of better answers to the
perennial problem of how it can more effectively advance the development process among the less advanced peoples of the world. New
institutional arrangements, perhaps better suited to the needs and conditions of the mid-1960's—such as the proposed National Institute of
Educational and Technical Cooperation proposed in John Gardner's
report, *AID and the Universities*—are being more actively discussed.
And as the role of the federal government in this area grows larger and
more pervasive, the more urgent it becomes for the private foundations
to re-evaluate their own approaches and programs.

Within the higher educational community itself, the universities
long-committed and -engaged on the world affairs front continue
active, reviewing their institutional arrangements, refining their techniques, and often extending their involvement. And with every passing
month, they are joined by new universities seeking paths into this
intriguing, frustrating, yet promising and enriching area of international activity. On every sector of the front one finds portents of new
developments in store for the years ahead. Hopefully they will
strengthen the work of American colleges and universities in world
affairs, but in any event, they are bound to affect it deeply.

Section III-6

Quality in Higher Education

JOHN W. GARDNER

No one can say that life has been dull for American educators since the dawn of the space age on October 4, 1957. The clamor has been deafening. And a good deal of the uproar has been produced by individuals who never had two consecutive thoughts on education before that fateful day. Characters we had never heard of went into orbit and started beeping. But those of us who are professionally involved in education are not exactly taciturn types and we have cheerfully added to the racket.

Looking back on its I think we would all agree that nothing really surprising has come out of all the commotion. The wise men said some wise things; men who were not very well informed said some uninformed things; and silly people said silly things. The proportions of wise, uninformed and silly contributions were probably not very different than they usually are. The chief difference was that the spirit of the times turned up the volume control considerably, or to put it another way, there were many more people listening. To those of us with a lifetime concern for these matters, it often seemed that the foolish comments rang more loudly, but that may have been an illusion.

At any rate, the first flush of excitement is now over, and we have the opportunity to appraise our problems a bit more calmly. One is reminded that when Thomas Babington Macaulay, the English historian and poet, was four years old, a maid spilled some hot coffee over his legs. She quickly set the coffee-pot down and made a great fuss over him, but he pushed her away saying, "Thank you, madam, the agony is somewhat abated."

One of the issues which has been most frequently raised in the public discussion of recent months has been the question of quality in education. I propose to discuss this question as it bears on higher education.

From *Current Issues in Higher Education*, the Association for Higher Education, 1958, pgs 9–13. Reprinted by permission of the Association of Higher Education.

Arguments about quality in higher education tend to be rather heated and, it must be said, rather pointless. There are many reasons why such conversations become muddled, the foremost being that they so often degenerate into arguments over "elite" versus "mass" education. People who engage in these arguments remind me of the two washerwomen whom Sidney Smith observed leaning out of their back windows and quarreling with each other across the alley; they could never agree, Smith pointed out, because they were arguing from different premises.

In the case of arguments over "elite" versus "mass" education, I am convinced that both premises should be abandoned because behind the arguments is the assumption that a society can choose to educate a few people exceedingly well or to educate a great number of people somewhat less well, but that it *cannot do both*.

The fallacy of this assumption is obvious. A modern society such as ours cannot chose to do one *or* the other. It has no choice but to do both. Our kind of society calls for the maximum development of individual potentialities *at all levels*.

It is unquestionably true that in recent decades we have worried all too little about individuals of unusual talent or potentialities. To make such an assertion, however, is not to deplore the unprecedented time and money we have devoted to the average youngster. It will serve no purpose to replace our neglect of the gifted by a neglect of the average. We are all to prone to such wild swings of the pendulum in our national life. Martin Luther said that humanity was like a drunken peasant who is always ready to fall from his horse on one side or the other; and in that respect we Americans are all too human. We must learn to see the achievements and shortcomings of our educational system in some sort of embracing perspective which will permit us to repair one omission without creating others.

The notion that so-called quality education and so-called mass education are mutually exclusive is simply archaic. We distort present-day reality when we try to force it into archaic molds.

This is not to say that there are not a few remarkably archaic characters in our midst. We all know that a few of the people calling most noisily for quality in education are those who were never reconciled to the widespread extension of educational opportunity. To such individuals there is something inherently vulgar about large numbers of people. At the other extreme are the fanatics who believe that the only possible objective in higher education is to get as many youngsters as possible into college classrooms, regardless of their ability. Such individuals regard quality as a concept smacking faintly of Louis XIV.

But make no mistake about it, neither extreme speaks for the American people. And neither extreme expresses the true issues and the true difficulties confronting us today. It would be fatal to allow these archaic voices to speak for us. It would be fatal to allow ourselves to be tempted into a debate over anachronisms.

The demand to educate everyone up to the level of his ability and the demand for excellence in higher education are not incompatible. We must honor *both* goals. We must seek excellence in a context for all. A democracy, no less than any other form of society must foster excellence if it is to survive; and it should not allow the emotional scars of old battles to confuse it on this point. Democracy will have passed an important milestone of maturity when those who are the most enthusiastic proponents of a democratic way of life are also the most vigorous proponents of excellence.

This is easy to say, but it is not easy to bring about. We might as well confess that as a people we have some difficulty in coping with the concept of excellence. It is a difficulty worth exploring.

The difficulty does not lie at an ideological level. The 18th century philosophers who made *equality* a central term in our political lexicon never meant to imply that men are equal in all respects, in all dimensions, in all attributes of their persons and their lives. Nor do Americans today take such a view. It is possible to state in fairly simple terms the views concerning equality that would receive most widespread endorsement in our country today. The most fundamental of these views is simply that in the final matters of human existence all men are equally worthy of our care and concern. Further, we believe that men should be equal in enjoyment of certain familiar legal, civil, and political rights. They should be, as the phrase goes, equal before the law.

But men are unequal in their native capacities and in their motivations and, therefore, unequal in their attainments. In elaborating our national views of equality, the most widely accepted means of dealing with this problem has been to emphasize *equality of opportunity*. The great advantage of the conception of equality of opportunity is that it candidly recognizes differences in endowment and willingness to work and accepts the certainty of differences in achievement. By allowing free play to these differences it preserves the freedom to excel which counts for so much in terms of individual aspiration, and has produced so much of mankind's greatness.

In short, our cherished views with respect to equality do not deny the fact of individual differences.

It is understandable that Americans should be cautious about excessive emphasis upon the differences in native capacity between one individual and other. Enemies of democracy have often cited the un-equal capacities of men as justification for political and social philoso-phies which violate our most deeply held beliefs.

But we cannot escape the fact of individual differences, and we cannot escape the necessity for coping with them. Whether we like it or not, they are a central fact in any educational system and indeed in any society. The good society is not one that ignores them but one that deals with them wisely and compassionately.

If we are really serious about equality of opportunity, then we should be infinitely serious about individual differences; because what consistutes opportunity for one man is a stone wall for the next man. Individuals differ vastly from one another, and they differ in in-numerable ways. If we are to do justice to the individual, we must seek the kind of education which will open his eyes, stimulate his mind, and unlock his potentialities. There is no one formula for this.

If we did develop such an indomitable concern for individual dif-ferences, then we would learn to laugh at the assumption that a college education is the only avenue to human dignity and social worth. We would educate some young people by sending them on to college. We would educate others in other ways.

Properly understood, the college or university is the instrument for *one kind of further education.* It should not be regarded as the only passport to a meaningful life or the sole means of establishing one's human worth. And we have come periously close to that.

Human dignity and worth should be assessed only in terms of those qualities of mind and spirit that are within the reach of every human being. This is not to say that we should not value achievement. We should value it exceedingly. It is simply to say that achievement should not be confused with human worth.

The more we allow the impression to get abroad that only the college man or woman is worthy of respect in our society, the more we contribute to a fatal confusion, which works to the injury of all con-cerned. If we permit the faulty assumption that college is the sole cradle of human dignity, need we be surprised if every citizen demands to be rocked in that cradle?

A genuine concern for individual differences would lead us to two extremely important emphases in education. (1) We would place greatly increased emphasis on the many kinds of human talent, upon the immensely varied ways in which individual potentialities may be realized; and (2) we would place equivalent emphasis upon the great diversity of educational paths required by this diversity of talents. And no particular kind of ability or educational path would be regarded as socially superior or involving greater human dignity than any other.

The sort of capacity measured by the conventional college aptitude test is very important, but instead of putting a more and more monolithic emphasis upon this sort of talent, we should encourage all kinds of individuals to run on all kinds of tracks. In this way we can distribute very widely the rewards of self-esteem and self-respect, and can encourage on a broader scale the release of energy and positive motivation on the part of the individual, which have been the great strengths of our society.

Having accorded this recognition to individual differences, we should recognize the great variety of educational paths required to serve these differences. At the level of higher education this means many kinds of institutions, and it means diversity within institutions.

But we cannot hope to create or to maintain such diversity unless we honor the various aspects of that diversity. We must recognize that each of the different kinds of institutions has its significant part to play in creating the total pattern, and that each should be allowed to play its role with honor and recognition.

We do not want all institutions to be alike. We want institutions to develop their individualities and to keep those individualities. None must be ashamed of its distinctive features so long as it is doing something that contributes importantly to the total pattern, and so long as it is striving for excellence in performance. The small liberal arts college should not be afraid to remain small. The large urban institution should not be ashamed that it is large. The technical institute should not be apologetic about being a technical institute. Neither coeducational nor noncoeducational institutions should feel it necessary to explain why they are one or the other. Each institution should pride itself on the role that it has chosen to play and on the special contribution which it brings to the total diverse pattern of American higher education.

Such diversity is the only possible answer to the fact of individual differences in ability and in aspirations. And furthermore it is the only means of achieving *quality* within a framework of quantity.

For we must not forget the primacy of our concern for excellence. We must have diversity, but we must also expect that every institution which makes up that diversity will be striving, in its own way, for excellence. This may require a new way of thinking about excellence in higher education, a conception that would be applicable in terms of the objectives of the institution. As things stand now the word *excellence* is all too often reserved for the dozen or two dozen institutions which stand at the very zenith of our higher education in terms of faculty distinction, selectivity of students, and difficulty of curriculum. In these terms it is simply impossible to speak of a junior college, for example, as excellent. Yet sensible men can easily conceive of excellence in a junior college.

The traditionalist might say, "Of course! Let Princeton create a junior college and one would have an institution of unquestionable excellence!" That may be correct, but it leads us down precisely the wrong path. If Princeton Junior College were excellent in the sense that Princeton University is excellent, it might not be excellent in the most important way that a community college can be excellent. It would simply be a truncated version of Princeton University. A comparably meaningless result would be achieved if General Motors tried to add to its line of low priced cars by marketing the front half of a Cadillac.

We shall have to be more flexible than that in our conception of excellence. We must develop a point of view that permits each kind of institution to achieve excellence *in terms of its own objectives.*

In higher education as in everything else there is no excellent performance without high morale. No morale, no excellence! And in a great many of our colleges and universities the most stubborn enemy of high morale and, therefore, of excellence, has been a kind of hopelessness on the part of both administration and faculty, particularly the latter, hopelessness about ever achieving distinction as an institution.

Not only are such attitudes a corrosive influence on morale, but they make it virtually certain that the institution will never achieve even that kind of excellence which is within its reach. For there *is* a kind of excellence within the reach of every institution.

In short, we reject the notion that excellence is something that can only be experienced in the most rarefied strata of higher education. It may be experienced at every level and in every serious kind of higher education. And not only may it be experienced everywhere, but we must *demand* it everywhere. We must expect excellence of every form which higher education takes. We should not demand it lightly or amiably or good naturedly. We should demand vigorously and insistently. We should assert that a stubborn striving for excellence is the price of admission to reputable educational circles, and that those institutions not characterized by this striving are the slatterns of higher education.

We must make the same challenging demands of students. We must never make the insolent and degrading assumption that young people unfitted for the most demanding fields of intellectual endeavor are incapable of rigorous attention to some sort of standards. One of the most appalling and unhappy errors of much popular education has been to assume that young men and women incapable of the highest standards of intellectual excellence are incapable of any standards whatsoever and can properly be subjected to shoddy, slovenly, and trashy educational fare. Though we must make enormous concessions to individual differences in aptitude, we may properly expect that every form of education be such as to stretch the individual to the utmost of his particular potentialities. And we must expect that each student is striving for excellence in terms of the kind of excellence that is within his reach. Here again we must recognize that there may be excellence or shoddiness in every line of human endeavor. We must learn to honor excellence (indeed to *demand* it) in every socially accepted human activity, however humble the activity, and to scorn shoddiness however exalted the activity. There may be excellent plumbers and incompetent plumbers, excellent philosophers and incompetent philosophers. An excellent plumber is infinitely more admirable than an incompetent philosopher. The society which scorns excellence in plumbing because plumbing is a humble activity and tolerates shoddiness in philosophy because it is an exalted activity will have neither good plumbing nor good philosophy. Neither its pipes nor its theories will hold water.

Section IV

Structural Accommodation

The prevailing forms of American higher education during most of its history were the independent college and the independent college with graduate and professional schools grafted onto it. Administration was relatively simple and generally restricted to a single campus. Enrollment growth was stable, and changes in governance could evolve. Financing, always a serious problem, did not involve large amounts, or untapped, unorthodox sources. But changes in size and purpose have required changes in structure and in relationships; new techniques of governance, new concepts of optimum size, and new relationships with the Federal government are now commonplace in higher education. The three essays in this section illustrate implications of these shifts.

Section IV-1

New Organizational Patterns in American Colleges and Universities

Joseph Axelrod

The observer of higher education must overcome several obstacles if he is to succeed in identifying the new patterns on American campuses. Through much that is new is taking place, everything that is new is not destined to be a new *pattern*. How is he to judge which are the emerging patterns and which are not? How many cases of year-round operation, for example, does he need in order to declare with confidence that this will become one of the future patterns in American colleges? (Even as he poses the question, he wonders whether the matter *is* quantitative.) Moreover, how can he be sure that a given innovation on one campus—an independent study program, or the requirement of a comprehensive examination for the bachelor's degree—is identical with innovations carrying the same label on other campuses?

Part of the difficulty arises out of reports both in the professional literature and in the popular press which attempt to create or preserve a particular institutional "image." Such reports often begin as distortions of the truth. Usually they remain so; but occasionally the publicized image serves as a pressure to establish itself in reality. Such phenomena complicate the task of identifying a new pattern, but the conscientious student of higher education must recognize that he cannot remain blind to them.

After other obstacles, one still remains. How shall he interpret the word "new," since it is *new* patterns he proposes to identify? "New" for how long? Since the end of World War II? Since the mid-fifties? Or since the turn of the decade, perhaps? We shall arbitrarily say: Since the first Sputnik, for with it, a new

From *Emerging Patterns in American Higher Education,* edited by Logan Wilson, American Council on Education, Washington, D. C., 1965. Reprinted by permission of the American Council on Education.

era in American higher education began. It was about the beginning of this era that the first National Defense Education Act was passed, that the educational profession realized the temporary relationship of the forties and fifties between Government and higher education had become permanent, that the Federal grant university, as Kerr calls it, had come to stay.

There were also other signs of the new era. There was unrest in the undergraduate schools; the old-fashioned liberal arts college seemed unable to find its place in a rapidly changing world. "The liberal arts tradition is dead or dying"—Jacques Barzun's words were quoted everywhere, and few educators disagreed. [28] Literally scores of new colleges came into existence in the late fifties and early sixties, many of which devised plans that openly rejected the organizational patterns dominant in the mid-fifties.

More broadly, the beginning of the new era was marked by the rise of state master plans for higher education. The California master plan was drawn up in 1959 and enacted into law in 1960. [15, 4, 22] Concurrently, state boards responsible for teacher certification began to modify requirements, explicitly rejecting the philosophy that had dominated teacher education in the thirties and forties. At this time, too, the teachers college, as an institution, is alleged to have died. [66]

The general education movement, too, came to its end, and the term itself has almost fallen into disuse. Colleges have adopted a more neutral phrase, like "basic studies," to describe their broad-area programs. The Association for General and Liberal Studies—a new organization of college and university faculty who had been active in the general education movement—avoided the term when, in 1961, it selected its name. [3]

The general education reform in lower-division curricula and the molding of normal school into teachers college into multipurpose institution can both be seen as movements that emerged sometime around 1920, reached maturity in the forties, and approached old age in the fifties. Only after these preliminary questions—What is a pattern? and, What is new?—have been answered can the student of higher education approach the problem of identifying the emerging organizational patterns.

OLD PATTERNS, NEW RECOGNITIONS, AND PLANS FOR REORGANIZATION

A selection of a handful of the published works that most accurately reflect the state of higher education in the late fifties—the last years of the old era—would, I believe, include: for the junior colleges,

Medsker's study [52]; for the four-year colleges, the collection of essays edited by Sanford [60]; for graduate education, the works of Berelson and Carmichael [12, 18]; and for the professional schools, a study by McGrath. [48]

What does the picture reflected in these studies reveal about American higher education in the late fifties? It reveals a general failure. The junior college, forfeiting its identity, had done less than was minimally required to meet its major objectives. Four-year colleges, judged by any reasonable standard of accomplishment, were failing. Graduate programs were a mish-mash of sense and nonsense which provided for doctoral candidates, in addition to the experiences particular to each, the common experience of humiliation. And the professional schools admitted that their programs were falsely based, attempting, as they did, to contain an accelerating knowledge impossible of containment.

This was the verdict of the late fifties. By the mid-sixties, the situation has changed on every front. The years 1959–64 are the beginning years of a period of reorganization in higher education.

The Junior College

The American Association of Junior Colleges was about forty years old when the junior college came under the scrutiny of Medsker and his staff. The judgment which the study reached concerning achievement of general education goals—"In the majority of two-year colleges, relatively little had been done to meet the objectives of general education"—is echoed in its judgments of other major functions. [52, pp. 23–27] A basic cause for the failure was the mounting pressure to offer courses exactly parallel to those in four-year institutions. "When this happens," Medsker declared, "the junior college forfeits its identity." [52, p. 53]

Loss of identity led to even greater loss of prestige. The other segments of higher education regarded the junior college as existing primarily to give inferior students *some* college training. A University of California chancellor, speaking at the end of the old era, expressed this thought exactly. He thanked the California junior colleges for their role "in building a great University of California"; because the junior college had performed the chore of providing lower-division education to the less talented student, "the University has been allowed to continue its pursuit of distinction," he stated. [55, p. 7]

This was the attitude dominant in the fifties. In the sixties it is dominant no longer. The state master plans have come into existence, and the junior college is destined to play an extraordinarily significant role in the future development of the nation. Like the university and the four-year college, the junior college is considered in the new age to have its own excellence which it, also, must pursue.

Growth in junior colleges during the first half-decade of the new era has been phenomenal. In New York State, for example, between 1953 and 1960, community colleges were established at the rate of about one a year. But this was too slow, reported Kenneth Doran, and in 1960 the Heald Committee report and the State University master plan called for more. From 1960 to 1964, ten were established. [21, p. 16] In early 1964, the Educational Policies Commission declared that junior college education must become universal in America and that the content of studies must change—must now be "aimed at *intellectual* growth." [25, p. iii, italics added]

Experimentation in junior colleges with new organizational patterns has thus far, however, been limited. B. Lamar Johnson, who recently made a ninety-college survey focusing on the new patterns, concludes that many institutions have given "increasing attention to improving the processes and organization of teaching." As for concrete change, however, Johnson reports that "only a few faltering steps have been taken." [38, p. 14] Still, his report describes many innovations in physical facilities—push-button lecture halls, auto-learning laboratories, new television production and reception areas, facilities for live long-distance interviews—and some curricular experimentation: programed learning, team teaching, independent study, and work-study programs. Only rare instances were found "of any attempts to break the lockstep of the traditional calendar." [38, p. 14] In late summer 1964, however, the Los Angeles Board of Education authorized a study to explore the possibility of year-round operation for the seven junior college campuses in Los Angeles, and similar steps are being taken elsewhere.

Though late in starting, the swell in developments in the public junior colleges has begun. The private junior colleges have traditionally participated in experimentation. The four-building Learning Center at Stephens College, for example, has resulted from new conceptions of both physical facilities and the organization of student out-of-class time. [62]

The Four-Year College

The pattern in recent junior college history—a general failure in the late fifties, followed by plans for revising the form and content of

the educational experience—has reached a considerably more advanced
stage on four-year campuses.

When Sanford's *The American College* appeared, it attracted the
attention of college administrators and faculty throughout the nation.
They were struck by the collection's new approach to higher education
and were stunned by the picture it portrayed: "American colleges are
failing rather badly. They fail to achieve their own stated purposes;
and they fail by other reasonable standards of accomplishment."
[60, p. 2]

Just as the junior college, by 1959, had lost its identity, seeking to
shape an amorphous product, hoping every variety of four-year school
would find it acceptable, so the undergraduate college by 1959 had lost
its identity, supplying its students with a huge cafeteria of specialized
courses designed in some vague way to meet the demands of the graduate schools. That the demands were often contradictory and sometimes
more imagined than real only made matters worse.

But about the time *The American College* appeared, a myriad of
new colleges came into existence. The sound of saw and hammer, argument and compromise, was heard everywhere—from Hempstead on
Long Island, to Detroit to San Diego and Santa Fe; from Oakland in
Michigan to Santa Cruz to Tampa and Sarasota. The new colleges all
began by rejecting old patterns, even the best of the *old* patterns.
Three gave themselves the name "New College," for their intention was
—and is—to be born new and to remain perpetually new.

In April 1964, a conference on the experimental college, sponsored
by Florida State University, took place at Wakulla Springs. Ten campuses were represented: Antioch, University of California (Cowell
College on the Santa Cruz campus), Florida Presbyterian, University of
Michigan (Dearborn campus), Michigan State, New College at Sarasota, Pacific (Raymond College), Parsons, Stephens, and Wayne State
(Monteith College).

The colloquium concluded with an analysis of the over-all patterns
in the ten institutions: Five are experimental entities within larger
institutions. Nine base their curriculum in the liberal arts and general
education. All have selective admission policies, include independent
study both as a means of learning and as a goal of education, plan programs that are flexible in both content and rate of learning, specifically
include evaluation officers to appraise the effectiveness of the program
(and in some cases the achievement of individual students), give the
library a central and unusually important role in the educative process,
and set special criteria for the selection of faculty. There was much

discussion about the elimination of grades and credits. There was a general recognition that the experimental college is and must be in a state of constant flux and change.[1] [37, pp. 3–7]

The curricula in all these colleges express dissatisfaction with traditional ways of organizing undergraduate instruction. The source of their inspiration is, rather, the rich tradition of nonconformity in American higher education, a tradition that produced such great experiments as the Meiklejohn college of the early thirties, the Hutchins college of the middle forties under Faust's deanship, and the Harold Taylor college of the late forties under Raushenbush's deanship. These three no longer exist as experimental colleges, but their influence has been incalculable.

The Small College to be established in 1969 on the campus of the California State College at Palos Verdes is illustrative of the new movement. The parent institution will not open until 1965, but already Small College is part of the plan. It will enroll 500 students and offer a specially designed three-year (twelve-quarter) B.A. program requiring year-round attendance. The student body will include the full range of abilities and backgrounds present in the total campus, which is being master-planned for 16,000 students. Small College will not set any blanket requirements for the degree (other than the minimal requirements of the State Education Code) because it plans to tailor-make each student's program. Instructional means will include independent study, programed instruction, and credit by examination. In addition, it will provide observation-internship experiences for graduate students in the regular college who plan to become college teachers. As at New College at Hofstra and Cowell College at Santa Cruz, it is anticipated that the operation of this separate experimental college will cost no more per student than the traditional program. [9, 13, 14, 36, 49]

While some of the new answers are being sought in the small, experimental college, other patterns are being created at larger institutions newly in operation or about to come into existence—at Boca Raton, Florida; Irvine, California; Oakland, Michigan; Stony Brook, New York; San Diego, California; Tampa, Florida; and at scores of

---

[1]As early as 1958, Hatch began to collect data about ten experimental colleges of the late fifties: Austin, Bard, Goddard, Hofstra, New College (Amherst, Mount Holyoke, Smith, and University of Massachusetts), the Michigan State campus at Oakland, University of South Florida, Wayne State's Monteith, and Wesleyan University. Hatch's report states seventeen aspects of experimental colleges. Many of these anticipate the listing which emerged from the Wakulla Springs conference. [31] The experimental programs at Bard, Goddard, Monteith, New College (Massachusetts group), and Wesleyan were also described by Baskin. [10]

other sites.   These larger institutions also reject the organizational patterns dominant in the fifties.

A 1963 workshop at Boca Raton hammered out the philosophic framework for the new Florida Atlantic University.   Participants recommended that the new institution "give major attention to the elimination of the lock-step, time-serving characteristics of conventional programs." They suggested the new university "organize student learning experience around substantial blocks of time" and "give more than usual attention to interdisciplinary study." Above all, it must seek "to avoid over-specialization which limits the breadth of intellectual understanding and reduces effectiveness in coping with the urgent problems of our generation." The recommended plan, moreover, emphasized the development of independent study programs and comprehensive examinations by means of which students are to demonstrate they have attained the goals set for the degree. [27]

The new patterns are stimulating curricular reform on hundreds of older campuses, from the University of Santa Clara to Southwest Missouri State College to the University of Toledo; from Coe and Beloit and Antioch to Southern Methodist and the City University of New York; from Montana State University to Pennsylvania State to the California State College at Hayward.

On some campuses, the reform is piecemeal; but on others, a complete overhauling is in process. The new curriculum at Beloit College, for example, will revolutionize every aspect of the instructional program. It is based on twenty-nine principles, among them the following: Course credit will replace hour credit. The interrelatedness of knowledge will become a basic mode of organizing the curriculum. Student achievement will not be measured merely by the passing of courses; area examinations and a comprehensive examination in the major will be required. Instead of admitting and subsequently graduating "peas in a pod," the college will accept a variety of students and help each to develop his maximum potential. Students will spend a smaller proportion of their time in class than formerly. During "vacation" terms, students will be involved in activities relevant to their education. High school and college will be looked upon as an eight-year unit rather than as two independent four-year units. Students will share a common academic experience both at the beginning and near the termination of their undergraduate careers. The degree program covers eleven "terms," each fifteen weeks in length: three underclassman terms, five middleclassman terms (two on campus, one on a field project done either in this country or abroad, two "vacation" terms), and three upperclassman terms. The content of the five middleclassman terms is to be tailored individually for each student. [11, 33]

Thus are the American campuses, old and new both, in ferment. This is the reply of the sixties to the standardized curriculum which the fifties inherited and proliferated. In the late fifties the liberal arts were said to be dead; in the mid-sixties, they are vigorously alive.

What has happended is simply that the liberal arts needed the time to redefine themselves for the new era. McKeon stated the point precisely: "The true function of the liberal arts ... is to liberate men. They have performed this function in the past by adapting themselves to the problems men have faced, and they have become obsolete and ineffective from time to time by elaborating old methods without consideration of new facts or problems. New liberal arts must be devised for the problems of the modern world." [50]

In the new liberal arts college, both *form* and *content* must change. The external forms have already undergone palpable change. One takes no risk in predicting that the fifty-minute hour, the three-hour course, the two-semester year, and the four-year degree will have become old-fashioned before the end of the decade. But deep-seated change cannot occur unless the content of the curriculum as well as its external form is modified.

The content of each of the disciplines is itself undergoing rapid change. By the mid-sixties, even the traditional colleges are recognizing that a discipline is not a collection of subject-matter information, but a set of tools and methods by which a changing subject matter can be explored. Some recent changes in curricular *content* are so common they need only brief mention. Humanistic and societal studies now focus beyond the arts, letters, and social institutions of Western man. Structural linguistics revolutionizes the teaching of English and foreign languages. Basic studies science courses emphasize the tools and methods of science rather than current but changing factual information. Behavioral science emerges as an integrating framework for the several social sciences. The new biology is a new world. There is a new relationship between knowing and doing in fine arts courses.

On the whole, however, change in form alone—*old* content poured into new molds—has been a trap for many colleges during the first half-decade of the new era. Language staffs discover that the language laboratory is a troublesome space-eater because the courses have remained unchanged. A good proportion of the 250 colleges and universities offering credit courses on television to 250,000 students discover that their telecourses must be something more than a TV camera focused on a man in a classroom. The new forms demand a new organization of content—indeed a *different* content. The independent study program results in more harm than good if the same mediocre readings on the same insignificant topics continue to be required.

But curriculum planners have another dimension in mind when they seek to change the content of a learning experience. This is the relationship which the student establishes between himself and the subject matter of the course—his "involvement." The profession, unfortunately, is still in the first stages of knowing how to explore this crucial aspect of the teaching-learning process. Pioneer work was done by five University of Chicago faculty members in 1949. [8] This early study helped focus attention on the different roles the effective instructor plays during a class hour; as he varies his role, the student's involvement is variously affected. This study also suggested that it is not the *fact* of overt student participation that matters, but the *nature* of his participation, and especially of his non-overt participation. This variable was identified as more significant in effective learning than other variables such as class size, which had attracted more attention. Much research has since been done, but, as McKeachie pointed out recently, no major break-through has yet occurred. [60, chap. 8]

An even more difficult problem must be solved by the new liberal arts college of the sixties: how to chain the powerful noncurricular forces. These appear to constitute even more effective educational means, along many lines, than the curriculum itself. "To design a college with only courses in mind," one observer writes, "is to overlook the most influential forces available for teaching." [39] These noncurricular forces have been studied in recent years, but as yet no mechanisms have been discovered for controlling and channeling them. [46, 54, 61, 63; 60, chaps. 13–15]

The Graduate School

At the close of the fifties, the over-all attitude toward the graduate school was one of ambivalence—severely critical and highly approving. In the academic world, much dissatisfaction was expressed, except by the graduate faculties themselves. The graduate school was, for the most part, looked upon good-naturedly as an antiquated system that slowly and patiently met every new condition with another patchwork reform. The graduate schools have the highest status in and out of the academic world, and those responsible for their programs are among the nation's best minds.

Researchers who studied the system in the late fifties found serious shortcomings. A 1958 article on graduate education summarized the recommendations of the Truman Commission of 1946: "The Commission pleaded for a larger conception of scholarship which would include 'interpretive ability as well as research ability, skill in synthesis as well as in analysis, and achievement in teaching as well as in investigation.'" Nevertheless, the article continued, "there is little present evidence that the recommendations of the Truman Commission have had practical effect, although there is continuing ferment over the issues raised." [45, p. 601]

Those who scrutinized the graduate schools a few years later were still impatient. "For more than fifty years," charged Carmichael in 1962, "the organization, methods, and policies of graduate schools have remained essentially unchanged; the policies and practices adopted in the nineteenth century are, in the main, still in force." [18, p. 159]

But change could not be held back. By the mid-sixties, many of the lines which had separated fields of knowledge had broken down. In area studies programs, space science, biology, behavioral science, and linguistics, traditional discipline boundaries are largely ignored in the most fruitful research being done. New degree programs are demanding combinations of skills and tools formerly fragmented by departmental walls; for example, advanced linguistic study now requires mastery of tools which have been developed jointly by humanist philologists, anthropologists, and mathematicians. [7, pp. 24–34] This cross-departmental communication is the wellspring for the great changes destined to reshape the graduate schools of the coming years.

The graduate schools of the mid-sixties take more seriously than those of the mid-fifties their responsibility in the preparation of college teachers. Leaders in higher education in the fifties became deeply concerned about the imminent, critical shortage of college teachers. The 1954 meeting of the Committee of Fifteen [29] was followed, in 1958, by another national conference, sponsored by the American Council on Education, where everyone admitted the situation was grave. [5] In 1959, the master plan survey team in California estimated their state alone would need an average of more than *three thousand* new faculty per year during the next fifteen years. [15, p. 121] But that same year, all forty graduate departments at Columbia University did not yield even a score over *three hundred* Ph.D.'s. [58, p. 179]

The 1958 Council conference joined other national groups in criticizing the graduate schools for having been slow to reorganize, but opinion differed about whether the change needed was a series of minor adjustments or a complete overhauling. Out of this Council conference came a number of specific recommendations that would lead to greater breadth in the doctoral program, to reduction in time spent in the program, to an emphasis on significance rather than novelty in the dissertation, and to a redignified master's program. [5,26]

During the years following, important changes in graduate studies were made, but too slowly and too few to satisfy many of the critics. Rosenhaupt summarized the developments in the early sixties: "While new growth is stirring everywhere, powerful factors restrain it." [58, p. 179] And Orlans reported disquieting facts: In some universities, it took some graduate students several months to arrange an appointment with their thesis adviser. [53, p. 52] In the dozen universities receiving the largest sums of money from the Federal Government, a *fifth* of the faculty sample could greet few or no advanced graduate students by name. [53, p. 49] A survey of Woodrow Wilson fellows in the early sixties disclosed that those who attended the four graduate schools judged best in the country by a group of liberal arts chairmen (Berkeley, Columbia, Harvard, and Yale) were less satisfied with the size of classes and with faculty guidance than were the fellows attending other institutions. [53, p. 52]

One cause for the slowness of change appears to be ignorance about higher education. First of all is "ignorance of simple facts about graduate education" by the graduate faculties themselves [58, p. 179]; second is ignorance about the graduate school—and the university in general—as a social institution. Thomas W. Hamilton wryly remarks: "Perhaps some day we shall know as much about our colleges and universities as we now know about corporations, political parties, and teen-age gangs." [51, p. vii] Another cause for slowness rests in the delicately balanced system by which universities are able to support doctoral candidates and simultaneously instruct lower-division students at relatively low cost. The unsupervised teaching assistant, notorious in the forties and fifties, is now becoming somewhat less common, as a result of efforts made by some of the graduate schools and national discipline associations. Among graduate schools, Harvard has led the way in reforming this vicious pattern. [64] Among discipline associations, the Modern Language Association of America is one which has urged the graduate faculties in the foreign language field "to stop assuming that good teachers simply happen." [47, p. 7]

At the master's level, two developments have attracted wide attention. The first is the series of high-level master's programs, developed on about eighty campuses, designed for prospective teachers. Thirty of these programs carry the specific title "Master of Arts in

Teaching." According to U.S. Commissioner of Education Francis Keppel, these programs "encourage high standards of scholarly achievement, professional competence, and long-term career commitment." [40, p. 253]

Second, special *three-year* master's programs are being conducted on some forty campuses. This attempt to break the old pattern, in which a single-year master's program disconnectedly follows two years of upper-division work, is worth looking at more closely. Typical of the movement is the three-year master's program at the University of Arizona. University officials hope that students who complete it "will have received a more thorough and demanding education and will have enjoyed experiences not available to most students in this age of mass and patterned education." Like other such programs, it is an integrally planned course of study covering three years of work. It retains students only so long as they maintain the program's high standards. The senior year includes an honors project and an apprenticeship; the graduate year includes training in independent research and experience in a supervised graduate assistantship. [2]

The Professional School

The history of the professional school during the late fifties and early sixties is as complex as that of the graduate school. In the late fifties, according to McGrath and Henderson, professional school curricula were moving away from a professional orientation toward a liberal arts framework. [48, 35, p. 142] A distinction between "pure" and "applied" knowledge originally provided the basis for the uniqueness of their curricula; but since World War II, this distinction has been found to be no longer functional or philosophically defensible.

As the years moved toward the mid-sixties, the professional school's programs—we refer here to those that are still a vital part, psychologically and physically, of today's campus—tend to become indistinguishable from programs in the main body of the university. [48, pp. 50–59] It seems likely that the professional schools will carry on their separate existence for a time, but the pressures of economy and efficiency may bring about their demise eventually. Many of the institutions now coming into being are not planning to have separate professional schools or even separately designated professional curricula. For example, the California State College at Palos Verdes is departing from the older state college pattern by planning neither a school or division of education nor one of business; this principle will apply to both its undergraduate and graduate programs. [14]

It thus appears that the professional school and the ivory tower will collapse together. This is a repetition, with variations, of the 1919–59 history of the teachers college.

THE NEW PATTERNS: THE REPLY TO STANDARDIZATION

The intellectual in America has always been closely related to higher education. By the end of the fifties, the intellectual had finally arrived. He was highly respected in the workaday world. He was better paid than ever before. He was influential in government and industry.

Still, he was troubled. Although he was influential, he felt impotent. The campus intellectual of the fifties railed against loyalty oaths; in the end he signed them. He did not like the news that nineteen of the ninety-three fraternities and thirty-six of the fifty-five sororities on the University of California campuses refused to sign the nondiscrimination pledge,[2] but he did not allow it to interfere with his work. He was happy, at least, to hear the platforms on his campuses ring with the slogans of anticonformism. The watchword was "pluralism of values," and it was everywhere said that no single view could ever dogmatically be declared "the American view." But the nation as a whole craved an identity—craved one so badly, it was willing to pay any price.

The price was standardization. Could the colleges and universities of the fifties resist the onslaught? Could they keep their students, their faculty, their curricula—and, what is more important, the administrative relations among these—free from standardization? They could not. The platforms of the campuses of the late fifties continued to ring with the slogans of anticonformism, but the studies of college and university students—many of them unpublished—reveal the crushing fact: the primary effect of college and university experiences on students was simply that they had become more like one another.[3]

A student entering college in the fifties who did not wish to be molded to a norm faced a wretched alternative: "Submit, or seek your education (without portfolio) elsewhere." Some of the most creative minds of the generation were expelled from the academic garden.

---

[2]This requirement was set by the Regents in 1959. The houses have until the fall of 1964 to comply. [59]

[3]Aside from the pioneer work of Newcomb and Jacobs, over half of the chapters (sixteen out of twenty-nine) in *The American College* bear on this question, as well as a substantial portion of the titles listed in the bibliography of the Center for the Study of Higher Education at Berkeley. [16] My thanks to Paul Heist for his help in interpreting for me some center data on this point.

Gamesmen, plodders, nonentities remained. They were turned out "capable" and "sharp" by the campus assembly line. "He's going to go places" was a phrase of approval, and it signified the student would take the path of involvement without commitment.

These students grew up to become the young faculty of the late fifties and early sixties—"a generation of gamesmen," Riesman called them, "bright but unconvinced men, who are erudite but poor specimens of mankind." [30, p. 20]

Higher education's achievement in standardizing the students of the fifties is commemorated in a folksong that became a hit in 1964. It begins with a description of the houses that, made of "ticky-tacky," look like a series of little boxes. The second stanza runs: "And the people in the houses/ All go to the university/ And they all get put in boxes, little boxes, all the same—/ And there's doctors and there's lawyers and business executives/ And they're made out of ticky-tacky/ And they all look just the same." [57]

But when the song reached its greatest popularity, the words were less true than when they were first sung. In the mid-sixties, students are becoming destandardized on many campuses. There is immense activity under the names of "honors programs" and "independent study programs." [10, 19, 32, 44] Moreover, the 1919–59 pattern that built a wall between the high school and the college is broken. The trickle of high school students taking courses on college campuses in advance placement programs in the early sixties will likely become a stream later in the decade. [56]

Admissions offices are concerned about the "creative" youngster who is not allowed in because he does not meet standards. The standards have not yet been changed, but students who are allowed in are not as quickly evicted as in the pre-1959 period. Administrators hope that the dropout rate among the more creative students, so great in former years, will decrease. Indeed, it is anticipated that the number of dropouts—which, in the forties and fifties, the process of standardization had brought to almost *half* of those who entered college [60, p. 631]—will decrease markedly as students become destandardized.

The first and most significant trend on American campuses during the current decade is thus the deconforming of students. The second is the deconforming of curricula.

The content of college and university curricula—especially during the crucial initial months when student attitudes toward the higher learning are being formed—has undergone rapid alteration during the last half-decade. In 1963, for example, a Harvard faculty committee declared its three-year-old freshman seminar successful, and the education editor of the *New York Times* saw a sign of the "beginning of an entirely different kind of general education—less uniform, less 'balanced,' less superficial, more tolerant of individual detours." [34]

At the close of the fifties, a university president, looking at curriculum change, said it "entails all the physical and psychological difficulties of moving a cemetery." [65] The major difficulty appeared to reside in a curious historical circumstance: the curriculum was grounded in the concept of number. Everything was by count: class hours, grade points, credits and courses, semesters and quarters and trimesters. So many credits for so many hours for so many weeks for so many years would earn a degree. Even some of the newest plans— the 3-3 of Dartmouth or the 4-1-4 of Gustavus Adolphus—suffer from dependence on counting. [20]

Leaders in higher education knew, as they faced the opening of this decade, that once the curriculum was freed from the yoke of number, they could manage the other curricular problems. But they understood the total problem well enough to know that this freedom could not come until the instruments measuring a college student's knowledge, in the fullest sense of the word, were perfected.

These two developments—dequantifying the curriculum and perfecting knowledge-assessing scales—are now moving toward one another, ready to join into a single movement. The pioneer work in joining these two was done at Chicago in the forties and at Michigan State, Shimer, and various other campuses in the East and Midwest in the fifties. Now it is the colleges and universities in Florida, Michigan, and New York that are leading the way.[4]

The response in the sixties to the standardization of the fifties affects faculty also. The large movement to destandardize is providing the motive force in bridging the gulf between teaching and research. By 1959, this gulf had become immense. By the mid-sixties, the ends of the teacher-scholar and the ends of the research-scholar, long due for re-examination, are beginning to be redefined, and the fields common to both are being rediscovered.

---

[4]As new campuses are being planned in these states, the organizational pattern calls for an officer in charge of coordinating measurement of student achievement and campuswide efforts to evaluate the effectiveness of the educational program. Such officers are not new on American campuses. A 1959 volume on testing carries descriptions of seven programs of the fifties, several of which had such officers. [1] But on the whole, the system of grading on the basis of vague and often contradictory criteria dominated the fifties. [6] It is, therefore, significant that the pattern of the fifties is being broken in these three states and elsewhere. [42]

Recent exploration of the ends of higher education points to three major goals for colleges and universities, all revolving around knowledge: its daily production, its continuous reinterpretation and transformation, and its daily diffusion. The central concern of the true scholar is seen to lie, first and foremost, with reinterpreting the body of knowledge, assimilating the new into the old, reassessing and transforming the shape of the whole. Only after he achieves this central objective—and is habitually performing it—is he considered ready to move to his own particular function. The research-scholar moves to the augmentation of knowledge, the teacher-scholar to the transmission of knowledge. Let the former neglect the center and attend only to augmentation, he becomes a researchist. Let the latter neglect the center and attend only to transmission, he becomes a classroom manager. Worse still, having no intellectual life in common, each must then mistrust and belittle the other.

In 1959, there were probably fewer research-scholars on American campuses than researchists, and probably fewer teacher-scholars than classroom managers. It may take several decades to correct the imbalance in institutional ends, but the sixties have seen the beginning. Universities famous for publish or perish are beginning to look for teacher-scholars for their faculties. New criteria for promotion will have to be worked out; but the problem will be surmounted. Dean E. McHenry, chancellor at the new Santa Cruz campus of the University of California, admits that "recruiting a qualified teaching staff, because of the emphasis on instruction rather than research, might be a problem." But he has announced that he has worked out a plan which "calls for a new system of staff evaluation and promotion." [17] The president of that multiversity dares to predict what lies beyond: "The last twenty-five years have been the age of the specialist," Kerr declares, "but I have a hunch—a very strong one—that the next twenty-five years will see a rebirth of the generalist. It's inherent in the very nature of things. It *must* happen." [43]

The age of overspecialization, of rivalry and misunderstanding between researcher and teacher is beginning to end. In the late fifties, educational leaders like Meredith Wilson and Peter Elder knew that was going to happen. This snatch of dialogue which took place in 1958 shows how they anticipated the current trend:

WILSON: What is "research"? Veblen, in his *Higher Learning in America*, makes the comment that the real business of a university is not teaching but study. Now, what kind of study is appropriately research? Mr. Elder, I would like to find out where you separate these.

ELDER: I am not sure I can help you. I personally generally avoid the word "research" and use the word "study." I merely mean some people's individual study is "published" before a group of undergraduates in oral communication. Other people's study is published that way and also another way in order to help people living thousands of miles away and a number of years from the present time. I therefore haven't made any distinction between research and study and really do not wish to. [5, p. 18]

In 1963, Kerr listed a number of institutional changes which he believes are coming, in spite of much faculty hesitation and "even some resistance": the revamping of curricula and calendars; the renovation of undergraduate teaching; the revolutionizing of some fields of study (for example, biology); the mechanization of some aspects of instruction. But two changes, he believes, will be readily accepted: "One will be directed toward overcoming the fractionalization of the intellectual world, and the other will call for procedures devised to make administration more personal, including faculty administration." [41, p. 101]

We have just seen, briefly, the paths by which fractionalization in the intellectual world is being combated. But destandardization of faculty-administration relationships will come less easily. The progressive formalization of these relations in the fifties became too well-paved a road to be quickly replaced. During the last decade, faculties were increasingly caught up in the formal procedures of rights and privileges, tenure and free speech, loyalty oaths and due process. "Faculty government has become more cumbersome," Kerr declared, "more the avocation of active minorities; and there are real questions whether it can work effectively on a large scale, whether it can agree on more than preservation of the status quo." [41, p. 43]

There are notable exceptions, but a great deal of the interchange between faculty and administration (including the superadministration, that is, systemwide heads and governing boards of institutions and systems) is formal or threatening or bitter. Reasonable dialogue between the parties is the exception. The observer notes that both sides invoke truth, justice, democracy, and America. And in invoking these clichés, they choke off dialogue. But if dialogue is not kept alive and flourishing between faculty and administration, how can higher education's total contribution to society be kept flourishing?

To recognize this principle, however, only intensifies the dilemma. No one seems to be sure how the principle is to be implemented, how dialogue is to be kept alive. During the fifties, relations between faculty and administrators underwent cycles of tension and relaxation as procedures were established to safeguard faculty rights, ensure justice, guarantee academic freedom. [24] No one can possibly wish these undone. But it cannot be denied that the growth of these procedures played a major role in the progressive impersonalization of faculty-administration relations. Is it possible, during the years immediately ahead, that the power of these procedures can be harnassed and made to contribute toward the humanization of these relations? Perhaps we can take a lesson from the giant computers—themselves symbols of standardization—that are actually learning how to differentiate and individualize rather than standardize. J. A. Easley, for example, told participants at a 1964 conference how PLATO, a new computer system, meets the needs of its users not *en masse* but individually. [23] Perhaps the answer lies not in combating bigness but in channeling its power.

The solution currently being offered, however, takes a different line of reasoning. If progressive impersonalization in faculty-administration relations comes from ever-increasing bigness, then humanization should occur if the structure, even as it grows larger, is made to appear smaller. This is the solution of decentralization. Decentralization is taking place on several older campuses[5] and on some new ones. At the University of California, Santa Cruz, for example, twenty or so small, liberal arts colleges will be established (about four in each half-decade) and a "campus core" will provide the home for the graduate school, the library, and certain facilities requiring elaborate paraphernalia. Cowell College, the first of the undergraduate colleges at Santa Cruz, will open next year with about six hundred students and thirty-five faculty fellows.

The concept of "modular" growth, according to Chancellor McHenry, although "new in an American state institution, is really medieval in conception." [49] Thus, possibly, a medieval concept of university organization holds the key for the solution to today's grave dilemma in faculty-administration relations.

These, then, constitute the four-dimensional response to standardization which we see emerging in the first half-decade of the new era: individualizing the student; freeing programs of study from the yoke

---

[5]For example, at the University of the Pacific. The Claremont group, incidentally, is not a case in point, since the Claremont colleges have not *moved* from centralization to decentralization. Nevertheless it should be said that recent developments in academic decentralization could not have taken the shape they have, without the benefit of the experience of Pomona and her sister institutions.

of number; rediscovering the central and common goals of researcher and teacher; and humanizing faculty-administration relations.

But there is a larger context, and I should like to close by stating my conception of it.

The leading minds in America know that education, and higher education in particular, is the most powerful instrument our society possesses for effecting social change. Both in the era ending about 1959 and in the present era, educators have sought to discover how that instrument can best be shaped toward that end.

The search for this answer during the era just ended was exciting, haphazard, energetic, disorganized, and eventful. And, as we have seen, the verdict of the profession was that it was not successful. There appear to be four causes for its failure. Three were internal: insufficient information about education, particularly higher education, as a functioning institution in our society; a general misconception of the processes by which knowledge is transmitted; and an emphasis on the constant production of new knowledge at the expense of the continuous reinterpretation of the whole body of knowledge. One cause was external: a society at war.

The search for the answer during the years following 1959 promises to be exciting, systematic, energetic, organized, and eventful. Let us hope that historians of American higher education, judging this search with the eyes of, say, 1999, will declare it was successful.

REFERENCES

Note. — This is a list of the literature cited in the paper; it is not intended to be a selective bibliography.

1. American Council on Education. Committee on Measurement and Evaluation. *College Testing: A Guide to Practices and Programs.* Washington: The Council, 1959.
2. Arizona, University of. *The University of Arizona's Special Master's Program.* Prepared by T. W. Parker. Mimeographed. 1963.
3. Association for General and Liberal Studies. *Common Goals of Liberal and General Education.* Proceedings of the First Annual Meeting of the Association for General and Liberal Studies, Oct. 25–27, 1962. East Lansing, Mich.: 1963.
4. Axelrod, Joseph. "Coordinating Higher Education in California," *University College Quarterly*, May 1964.
5. _____ (ed.). *Graduate Study for Future College Teachers.* Report of the Conference on College Teacher Preparation Programs Sponsored by the Committee on College Teaching of the American Council on Education in Washington, D.C., April 30 and May 1, 1958. Washington: American Council on Education, 1959.

6. _____. "What Do College Grades Mean? A Survey of Practices at Four Institutions," *College and University Teaching*, Herman A. Estrin and Delmer Goode. Dubuque, Iowa: William C. Brown Co., 1964.

7. Axelrod, Joseph, and Bigelow, Donald. *Resources for Language and Area Studies.* Washington: American Council on Education, 1962.

8. Axelrod, Joseph; Bloom, Benjamin S.; Ginsburg, Benson; O'Meara, William; and Williams, Jay C., Jr. *Teaching by Discussion in the College Program.* Chicago: College of the University of Chicago, 1949.

9. Baskin, Samuel (ed.). "Higher Education: Some Newer Developments." MS in press. New York: McGraw-Hill Book Co. (See especially chap. 2, "The New Colleges," by Lewis Mayhew.)

10. _____. *Quest for Quality: Some Models and Means.* U.S. Office of Education, New Dimensions in Higher Education, No. 7. Washington: Government Printing Office, 1960.

11. Beloit College. *The Beloit Plan.* Prepared by Sumner Hayward. Mimeographed. Beloit, Mich.: The College, 1964.

12. Berelson, Bernard. *Graduate Education in the United States.* New York: McGraw-Hill Book Co., 1960.

13. Cain, Leo F. "The Small College at the California State College at Palos Verdes." Address given at the National Conference on New Directions for Instruction in the Junior College, Los Angeles, California, July 16, 1964.

14. California State College at Palos Verdes. *The Academic Plan for the California State College at Palos Verdes.* Palos Verdes: The College, 1964. (Presented to the Chancellor and the Trustees of the California State Colleges, Feb. 26–27, 1964.)

15. [California, State of.] *A Master Plan for Higher Education in California, 1960–1975.* Sacramento: California State Department of Education, 1960. (Prepared by A. G. Coons, A. D. Browne, H. A. Campion, G. S. Dumke, T. C. Holy, D. E. McHenry, H. T. Tyler, and R. J. Wert.)

16. California, University of. Center for the Study of Higher Education. *Bibliography of Publications.* Mimeographed. Berkeley: The Center, 1946. (The list contains 130 items written by center staff or based on research conducted at the Center.)

17. California, University of. Santa Cruz Campus. University of California press release, dated November 1962.

18. Carmichael, Oliver C. *Graduate Education: A Critique and a Program.* New York: Harper & Bros., 1961.

19. Cole, Charles C., Jr., and Lewis, Lanora G. *Flexibility in the Undergraduate Curriculum.* U.S. Office of Education, New Dimensions in Higher Education, No. 10. Washington: Government Printing Office, 1962.

20. "Colleges *Can* Operate All Year," *Saturday Review*, Dec. 15, 1962. (A series of four articles by Edward H. Litchfield, University of Pittsburgh; Weimer Hicks, Kalamazoo College; Marjorie Freed, Antioch College; and Joseph E. McCabe, Coe College.)

21. Doran, Kenneth T. "New York's Two-Year Colleges," *University College Quarterly*, May 1964.

22. Dumke, G. S. "Higher Education in California," *California Historical Society Quarterly*, June 1963.

23. Easley, J. A., Jr. "PLATO: A Computer-Controlled Teaching System." Paper presented at the Nineteenth National Conference on Higher Education sponsored by the Association for Higher Education, Chicago, April 21, 1964.

24. Eckert, Ruth E. "The Share of the Teaching Faculty in University Policy-Making," *American Association of University Professors Bulletin*, Winter 1959.

25. Educational Policies Commission. *Universal Opportunity for Education Beyond the High School.* Washington: National Education Association, 1964.
26. Elder, J. P. "Revising the Master's Degree for the Prospective College Teacher," *Journal of Higher Education,* March 1959.
27. Florida Atlantic University. *A Proposed Statement of Beliefs for Florida Atlantic University.* Mimeographed. Boca Raton: The University, 1963. (Prepared by Samuel Baskin and revised to include comments from workshop participants, Sept. 23, 1963.)
28. "The Future of Liberal Education," *Saturday Review,* April 18, 1964.
29. *The Graduate School Today and Tomorrow.* Written by F. W. Strothmann on behalf of the Committee of Fifteen. New York: Fund for the Advancement of Education, 1955.
30. Habein, Margaret L. (ed.). *Spotlight on the College Student: A Discussion by the Problems and Policies Committee of the American Council on Education.* Washington: The Council, 1959.
31. Hatch, Winslow R. *The Experimental College.* U.S. Office of Education, New Dimensions in Higher Education, No. 3. Washington: Government Printing Office, 1960.
32. Hatch, Winslow R., and Bennet, Ann. *Independent Study.* U.S. Office of Education, New Dimensions in Higher Education, No. 1. Washington: Government Printing Office, 1960.
33. Hayward, Sumner. "Five Experimental Programs in Undergraduate Liberal Arts." Paper presented at the Nineteenth Annual Conference on Higher Education sponsored by the Association for Higher Education, Chicago, April 20, 1964. (The five colleges described are Raymond, Oakland University, Kalamazoo, Earlham, and Beloit.)
34. Hechinger, Fred M. "A Move to Free College Freshmen," *New York Times* (Western Edition), March 13, 1963.
35. Henderson, Algo D. *Policies and Practices in Higher Education.* New York: Harper & Bros., 1960.
36. Hofstra University. *A Proposal for a 3-Year Autonomous Undergraduate Degree-Granting New College at Hofstra University.* Prepared by the staff at New College and the Bureau of Institutional Research at Hofstra University. Hempstead, L.I., N.Y.: The University, 1964.
37. Johnson, B. Lamar. "Behold You Have Created a New Thing: A Conference Summary and Critique." Address delivered at the Colloquium on the Experimental College, sponsored by Florida State University, Wakulla Springs, Florida, April 8, 1964.
38. ———. "Islands of Innovation," *Junior College Journal,* February 1964. (The full report of this survey appeared in March: *Islands of Innovation: A Report of an Exploratory Survey of the Utilization of Junior College Faculty Services.* Los Angeles: University of California, 1964.)
39. Keeton, Morris. "The Climate of Learning in College," *College and University Bulletin,* Nov. 15, 1962.
40. Keppel, Francis. "Master of Arts in Teaching," *American Education Today,* ed. Paul Woodring and John Scanlon. New York: McGraw-Hill Book Co., 1963.
41. Kerr, Clark. *The Uses of the University.* Cambridge, Mass.: Harvard University Press, 1963.
42. Kurland, Norman D. "New York College Proficiency Examination Program," *Current Issues in Higher Education,* 1963, ed. G. Kerry Smith. Washington: Association for Higher Education, 1963.

43. Leonard, George B. "California: What It Means," *Look*, Sept. 25, 1962.
44. Lewis, Lanora G., in cooperation with Bryan, J Ned, and Poppendieck, Robert. *Talent and Tomorrow's Teachers: The Honors Approach.* U.S. Office of Education, New Dimensions in Higher Education, No. 11. Washington: Government Printing Office, 1963. (A statement based upon the transcript of proceedings of an April 1962 Conference of the Inter-University Conference on the Superior Student.)
45. Little, J. Kenneth. "Graduate Education," *Encyclopedia of Educational Research*. New York: Macmillan Co., 1960.
46. Lunsford, Terry F. (ed.). *The Study of Campus Cultures.* Papers Presented at the Fourth Annual Institute on College Self-Study, University of California, Berkeley, July 24–27, 1962. Berkeley: University of California, 1963. (By R. W. Tyler, H. S. Becker, B. R. Snyder, B. R. Clark, C. R. Pace, T. Newcomb, M. A. Trow, J. Floud, J. King, and R. H. Sullivan.)
47. MacAllister, Archibald T. (ed.). "The Preparation of College Teachers of Modern Foreign Languages," *Publications of the Modern Language Association of America*, May 1964.
48. McGrath, Earl J. *Liberal Education in the Professions.* New York: Teachers College, Columbia University, 1959.
49. McHenry, Dean E. "The University of California at Santa Cruz." Address given at the National Conference on New Directions for Instruction in the Junior College, Los Angeles, California, July 16, 1964.
50. McKeon, Richard P. "The Future of the Liberal Arts." Paper presented at the Nineteenth National Conference on Higher Education sponsored by the Association for Higher Education, Chicago, April 20, 1964.
51. _____. *The Smaller Liberal Arts College.* Washington: Center for Applied Research in Education, 1962.
52. Medsker, Leland L. *The Junior College: Progress and Prospect.* New York: McGraw-Hill Book Co., 1960.
53. Orlans, Harold. *The Effects of Federal Programs on Higher Education: A Study of 36 Universities and Colleges.* Washington: Brookings Institution, 1962.
54. Pace, C. Robert. "Images of American Colleges and Universities," *Higher Education: Its Multiple Facets*, A Report of the Eighth Far Western Conference of Fulbright Scholars. Los Angeles: University of California, 1963.
55. Peterson, B. H. "The Role of the Junior College in California," *California Education, October* 1963.
56. Radcliffe, Shirley A., and Hatch, Winslow R. *Advanced Standing.* U.S. Office of Education, New Dimensions in Higher Education, No. 8. Washington: Government Printing Office, 1961.
57. Reynolds, Malvina. "Little Boxes." Discs issued by Columbia, #4-42940, and by Victor, #47,8301.
58. Rosenhaupt, Hans. "Graduate Education," *American Education Today*, ed. Paul Woodring and John Scanlon. New York: McGraw-Hill Book Co., 1963.
59. *San Francisco Chronicle*, May 29, 1964.
60. Sanford, Nevitt (ed.). *The American College.* New York: John Wiley & Sons, 1962.
61. Selvin, Hannan C. "The Impact of Higher Education on Student Attitudes," *Unity and Diversity in Higher Education.* A Report of the Seventh Far Western Conference of Fulbright Scholars. Berkeley: University of California, 1962.
62. Smith, Seymour M. "New Logs and Old Learning," *Improving the Efficiency and Quality of Learning*, ed. A. E. Traxler. A Report of the Twenty-sixth Educational Conference Sponsored by the Educational Records Bureau and the American Council on Education. Washington: American Council on Education, 1961.

63. Stern, George G. "Student Values and Their Relationship to the College Environment," *Research on College Students*, ed. Hall T. Sprague. Boulder, Colo.: Western Interstate Commission for Higher Education, 1960.
64. *Teaching Fellowships in Harvard College: A Survey by the Committee on Teaching as a Career.* Cambridge, Mass.: Harvard University, 1960.
65. Wilson, Logan. "A President's Perspective," *Faculty-Administration Relationships*, ed. Frank C. Abbott. Washington: American Council on Education, 1958.
66. Woodring, Paul. "The Short, Happy Life of the Teachers College," *American Education Today*, ed. Paul Woodring and John Scanlon. New York: McGraw-Hill Book Co., 1963.

Urban Sprawl in the Academic Community

Alleviating the University's Growing Pains

JOHN K. FOLGER

It is now generally recognized that the United States has become an urban society. Cities are dominant in our economic life and culture and are even assuming a dominant role in our politics, long the stronghold of rural influence. With this development has come an increasing concern for urban problems. Slums, traffic and expressways, suburban uniformity, juvenile delinquency, and related problems have become commonplace subjects of discussion and analysis by the press, radio, and television.

Similar developments in higher education have received much less attention. The growth of college enrollment in the country as a whole has been widely publicized, but few persons have stopped to realize what the national tidal wave of students means for the individual institution. There has been little recognition of the extent to which our students are concentrated in large universities: a concentration that will soon be higher than the concentration of our population in metropolitan centers. A few pertinent facts will set the stage for a consideration of some of the problems created by academic growth.

In the last thirty years, enrollment has been increasing much more rapidly in the United States than has the number of higher educational institutions, particularly in the period since 1952 (the point at which the influx of veterans following the passage of the GI bill was subsiding). Between 1953 and 1960, enrollment rose by about 65 per cent, and the average size of institutions increased by about 55 per cent. The average size of colleges more than doubled between 1940 and 1960. The average number of faculty members (including all professional staff–administrators, research workers, and teachers) increased somewhat

From *The Journal of Higher Education,* Ohio State University Press, November, 1963. Reprinted by permission of *The Journal of Higher Education.*

faster than the number of students, because research and extension personnel were multiplying more rapidly than the teaching faculty.

The distribution of colleges by size is markedly skewed. The largest 10 per cent of the institutions enroll over one-half the students and have an average enrollment of over 10,000 students. Nearly all of these are classified by the Office of Education as universities. There is likely to be a continued rapid increase in the average size of institutions. Although it is impossible to foretell with any accuracy how many new colleges or universities will be established in the next twelve to fifteen years, it is improbable that the number will be large. The rate of formation of new colleges was lower in the fifties than in the two preceding decades, despite the much more rapid increase in enrollment. A primary reason for this appears to be the extremely high cost of launching a new institution, even one of modest size. In addition, there are large continuing costs if an institution of reasonable quality is to be developed and maintained.

In spite of these barriers, new institutions are being established every year, and will probably continue to be, although public funds may be the main source of support for them (whether they are publicly or privately controlled). We have prepared two projections of the number of new colleges formed. Our low projection of the number of institutions implies the same rate of increase as that which occurred between 1950 and 1960; the high one, the rate of increase observed between 1930 and 1960. The low projection would add about 200 more institutions by 1975, or about 14 a year, on the average. The high one would add about 400, or about 28 a year. If we divide the projected number of institutions into the projections of college enrollment in *Current Population Survey* (Bureau of the Census, No. 232, p. 25), we get projections of the future average size of institutions.

The projections of average institutional size range from 2,500 to 3,800; a median figure would be slightly over 3,000. With an over-all ratio of students to professional staff of 10 to 1 (this implies a ratio of students to full-time teachers of over 20 to 1, since full-time teaching faculty make up less than one-half the professional staff), the average institution would have over 300 professionals on its staff by 1975.

Averages do not really mean very much when there is such a wide range in institutional size. We already have a class of institutions— universities—that are very large and complex. In many ways they correspond in the world of higher education to cities in the general culture. They are the dominant type of institution in higher education today, not only because of their size and the high proportion of all students they enroll, but because they educate most of the college teachers and administrators and produce most of the research and textbooks, thus influencing the character of every college in the country. If the large universities retain their present proportion of total enrollment, they will grow very large indeed, reaching an average size of 20,000 to 25,000, according to the high projection. If they set limits on enrollment (as some have already done), there will be additional pressure on the smaller institutions to enlarge, and many more of these will grow to university size.

By 1975 there may be five hundred to six hundred institutions enrolling 5,000 students or more, three-fourths of all students in attendance. A very rapid growth of public junior colleges would modify these projections, but it is unlikely that the percentage of students in institutions with more than 5,000 students will fall below 60 to 65 per cent of the total.[1] These figures make it clear that universities[2] are becoming dominant in higher education much more rapidly and more completely than the metropolis has come to dominate American society.

This rapid growth in higher education has created problems for the universities comparable to those that face our metropolitan areas. Some of the problems of institutional growth are strikingly similar to problems of urban growth; the university is spared certain others, however, that face the metropolis. For example, it does not keep its failures (who constitute a large proportion of the total), whereas the city does, swelling its relief and welfare rolls and adding to the statistics of crime and delinquency. It is beyond the scope of this paper to describe all of the problems and advantages that size brings to an institution, but a few can be discussed.

A typical university today has three hundred to three thousand faculty members, administrators, and other professional staff, divided into fifty to one hundred specialized departments for administrative purposes. This large and heterogeneous group is specialized as to field of teaching and research but shows great resistance to specialization in administration and management. The faculty strongly favors a direct, town-meeting, democratic type of organization. This system of governing is well suited to the idea of a community of scholars but presents obvious difficulties when applied to a university with over five hundred faculty and staff members. The stresses and strains between the faculty ideals of democracy and fellowship among colleagues and the requirements for management of a large, complex organization are

---

[1]About one thousand new junior colleges enrolling 1,000 students each would be required to reduce the per cent of students in institutions of over 5,000 from 75 per cent to 60 per cent by 1975, assuming that all their students were drawn from the institutions with over 5,000 students.

[2]Obviously, not all large institutions are universities, but we shall call them that for the sake of simplicity.

intensified by rapid growth. Our figures on institutional size indicate that this problem of institutional management will be magnified in the future. The difficulty of reconciling faculty values with the direction and control of large university organizations is succintly stated by John Corson:

> As institutions grow large and complex—be the institution an industrial firm, a business enterprise, a religious institution, a government bureau, or a university—each faces a plaguing dilemma. Can it, on the one hand, develop a systematic organization to coordinate all its members in achieving its purpose while, on the other hand, stimulating and facilitating the enterprise of each member?[3]

The administrative specialization required in a large organization presents special problems in a university. As they have grown in size, large universities have been employing more staff specialists, who tend to usurp what the faculty regards as its own policy-making prerogatives. This is particularly true in the areas of business operations and student personnel services. We have here an illustration of the conflict between the citizen generalist and the bureaucratic specialist. As the institution expands (certainly by the time it reaches the size of the smallest of our present universities, 3,000–4,000 students), it becomes so complex that specialists are essential, and the president, vice-president, and deans become increasingly dependent on them. The area in which faculty advice and decision are sought narrows.

For example, take the area of student admissions. University faculties generally expect to control admissions policies. The policies are implemented by the director of admissions and his staff. In the last two decades, an elaborate body of knowledge and a technology have grown up in the admissions area. Today, in an institution which has a real selection problem (and more universities will, if they limit their size), the process of admissions requires a basic knowledge of the psychology of learning and personality development, an understanding of multiple-regression techniques, and a minimum understanding of probability theory, test-construction techniques, and the use of biographical inventories and attitude tests. Familiarity with the design and interpretation of prediction studies is also important. Since most faculty members are short on one or more (or all) of these skills and knowledges, there is a tendency for the admissions officer to take over more and more control of the admissions process, including the policy

---

[3]*Governance of Colleges and Universities* (New York: McGraw-Hill Book Company, Inc., 1960), p. 18.

decisions. A common reaction of the faculty is to depreciate all the technology (admissions tests are no good, and so on) and to insist on a continuation of the intuitive procedures they feel comfortable with. Thus one of the university's problems in growing bigger is to learn how to use the specialist in such a way that he can contribute his skills without undermining the policy-making role of the faculty. Since this role is often ill defined and viewed differently by different people, the problem is a complex one, regardless of the size or rate of growth of the institution. Rapid growth and large size merely intensify these issues.[4] Other examples of problems faced by faculty and staff in adjusting to conditions created by large size could be cited, but this one illustrates the problem.

At present, the prevailing faculty attitude seems to be one of cynicism; the current situation in the large university is obviously at variance with faculty ideals, but a new set of values more consistent with the realities of a large complex university has not emerged. Since the development of a new ideology is a very complicated process, dependent on many things in addition to the changed conditions created by size, it is unlikely that the emergence of new values will keep pace with the growth of universities.

The conflicts between community values and bureaucratic conditions will be one factor in the high mobility of faculty members in the next decade. As faculty salaries become more adequate, the noneconomic aspect of work will become a bigger factor in the choice of positions. Among these aspects, the system of management and the faculty's role in institutional government will be important.

A big problem in the metropolis is to give the citizen a sense of importance and of participation in his government. The universities are in the same predicament, and to the degree that they are successful in coping with it they will retain their teachers and attract new ones. The solution is to develop a bureaucracy that is effective without robbing the faculty of a voice in institutional government and a sense of having an influence on problems of concern to it.

Learning in the large university can be a very impersonal thing. Crowded lecture sections, instruction via the mass media, and specialization which restricts the student to brief and perfunctory contact with a large number of professors make instruction formal and impersonal. The chance for an undergraduate to know any teacher well as a person is slight. The student learns to separate his social life and living ar-

---

[4] *Ibid.*, p. 110.

rangements from his formal classroom learning activities in much the same way (psychologically) that the city dweller separates work from residence and recreation. Like the big city, the big university typically has elaborate recreational and social opportunities available to those who can pay the costs. The costs of recreation are paid chiefly in money in the city and in time in the college.

The large university is well organized to provide specialized technical education of high quality at reasonable cost. Its impersonality is not a serious impediment to education for those students who are strongly motivated to acquire the knowledge it offers. For students without such motivation, however, it creates serious problems. There is a good deal of evidence that most students lack the appropriate motives for acquiring a liberal education (as contrasted with a technical, professional one) in an impersonal educational environment. Students come to college chiefly for vocational reasons—to get a good job, to get ahead in life—not for intellectual growth.

It is obvious that four years of college or university life will not transform every student into an intellectual. It is also clear that most students experience some intellectual growth in college. Research findings suggest that students do not, however, reach a reasonable level of intellectual growth in the light of their own potential and the requirements of modern society for persons with the ability to solve problems and make critical evaluations, and with the other intellectual characteristics that are the goals of a liberal education.[5] The current deficiencies of our colleges and universities in motivating students to seek intellectual growth are likely to become even more serious in the future, when the student body will be more heterogeneous and contain an even larger percentage of students who come to college chiefly for vocational reasons.

Although the small college, as well as the large university, often fails to develop this intellectual potential of its students, it is significant that the institutions that have had the greatest impact on their students' attitudes and values are small colleges. The development of intellectual potential in most students depends on changes in values and motivations. These are modified mainly through personal contact with family, friends, teachers, and other close associates. By contrast, impersonal

---

[5]Relevant studies are reported by Harold Webster, Mervin Freedman, and Paul Heist, "Personality Changes in College Students," *The American College*, edited by Nevitt Sanford (New York: John Wiley and Sons, Inc., 1962); Philip Jacob, *Changing Values in College* (New York: Harper and Brothers, 1957); and Nevitt Sanford, "Ends and Means in Higher Education," *Proceedings of the Association of Higher Education, 1962* (Washington, D.C.: The Association, 1962).

contacts through radio and TV, newspapers, and lectures usually have little impact. The problem of the big university is not that it is big, but that the relations between students and teachers in it are usually impersonal.

What is to be done about these problems of size in our universities? We cannot go back to the small liberal-arts college for the solution, although there are those who propose this. Like the city in modern society, the university has developed because it fulfills important functions better than the small school. It can provide specialized and professional education of great variety and high quality. It advances knowledge through research and scholarship, in addition to transmitting it. It is generally more efficient from an economic point of view. The answer is not to do away with the university but to overcome some of the difficulties its size presents.

The most widely attempted, and in many ways the most successful, approach to improving the intellectual development of students is to select those with high potential and give them specialized personal treatment. Recent years have seen a resurgence of honors programs, a good example of this technique, partly through the stimulation of the Inter-university Committee on the Superior Student. Graduate students (a group with higher than average motivation toward intellectual development) also get special treatment in the university. In fact, graduate students and superior undergraduates in honors programs may receive most of the time and attention of the faculty, making education for the remaining undergraduates routine and impersonal.

Special programs for selected students at the undergraduate and graduate levels are excellent, but they do not touch the problem in its more difficult aspects. Another approach is to enlist students who have intellectual orientation in the job of motivating other students who lack it. The house plan at Harvard and variations on this idea (such as the Wesleyan plan for colleges within the university) in a number of other institutions are designed to provide the student with an intellectual orientation by bringing him into personal contact with intellectually oriented students and faculty, not exclusively in the classroom, but in a broad range of college activities. This idea has been used chiefly in institutions which have a very capable student body to begin with, with strong intellectual tendencies. Whether it would work with a student body with more heterogeneous motives is difficult to say, but the approach has great promise. If we can create within our large universities student communities which have an intellectual as well as a social component, a basis for achieving the goals of liberal education in the large university will be established.

The construction of housing for students which is designed to make a positive contribution to the university's educational goals is a large and costly endeavor (one undesirable aspect of the Harvard house plan is that it is expensive), but in this period of rapid growth of higher education when many new dormitories and other facilities are being built, we have an excellent chance to try out new plans. There are numerous ways, however, of establishing informal student groups that will promote the goals of the institution without the expense of new or rearranged living quarters. In the pyramid plan at Pennsylvania State University, for example, small groups of freshman and sophomore students meet periodically with upperclassmen and graduate students who act as leaders for the purpose of academic and vocational counseling. Groups of this type are relatively inexpensive to establish and have great potential for furthering the intellectual aims of the university.

The organization and management of the large institution by the faculty and administration can also be improved by attention to the informal organization of the faculty. Just as the informal life of the students is of great importance in determining what and how much they learn, so the informal organization of the faculty in the university is very important in determining how well the formal organization will function and what attitude the faculty will take toward the increased bureaucracy made necessary by growth. This fact is widely recognized but seldom applied in such matters as the design of faculty offices, the nature and location of the faculty club, and so on.

The high rate of faculty turnover that can be anticipated in most universities in the next decade will make it difficult for universities to maintain an effective organization, but it will provide the opportunity for better orientation of new faculty. New faculty members are likely to be amenable to the necessities of organizational responses to change and growth. In general, universities do not take advantage of the opportunities they have to give newcomers to the faculty an understanding of the organization and its operation.

One organizational response to growth is increased decentralization and the concomitant increased autonomy of the individual units. In the university, this has taken place unevenly: some decisions are usually decentralized (what to teach); some are seldom decentralized (budgeting, purchasing). Many are shared in elaborate and often confusing ways, so that they are both centralized and decentralized (personnel selection, promotion). Decentralization works well for some functions (research and graduate instruction) but presents knotty problems in others (the general education of undergraduates, development

of interdisciplinary specialties). Sometimes decentralization of authority reduces morale and organizational effectiveness. For example, a
democratic president may delegate the responsibility for making decisions to an authoritarian dean. Again, in some cases it increases morale
(at least temporarily) but reduces effectiveness (the popular department
head who promotes peace and harmony but cannot bring himself to get
rid of incompetent members).

These comments should make it clear that decentralization is no
panacea for the problems incident to growth in the size of a university,
although it may often be a solution.[6] One conclusion can be drawn,
however, which appears to have universal validity. If the university is
to avoid the institutional equivalent of urban sprawl in the metropolis,
it must do a much more effective job of planning than it has done in
the past.

Just as nearly every large city now has a plan for development, so
nearly every university has one. Unfortunately, most university plans
have serious limitations. A common defect of university and metropolitan plans alike is that they are limited to the physical aspects of
growth. A university usually has a long-range plan for new buildings,
but these may not reflect the institution's underlying educational objectives and programs. A fine physical layout for classrooms and
laboratories may be seriously inadequate in serving the purpose of
creating decentralized communities of students in which intellectual
motivation can be developed. A plan may be efficient as measured by
cost per square foot but very inefficient as a means of promoting contacts within the faculty and between faculty and students.

Unless an institution has a plan that takes account of all aspects
of university development as they affect its educational objectives,
growth will create the academic equivalent of urban sprawl. A poor
plan may be as bad as no plan; and viewed against the complexities of
the problems discussed here, most university plans appear to be inadequate. The application of technology to educational growth (TV,
teaching machines, and so on) is only a partial solution, and if widely
adopted may make the university of the future even more impersonal
and standardized. Inefficiency in the presentation of information cannot be defended, but the educational consequences of economic efficiency must be assessed.

The results of helter-skelter growth in universities may be as serious as the effects of slums in our big cities. The consequences may be

---

[6]Corson, *op. cit.*, pp. 85–86.

more serious because they are not obvious. We can do something about the problems created by growth in the size of the university if we recognize them and get to work. If we do not, the ideals of a liberal education and a community of scholars will become a more distant dream than they are today.

Section IV-3

Harvard and the Federal Government

Ever since the burgeoning of Government research expenditures during and following World War II, Harvard University, like other American universities, has become increasingly involved in Federal programs. During the 1960–61 academic year Federal funds accounted for slightly more than a quarter of Harvard's budget, the high point in a steady upward trend.

While this new relationship with the Government is a clear indication of the extent to which Harvard and her sister universities in the twentieth century have been called to respond to the demands of society, it has raised complex policy and administrative problems, so complex indeed that it has been increasingly difficult to view the relationship as a whole. The Harvard Governing Boards and Faculties have watched with deep interest and concern the institution's growing involvement with the Federal Government, particularly in recent years. In order to assess the significance of this new relationship, which has developed, without much overall planning, in response to specific opportunities or obligations, Harvard recently undertook to study the impact of Federal programs on the University and then to cooperate with the Carnegie Foundation for the Advancement of Teaching in a broader study of the subject.

This present summary is part of a larger report on the Harvard situation, made by Dr. Daniel S. Cheever, who served as Special Research Assistant to the President during the period of its preparation. Similar studies have been undertaken at 22 other institutions of higher education of varying size, and the form and direction of these self-studies have been encouraged and guided by the staff of a special committee of the Carnegie Foundation, of which I have been the chairman.

From *Harvard and the Federal Government*, A Report to the Faculty and Governing Boards, Harvard University, Cambridge, Massachusetts, September, 1961.

191

Eventually the committee will publish a detailed report on the 23 self-studies and, hopefully, will be able to draw some significant conclusions about the relationships between Government and higher education in this country. Meanwhile I recommend to the attention of the Faculties and Governing Boards of Harvard this summary document of Harvard experience, the product of many months of work on the part of many people. It illuminates for the first time a new aspect of Harvard's manifold activity which calls for our vigilant concern.

NATHAN M. PUSEY

(A report to the Faculties and Governing Boards of Harvard University, September, 1961.)

Harvard is by no means unique in its new relationship with Government. At least 80% of the institutions of higher education in the United States now receive Federal funds, and Harvard is one of those heavily involved in Federal programs. It is difficult to obtain precise totals but a sampling of seventeen institutions with large Federal programs showed Harvard in ninth place both in the amount received and in the relation Federal money bore to the total university budget.

Government funds tend to concentrate in the relatively few institutions with strong graduate and professional programs in the natural sciences because of the heavy national emphasis on research. A recent study of Federal expenditures for research in 287 institutions showed that 5 institutions received 57% of the total, while 20 institutions received 79% and 66 received 92%. In Harvard's sampling of seventeen institutions there were three administering Federal laboratories as a public service where Federal funds comprise more than two thirds of the annual university income budget and there were three others where the proportion was greater than a half of the total, based on 1960–61 figures.

Federal programs involve various parts of Harvard University in different degrees. Whereas Federal funds in 1959–60 supplied one quarter of the budget of the University as a whole, they supplied 55% in the School of Public Health, 57% in the Medical School and 30% in Arts and Sciences (of which almost half, however, went to the Cambridge Electron Accelerator, operated jointly with M.I.T.).

This new relationship with the Federal Government began only with the Second World War, the Office of Scientific Research and Development contracts, and the "GI bill of rights." Since then, in the country as a whole, science and defense have brought Government and the educational community together to such an extent that 20% of the total expenditures in higher education in the United States now comes from Federal sources.

While the use of Federal funds at Harvard has, up to the present, served the interests of both public policy and the advancement of knowledge, there are enough potential difficulties in the relationship to warrant taking a careful look at where we are and where we seem to be going.

THE NATURE OF FEDERAL PROGRAMS

With the First Morrill Act of 1862, the Congress turned from the idea of a national university that had intrigued a number of the Founding Fathers and adopted two policies that have persisted as the basis of Federal programs in higher education. It decided to give land grants to both private and state institutions, and to this day Federal grant programs do not discriminate between them. At the same time it decided to give support not to the general purposes of education, but to the improvement of the "agricultural and mechanic arts," and Federal support is still granted not for "education" but rather to further the specific purposes of particular Federal departments and agencies. For example, the national programs in which universities are now involved are not confined to the field of defense; they are also growing wherever the advancement of knowledge may make a contribution to the solution of social problems or the advancement of human welfare. For instance, Congress has multiplied by ten times in eight years the resources of the National Institutes of Health whose grants have done so much to support research, and provide research facilities, at Harvard.

Research Projects

Federal support is most conspicuous in the research portions of the University's budget. For example, the Division of Engineering and Applied Physics supported 95% of its research, but only 44% of its total expenditures, with Federal funds. Federal funds similarly supported 67% of the research and 48% of the total expenditure of the Chemistry Department; and in the Physics Department 90% of the research and 63% of the total. Even though some parts of the University have a larger proportion of private money in their research funds than do the departments noted above, none could carry on anything like the present level of scientific investigation without Federal aid.

During 1959–60, Harvard received more than $18 million from the Government of which $11,860,000 was solely for research purposes. This total included $6,512,000 from the Department of Health, Education, and Welfare, of which $5,495,000 came from the various National Institutes of Health for research toward the cure of specific diseases,

$826,000 from the Division of General Medical Science, and $132,000 from The Office of Education. The other major sources were The National Science Foundation, established to foster basic research, which provided $1,155,000, and the Office of Naval Research which provided $1,704,500.

The several Faculties of the University obviously did not share equally in Federal support for research. The principal benefactors . . . were the three schools in the Medical area and the Faculty of Arts and Sciences. Moreover there are variations among the departments within the Faculty of Arts and Sciences, with the chief research support going to departments in the Natural Sciences, including the Division of Engineering and Applied Physics, and to the museums. But small amounts do come to the Russian Research Center and the Laboratory of Social Relations, and programs in mental health are beginning to bring some support to the social sciences. . .

Research Facilities and Equipment

The Federal Government has been even more generous, in certain specialized fields, in the construction and operation of research facilities. The Cambridge Electron Accelerator will be completed in 1962 at an estimated cost of $11,630,000. This sum will have come from the Atomic Energy Commission. While the Commission will retain title to this facility for 25 years, Harvard and M.I.T. will operate it jointly so as to provide new research opportunities not only for their own faculties, but for an additional research staff. The work made possible by this new facility is of such importance that the Atomic Energy Commission will support additional research staff and the entire operating costs, which are expected to total approximately $5 million annually by 1963–64.

Here clearly is a wholly new dimension in higher education. Advance in nuclear physics requires expenditures beyond the capacity of private donors. In the main, Federal backing does not in this case involve financial cost to the University nor does it impose limitations on freedom of inquiry or the right to publish. The scientific community in Harvard, in M.I.T., and in the Government agreed that a facility of this sort should be built. Its presence near the Harvard Yard is eloquent testimony to the joint concern of the university world and the Federal Government for the advancement of nuclear physics.

Other research facilities have been made possible by generous sums made available by the National Institutes of Health through its Division of Research Grants. In the Faculty of Arts and Sciences, the Chemistry and Biology Departments have acquired new facilities, notably the new James Bryant Conant Laboratory for Chemistry, a portion of the cost of which was paid by the U.S. Public Health Service. In the Medical School the Departments of Anatomy and Pharmacology have been rehabilitated, and animal research facilities provided. Similarly the National Institutes of Health has contributed to the cost of constructing the new University Health Center. In every instance more than matching of funds from non-public sources was required.

By 1962 it is estimated that the Federal Government will have contributed nearly $14 million to the construction, modernization, and remodeling of research facilities which will be owned and operated by the University. Of this total the National Institutes of Health will provide nearly $12,883,000 and the National Science Foundation something over $1 million.

To complete the account it should be mentioned that, in addition to the construction and modernization of these research facilities, Harvard received from the U.S. Public Health Service (including the National Institutes of Health), the Atomic Energy Commission, and the National Science Foundation roughly $35,800 worth of research equipment and material during the same academic year; and substantial grants were received, soon after the fiscal year we are considering, from the Advanced Research Projects Agency.

While many colleges and universities have benefited from the Federal housing and loan program which has aided in the construction of dormitories and non-instructional and non-research facilities, Harvard has not yet done so. On the other hand, Harvard from its own resources is contributing indirectly to the Federal Urban Renewal program by participation in, and contributions to, the Citizens Advisory Committee of Cambridge. Harvard has expended $800,000 in land acquisition since 1955 in Federally approved urban renewal areas. This sum and other sums to be expended, according to Section 112 of the National Housing Act of 1959, become a non-cash urban renewal credit to the City of Cambridge in the amount of $1,000,000. Harvard's share will thus materially reduce the City's cash expenditures for urban renewal. Similar urban renewal credits are in prospect for Boston in the Medical area.

Instructional Programs

While it might seem the Federal Government makes an arbitrary distinction in favor of research and against instruction, there are exceptions. The School of Public Health received from the Public Health Service in 1959–60 almost $154,000 to support its general instructional programs. Furthermore, support for instructional programs in certain foreign languages was provided by the Office of Education. Under the National Defense Education Act, that office paid out over $80,000 for instruction in Far Eastern and Middle Eastern Languages, on condition that this be matched in equal amounts by the University. The three Armed Services contributed nearly $130,000 toward the ROTC program. The School of Public Health participated in a program, aided by a $23,000 grant from the International Cooperation Administration, for teachers of preventive medicine and public health. The Atomic Energy Commission and the National Science Foundation sought to promote the training of science teachers by furnishing the School of Education and the Faculty of Arts and Sciences something over $283,000.

Consultation and Leaves of Absence

In addition the Federal Government has turned to universities for specific advice on important issues. In the summer of 1960, for example, the Senate Foreign Relations Committee asked the Harvard Center for International Affairs to prepare studies on certain problems in American foreign policy at a cost of approximately $20,000 to the Government.

Far more often, however, the Government turns to individual Faculty members, through consulting arrangements which may benefit both the Government and the University. So long as a Faculty member is able to carry out his academic responsibilities, he is free to consult as much as he wishes. Practice varies from Faculty to Faculty. The Business School alone chooses to place the consulting activity of its Faculty members on a formally organized basis and places a limit on the amount of consulting done by the Faculty during the academic year. When Departments are considered as a whole, the average number of days of off-campus consulting per month per Faculty member is surprisingly small. In the Faculty of Arts and Sciences, it was exceptional to find that the average number of days per member spent on Government business exceeded a day a month. It is true that the University continues to pay fringe benefits[2] and salaries to Faculty members while they are consulting in Washington or elsewhere. Unreimbursed costs of this kind were estimated to amount to $211,310 for the academic year 1959–60. Such an amount, however, cannot properly be considered an unreimbursed cost in the sense that reimbursement should be expected or desired. Nor is such Faculty consulting without benefit to the University or to the Faculty member. The figure is simply a measure of the University's involvement with the Federal Government through consultation by Faculty members on an individual basis.

In any year a number of Faculty members are likely to be on leaves of absence working for Federal agencies. The year 1959–60 was no exception, and twelve permanent members of the Faculty were so engaged. In addition, twenty-one Faculty members received travel grants from Federal agencies. The University continued to make the necessary contributory payments toward the retirement of these Faculty members, even if they were on leave without pay to accept Federal salaries. Here again, such unreimbursed costs are simply an index of the extent to which the University renders a public service. Such leaves of course also provide new knowledge for instruction in the University as well.

Training Grants, Fellowships, and Exchanges

Particular mention should be made of other programs that are intended to contribute to student and professional advancement. For example, the Department of Health, Education, and Welfare provided in 1959–60 nearly $1,753,000 for Training Grants to the three schools in the Medical area (Medicine, Dental Medicine and Public Health) and the Faculty of Arts and Sciences. About 300 individuals, of whom about three-quarters already had doctoral degrees, were supported while studying at Harvard by this important program. Most of these trainees were being prepared for careers in research rather than for the practice of medicine. This large effort, moreover, was undertaken at considerable expense to the University in terms of Faculty supervision and facilities—amounting to a total of $310,390 in unreimbursed costs, a figure that fails to take into account such problems as crowding, staffing, and possible impingement on the training of medical students.

In addition to those who received Training Grants through the University, hundreds of graduate and post-doctoral students came to Harvard either on Federal fellowships, or under some Federal program for the advanced training of its Military, Foreign, or Civil Service, notably in the Graduate School of Public Administration. The University, of course, retains the right to accept or reject these students. The list of agencies awarding fellowships is a long one. The natural science departments in the Faculty of Arts and Sciences have had a considerable share of the total available National Science Foundation Fellowships. A number of National Defense Foreign Language Fellowships encourage study of Far Eastern and Near Eastern languages. By bringing able professional men and women, including government officials, to many parts of the University, these programs have contributed heavily to our academic life.

There is very little Federal assistance for undergraduates. A National Science Foundation program a year ago did permit twenty undergraduates to participate in research in biochemistry and biology during the summer months. But this is about the extent of it. It seems to us at Harvard that the country needs and would welcome a Federal undergraduate scholarship program based on both need and ability.

Harvard has found it impossible to participate in the loan program of the National Defense Education Act (Title 2) on account of the objectionable disclaimer affidavit requirement. It is a source of concern to us that the Congress has completely failed to understand the position of Harvard and the Association of American Universities in the matter. There is a danger signal here.

By intervention of one kind or another, the Federal Government has enabled the University to play a considerable role in world affairs. During 1959–60, for example, there was an exchange of a few Soviet and American students involving the Faculty of Arts and Sciences. A Fine Arts professor and a member of the Faculty of the School of Education also participated in an international exchange of faculty with the Soviet Union. A considerable number of foreign faculty members taught at Harvard, and hundreds of foreign students received instruction. The Graduate School of Design, the Business School, and the Law School entered into cooperative programs with foreign universities, while the Graduate Schools of Education, Public Health, and Public Administration provided technical assistance to foreign governments. It should not be hard to demonstrate that long-range purposes of our Government are clearly served by these exchanges.

MANAGING THE RELATIONSHIP

By 1960 Harvard was participating in at least thirty-four categories of programs managed by two score Federal agencies, under the general oversight of a dozen Congressional Committees. Since all the Faculties were involved, though in widely varying degrees, Harvard's relationship with Washington was clearly managed on a highly decentralized basis.

While this decentralized pattern, with its heavy emphasis on particular fields and specific activities, has brought about a great many difficult problems, it has probably made it easier to maintain the essential academic freedom of the University. The Federal Government has clearly not interfered in the direction of Harvard's research projects. It has certainly sought to encourage, in fields colored by a national interest, research which our Faculty members wished to undertake. The variety of sources of support helps make it possible for a distinguished scientist in a respected institution to obtain backing for his research on terms acceptable to him and his university. The image of a coercive government dictating what shall and shall not be done in university laboratories and libraries simply does not fit Harvard's experience with Washington.

The nature of the relationship becomes clearer if we examine the ways in which support for research is obtained. The University's basic purposes have been well served by Federal programs because the University is encouraged to assist in defining the terms of participation. Typically, a Faculty member develops his own project and then seeks funds for its execution. A key role in the awarding of funds is played by various advisory boards and panels, established by the various agencies, which permit men from institutions of higher learning to advise in managing Government programs. In deciding on the scope of a research project, Faculty members deal with professionally trained personnel in agencies themselves and with professional colleagues from the university world who serve on these boards. As a consequence, communication and understanding between the University and the Government regarding the conduct of the research are generally satisfactory, and the impact of Federal funds on a particular research project does not seem to differ basically from the impact of money in similar amounts from private sources.

The procedure of the National Institutes of Health affords an example of the satisfactory University-Government relations in fostering basic research. Although established to combat specific diseases, the National Institutes have administered their funds so as to encourage basic research in such disciplines as Chemistry and Biology. The goal of independent uninhibited research is served by a combination of specific disease institutes and advisory panels of scientists. The Institutes secure public funds, which the panel allocates to best advantage. Similar procedures link the defense interests of the nation with the University in mutually beneficial ways.

This degree of decentralization and of initiative by individual Faculty members is desirable as long as we follow clear policies to maintain the basic purposes and principles of the University as a whole. Such policy with respect to acceptance of Federal funds is established in broad outline by the President and Fellows of Harvard College, with the advice of the Faculties and Deans concerned, and is applied uniformly throughout the University. Harvard's practice of not undertaking classified research except in times of grave national emergency affords one example. While such projects were undertaken during the Second World War and would undoubtedly be undertaken again under similar circumstances research that cannot be published immediately seems incompatible with the University's basic purpose to seek and disseminate knowledge. This policy, however, does not preclude the participation of Faculty members as individual consultants in classified work.

The University will apply for a Federal grant or contract only after careful consideration. An individual research project must be selected for professional reasons by the individual investigator, who must be free to decide whether to publish or not and must have the right to do so. Such investigators are free to receive Government or other support for their research projects provided there is no interference with Harvard's role as an educational institution.

It has been necessary to provide some measure of direction and coordination in such matters, in order to preserve the basic character of the University as a whole, without infringing on Faculty responsibility and individual initiative. Among the coordinating instruments are the Committee of Deans and the Committee on Research and Development, with the President of the University serving as chairman of each. The Administrative Vice President has special responsibility for all Federal programs in any department of the University, although his responsibility in the Medical School is shared in some measure with the Associate Dean. When it was decided, after World War II, to continue to accept Federal funds for research under contract with the Government, a single office, the Office for Research Contracts, was established to administer the details of research contracts formerly handled by the Treasurer's office. The present Office has been of immense value to the University in maintaining a uniform policy, protecting it against improper commitments, assuring its reimbursement of proper costs, and providing assistance to Faculty members in the negotiations that lead to a contract. Every contract must have the approval of the Department Chairman concerned and of the Dean of the appropriate Faculty, and must be drawn so as to be compatible with University policy, before being presented to the President and Fellows for approval.

The Office for Research Contracts deals with all Federal grants and contracts for research and development, with the exception of grants from the U.S. Public Health Service. For these the Administrative Vice President or, as appropriate, the Associate Dean of the Medical School signs grant applications. Although there are a number of reasons, historically speaking, why grants from the United States Public Health Service should be handled separately, an argument can be made that all grants and contracts should be administered in a single office in the University.

PROBLEMS AND OPPORTUNITIES

The decentralized nature of Federal research programs may help the university protect itself against deliberate encroachment, but it makes it all the more difficult to preserve the proper balance either among various schools and departments, or within each of them between research and teaching. The availability of Federal grants for project research tends in any university to divide the responsibility of the faculty, and to weaken the influence of the president and the deans, in planning the content, emphasis, and direction of research and teaching. Individual faculty members tend to be influenced less by their colleagues and the needs of their faculty or department as a whole than by the interests they discover can be implemented through their channels of communication with Government agencies. Is it possible to get the tremendous advantages of Federal support and at the same time to maintain a proper balance among the several interests of the University?

Harvard seems to have done so, but it may nevertheless be useful to review our problems as well as our opportunities.

One of the most serious of questions in Federal programs is that of unreimbursed indirect costs on grants. Most spectacular in 1959–60 were the unreimbursed costs arising from research grants, which made satisfactory allowance for direct, but not for indirect costs. While spending $11,860,836 of Federal funds for project research, the University incurred $687,500 in unreimbursed indirect costs.

What a university thinks about the issue of indirect costs depends a great deal on the size of the grants. If a faculty looks to Washington for little of its support, indirect costs are negligible and may in fact be difficult to identify. In sufficient magnitudes, however, Federal grants can make a university poorer rather than richer by building up unreimbursed costs. More than one Faculty at Harvard has found it necessary to limit its participation in desirable programs lest their indirect costs drain away its unrestricted income.

Government agencies differ in their attitudes toward this problem. For the year in question, Harvard, on the basis of the formula of the U.S. Bureau of the Budget, determined that 28.5% of the total direct costs was an allowable charge for indirect costs. Some Federal agencies were willing to pay this figure. Congressional appropriations for the Department of Health, Education, and Welfare, however, limited by a legislative rider payment of indirect costs to an arbitrary 15% of direct costs. Some agencies have not felt obliged to pay the full institutional rate for indirect costs, either because they believed that the university ought to share in the expenses or because their scientists wished to have as large a share of the limited funds as possible go to direct research costs in their special fields.

The Federal policy of encouraging construction and modernization of research facilities by a "matching fund" formula, with the University and the Government sharing costs on a dollar for dollar basis, also presents a complex of opportunities and difficulties. A lack of space in some areas of the University has forced the postponement of important research and instruction. Meanwhile, unreimbursed costs of Government-sponsored research have delayed the accumulation of funds that could be used to match the Federal contributions for construction.

The matching fund formula has, of course, long been used by private donors. Whether used by them or the Government, the formula tends to channel funds to the stronger institutions with adequate financial and research resources for facilities which they are fully equipped to support. The matching requirement also helps to prevent universities from becoming dependent on any one source of financial support, thus protecting their freedom of scientific investigation. At present, the matching requirement seems most feasible in construction grants for research facilities, in which private corporations and foundations seem also to be primarily interested. Matching funds for teaching facilities from private sources are manifestly more difficult to obtain. The School of Public Health, for example, has found private foundations, industries, and individuals extremely reluctant to finance the kind of teaching facilities required to train individuals for careers in the public health field. As a result of similar experience, the Association of Schools of Public Health has suggested a Federal share of 85% for teaching facilities construction. It should also be noted that the Association of American Medical Colleges proposed a Federal share of 75%.

Even with respect to research facilities, there is a real question whether the need in all institutions of higher learning can be met in the next ten years by a rigid application of the fifty-fifty matching formula. Estimates have been made that more than one billion dollars will have to be invested in graduate research facilities in the next five years in order to provide space for graduate students who are already in school and college. The matching formula would require that some $500 million, or $100 million a year, be forthcoming from non-Federal sources to meet this need; but it seems doubtful whether this can be realistically expected.

THREE DANGER POINTS

Federal grants for research and for construction have brought great benefits to Harvard yet there is a danger that the total program of the University could be affected by the extent that the unreimbursed costs and matching funds involved in such grants use up the precious unrestricted funds that would be available for other purposes.   The three greatest threats posed by Federal aid are likely to be in the balance among the several fields of learning; in the balance between teaching and research; and in the balance within the Faculty between those with and those without tenure appointments.

On the first point, the problem is obvious. An overwhelming proportion of Federal support goes to the sciences. To maintain a balance, a university must make a special effort to provide support from private sources for other fields of knowledge.   Harvard has been relatively successful in this effort.   The growth of the humanities and social sciences has been maintained at a respectable rate with the support of private funds . . .

The second and third points, while no more important, are more complicated and difficult to assess, in part because the problems of the balance between research and teaching, and between tenure and non-tenure personnel, are interwoven. Moreover, the relationships in each case have varied considerably from one part of the University to the other. In some Faculties, Federal funds have brought about a marked increase in the total teaching and research staff. While our tenure ranks have not been increased directly by Federal support, some indirect increase, impossible to measure, may have occurred as a result of the capitalization of funds made possible by Federal support of various activities in the University. There has however been a marked upward trend in the number of non-tenure appointments since Departments and Faculties have employed Faculty members who are paid from Federal funds for the portion of their time spend on federally supported research, and from University funds for the time spend on instruction.

The Medical School and the School of Dental Medicine have estimated that 60% of their teaching and research staff are available owing to Federal funds. In these two Schools, the staff has increased over a twenty-year period at a faster rate than the size of the student body, and as a consequence the teaching load has decreased. However, Federal policy distinguishes between medical teaching and research and devotes most of its support to the latter. The experience of the School of Public Health, however, has been more satisfactory because the teaching of public health, unlike medical instruction, is supported by

Federal programs. In this School during the past twenty years, the Faculty and the student body have each doubled in size, while the amount of teaching time per man has also increased substantially.

The most obvious increase in staff has been in the number of post-doctoral fellows. The Chemistry Department in Arts and Sciences, to take a notable example, had one hundred such fellows, most of them employed specifically to work on Federal programs. Their availability has encouraged that Department to institute undergraduate tutorials, although it must obtain special funds to reimburse the post-doctoral fellows for time spent in instruction.

It would be a great mistake to assume that because large amounts of Federal money are available for research, instruction is bound to be neglected. Project directors are normally Faculty members, and the results of their research contribute toward lively instruction for both graduates and undergraduates. There are hopeful signs, moreover, that the Federal Government is recognizing that the distinction between research and teaching is arbitrary and dangerous. Certain post-doctoral fellowships and project training grants of the National Institutes of Health, for example, permit those funds to support teaching as well as research. In a number of instances scholars who have been employed in part for research supported by Government grants and contracts have also offered stimulating new courses available to both graduate and undergraduate students. On balance, however, instruction is in danger of neglect unless a Faculty is sound enough financially to avoid committing its unrestricted money to underwrite research inadequately financed by the Government.

The availability of research funds does not appear to have caused any major reduction in the teaching loads of Faculty members in science in the period since 1940. The availability of Federal support has not led Harvard to set up separate faculties for research and teaching. No one is expected to teach without time for research. In the Faculty of Arts and Sciences, a single staff teaches both graduate and undergraduate students, and every Department, with occasional exceptions to meet special circumstances, has a strong tradition that senior members teach undergraduates as well as graduate students.

It seems clear, however, that there has been a slight reduction in the teaching load of most Faculty members in science over a twenty-year period. While more time is now probably spent by Faculty members in research, particularly in those departments where research has been financed by the Government, it is also true that formal teaching loads seem to run somewhat higher in the social sciences and the humanities than they do in the natural sciences.

These facts by themselves, however, do not tell the whole story. The Faculty spends a great deal of time, which is difficult to measure, in directing doctoral dissertations or other individual graduate instruction. This point is of special importance in all science departments of the University, where the number of graduate students and post-doctoral students has enormously increased. What is more, the altered structure of the student body has been accompanied by changes in teaching methods so that there is now more individual instruction than used to be the case twenty years ago, particularly in the medical area and in some parts of the Faculty of Arts and Sciences.

As a result of the emphasis on research in the sciences, graduate and postgraduate students benefit far more than undergraduates from the various Federal programs. They have apparently been restricted very little, if any, by the conditions of Federal grants in their free choice of subjects. Like the grants for research projects, the Government fellowship programs in science, such as the National Science Foundation Fellowships and the National Institutes of Health Fellowships, are neutral with respect to the special fields of investigation within a major branch of science.

The so-called "regular" National Science Foundation Fellowships have until very recently imposed a handicap on undergraduate teaching by requiring that a student holding such a Fellowship may not receive additional pay from the University for assisting in instruction. These Fellowships have therefore diminished the attractiveness of Teaching Fellowships, so that in some Departments graduate students of the very first rank have not always been available to serve as course assistants. The Government's concern is to enable a student to complete his doctorate in short order, for which, it must be said in fairness, Harvard does not count performance in teaching. Even so, there is a real question whether the able graduate student should not be encouraged to obtain teaching experience in order to meet the Government's objective of raising the general level of scientific achievement in the country at large. It should be noted in this connection that some National Science Foundation Fellows have chosen to serve as course assistants without pay, and this fall new administrative rulings now permit National Science Foundation Fellows to earn up to $600 annually by teaching.

Many graduate students are supported, especially during their third and fourth years, by employment as Research Assistants on projects financed by Federal funds. (In some Departments, a minority of these appointments go on a part-time basis to graduate students who also serve as Teaching Fellows; University funds are of course used to pay for the share of time devoted to instruction.) It has been estimated, for example, that half of all research in the Division of Engineering and Applied Physics is used in the preparation of doctoral dissertations. An appointment as Research Assistant can thus serve the purpose of a fellowship as well. This arrangement is wholly satisfactory to the Federal agencies, and most important for scientific achievement at Harvard.

Some Departments have been reluctant, however, to allow any graduate students to be supported with funds from research projects, lest senior Faculty members be put in the position of "buying" their students. This point of view doubtless originated at a time when fewer Faculty members had research funds at their disposal, and to most Faculty members it seems less valid today.

Undergraduate students, in contrast, however, as stated earlier, receive little direct benefit from Federal programs. The point that should be made here is that the Federal government, by distinguishing between teaching and research, often handicaps the effort to bring the knowledge gained from research into the undergraduate classroom. For example, the "facilities program" of the National Science Foundation and the National Institutes of Health cannot be used to aid undergraduate instruction; consequently, the Government was recently unwilling to match part of the money Harvard was prepared to make available to the Biology Department, because the proposed facilities were to be used in part for undergraduate instruction. This policy seems particularly unwise to Harvard since we draw upon the same instructors for graduate and undergraduate instruction, believing that the combination makes for better research and better teaching.

There is a suspicion that the increased emphasis on research, postdoctoral scholars, and graduate students in our science Departments has contributed to a remoteness between Faculty and undergraduates. Whether this stems from Federal research support, or from the general characteristics of modern science, or from other factors is hard to say. Science seems to play less of a role than other fields in the undergraduate Houses, and some of the Departments not involved in Government programs, such as the English Department, actually offer more undergraduate tutorial instruction. It is perhaps inevitable that a scientist eager to concentrate on his research will be reluctant to take on the hard work of teaching a large introductory or General Education course. Nevertheless, undergraduate work in a laboratory is analogous in many respects to an individual or group tutorial in the humanities or social sciences, and much Faculty time is devoted in the scientific Departments to supervising such work. And against distractions of Federal programs must be balanced the enormous interest students of all ranks take in a teacher who is known to have made a significant discovery, or to have played an influential role in public affairs.

While all Harvard professors are expected to engage in research, the University community, as a result of Federal funds, now includes a large and growing proportion of research workers who are not members of the teaching Faculty. In view of the type of work they do, Harvard may now have to adjust some of the rules that were designed to maintain the proper balance between those Faculty members with, and those without, permanent tenure.

The problem arises especially in connection with the growing numbers, in many Departments, of Research Assistants, Research Associates, and Research Fellows. These staff members, most of whom are scientists, are recognized as important members of the University community. Most of them (with the exception of the Research Assistants who are primarily students) have Corporation appointments, and receive the same fringe benefits as regular Faculty members. The quantity of Federal funds for research has greatly increased the numbers of such staff members, and thus intensified the perennial problem that a great many more able scholars are attracted to Harvard by temporary positions than can possibly be given tenure appointments. The temptation is very great to use the short-term Federal funds to keep at Harvard scientists for whom there is no prospect of a permanent position being available, to an age when their opportunities elsewhere diminish.

To protect against this danger, we have a general rule that non-tenure appointments for Faculty or research personnel shall not be extended beyond a total of eight years (eleven in the Medical area) or beyond a total of three years for those 35 years of age or older. A facility such as the Cambridge Electron Accelerator, however, will require the continued presence of skilled personnel. At least some of the scientists who are being attracted to this facility are doubtless the equal of scientific colleagues who hold Faculty appointments. Although both groups will be working together on research projects, only one will have Faculty status. It may well be necessary, therefore, to introduce some flexibility into our personnel practices so as to retain key research personnel beyond the usual limit of annual appointments whenever it is necessary in order to make the most effective use of research facilities. Harvard has for some time been prepared to make exceptions to normal procedure so that a few highly-qualified individuals may be given appointments without limit of time without being tenure members of the Faculty. It should be possible to continue these appointments so long as contract funds are available.

Science has become increasingly complicated, expensive, and dynamic, and new fields and subjects appear on the scene with astonishing rapidity. As a result scientific instruction today doubtless requires more hours of preparation and research than formerly. A first-class Faculty is dependent on moderate teaching loads and on ample opportunity for research. In the scientific areas, in particular, such a Faculty also needs the carefully planned growth that avoids proliferation of highly specialized courses to the detriment of scientific education of appropriate depth and breadth. In order to encourage the closest relations between research staff and regular Faculty, and to take maximum advantage of research programs for instructional purposes, Harvard is planning to make a few teaching appointments by means of one-year lectureships, granted strictly on individual merit, to staff members employed and nominated by a research facility, with the endorsement of the Faculty concerned.

But the most difficult problem is that of the relation of the massive research programs to the permanent Faculty. The traditional policy at Harvard has been to pay no permanent Faculty member from short-term research funds. If Federal funds were to be cut off tomorrow, Harvard would be able to honor its commitments to all its permanent Faculty members. Whether this rule now needs to be so rigidly followed, in order to protect the essential values of academic freedom and intellectual independence, may be open to question. There is clearly a serious shortage of tenure members in some Departments and Faculties, notably those in the Medical area, even though those very Faculties have received their research funds largely because of the quality of their tenure Faculty members. All the evidence suggests that Federal funds for these fields will be forthcoming for the foreseeable future and on increasingly acceptable terms, provided, of course, that the quality of the Faculty is maintained.

That quality, however, cannot be maintained by endowment funds alone, since a first-rate scientist is not attracted mainly by his salary, but by all the facilities and resources that make for a desirable scientific environment. The research facilities, training grants, graduate and post-graduate fellowships, and the international exchanges of students and Faculty which are so important in attracting able scholars to Harvard are now heavily dependent on Federal funds. While no Faculty member likes the necessity of spending valuable time and energy in making appeals for the renewal of such support, it is generally conceded that to get comparable aid from private sources would involve equal or greater difficulties.

In order to maintain the essential quality on which all the rest of our scientific and medical activities depend—the quality of our tenure Professors—it may be necessary for us to experiment cautiously to achieve greater flexibility by paying tenure salaries from Federal funds in certain Departments, for whose fields of interest steady and continuous Federal support may be most confidently predicted for the future.

THE UNIVERSITIES' POINT OF VIEW

University and Government people alike have been slow to realize the significance of their new relationship. The Government now calls on the universities for achievements that depend on the highest qualities of creativity, but sometimes through purchasing procedures that could destroy the environment in which such qualities flourish. This is not from any wrong intentions on the part of individual agencies; in general, they have bent over backward in favor of academic freedom, and have done a great deal to adapt Government methods to the requirements of a university. Indeed, in the process of asking Congress for funds, they sometimes exaggerate the potential practical achievements of the basic research they propose to support. But a relationship based on a short-term grant for specific purposes, which was perfectly sensible when such grants were only a tiny increment to an academic budget, may be self-defeating when the grants have become a major reliance of the university. At that stage, the donor would do well to consider the general health of the institution which he is building up, if only in order to protect his investment.

This first becomes apparent in such practical details as the payment for overhead expenses, or the requirement of matching funds. But it is true in a more profound sense. For research can be carried on effectively in the long run only if a university maintains its overhead in an intellectual and academic, as well as an administrative, sense. This is the case for asking the Government to support basic as well as applied science, and teaching as well as research. It is not a question of asking the Government for more money, but, rather, of asking it to give its funds with a proper regard for the total function of the university.

As universities recognize that there is no substitute today for Federal support in many fields of science, they must ask the Government to recognize, in the way it makes its grants, that the university is a creative force because it is concerned with all fields of knowledge, and because it offers scholars the intellectual independence that goes with permanent status. If they are to make this clear, universities themselves need to understand their relationships with Government, and to set up proper channels through which to inform Government of their point of view on the issues which may well affect their basic character in the future. This is the real point of the affidavit controversy.

A half-dozen major organizations represent institutions of higher education in Washington, including the American Council on Education and associations of urban, state, land-grant, and church-related institutions. In particular fields, the Association of American Medical Colleges and the Association of Schools of Public Health have presented their views to the Executive agencies and the Congress, and a committee of the Federation of College and University Business Officers Associations has served as a useful "listening post" in Washington. Most suitable to represent Harvard's point of view, potentially speaking, are the Association of American Universities and its sub-group, the Association of Graduate Schools.

Harvard does not favor the establishment of separate organizations to present the particular views of private, as distinguished from public, institutions in Washington or elsewhere. This University has as much in common with the major state universities as it has with independent universities. On the familiar issues in our relations with the Federal Government—overhead, flexibility of contract terms, long-term support, the construction of facilities—there is scarcely any important difference between what Harvard thinks and what is thought in the major public universities. Differences in point of view arise not so much between public and private institutions as between strong and weak ones. While public and private institutions obviously differ on significant points, these differences seem much less important than their common ground. The Association of American Universities has already provided a platform from which testimony was presented to a Congressional Committee on the NDEA disclaimer affidavit. It goes without saying, of course, that the academic side of a university must be represented as carefully as the financial side.

The close relationships between universities and Federal Executive agencies have already been discussed. To an unfortunate degree, however, there is too little communication in important matters between the universities and Congress. If this had not been true, for example, the objectionable affidavit provision of the NDEA would never have been enacted without more thorough consideration. University spokesmen must understand Congressional politics and policy-making and be prepared to discuss with Congressmen and Senators the basic issues confronting higher education. Unfortunately, university spokesmen often disagree among themselves on points of fundamental importance. We must, therefore, try to reach a consensus on important issues within our own family and with like-minded institutions, if we are to develop satisfactory relationships with Congressional Committees as well as Executive agencies. It is in Congress that the crucial decisions are made on Federal-university relationships, and Executive agencies cannot be expected to represent the universities' interests on every point.

If universities are prepared, individually and cooperatively, to affirm and defend their central educational purposes, and to resist the temptation to expand particular functions at the expense of their primary obligations, they will then be in a position to urge the Federal Government to show some concern for higher education as a general element in the national interest. Representatives of the Government might well be able, then, to agree with universities in a general approach to their future relationship, along lines which might guide the programs of the Federal departments and agencies. A start has been made by the Government itself through several excellent reports, such as the statement of the President's Science Advisory Committee entitled "Scientific Progress, the Universities and the Federal Government," the studies through which the Office of Education planned its administration of the National Defense Education Act, the report of the National Science Foundation on "Government-University Relationships," and the reports of various White House conferences. Under the leadership of the Executive Office of the President (including the President's Science Advisory Committee), the National Science Foundation, the Office of Education, and some of the interested executive departments and agencies should be asked to consider what type of long-range policy might be adopted by the Federal Government for the support of university programs at a high level of excellence. Such a government policy should emphasize, among other points, at least these four:

(1) The support of university programs by the Government should not be conditional on any terms which infringe the educational independence and academic freedom of a university. In view of the generally excellent record of the Government to date, agreement on this point may be expected.

(2) Universities should not be asked to carry on work which is not in harmony with their essential purposes, except in cases of extraordinary national need that cannot be otherwise met. The types of activity which properly require close direction by government, or need only those skills generally available in non-academic institutions, should be performed in government, industrial, or special institutional facilities.

Any function which should be carried out in a university, on the other hand, should be carried on with a high degree of freedom, such as is appropriate for research in an academic institution; it should emphasize the search for basic knowledge and it should be connected as closely as possible with the teaching function.

(3) The method of granting aid should be calculated to support the highest standards of excellence in instruction and research. It may well be in the interest of the nation to build up additional centers of academic excellence in greater numbers, and with more adequate geographical diversification. To this end special expenditures by private foundations and other donors, or by the Congress, may be warranted. But this purpose would not be advanced by the award of individual fellowships or grants for specific projects on any other standard than that of highest merit.

(4) Care should be taken to make the financial terms of university grant programs support the entire cost of such programs, and not outrun the ability of any university to retain general managerial and educational responsibility for them. This requires the payment of full overhead costs; grants for the construction of facilities on formulas that are realistic in terms of the university's private sources of funds; and some method of supplementing project grants and contracts, in reasonable proportion, to strengthen the ability of the university to discharge its general educational function.

To accomplish this last purpose, some have suggested, taking the British University Grants Committee as a model, that the Federal Government change to a totally new system, giving only general support through a single block grant to each university, to be used for purposes of its own choosing. From the point of view of the Government, this method would not promise to accomplish the special program purposes for which the Congress has been willing to appropriate funds. From the point of view of the universities, it may be better to live with the difficulties of the present disorganized system than to increase the risk of political interference with university independence by putting all our eggs in one basket. Even if the general-purpose grants were intended to supplement, rather than replace, the project grants, however, the scheme would have its difficulties. For the project grants have one great merit that is not to be underestimated: they can be appraised on scientific and professional standards by the academic peers of the applicants, whose judgment can be accepted and respected by scientists, university presidents, and Congressmen alike. But how would general grants be allocated? It is difficult to imagine that the Government would permit some private accrediting board, in effect, to certify institutions for Federal support, or that other institutions would accept its verdict with equanimity. It is difficult to imagine the Federal Government itself taking the responsibility for rating universities according to their general academic excellence. On the other hand, it is all too easy to imagine, after a period of general logrolling, the enactment of a statutory formula to give aid to all institutions equally, or some formula based on population or geography, regardless of scientific or academic standards.

Without getting into such difficulties, however, a great deal could be done to reduce the dependence of universities on project grants, which always tend to make the strong Departments stronger, and weaken the university's ability to develop with a proper balance. One way would be to develop a system of institutional grants for unrestricted purposes in particular areas of learning, such as—to take random examples—mathematics or language study. Such a system, supplementing project grants, would enable universities themselves to make the basic decisions on their academic programs within very much broader limits than they can today. It would be only a reasonable extension of a course of action already marked out by the Institutional Grants Programs of the National Science Foundation and the National Institutes of Health, which provide general grants to a university in some proportion to the amount of money received through research grants and contracts.

CONCLUSION

Harvard's particular experience suggests that the universities generally have been important to the Federal Government, at the same time that Government support promises to become indispensable to the universities. It is not merely that the Government needs to buy certain specific services, while universities need money—although both are true. It is rather that the Government needs from the universities something that industrial or Governmental laboratories cannot supply, the creative activity that takes place most naturally in an institution where the arts, sciences, and letters are joined in an atmosphere of intellectual freedom. The money that the Government spends on specific projects will be wasted if it is not spent in ways that will sustain these special qualities of the university.

At the same time, the university is led to a new relationship with Government by more than a need for money; if only that were involved, it might be desirable to renounce Federal grants in order to avoid any risk to academic freedom. But science and technology have done more than make academic research and teaching expensive; they have made them a necessary ingredient in national policy and in the advancement of human welfare. The university no longer expects to avoid involvement in public affairs, for it is by now all too clear that free universities and free political institutions are interdependent and their futures intertwined.

The role of the university cannot be one of withdrawal from the world. But it will serve society well only as it remains true to its essential nature—a university, not an agency of government. It is entitled to demand complete intellectual freedom. To this end it must ask for a measure of detachment from current crises and routine procedures as necessary conditions of fulfilling its fundamental purpose in civilized society.

Section V

Problems and Dislocations

When rapid change is forced upon a social institution, as has happened to American higher education, it will manifest many dysfunctions and needs for reform. Some of these are extensions of problems which have long plagued colleges and universities. Others derive directly from the revolutionary decades. These problems and issues must concern all of higher education in the late 1960's, for its future viability will be determined by how well they are resolved.

General Education: A Definition

By LEWIS B. MAYHEW

General education, while not a new term nor concept (the earliest use noted is in 1837), has come into common use just in the past several decades. It represents one more step in the long line of changing educational patterns which man has evolved in an effort to keep education abreast with other cultural and technological changes. As has been true of other developments in the past, general education became a dynamic force in protest against existing practices which had become obsolete but which were still being widely employed and defended. Perhaps the clearest notion of what general education is or what it intends to be can be seen by noting those things in American education which have been severely criticized. Actually, the origins of the theory underlying the movement and the techniques for achieving its objectives can almost all be inferred from the criticisms of education made by educators, social theorists, and laymen.

Possibly the most significant factor in this regard is the unbelievable expansion in human knowledge which has come about in the twentieth century. Early in the middle of the nineteenth century, scholarly men in many walks of life could justifiably claim to know at least the elements of all spheres of human knowledge; by the middle part of the twentieth century even trained scholars could comprehend only the barest outlines of a tiny portion of what was known of the universe. This expansion of knowledge, coupled with an increasingly complex industrial society demanding many and varied skills from its people, resulted in marked proliferation of college courses. In 1829 the entire curriculum of Yale University was printed on one page. In 1955 two hundred pages were required to list the available offerings. Obviously no single student could study even a fraction of the available curriculum. And with the rise of the free elective system, which allowed students to select as their individual interests dictated, there was scant assurance that students would even elect samples from each of the major subdivisions of the curriculum. With such freedom to choose, with such riches of course offerings, higher education came to resemble an intellectual cafeteria with no guiding principles and with no means of conveying to students any feeling for the unity of life.

A second quality about which protests were made was the caliber of college teaching. In the liberal arts colleges in the early nineteenth century, teachers were very much a part of the total lives of their students. They conceived of themselves as responsible for the students' moral and spiritual welfare as well as their intellectual development. Teaching (and not infrequently preaching to) students was judged the primary occupation of the college professor, and for that matter of the college president as well. While there were always ineffective teachers, as Henry Adams has so clearly shown in his account of his undergraduate days at Harvard, such ineffectiveness was a result of a lack of talent—not a lack of concern with the responsibilities of teaching. Gradually, however, the complexion of American education changed. The German conception of the university as a center for scholarly research was transplanted to the American scene in the form of the graduate school. This, through its direct influence on the institutions of which it became a part, and through its indirect influence on the liberal arts college through the professors it trained, revolutionized collegiate education.

Research became the most satisfying, respectable, and rewarding activity open to a college professor. Nonessentials, such as teaching, which interfered with research were to be accommodated with the least possible expenditure of time and energy. Indeed many undergraduate colleges which were part of a university were tolerated because they provided the raw material for future graduate students and because they provided, through teaching opportunities, subsidy to graduate students and thus to research projects of the graduate faculties. Since the rise of the research-oriented university was associated with the growth in significance of the Ph.D. as a qualification for college teaching, the ideals of the graduate schools were spread over the academic map. Young men trained by graduate faculties picked up the conception of research as the highest type of human activity and carried it with them into the liberal arts colleges to which they moved. Wanting to make a name for themselves in research in order to qualify for university appointment, they drew farther and farther away from any but the absolutely required teaching responsibilities. Such conditions could not help but result in poor or half-hearted teaching by any but the most talented and inspired professors. The lecture technique became the most frequent vehicle by which the professor communicated the results of his own or someone else's research to relatively passive undergraduates. Outside of class, personal contacts between the teacher and his students became rare.

Early American education had been based on a psychological theory that transfer of training was possible. Indeed the mind was frequently likened to a muscle which could be toughened on one set of exercises in preparation for actual work on other completely different activities. The classical languages were offered as much for the disciplinary values of study of their syntax as for any substantive values. Memorization was good training for all manner of adult tasks. The limited, required curriculum made no attempt to train directly for the actual activities of the ministry or law because it was assumed that the rigors of moral and natural philosophy and classics would develop powers directly transferable to professional work. Gradually, however, experimental psychology exploded this belief. It was shown that study of German did not increase one's ability to learn French. Developed facility in arithmetic did not make formal logic any easier. The implications of these results for the curriculum were profound, and fitted right into the increasing number of courses. As one wag remarked, there seemed to be solid psychological ground for offering a course in baton waving for right-handed people and another for left-handed people, with second sections of each to provide for sex differences. Curriculum builders, not understanding the full significance of newer psychological discoveries, went too far in providing separate courses for different skills. They overlooked what was later to be found—that transfer was possible so long as it was directly taught for, and so long as there were perceivable common elements in the areas considered.

At least partly as a result of these and other conditions, the graduates of colleges and universities in the 1920's and 1930's did not appear in good light. For one thing the colleges were losing large percentages of students who enrolled. Some of these of course were lacking in ability, but more dropped out of college because it did not seem to be meeting their expectations. Those who did finish college did not seem to be appreciably different from people who had never seen the ivy-colored walls. College graduates did earn more money, but their reading habits, their citizenship practices, their use of leisure, did not differ appreciably from the rest of middle-class America. Clearly something was wrong if as a result of the great expense and effort expended in giving young people a college education, the only gain was a somewhat greater earning capacity.

Still another characteristic of the American collegiate scene was the fact that colleges and universities were not providing a common universe of discourse for their graduates. One of the strengths of the English Parliament in the eighteenth and nineteenth centuries was the fact that its members were all products of the same intellectual environment, hence had a common language, a common ideology, and a commonly possessed set of symbols and allusions with which they could communicate with each other. The American college in the twentieth century was failing to do this. In a university of 14,000 students, with a curriculum of 2,000 courses and the free elective system operating, the chances against any two students taking the same pattern of courses were astronomical. Husbands and wives who attended the same liberal arts college frequently found that they had taken only one or two courses in common out of a four-year curriculum. The results of such a system of education were doctors who could scarcely communicate with their patients, engineers who had no feeling for the arts-training of their wives, and psychologists who could not understand sociologists even in common conversation. If an important responsibility of education is the transmission of the cultural heritage from one generation to the next, American collegiate education appeared to be failing miserably.

The changing technological and social world of America revealed still one more glaring weakness. Each generation of Americans, from the turn of the twentieth century on, was finding more leisure time. The urban movement with its accompanying smaller families, the technological revolution with its labor saving devices on the farm, in the factory, and in the home, were freeing men and women from the burden of long hours of work. Yet the educational system was coming to be designed chiefly to train people to do specific kinds of work. It was giving no attention to educating man to do those things which commanded most of his time—being a member of a family, a citizen, and a leisure-using human being. Some readjustments in education were demanded if it was to meet the emerging needs of its people.

To rectify these and other conditions, theorists began to advocate, and some colleges and universities to experiment with, a new kind of education to which the name general education was applied. Early prototypes were created as early as the post-World War I period with John Erskine's course at Columbia. The 1930's saw a few more innovations as Robert Hutchins caused a revamping of the College at the University of Chicago, as Floyd W. Reeves carried the Chicago ideas to the University of Florida, as W. W. Charters led the establishment of a general education program at Stephens College, and as Alexander

Meiklejohn tried a bold experiment at Wisconsin. It was in the 1940's, however, that the general education movement really began to gain acceptance as a possible solution to the educational ills everywhere apparent. These programs as they developed varied from each other in important regards. They each developed out of indigenous conditions and reflected the diversity that is American education. However, the main current of development demonstrated some common elements which can be called characteristic of general education.

Programs usually tried to provide students with the broad outlines of human knowledge. For this purpose interdisciplinary courses were developed frequently in the areas of the humanities, sciences, social sciences, and the communicative arts. Sometimes these would be simply surveys of the high points of a fused course such as the history of western civilization. Sometimes they would sample in depth a cross-section of some part of the western tradition. The "block and gap" system of the science courses at Harvard exemplifies this. Sometimes, of course, students were simply required to take several different courses from the broad field of the social sciences. The general pattern, however, was to create new courses which if taken in their entirety would give at least a panoramic view of what man knows.

The theorists emphasized the importance of the teacher in these new courses and a number of colleges expended considerable energy in trying to train their faculties to be better teachers. A few places, such as Michigan State University, made the majority of its appointments to the general education program full time ones, with full salary and promotion opportunities. Some universities set up doctoral programs designed specifically to train teachers to handle interdisciplinary courses in general education.

Most programs assumed, either explicitly or implicitly, that a measure of transfer of training was possible. Thus it was assumed that courses in the social sciences could develop habits and attitudes which would be applicable to the person's life as a citizen. The humanities provided experiences thought to have direct relevance for the leisure time of the adult, and the sciences sought to develop a method of thinking which could be applied to many of the problems faced by adults. All courses in general education claimed as one of their objectives the development of critical thinking ability which, it was speculated, could be used in all fields with equal relevance. Indeed, Dressel and Mayhew[1] argued that critical thinking could well become the integrating theme or thread of general education. Their thesis clearly rests on the belief that the methods of thought taught in a communications course can be transferred to a social science problem.

Almost every program or course in general education seeks to change human behavior. Indeed, the concern for stating one's educational purposes in terms of human behavior is distinctly related to the rise of general education. Ralph Tyler and his colleagues at the University of Chicago taught that educational objectives must be so specified before either teaching or evaluation could ever realistically take place. The impact of his thinking through the Cooperative Study of General Education, the Progressive Education Association Eight-Year Study, and the leadership of the College of the University of Chicago on general education, has insured this point of view an important place in the entire movement. While there are of course major differences between institutions, most programs of general education have listed purposes somewhat in the form found in the 1947 *Report of the President's Commission on Higher Education* or the Armed Forces Institute's *Design for General Education.*

One of these purposes, which characterizes many courses and programs, is an attempt to provide a common universe of discourse for students regardless of their field of specialization. Despite differences in course titles or texts used, there seems to be an implicit attempt to provide a basic core of knowledge with which all students are familiar. Mikesell[2] found that certain basic concepts such as that of revolution were taught by most social science courses regardless of whether they were historical courses, problem courses, or some other type. Michigan State University may be thought of as exemplifying the characteristic with its Basic College. That college tries to provide what is basic or fundamental to the education of all men.

General education courses typically claim to educate for the non-vocational aspects of life. They purport to educate for effective citizenship, worthy use of leisure time, effective home and family living, and movement toward effective personal adjustment. They are based on the assumption that men and women need to have formal education to fit them first for the task of living personally satisfying and socially useful lives. Courses may try to do this through a study of great books in the history of western civilization or through courses in personal adjustment. But the entire general education movement as represented in theory and in practice claims this as its unique goal. Medical or engineering education has a clearly vocational purpose. General education courses attempt to achieve something else.

While the pattern varies, general education courses represent a tendency toward more requirements for students. Although some institutions seek to achieve the goals of general education through some modification of the free elective system, more seek them through prescribing a certain percentage of the students' time. This may vary from a completely prescriptive program as at the College of General Education at Boston University to something over a half of the curriculum at some Catholic institution or to a bare requirement of one course for some curricula at Drake University. This prescriptiveness prompts the most stringent reaction to the free elective system.

Part of the defense for prescription is the need to force students to explore at least the broad divisions of knowledge in an effort to enable them to make more judicious choices of fields for specialization. And this defense is fairly characteristic of a number of the better known programs. The argument runs that the free elective system was not really free because students were choosing to exclude things from their programs without knowing what they were doing. A free choice could be made with respect to science only after a student had experienced a broad course in science. Then he would have some valid basis for judgment.

These arguments seem to be characteristic of the general education programs which have been put into operation. This does not contend that these are ideal characteristics nor that they represent all of the characteristics found in programs labeled general education. Many programs and practices possessing a number of these characteristics would have to be judged ineffective and quite a few efforts possessing none of them would have to be judged excellent. It is to establish some acceptable criteria of effectiveness that this chapter is written—and in the expectation that the examples discussed in the subsequent chapters may illustrate the application of the criteria. By way of contrast, however, some of the qualities of general education judged weaknesses by critics of the movement ought to be presented. It should be clearly emphasized that the justice of many of these criticisms would have to be admitted even by the most sincere advocates of general education.

One major criticism is that general education is really a meaningless term since people define it in almost any way their fancies dictate. At Michigan State it means the program and courses of the Basic College, which differs in important respects from the General College at the University of Minnesota. At the latter institution the program of the General College differs appreciably from the offerings of the Department of General Education in the College of Science, Literature, and the Arts. At one institution the full process of stating objectives and constructing a new curriculum of courses specifically geared to those objectives has been followed. In another institution older courses are simply renamed and thus emerge as a new program of general edu-

224 HIGHER EDUCATION IN THE REVOLUTIONARY DECADES

cation. Boston University, Michigan State, and to a lesser extent the University of Florida operate required courses. At Harvard the requirements may be satisfied by taking some of a variety of courses offered, while at Stephens College there is no requirement save a course in Communications. To some, general education is rationalistic, with students being given principles assumed to be valid. They are then expected to deduce from these proper ways of behaving. To others, such an approach runs counter to the ways they believe human beings function, and thus courses are so organized as to proceed from students' own problems to the making of generalizations on the basis of them. For example, at St. Xavier College in Chicago the general education courses are all theoretical at the first level with recourse to empiricism in the second year. The course in Basic Beliefs at Stephens College, however, starts with a listing of students' questions, analyzes them in terms of their experience, and draws on the historical philosophical principles only when needed and when they can be validated by student experience.

The theory of general education is similarly subject to varied interpretation. To some, general education is the older liberal arts in modern clothes. To others it is the liberal arts without the aristocratic connotations of that term. To still others general education is but a segment of the older liberal arts curriculum. Critics of course say, "And not a very good segment at that." At any educational discussion of general education the question always comes up as to what this particular group means by the term. Critics again suggest that psychologists have little trouble defining their area of concern, nor do engineers. They question whether there can be much validity in an educational enterprise possessing such obscure lines of definition.

A second widely advanced criticism is that general education is superficial, that it is "watered down," that it deals in generalities possessing no real substance. Frequently using the survey course as the arch-type of general education these critics show quite vividly how the sheer volume of information covered and the speed with which it is done preclude any lasting impact on the knowledge or understanding of students. Or they will suggest that the apparently undisciplined use of information from a number of fields to study one problem, leaves serious gaps in student knowledge and may further leave students with a feeling that they know a field when actually they don't. Another facet of the position is that teachers are forced so to reduce the essential content of a field for the sake of the general student, that the emasculated result does no good for anyone. The science courses have been particularly vulnerable in this regard, as they have had to reduce the amount of mathematics demanded of students taking the course. Many general education courses are vulnerable and well deserve the criticism. While most administrators of colleges having general education programs will claim that they do not offer survey courses, closer study of their curricula suggests that they do. The general education courses are frequently great catalogues of information hung together by some theory such as the historical development of the west, or man as a biological organism functioning in a physical environment. Even when courses possess some logic which removes them from the category of a survey course, the teaching of them sometimes places them back in the proscribed camp.

In a similar connection, not a few courses of the problem-centered variety seem frequently merely to rearrange student prejudices rather than to force them to examine their beliefs in the light of new evidence. Social science courses occasionally err in this regard with students thoroughly enjoying expressing their opinions but without being stimulated to do the study necessary to test their own convictions. Courses in communication skills, which attempt to teach a new field such as listening, do not have a tested body of fact and theory as yet (although this is being accumulated). As a result time spent on this topic seems to the student a great waste. They feel that each one's opinions about how to listen are quite as good as the next person's.

Some critics scrutinize the newer types of social science offerings and judge them to be lacking the rigor of more orthodox disciplines. Courses such as those on personal adjustment, marriage and the family, and effective living have come in for a major burden of blame. They are contrasted—to their disadvantage—with courses in economics, history, and political science. Learning about the American Constitution is seen as more demanding than learning about how a late adolescent meets and solves his problems.

An aspect of this charge of superficiality is the belief that general education courses attempt to develop intellectual skills before the students have sufficient knowledge. People, to learn to think critically, the argument runs, must first be deeply immersed in the substance of a field. Before one can invent hypotheses as to how communities develop, he ought to learn everything which is known about communities. Students should not attempt to explain the origins of the Carolina Bays unless they have had a great deal of substantive information in geology, physics, chemistry, and astronomy. In the humanities it is claimed that students should not be expected to handle the Greek tragedies until they have been grounded thoroughly in ancient history and preferably in ancient languages as well.

Joel Hildebrand, chemistry professor emeritus from the University of California, is a major spokesman for this point of view. He feels that it is unsound for students to be expected to apply knowledge in solving problems until they have fully mastered the field. He argues that rather than being allowed to use a bit of chemistry and a bit of something else, students should study chemistry alone until they appreciate in full its complexities. Arthur Bestor, criticizing the high schools, is caustic on the subject. He feels that the courses emphasizing life adjustment are dishonest in that they suggest that students can learn the hard substance of a subject while struggling with problems which bother their young lives. He feels that people can make adequate adjustments to life only after they have mastered the basic intellectual tools of language, mathematics, science, and history. (Mr. Bestor is an historian.)

And of course much of what such men say is warranted. In personal adjustment courses, students are sometimes given such things as the psychological mechanisms of adjustment (projection, repression, rationalization, and the like) with the implied suggestion that they can now use these concepts in analyzing their own behavior. Many students have been asked to use the information of the cultural anthropologists without knowing in the slightest the tenuous nature of the evidence that field has to offer.

Another criticism is that general education by teaching generalizations, does not provide students with solid information which can become part of their intellectual equipment. Students are taught that the Church was the custodian of culture throughout the medieval period. They never come in contact with flesh and blood examples of how that was done, so that they can appreciate the magnitude of the achievement. They are taught that culture is that which binds men together without developing a feel for what culture is like. Particularly do communication courses receive fire in this regard. Students are taught to communicate without learning the grammar and syntax of their language—which make effective writing or speaking possible.

The validity of this, claim critics, is established by the fact that general education courses do not prepare students for advanced work in a specialized field. Rarely has a department of chemistry, sociology, history or in any of the other disciplines felt free to modify their beginning work on the strength of what students learned in a general course. The general education course in science seems just so much waste of time for students who are going to take more science. Students have not learned to apply mathematics nor have they even learned the nature of study in a specialized field by being exposed to a few generalities about it.

Of a different order of criticism is the judgment that general education is just a device for obtaining cheap education. By teaching science courses in which there is no laboratory work, appreciable savings can be made in the instructional budget. By arranging large lecture classes in which surveys of knowledge are presented, much greater numbers of students can be handled than if they were allowed to enter smaller, more specialized classes. Forcing all students into large basic sections provides a relatively cheap way of screening out inept students before they get to advanced courses.

And, as a matter of fact, economics has led a number of institutions to consider general education. A common course, taught with a detailed syllabus, can be offered more cheaply than can a number of distinct courses each requiring a specialist as teacher. General education courses typically have a lower cost per student-credit-hour than do courses in the specialized fields and a much lower cost than professional courses. Some institutions have tried to cut costs of general education courses still further by assigning only younger faculty members or graduate students to them. In several institutions the task of each new faculty member is to do his turn in the general courses before he is allowed to teach upper-level offerings.

General education spokesmen have claimed a major interest in improved classroom teaching but critics say that this interest is not reflected in practice. Teachers required to teach a fused course embracing not only their own specialty but many dissimilar fields cannot be expected to do a good job. The historian expected to deal with philosophy cannot help but be quite superficial and in the end ineffective in teaching a field foreign to his own experience. The biologist forced to tackle physical science is going to feel so insecure that the effectiveness of his teaching is bound to decline. The policy of letting young and inexperienced teachers handle these courses also results in less effective teaching.

Here again some validity to the claim must be allowed. At one institution students overwhelmingly endorsed the idea of general education. At the same time they judged the teaching of the general education courses are less effective than in the upper schools. The writer has visited many college campuses and asked students whether the teaching was different in the general and specialized courses. Invariably general education teachers are judged less effective because (1) they are teaching things they don't like or (2) they are not familiar enough with the material outside their own field. The writer and a colleague visited a number of colleges in the winter and spring of 1952–1953 and attended general education classes at each one. With few exceptions the teaching seen was pedestrian, routine, and no more inspired than that found in other parts of the curriculum.

A last criticism is that general education courses are not as demanding of students as are upper-level courses. Not requiring precision of knowledge they foster a careless attitude on the part of students. By dealing with generalizations they encourage students to think in generalities. By covering a wide segment of human knowledge they foster a false sense of knowledge on the part of students. By dealing with knowledge at almost an opinion level they inculcate in students a faith in their own opinions and a disrespect for informed opinions. Further, by the way they are taught and the lack of prestige these courses enjoy, students are conditioned to put off studying them until after all other work is done. Especially for bright students, the work in general courses seems so uninspiring that they don't work at it. Such poor habits of scholarship then carry over to more demanding courses.

There is some evidence to justify each of these criticisms. And people interested in general education need to accept the evidence when it supports a criticism. However, the views of critics must be interpreted rather carefully. Many times critics will utterly destroy general education as they compare it with the liberal arts or specialized education. What they have done, however, has been to select the horrible examples of general education and contrast them with idealized recollections of the best examples of an older scheme. It is true that a poorly conceived course in biological science, taught by an uninspired man whose inadequate training thirty years previously was in physics, makes a sorry showing when contrasted with a chemistry class taught by a man of catholic tastes, great human understanding, and impeccable scholarship. Further it is true that some graduates of an orthodox liberal arts program consisting of separate disciplinary courses were well versed in language, numbers, and the skills of reasoning and that many products of general education today are not. Neither of these situations establishes a case, however. It is only when the full range of various types of education are appraised in the context of the society in which they function—and of the goals of the students they attract—that valid comparisons can be made.

In effect this volume is holding up some examples together with the goals they seek to achieve. These examples are not judged as perfect but they are ones which we would call effective. In selecting examples for inclusion we have used certain criteria. We feel that these must be satisfied if we are to make the judgment that this is an effective practice, course, or program in general education.

1. *Does the program or practice affect a substantial portion of the entire student body?* General education has as one of its purposes the establishment of a common universe of discourse—a common heritage for a group of students. In order to do this all members should be subjected to approximately the same set of educational experiences. This is not to say that they must all enroll in exactly the same course. But if they enroll in different courses, each such offering should actively seek the same goals in ways which are discernible to students. In the classroom if a given exercise is presumed to have general educational value, it should affect most if not all of the students in class rather than one or two. If, for example, discussion is held to be of value, it should be so conducted as to embrace a large number of the students in the classroom. If counseling is an important adjunct of the program, it should be so arranged as to aid most students and not just the few who seek it because of severe personal problems.

There are many excellent educational activities which do not reach all students and some of these may develop values of importance to general education. At Stephens College, for example, excellent courses in studio arts are offered which undoubtedly contribute something of importance to the general education of girls who take them. They are not, however, examples appropriate for this discussion. The late Clarence Lee Furrow often said the best general education course he had seen was an agriculture course on the use of manures as fertilizer. Again we would applaud breadth of vision on the part of such an instructor, but we would not select this for inclusion in our group of examples. At the level of classroom teaching a professor might do a brilliant job in stimulating his top students to do outstanding work. If this stimulation did not extend to the lower ability ranges we would reject the teaching as not being general education.

2. *Does the practice, program, or course realistically contribute to broadening students' views of human life?* A program of general education should be made explicit to students as a means of showing them more of human knowledge then they were aware of. If it is intended as exploratory so that students may make more intelligent choices for later specialization, this should be made clear. Further, the activity should provide a base from which students can move to these broader horizons. If a course in the humanities seeks to have students understand their debt to the Greeks, Romans, and the men of the Middle Ages, it should first help students understand where they are. If a course deals with the ways a small primitive society functions, ways of interpreting this information in other societies should be made ap-

parent to students. If mathematics or foreign languages are included in the general education curriculum, they may be justified only if they help students see more broadly the way human beings can communicate with one another.

There is room in the college curriculum for other orientations. Courses in statistics can be taught with a view only to developing certain skills. Courses in history may be included which seek only to lay bare the origin of some historical event. Courses in zoology may appropriately be offered and consist in nothing more than a deeper knowledge of sub-human mammals. These may be excellently taught but are not general education. General education must constantly relate the substance being considered with its broader significance for human living as it is perceived by students.

3. *Does the program, course, or practice have identifiable aims or objectives which can be stated in terms of human behavior?* General education is pragmatic education which aims to make discernible changes in people. It typically attempts to move an individual from one stage of development to another in full realization of what is being attempted. The objectives of general education—whether it be a course or a program or even a small segment of a course—should be made explicit, and then realistic attention given to those experiences most likely to achieve the purpose. If a goal of gaining facility in critical thinking is stated, it should contain specifications of what people do who think critically. If development of a satisfying philosophy of life is desired, this too must be spelled out. General education is predicated on the belief that there should be a direct relationship between what is sought and what is taught. General education further postulates that goals are more likely of achievement when they provide a definite rationale for the ways a curriculum is organized or a class is taught.

Emphasizing the importance of objectives does not imply that there need be a large number of purposes stated for a given activity. As a matter of fact, many courses and programs have erred through having too many, with the result that no *one* is consciously taught for. Actually one or two objectives in a particular course are about all that teachers can keep in mind in planning their work, and some six to eight are about all that are realistic for an entire program. A course in social science would do well to concentrate on inculcating a certain body of knowledge and developing such a thing as critical thinking instead of listing a variety of items such as developing habits of citizenship, changing student attitudes, and helping a person realize his obligations to society.

With respect to this criterion no clear distinction can be made between general education and other kinds of education. Presumably any program should have purposes and any course objectives. However, in practice tradition frequently rules in place of rational search for purpose. If a course did not have identifiable and used objectives, it could not be cited as an outstanding example even though the students in it were bright and hard working and the professor stimulating. If a program did not have stated purposes which were well understood by the teachers in that program, neither could it stand as an example of effectiveness.

4. *Does the program, practice, or course realistically recognize prior experiences of students?* General education theory is based on a belief that human learning evolves out of blending previous experience with new knowledge, skills, and abilities. It argues that whatever is attempted should bear a clear relationship to what students have experienced before. A course in the humanities would thus make explicit connections between students' own questions about the creative aspects of life and what was yet to come. A program would consider the kinds of homes and schools from which students originated and would capitalize on the base these sources provided. Thus a college deriving its student body from a rural population possessing a relatively low intellectual tradition would be quite different in form and in substance from a college drawing its students from a large metropolitan area. A college drawing its students from all over the United States would necessarily be different from one serving essentially students from one state. Similarly a teaching practice would differ with the kinds of experiences students had had. If most of the students in the class had had intimate familiarity with democratically conducted classes, a student-centered class would be appropriate. Had most come from more authoritarian situations, a different approach to the problem of teaching would be in order.

One can make some contrasts here with other kinds of education. Courses in internal medicine have as purposes to develop a common facility in diagnosis. Thus differences in background are accommodated as quickly as possible so that the course can get on with developing standard techniques of medical practice. Many strictly substantive courses such as entomology, or introduction to geology, can be and are taught on the assumption that the students have had no prior experience which is relevant save training in the skills of reading, writing, and arithmetic. The goals here are simply to acquaint students with a new field of knowledge. The goals of general education are not so clearly discrete. For a course to be truly reflective of general education there must be an expressed continuity with the students' past.

5. *Does the program, practice, or course make explicit the mechanisms for achieving integration?* In part general education appeared as

an attempt to restore some unity to collegiate education. The free elective system had allowed students to take just an accumulation of unrelated courses with very little attention given to what they represented in totality. General education rests on the assumptions that integrity can exist in the curriculum but that definite steps must be taken to achieve it. Thus in a program various institutional means must be present for doing this. The means may be a system of comprehensive examinations, a team system of teaching, a course emphasizing a major theological orientation, or a senior integrating course. Similarly, within courses there need to be built-in devices to facilitate integration. Such a device might be an historical framework showing how a variety of forces have served to create modern man. Another might be a series of examinations, each one cumulative with respect to materials covered on previous ones. Another might be asking teachers from another field to present introductory lectures in an effort to show the interrelationships among fields of learning. Such things as counseling centers and residence halls ought also to use definable techniques for achieving synthesis. It might be that counselors should teach academic courses in the general education program or it might be that the residence halls could be used as laboratories for social service courses, for example.

With respect to integration the difference from advanced specialized work or professional work is clear. There is room in the curriculum for a course on actuarial science even though this is unrelated to any other subject. The advanced courses in the sciences, literature, or the arts can achieve these specialized purposes without giving too much attention to equally specialized courses in other departments. Thus the teacher of a course on Constitutional Problems Under Lincoln need scarcely be aware that in Psychology a course on projective tests is given. For a general education course in social science to be conducted without awareness of the work in the humanities would be counter to the transcendent goals shared by both.

6. *Is the program or practice based on a holistic conception of human personality?* General education emphasizes integration of its manifold aspects out of a conception that the totality of human personality is rightly affected by education. It assumes that man's intellect is so related to his body and his emotions that one cannot be affected in isolation of the others. Courses in science are designed to demonstrate knowledge but also to foster scientific attitudes. Courses in social science not only teach the methods of inquiry peculiar to those disciplines but also to affect the feeling of students. Courses in the humanities seek as much to alter the students' feelings about art as experience as they do to provide them with tools of analysis and with

substantive knowledge. The fact that counseling has emerged as almost a full time partner of general education is not without significance in this regard. It clearly recognizes that an individual's success in his academic work is demonstrably related to his emotions and that how he feels derives from reaction to his academic work. Further, the kind of general education to be offered is a result not of the traditions of a particular institution and the talents of its faculty nor of the desires of its students. Rather there is an interaction going on between all of these factors which determines the nature of the offering.

An army course in rifle marksmanship, or a college course on I.B.M. operations or materials testing, does not depend for their validity on such a conception of a human being. One can view a human as nothing more than an accumulation of conditioned responses and still succeed in teaching students to translate medieval French. One cannot so view students and attempt to prepare them for successful home and family living.

7. *Does the program, course, or practice view as primary its own intrinsic goals?* General education should not be thought of as preparation for higher levels of training. These are goals which are valid in themselves and the efforts to achieve them should not be contaminated by competing goals of preparing students for more advanced work. The entire program for example should be so constructed that students will have received a defensible education if they never take another formal course. This does not mean that such a program should not be of value to higher order courses. Quite the contrary—It means that those courses should build on or take advantage of what the general education program does. But the general education program should not be adapted to fit the desires of the various upper-level courses. Articulation in other words should be initiated by the upper level, not by the general education program. Similarly, each course ought to set for itself the most valid purposes it can. In science courses these might consist of teaching students to read and interpret scientific information found in the popular press. To expect a course to do this and to prepare students for the detailed demands of zoology, chemistry, and the like for pre-medicine asks more than a course can supply. Again, saying this does not mean that a biological science course has no value for pre-medical students. But the specific needs of pre-medical students should not govern the biological science offering. In communications courses a research paper should not be justified because it trains students for upper-school report writing. Rather the communication needs of all students should be scrutinized and techniques developed most likely to meet those needs.

Introductory courses stressing the physiology of psychological behavior are appropriate in a sequence leading to a major in psychology. Introductory French stressing grammatical drill would be satisfactory for language majors. College algebra would be fine for those needing that skill or those going on into calculus. None of these would be general education courses no matter how well planned and how well taught.

8. *Is the program, practice, or course as well staffed and financed as other comparable parts of the institution?* If general education programs are to flourish, they must have strong administrative support. If the movement is to attract able young men who propose remaining with the movement, they must have their professional future secure. No program which assigned its general education teaching duties to graduate assistants or to the youngest or weakest faculty members could be classed as an effective program. No course which was less well planned than the best of upper-level courses could be accepted. No technique of teaching employed chiefly for extraneous reasons of finance could be cited as desirable general education practice.

9. *Does the teaching in the program or course reflect attention to sound scholarship, probing deeply enough into a subject to bring about significant changes in people's beliefs and a demand for students actively to practice the skills which are being taught?* A faculty which is not alert to the best thinking of the relevant fields of scholarship can serve only to bring discredit to the idea of general education. Thus a program which heaps the teaching of a general education course on the already overloaded professor of specialized courses would not be adequate. The program must allow time for teachers to understand deeply the fields they are trying to interrelate. Similarly, teaching which superficially hits the high points of some field is not satisfactory. It is more consistent with the theory of general education for three cultural epochs to be studied deeply in a course in the humanities than for twelve to be described so as to give a panoramic view of the West. Then again a program or course must provide time for students to practice skills. If critical thinking is taught, the materials covered should be few enough to allow for considerable class time for students to do critical thinking. If aesthetic judgment is desired, then an hour spent in studying one painting would be worth three hours spent in a lecture about the principles of aesthetic judgment.

10. *Does the program or practice make use of what is known of individual differences among human beings?* No two individuals are alike. Unless this is clearly understood, a passion for providing a common cultural heritage or a common universe of discourse can lead

one into an unrealistically rigid pattern. Each program should make some provisions for students deficient in basic skills just as each class should make provisions to help the weaker students. Similarly, each program should provide for the exceptionally well qualified students. This might take the form of acceleration, enrichment of courses, honors work, or some other means. Further, each program and especially each course should provide enough variety in materials as to stimulate a heterogeneous student body.

Again general education can be contrasted effectively with other types of general education. Advanced courses in professional fields can assume that individual differences have already been manifest in the selection of students into the course. It can be assumed that all students in a graduate seminar on research methods of history have a common background of study, somewhat common abilities, and even, within limits, a common purpose. No such assumption is warranted in general education courses.

11. *Does the program, course, or practice provide for regular evaluation and accept the need for periodic change?* This criterion is not limited to general education. All educational effort should be concerned with evaluation and change. However, we would argue that evaluation is an essential part of general education. Its rise as an important adjunct of education parallels the development of general education. We would argue that a program whose leaders did not make continuous systematic effort to appraise its progress could not qualify as effective. We would suggest similarly that courses and practices which were not scrutinized with respect to their achievement of the purposes for which they were organized were not general education. We would also reject as ineffective those programs and practices which were regarded as unchangeable.

Obviously no program, course, or practice can achieve perfection with respect to these criteria. They do suggest goals toward which general education can strive. They can suggest what effective general education really is.

REFERENCES

1. Dressel, P. L., & Mayhew, L. B., *General Education: Explorations in Evaluation* (Washington, A. C. E.), 1954.
2. Mikesell, Doyle, "Social Science General Education Courses," *Junior College Journal*, January 1954, 268–277.

Second Report to the President

I. THE REVOLUTION IN AMERICAN EDUCATION

Revolutionary changes are occurring in American education of which even yet we are only dimly aware. This Nation has been propelled into a challenging new educational era since World War II by the convergence of powerful forces—an explosion of knowledge and population, a burst of technological and economic advance, the outbreak of ideological conflict and the uprooting of old political and cultural patterns on a worldwide scale, and an unparalleled demand by Americans for more and better education.

These forces have created enormously increased educational challenges of which we have not yet taken full stock and which our educational institutions as a whole are ill-prepared to meet. The gap between this Nation's educational needs and its educational effort is widening ominously.

America would be heedless if she closed her eyes to the dramatic strides being taken by the Soviet Union in post-high school education, particularly in the development of scientists, engineers and technicians. She would be inexcusably blind if she failed to see that the challenge of the next 20 years will require leaders not only in science and engineering and in business and industry, but in government and politics, in foreign affairs and diplomacy, in education and civic affairs. A responsible exercise of our Nation's role in world leadership also requires a broadened citizen interest in and understanding of foreign relations and world affairs.

World peace and the survival of mankind may well depend on the way in which we educate the citizens and leaders of tomorrow.

From *The President's Committee on Education Beyond the High School* (Washington: U.S. Government Printing Office, 1957).

Four Educational Complexes

Without realizing it we have become a "society of students." More than 40 million of us—one-quarter of the Nation—are enrolled in formal education programs. Millions more are involved in less formal educational efforts.

No longer is there a single "American educational system." Four major educational complexes have evolved—our traditional system of schools and colleges, an elaborate educational program under the military, a mushrooming system of education operated by private business for its own employees, and a great variety of programs of continuing education under the broad title of "adult education." In addition, every individual's environment is crowded with powerful educational forces—newspapers, books and magazines, radio and television, libraries and museums, concerts and art galleries.

Strictly speaking, of course, no one of these is a system in the sense of being unified, closely coordinated or centrally directed. Moreover they are interlocked because the colleges and universities provide extensive services to all the others. No one knows their full dimensions, but the educational programs run by the military and by business are approaching in total expenditures all of our colleges and universities combined. Most of the military programs are 100 per cent Federally financed, and business firms recoup at least half their educational costs as deductions under the Federal income tax, whereas the heavy dependence of colleges and universities upon private funds and State and local tax revenue places them at a competitive disadvantage in the scramble for scarce resources, especially teachers.

In a recent year 400,000 armed service personnel received training in civilian-type specialties; 230,000 took a variety of correspondence courses; nearly 200,000 had college-level courses in the Resident Center Program, and 200,000 more received classroom instruction under the Group Study Program.

The number of students in business-sponsored educational programs now equals the total enrollments of all colleges and universities. Almost 90 percent of the 500 largest corporations have entered the field.

One out of every three adults, an estimated 50 million, participate in various sorts of adult education programs, some primarily vocational, others primarily recreational or cultural.

The rapid and parallel growth of these four educational areas reveals the enormous demand for education in our society and raises serious questions. To what extent do they overlap, or complement, or remedy one another's defects? How well are they coordinated,

and what can they learn from each other? What total economic resources are devoted to all four, with what efficiency and effectiveness,
and how is the total divided?

Answers to these and many other questions are needed, but we have
no answers now because crucial facts are lacking and the Committee
was not equipped to gather them. Accordingly, the Committee has
found it impossible to appraise systematically the total field of "education beyond the high school" or to make meaningful recommendations for certain important sectors, including that burgeoning but
amorphous field called "adult education." Hence this Report focuses
largely upon colleges and universities, about which more is known and
more can be clearly foreseen.

The Committee is acutely aware that the strength of education beyond the high school depends heavily upon the strength of our elementary and secondary schools. Much of what is said in this Report,
therefore, concerning the needs of higher education applies with equal
force to the lower echelons of education.

Demands of the Next 15 Years

Our colleges and universities are expected by the American public
to perform something close to a miracle in the next 10 to 15 years.
They are called upon to provide education of a continually improving
quality to a far larger number of students—at least 6 million by 1970
compared to 3 million now. The sharp rise in births which began in
the 1940's and which has already overcrowded the schools will shortly
begin to strike the colleges. Meantime, with the college age group in
our population at its lowest point in 25 years, enrollments in higher
education are at the highest level in history because a steadily increasing proportion of young people are going to college.

This great expansion of capable young people seeking education
beyond high school represents an enormous opportunity and challenge
for our society. But our institutions of higher learning, despite their
remarkable achievements in the past, are in no shape today to meet the
challenge. Their resources are already strained; their quality standards
are even now in jeopardy, and their projected plans fall far short of
the indicated need.

No good would come, the Committee is convinced, from presenting
a softer picture of the hard difficulties faced by our colleges and universities in the years ahead, but these difficulties are not so great that
they cannot be overcome by the American people if they set themselves
to the task.

Economic Realities

A stern reality to bear constantly in mind is that our colleges and universities must operate within the limits of the economic and educational resources available to them.

In round numbers colleges and universities are presently spending a little over $3 billion a year on educating students and on physical facilities—about three-quarters of 1 percent of the Gross National Product. (This excludes board and room, auxiliary services and special research projects, most of which are or should be self-financing.) If in 1970 the United States should devote to these same purposes the same proportion of its increased Gross National Product—estimated moderately at 630 to 650 billion dollars—the colleges and universities collectively would still have less than $5 billion per year with which to educate at least twice as many students and to expand facilities.

This increase would scarcely provide for the top priority need of insuring an adequate supply of good teachers. Nothing would remain, then or in the meantime, for new buildings, for strengthening services and for a host of other important needs.

To pay adequate faculty salaries and accommodate twice as many students—at present student-teacher ratios and with present amounts of building space per student—would require something like a trebling of the current level of expenditures. With greater efficiency this requirement can undoubtedly be reduced, but even then it will call by 1970 for half again the present percentage of the Gross National Product devoted to higher education.

Even if this many dollars were available, it is doubtful that enough top-quality teachers could be obtained to maintain present student-teacher ratios in view of the physical limits between now and 1970 upon the Nation's overall supply of highly trained manpower, the mounting demands for such manpower from all directions, and the difficulties of expanding the capacity of graduate schools to prepare more college teachers.

Findings

These considerations concerning the next 10 to 15 years lead the Committee to the following conclusions:

1. If the United States is to become increasingly a society of students it must also become increasingly a society of teachers. Ways must be found to harness into the service of education a far larger

number and variety of people, organized around a highly skilled group of professional teaching and administrative personnel.

2. The quantity of students and the quality of education cannot rise together unless basic educational resources also rise with sufficient speed. The American people must be willing to devote a significantly greater proportion of the Nation's rising income to higher education or else colleges and universities will be forced to choose between poorer quality and sharply restricted enrollments. In either event hundreds of thousands of able young Americans would be deprived of the opportunity to develop their full capabilities.

3. If an unwelcome choice were required between preserving quality and expanding enrollments, then quality should be preferred, because it would do neither individuals nor the Nation any good to masquerade mass production of mediocrity under the guise of higher education. But the choice between quality and quantity is not mandatory. The Nation needs more of both, and it can have more of both if it decides to do so. The decision rests much more with the public than with the educators, and the public's decision must be expressed in terms of greatly increased financial support for colleges and universities.

4. The educators in their turn have a heavy obligation to put these increased resources to their best use. Money alone will never be sufficient. Teachers must be enabled to increase their effectiveness, and buildings and all other educational resources must be used more efficiently, through improved management and more effective academic procedures.

5. By dint of strenuous effort by all concerned, the resources available to higher education can be greatly enlarged. Yet even then they are unlikely to be sufficient to meet in full measure every need and every desire. Therefore it is of the highest importance that priorities be wisely established and firmly adhered to, that careful and comprehensive planning be done, with a high degree of lay participation, and that the efforts of neighboring institutions be better coordinated than ever before. There will at best be much unfinished business in 1970—but meantime anything short of maximum efforts could place the long future of our democratic society in serious jeopardy.

6. The coming years will require greater public understanding and support, a strong and sustained effort to enlarge and improve higher education, a burst of imaginative experimentation and many changes in our conventional educational practices—changes comparable to the technological revolutions in industry and agriculture.

There follow those things which, in the Committee's opinion, must be started immediately.

II. TEACHERS—THE TOP PRIORITY

The most critical bottleneck to the expansion and improvement of education in the United States is the mounting shortage of excellent teachers. Unless enough of the Nation's ablest manpower is reinvested in the educational enterprise, its human resources will remain underdeveloped and specialized manpower shortages in every field will compound. Unwittingly the United States right now is pursuing precisely the opposite course. Demands for high quality manpower have everywhere been mounting, but colleges and universities have found themselves at a growing competitive disadvantage in the professional manpower market.

Our Nation, like the prodigal farmer, is consuming the seed corn needed for future harvests. The ultimate result could be disaster.

Salaries Must Be Raised

Over the last half century and especially since 1940, serious erosion has occurred in the real incomes of American college teachers relative to other professional groups and to wage earners generally. The greatest erosion has been at the highest ranks.

To restore teaching to a competitive position in the professional labor market comparable to that which it occupied before World War II would require an average increase in faculty salaries of something like 75 to 80 percent. And to maintain this position, once restored, would probably require by 1970 an average rise of 100 to 125 percent above present faculty salary levels.

The plain fact is that the college teachers of the United States, through their inadequate salaries, are subsidizing the education of students, and in some cases the luxuries of their families, by an amount which is more than double the grand total of alumni gifts, corporate gifts, and endowment income of all colleges and universities combined. This is tantamount to the largest scholarship program in world history, but certainly not one calculated to advance education. Unless this condition is corrected forthwith the quality of American higher education will decline. No student and no institution can hope to escape the consequences.

The Committee recommends to every board of trustees, every legislature, and all others responsible for academic budgets:

(1) That the absolute highest priority in the use of available funds be given to raising faculty salaries, with the goal of doubling the average level within 5 to 10 years, and with particular attention to increasing the spread between the bottom and the top of each institution's salary structure;

(2) That action also be taken to provide at moderate cost such benefits as health and life insurance, adequate retirement programs, faculty housing, assistance for the education of faculty children, and similar measures whose costs to the institution are small compared to the benefits and attractiveness to faculty members.

Higher salaries are essential but will not by themselves be enough. The problem of good teaching must also be attacked on three other fronts:

Recruitment Must Be Increased

High-powered recruiters descend upon campuses these days for nearly every career but teaching. The search for tomorrow's teachers must be intensified, and the best recruiters are today's teachers.

The Committee urges the faculty of every college and graduate school to join with national educational organizations in a nation-wide effort to recruit undergraduates and graduates of high talent for college teaching.

The Committee further suggests that clearinghouse machinery be established by national educational organizations with the support of private foundations to help colleges and universities locate other good manpower for teaching, including retiring professors, retiring professional personnel in business and government, and retiring military officers, with appropriate qualifications.

There is growing use of competent persons from industry and other fields for part-time teaching. This practice should be encouraged by regular employers and by colleges.

The Committee urges the colleges and universities, as soon as they can narrow the present salary gap, to reverse the present "raiding" process by industry and others, and to recapture some of the many excellent people who would have preferred teaching but who earlier bypassed or left the profession because of stronger financial inducements elsewhere.

Women comprise the greatest potential pool of additional college teachers for the future. Colleges and universities should overcome the cultural attitudes which have consigned women to a decided minority role in the ranks of higher education, resulting in an enormous waste of brain power and teaching talent.   Similar waste results wherever employment barriers exist against members of racial and religious minorities.

Preparation Must Be Expanded and Improved

The limited capacity of university graduate schools to prepare good college teachers threatens soon to become a critical bottleneck.

There is evident need to enlarge and improve existing graduate programs and to develop new types of teacher preparation programs involving the joint efforts of graduate schools and strong undergraduate colleges.

The graduate school faculties are properly concerned with their high and unique mission of expanding human knowledge through sustained scholarly research, but they carry also the equal obligation to insure the quality of tomorrow's undergraduate education upon which rest the graduate schools themselves and society's hopes for the future.

The Committee urges the administrators and faculties of graduate schools and of undergraduate colleges to collaborate more extensively than ever before toward improving and expanding present programs of college teacher preparation and developing new joint programs, and urges private foundations to consider support especially for experimental efforts and new developments of this sort.

Teacher Utilization Must Be Improved

Even with more good college teachers, well prepared and better paid, there will be great need for them to use their talents with maximum effectiveness.

Encouraging and increasing numbers of college and university faculties have lately begun to reexamine old practices and to experiment with new ones in a concerted effort to improve the learning of students and the effectiveness of teachers.

Among the promising approaches being explored are: (1) Giving students more responsibility for their own education through greater reliance on independent study and less on daily instruction from teachers; (2) relieving skilled teachers of tasks which can as well be done by assistants so as to release their time for more important and difficult teaching functions; (3) adapting different class sizes to accommodate most efficiently the various objectives in learning; (4) extending the reach of rare and unusual teachers to far more students by harnessing television and films to the service of education; and (5) simplifying the curriculum to reduce its size and raise its quality.

The Committee urges all educational institutions to continue to devise ways by which their available faculty may teach more efficiently without impairment of quality, and that educational organizations and foundations undertake to keep individual colleges fully informed about such experiments and new developments throughout the country.

Section V-3

Student Discontent and Campus Reform

By Paul Potter

On April 17th of this year, in Washington D.C., 25,000 people, mostly students, gathered to protest American involvement in the war in Vietnam and to demand an end to that gruesome and repressive struggle. The demonstration, which on the whole was played down by "responsible" media, constituted one of the most dramatic manifestations to date of what people have come to call "the student movement." By any standards it was large, three times as large as the student march in 1962 to demand an end to nuclear testing. But more important than size was the fact that the demonstration stood in polar opposition to some of the country's most sacred and deeply held principles—its unrestricted, unquestionable, unchallenged right to wage holy war against what it calls communism in whatever way, with whatever tools, seems most expedient. What happened in Washington in 1965 would have been called treason ten years earlier and may well be called treason ten years hence. Even five years ago it would have been difficult enough to get 25 people to that kind of demonstration—not to mention, or even imagine, 25,000.

If you can understand why the March on Washington happened in 1965, then you can understand a great deal of the basis of student discontent on the campus today. But comprehending Washington and the mood of the students who protested there means coming to grips with much that many Americans, including far too many of your own ranks, would rather ignore or simply write off with some such sweeping term as "communist-inspired," or "beatnik," or "misguided." In fact, one characteristic of the problems I want to discuss here is that so many otherwise intelligent people refuse to admit their existence.

From *Order and Freedom on the Campus*, Western Interstate Commission for Higher Education, 1965.

247

I have noted the size and intensity of the march on Washington as a foreword to underscore the fact that what we are talking about is real, is growing, and demands much more than categorical dismissal.   In fact, the reality of a student movement has begun to challenge those who would dimiss it.   The students who marched in Washington, or struck at Berkeley, or protested on numerous other campuses across the country, or left their schools to help organize movements in the South or among the urban poor in the North are, in a real sense, the actual conveners of this conference and similar gatherings, formal and informal, across the country.

And it is in this sense that I want to speak to you today—as one of the thousands who helped to call you here.   In doing so, I do not propose to describe or represent to you the entire diversity of groups and reactions that exist on the campus today.   Nor will I attempt to give a presentation which has academic authority or style.   Rather, to the extent possible, I want to speak to you with the voice and out of the experience of a person who has participated actively in the construction of the current movement and who believes deeply in its integrity and validity.   If my tone is not detached, it is because I find it difficult to detach myself from what I say and do, and I find with my compatriots one source of concern—a world in which men so easily detach themselves emotionally from the things they create.   If my comments are not always friendly or if I seem to fail at times to seek some common ground with you, it is because I see the distance between us as great and perhaps insurmountable, and I can see no virtue in constructing here a false sense of our capacity to reconcile our worlds through words or "understanding."

THE SOURCES OF DISCONTENT

It is a popular occupation these days for detractors of the student movement to concentrate their attack on the participants' dress, cleanliness, and length of hair.   Out of the accumulated residue of such reactions comes an impression of student radicals as some sort of rabble scraped from the bottom of the American social heap.   Disregarding for the moment the accuracy of the physical descriptions and the nature of a society that responds to basic challenges by commenting on the dress of the challengers, let me begin this presentation by stressing how false an impression that description gives of the background of most student radicals.

Interestingly enough, the "rabble," which the pundits so meticulously dissect, turns out to be the sons and daughters of the American dream.   Most of us were reared in families that had acquired the tools to harvest and enjoy the abundance of the world's most abundant

society and were given all that good Americans are supposed to want—
money, suburban living, cultural opportunities ranging from home environments carefully developed to provide stimulus to whatever
potential we had, to summer camps and trips to Europe. Our parents
were well educated, were most frequently professionally employed, and
had acquired moderately high, almost comfortable status. We grew up
believing that we would inherit all of these things—money, status,
security, cultural abundance—taking them for granted, which was a
reasonable thing to do, given their rich and bountiful array around us.

We grew up as well believing that we lived in a great nation which
had harnessed itself to the will of its people, providing them with education, the highest standard of living in the world, equality of opportunity, democracy, and the great middle class. We believed ours a
humble nation that awkwardly and reluctantly shouldered the responsibilities a much more corrupt world forced upon her, but dis-
patched those responsibilities, once shouldered, with integrity, honor,
and the most peaceful intentions.

We were, in short, the first post-depression, post-war generation
to emerge into the world with all the assists of the mildly permissive (in
some cases almost progressive) family culture of upper-middle-class
America. If our parents sometimes despaired at our inability to understand the austerity and struggle that made possible their achievements,
they were nonetheless pleased with the generally enthusiastic and alert
products of their work.

Somehow, and for reasons that are not entirely clear to me, this
group of young people, who had everything that their society could
give to them, found that gift hollow and rejected it. In their rejection
they began to fashion a movement which has comprehended many
issues and touched on a number of the nation's most exposed nerve
ends.

The experience of students in universities has had a great deal to
do with their disaffection. Somewhere earlier they had already begun
to understand that much of what they were supposed to cherish and
emulate was sham. The jolt of the college experience has been for
many, however, the event that brought discontent to the surface. That
reaction may stem partly from the fact that many of us had high expectations about what college would mean. There was an excitement
about finding an intellectual and personal seriousness in universities
which we frequently had not found in high schools, and there was a
sense that college offered independence in directing our education and
lives that had previously been missing. There was a vague yearning
for something in college that we had begun to sense was missing from
our backgrounds.

The reality of universities was, to a great extent, the opposite of what we had hoped for. In the place of intellectual and personal seriousness was substituted the academic grind of large classes, intense competition for grades, exams that were irrelevant and intellectually damaging, and an environment in which the chief academic occupation seemed at times to consist of learning how to beat the system and "psyche" out professors and exams. In place of personal independence in shaping life and education were substituted numerous requirements characterized mostly by dullness and massiveness, the confining and degrading existence of dormitories and their regulations, and the general recognition that less personal freedom was extended in the university than there had been in the home. Independence, university-style, meant isolation in an environment that was essentially callous to personal needs. For most, it was the first encounter with the full inflexibility of mass bureaucratic organization, the first experience with the rat race and a system of external pressures and deadlines that substitute for internal initiatives or concerns, the first invitation to take on the garb of hipster, to ask questions that you didn't really care about, to "bull" your way out of situations that were embarrassing or threatening. If, on occasion, students found good teachers or exciting classes, it did little more than underscore their sense that the rest were bad or useless.

Perhaps the most difficult thing to assimilate, however, was the phoniness of the presentation of the university experience. Most institutions insist on clothing themselves in liberal rhetoric, for whose benefit it is difficult to say. They begin with applauding the virtues of liberal education, continue with much ado about the importance of the student's assuming his educational responsibilities as an adult (the conclusion is difficult to avoid that adults are people who have learned to function well in such systems), and end with a system of junior residents who, the students soon learn, write regular reports that are kept in some central place; house mothers, who are most frequently caricatures of mother surrogates; counsellors, who help the misfits adjust; and disciplinarians, who mete out justice in a system that students soon learn is arbitrary, although somewhat manipulable with the aid of parents or through effectiveness as a hipster. On the whole, colleges seem to try to present themselves as permissive and mildly parental when in fact they are neither. The tired and elaborate rationalizations for keeping things as they are, are soon seen as just that.

I want to make it clear that I am talking about a very general experience. The terms I use to describe it are not necessarily those that most students would use to depict their experience, nor are these necessarily the areas in which student discontent is focused. What I want to stress is that, in general, the university experience outside of the classroom is the catalyst that begins to give students new insights into the way the society operates, the way people are treated, and the way cultural values are misrepresented. At some point students begin to understand that they have lived in a capsule which the university attempts to duplicate; its failure sharpens the discontinuity between past personal experience and aspiration and what the society has, in fact, to offer. It makes the student aware, consciously or unconsciously, of the simple fact that educational institutions exist to fit him to the system and not *vice versa*, and that is a recognition that all of his careful socialization to upper-middle-class values has ill prepared him to accept. We grew up feeling reasonably potent in influencing our personal milieu; and without our parents' deeper needs for economic and status security, we are in a much better position to challenge a society that promises to make us impotent.

THE EXPRESSION OF STUDENT DISCONTENT

To say that these feeling and discontents are widely shared among certain, if not all, groups of students is not to explain why in the 1960's they have crested in the current movement, or why in the 1950's they remained untapped or were directed into less socially significant arenas. I do not want to attempt to review the accumulation of forces that changed the fifties into the sixties. I want only to say that, by 1958 or earlier, the first signs of revived student interest in social and political issues had begun to appear. By 1960 they had built up to the point that unleashed in the same spring the sit-in movement, the San Francisco demonstrations against the House Un-American Activities Committee, and the West Coast vigils against the execution of Caryl Chessman. The same spring saw the awakening on a number of other campuses of more campus-directed reform activity, but in overall significance it paled beside the off-campus issues. Nonetheless, on a number of campuses, significant battles were being waged against compulsory ROTC, fraternity and sorority discrimination, and the loyalty and disclaimer affidavits in the National Defense Education Act—three of the more obvious and vulnerable indignities that universities had been content to tolerate.

The kinds of issues that came to the fore that spring, and for the most part since then, suggest that the university system was at once more encompassing and more difficult to get a handle on. Student life was a kind of gumpot that was difficult to move in or gain clear insight into. Students more and more found it easier to direct their protests off campus.

What has emerged out of five years of growing protest is a clearer critique of the society, a more articulate enunciation of some of the contradictions in American life. The naive belief in the myths of freedom and abundance that suburban life and patriotic school teachers had inculcated could now be confronted by the stench of southern justice or the burning flesh of children napalmed by American bombs in Vietnam. The myth of the great American middle class, which projected the image of an endless prosperous suburb, could be counterposed to the fact that 30 million Americans still live in poverty and that millions more live at the margin, with economic insecurity a constant element in their lives. Students could begin to appreciate the irony of being called rabble by the press, since the real rabble, the poor and dispossessed, were excluded systematically from the opportunity represented by university education because of the prejudices of class- and status-oriented education, not to mention just plain lack of money with which to purchase the educational tickets.

The myth of American benevolence in international issues stands exposed against the reality of American intervention in Vietnam and the ruthless subjugation of that nation to the game of power politics, the repression of the revolt of constitutional forces against military dictatorship in the Dominican Republic, and the public fabrications, distortion, and attempted control of information that have become a part of pursuing these policies. The myth of political freedom is juxtaposed to the reality of the persecution of unpopular political sects, the existence and continued operation of the House Un-American Activities Committee, the constant surveillance and frequent harassment of left-of-center political groups by local "subversive squads," the ready chorus of red-baiting which greets any serious questioning of the operation of the existing system. And out of all this comes a growing sense of a social, economic, and political system that has lost its ability to be responsive to the needs of ordinary people.

What is essential to understand here is that those problems which the existing movement has helped to dredge up for public scrutiny are not viewed by most students in the movement today as simple malfunctioning of a basically sound system. Students have been quick to understand the complicity of liberal institutions in the maintenance of those problems—for example, the extremely limited, yet dogmatically defended, concepts of education that do exclude the poor, do freeze the class system, do cut millions of people off from participation in the mainstream of society. The disaffection that has grown over the last few years is deeper and more dramatic than most people like to admit, and its roots are as deep in the middle-class institutions of the society as they are in the agenda of social problems this generation of students has exposed.

The first bold acts of protest in 1960 helped to establish a dynamic that has shown no sign of playing itself out. For what those protests did was to break through the kind of isolation existing in universities which made people feel that effective political participation is impossible or self-destructive. It has helped to create an environment in which the accumulated discontents, not only of students but of Negroes and other poor people—and increasingly of faculty and other professional groups—could be expressed without fear that the statement of radical concerns would lead to political persecution. An independent political community is being built in this country which has the power to sustain those who want to challenge the great Johnsonian consensus or who want to at least partially dislodge themselves from the tyranny of the institutions on which they are dependent for work.

There is another critical function that the movement has performed for its adherents. It has created for us all a greater sense of the reality of America; it has provided a tool with which to cut through the shrouds of sophistry that allow people to rationalize their dehumanization and that of others. It accepted as one of its tenets a moral and logical clarity and an insistence on the unity of ends and means that have made its demands and its critique clear and uncompromised on the one hand and on the other have kept it away from the pitfalls of striving for respectability and institutionally sanctioned legitimacy. It was the clarity and simplicity of the sit-ins and the Chessman vigils that drew so many students to them—students who in many cases had seemed apathetic when approached by the safer, more legitimate round of campus political disputes and student government politics. The arguments were simple and to the point. Segregation was a clear evil and should be ended, regardless of what the law said or local custom dictated. No society had the right to take the life of one of its members, to perform such an ultimate and irreversible act on even the most tortured of its creations. And the clarity of the issues was critical in exposing the unclarity in the society that had allowed these issues to lie submerged so long.

It is part of this search for clarity that has sent students into the cotton fields of Mississippi and the deep South, and into the urban slums of the North. These reservoirs of social repression and neglect represent to us much of what is most real about America. It is in attempting to understand what this society does to the people whom it can't incorporate into the system that one can begin to comprehend the extent to which this society is in need of change. It is the assertion that, so long as the least of us remains exploited and repressed, all of the rest of us must be dehumanized by the construction and justification of a system that allows his exploitation. And there is a determination to build on that assertion the kind of movement that will bring about a decent society for all people.

It is the same search for the reality of America that has led so many students into absorption with the war in Vietnam. For in understanding that war, one must begin to understand the way society has come to believe that its own freedom can only be defended by sacrificing the lives and opportunity for self-determination of an entire nation of people.

There is a very deep sense that the country has lost its capacity to tell the truth, that the honesty and integrity of people will be evoked only by cutting through cultural lies and by beginning to speak what seems to be true, regardless of its acceptability, regardless of its consequences.

What I hope you begin to see from this picture is that the kind of discontent which is emerging on the campus is neither sporadic and disconnected nor inexplicable. I hope that you will attempt to understand as well the depth of the disaffection which I am describing.

The actual amount of energy that to date has been directed at campus reform has been relatively slight. Berkeley has come to symbolize an important wave of protest, but it is only the beginning and not necessarily a representative example of what has come before or what will follow. There are good reasons why the campus has been relatively neglected. In the first place, the issues at stake on the campus seem less important than the national and international problems which have absorbed so much student energy. And second, as I have already indicated, problems on the campus are too close, too difficult to define, too integral to the personal biography of the students to easily gain insight into or leverage on. There is a kind of inarticulateness that plagues the movement when students begin to talk about their own situations and what they want to do to change them.

I was recently in a conversation with a number of thoughtful, well versed, deeply involved student radicals, and the conversation turned to the question of why students join the movement. There was a real hesitation among all the people in the room to bandy around the glib formulations that most frequently are offered to answer that question. But, try as we would, no one was able to get beyond the old formulations, to add a new dimension to the discussion that had only to come from reflection on one's own experience.

That strange muteness about ourselves and our needs is remarkably contrasted to the articulate and exciting insights that these students and many thousand others have developed in talking about the political and social problems of the nation.

It is this inarticulateness that has kept students from dealing effectively with their own condition, and all I can do by way of explanation is to suggest that the accumulated experience of living in a society that refuses to look at people and take them seriously *as people* eventually destroys the individual's capacity to take himself seriously. What the movement provides is a new experience to dislodge students from their old self-conception (or lack of it) and make possible the beginnings of something new. It is the dialectic of new experience constantly counterposed to what went on before that makes me confident that the next few years will see a marked increase in the capacity of students to deal directly with their own condition in the university.

In a way Berkeley provided an insight into how much of this may come about, not so much in the nature of the action as in the source of the action, the basis for militant and uncompromised student action. It is essential to understand that there would not have been a Berkeley Free Speech Movement, or at least not a movement of any proportion, if there had not been a civil rights movement. It was the interference of the administration in the capacity of civil rights groups to carry on their struggle—to continue to deal with one of the few things students are confident is real and worthwhile in the society—that triggered the confrontations and led thousands of students to support these groups. In a sense the Free Speech Movement is a misnomer for what happened in Berkeley, for it implies that what moved students was an abstract concern for free speech. In fact, what moved students was a passionate concern for the very immediate, very real struggle in which they were involved, and what infuriated them was the notion that petty bureaucratic regulations could be allowed to interfere with that struggle.

Free speech, I suspect, can never be an issue if no one has anything to say. What the last five years have demonstrated is that, when people really do have something important to say, they will find a way to say it, even if that means losing a job or going to jail or dying.

The reason why the Filthy Speech Movement failed to arouse the kind of support that the Free Speech Movement elicited was not that it lacked an issue or principle. Anyone who bothers to explore the history of the Filthy Speech episode will find that, contrary to the impressions press reports gave, there was merit and principle involved in the issue. Students were not so much demanding the right to shout filthy words as they were illustrating another piece of the hypocrisy of the system. Students failed to support the effort massively because the issue, although principled, was not that important, was not that central to anything that was happening. Similarly, the failure of students as yet to challenge massively the content of courses that are taught in classrooms, or the status system that keeps people in a university from talking to one another, or the mountains of banality that corrode the university in dozens of areas and make life there unrewarding, has occurred because all of this too, ironically, seems irrelevant.

But of course, it isn't irrelevant, and that is precisely the point. Gradually students are seeing just how it isn't irrelevant. For example, the introductory economics course, which seems stupid and dull, must increasingly be seen as more than that—for it is dangerous as well. More frequently than not, it is directed at rationalizing the necessity for an economic system that has failed—that has created hardcore poverty and "structural" unemployment as well as the abundance that the textbook talks about. It is important to find some way to break through the academic intrigue long enough to appraise people of the fact that the economic system has failed and to see if there is anyone who is interested in reconstructing it. There must also be ways to begin thinking about questions such as these: Must work always be organized from the top down? Must men always be trained to spend their lives doing tasks that damage or destroy their human potential? Can we create an economic organization in which men do work, not from necessity or through coercion but because it is fulfilling? These are not abstract questions. They are only abstract in the encapsulated, make-believe "real" world that thrives on defending and entrenching the *status quo*. In the world that the student movement is trying to create, where problems are not hidden, these questions and endless more like them must be faced and answered.

RECONSTRUCTING UNIVERSITIES

One of the debates that goes on constantly within the movement, you will be interested to know, is whether or not it makes sense to attempt, in a major way, university reform. There are many who have felt for a long time that the university is too formidable and entrenched an adversary for students to take on. There are others who feel that the kind of compromises we can exact from the universities are so minimal in their nature as to make the effect of gaining those concessions and making commitments to explore them distracting and thus destructive to the basic work of building a political and social movement for basic change.

Both of these arguments contain interesting insights which I want to explore. Let me begin by saying that very few, if any, schools in this country exist for their students. Those liberal arts colleges which are most frequently credited with being student-centered are still built around an image of what they want to do for students or, as the jargon has it, what kind of a finished product they want to produce. Whether that image is shared with the students is a matter that can never be determined, since the students are almost never consulted or, if consultation does take place, it is done within the context of a system whose basic assumptions are already incorporated as given. It seems to me not a disrespectful thing to say that institutions of higher education exist to prepare students to take their place in the going system and that even the most liberal of institutions are concerned with developing an "enlightened" commitment, but nonetheless, a commitment to it. To say that they exist to pursue truth, or some such higher value, is naive and unbecoming to many of the distinguished intellects who propound that statement.

The influence of organized corporate and institutional interests on the universities is clear, as is the willingness of the universities to cooperate in numerous ways with almost anyone who has the money to buy their facilities. Students more and more call this whoring; others call it research. The federal government continues to be the biggest buyer; and, although there are occasional rumblings about the distorting influence of government spending on the whole structure of higher education, no one as yet has mustered the political or financial will to really come to grips with the impact of federal involvement. In the end, it seems simplest to accept the close and historic ties between the university and established power and values, not necessarily as immutable but certainly as dominant and entrenched in the existing situation.

Educators enjoy emphasizing the unique qualities of the university as an institution, but what I have just noted in conjunction with other aspects of the university makes it worth while to understand the extent to which the university can also be viewed as a photograph of the existing system. Universities, especially the large ones, have more and more come to resemble the giant corporate entities that now dominate our educational system. This phenomenon has been described by many people, but I note it here again just to underscore the difficulty that confronts anyone who is interested in serious reform or reorganization of the university. We are talking about a highly organized, bureaucratized system that is controlled from without, that is primarily responsive to external pressures, that is involved in inter-institutional competition for resources, and that is mightily committed to the going system.

However, this barrier is matched by another closely related factor, the internal organization of the academic life of the university and, within it, the place of the student. I touched on this subject earlier, but I want to explore the problem further at this point because I think it is central to the development of any significant reform effort on the campus. As yet, I know of no significant effort directed at the academic organization of the university. It is important to understand why this is so.

Probably the most intimidating and effectively stifling element of any university is the environment that exists in the classroom. From the outset the student is reminded that he is in the university to gain some minimal exposure to the accumulated wisdom of the various disciplines with which he will come in contact. He is made to understand that the most he can hope to master as an undergraduate is some small appreciation of the complexity of the fields he chooses to concentrate in. He is frequently told by professors that, if he wants to take up their time during office hours to discuss some point raised in class, he should come fully prepared to enter into academic discussion. Under no circumstances should he disturb a professor if it is only to display his ignorance. In short, he is made painfully aware of his status as an untested and unworthy novice who can only hope after years of work to acquire the tools to talk intelligently about some area of specialty. Students who fail to respond to these warnings, who instead persist in asking ordinary questions that come out of natural curiosity and not out of the intention to comprehend the discipline, are subjected to withering comments and looks. They are embarrassed or, if they refuse to be embarrassed, are ignored.

Not all professors, of course, are this severe in their description and enforcement of the academic system, but most come close enough to accepting these terms to concede the definition of the classroom experience to their more vocal colleagues who do quite literally subject the undergraduate to the kind of harangue just described. There are very few teachers who can always resist the temptation to pull academic rank in order to put down irritating questions or in order to feel more secure in front of a class.

After awhile, even the professors who want to break through the constraints of the system are confronted by students who have been so well socialized to it that they re-impose constraints and seem to feel more comfortable within the protective confines of the system. I once had the opportunity of sitting in on a seminar in which the teachers were obviously quite anxious to stimulate a free-wheeling discussion of a number of social problems. Throughout a semester, the students refused to detect many cues to this effect and kept bouncing back with academic concepts and jargon which no one particularly understood or cared about.

The student who seeks practical insight into personal and public issues is frequently cautioned against any attempt to connect his classroom experience with life experience. Political scientists go to great lengths to make their students understand that their courses have nothing to do with practical politics. Introductory psychology lectures most frequently start with the caution that it is a dangerous thing to go around attempting to apply concepts learned about neuroses and such. And then, of course, the lecturer goes on to discuss the nervous system of the rat.

Middle-class child-rearing habits are credited with preparing children to postpone gratification, and it is fortunate for the universities that this is true. Few undergraduate classes I know of could be endured a day without that capacity. It is amazing how many students start off on their academic apprenticeship convinced that they must learn to like it, anxious for the day when they too will be able to speak the language and manipulate the esoteric symbols of their discipline. Some don't last, like my friend who finally gave up after three years of waiting for psychology courses to move from rats and flatworms to people. Others, of course, do make it, winding up in senior honors seminars, sounding like young professors and having forgotten long ago any genuine questions from their own experience that they might have wanted to answer, once they got the tools.

Graduate students should have a more open and exciting educational experience, according to the terms of the system. But again, in the vast majority of cases, this seems not to be true. Indeed there is much to be said for the notion that the graduate student is the most cruelly exploited member of the academic community. He is completely exposed to all of its pressures, being more often than not dependent upon it for money and, more important, the kind of recognition that will lead to a good thesis committee, good recommendations, and a chance to get into the publishing scramble with the junior faculty at some good university. He is aware that professors talk about their graduate students and thus is hesitant to offend any of the fraternity by impertinence lest they brand him a trouble-maker. He is aware that a teaching assistantship is the kind of low-status brand that may make it difficult for him to gain access to the powerful professors in the department. He is aware of the competition he is locked into with every other graduate student in the department, and he is therefore an active participant in the competition that has deprived many of the "best" graduate schools in the country of any graduate student community.

At least we might hope that the student is now more free intellectually, but again this turns out not to be true. Internal competition and the expectations of professors place a heavy emphasis on internal documentation of papers and the selection of subjects, not by interest or importance, but by their capacity to be thoroughly researched and convincingly presented. Nor is the graduate student's relationship with faculty necessarily improved.

By way of illustration, let me tell you about a friend who, after much preliminary investigation, came up with some hypotheses for a doctoral dissertation and then went to the most logical member of the department to see if he would oversee her thesis work. After much fumbling, he agreed to act as her thesis advisor, but he announced at the outset that she should expect very little help from him. When she asked why, he finally admitted that he was deeply interested in the area she had selected for her thesis topic, hoped to publish in that field some day, and had a number of ideas which he was concerned she should not steal. Therefore he found it impossible to talk.

That, of course, brings us to another dimension of the problem. Faculty are themselves locked in their own kind of competition for grants and academic honors and for the kind of research record that leads to promotions and prestige. Eventually the pressure of the system reaches a point where a professor is no longer willing to explore his ideas with his students, and undoubtedly his colleagues as well, for fear they will steal from him all that he has—his intellectual productions. What kind of academic community can exist in a situation such as this? And what kind of learning can go on where people find that what is new inside themselves and in the process of creation must be hoarded, like space in an air raid shelter, against all those who might benefit from sharing it.

Any university reform that is worth the name must deal with this problem. It is little wonder that students have balked at entering this arena. How, after all, can one challenge the system of intellectual competence that allows the professor to lecture from the front of the class after years of study and diligent application? Students do sense their ignorance, are quick to doubt themselves and the worth of their own ideas, are fascinated by the academic flourish that some professors manage to acquire. There must be something powerful that motivates students to challenge a system that so effectively reinforces itself and so convincingly challenges the student's own self-confidence.

And as I indicated earlier, the movement has begun to provide those kinds of questions, is giving students the equipment and the conviction to challenge professors—not on an academic footing but in the human dimension that is so uniformly rejected by the university. This is something to stand on, and its appeal is strong enough to attract many faculty who are themselves fed up with the confines of the university niches and have themselves begun to question the relevance of their disciplines to the things in life that are important. The teach-in movement tapped a great deal of this sentiment and, interestingly enough, has split internally on the issue of how academic and correct the teach-ins should be. Out of this spring's experience has come a much more self-conscious group of young faculty who are in contact with one another and are looking for ways to expand their ranks and the scope of their concern.

Students too have come closer to a real engagement with the issue of education. The Yale protest over the firing of a good and popular teacher was a move in the direction of questioning the way classes are organized. In contrast to previous student efforts, which have concentrated much more on social rules and superstructural changes such as the representation of students on faculty and administrative committees, the Yale uprising was a direct challenge, although it still fell far short of a full-fledged confrontation.

Here we should pause once more, because a full-fledged confrontation entails the demand that higher education be progressive, that it be structured around the needs and problems that students define out of themselves and out of their own experience—and this is the exact antithesis of what we have today. The intensity of the struggle posed by the notion that higher education should be progressive is certainly much more severe than anything we have seen to date. And yet I genuinely believe that the day is soon coming when students will stand up in classrooms and demand that their professors lay aside their esoterica and begin to talk to them in their own terms about problems that can be jointly defined as important. A non-dramatic indicator of what is to come occurred this year when a group of students at Oberlin began an effort to get the student body to hire its own professor who would be explicitly instructed to talk about the things that aren't discussed in the classroom.

What begins to emerge are two highly conflicting and polarized images of what higher education should be. The first, which exists today, is that of a university controlled externally by financial and political as well as social forces which are not responsive to the needs or interests of the people in the university, and organized internally around a system of very open competition, status sanctions, and authoritarian teaching methods. By contrast, I see emerging out of the movement today the demand for education that is directed toward the concerns of the people involved in it, organized democratically, and conducted in the most open and cooperative fashion. I do not believe that the educational system that I envisage can exist in this society. And I am in this sense pessimistic about the possibility of any reform movement actually accomplishing these goals.

It is this pessimism that has led many students to talk about the need for counter-institutions or the enactment of educational programs that deal with the problems we are talking about—with or without the cooperation of the university. There is a sense that a commitment to see reform accomplished within the existing system may be a commitment to never seeing the educational needs that people are beginning to express dealt with.

By counter-institutions I mean two things. First, an operation that works outside of the sanctions of the existing system. And second, a program that is designed to challenge the system it is rejecting by setting up an alternative in such a way that people in the system are actually challenged to leave it. Some of the teach-ins were good examples of what I am talking about. They were exciting educational experiences that broke down all sorts of barriers, but at the same time they were counterposed effectively against the day-to-day university routine, so that many students drew from the teach-in a clearer sense of what education could be. Counter-education in the long run becomes a tool for reform or reconstruction of the existing institutions. In the short run it becomes a way of thinking about problems that the society will not deal with and sharing in an experience that can give people more personal and intellectual independence.

Many students will choose and are choosing a more dramatic course. They are simply leaving the university and moving into full-time work in the movement where education comes from first-hand experience of the range of issues with which people are struggling. There is a hint of nihilism in this more sweeping rejection of the system and its sanctions which I sense is the most perplexing and disturbing aspect of the student movement for many liberal educators. But that negation was not created by the movement. It was born in a society that refused to confront its most basic problems, and it is the inherited burden of this generation of students to play out that negation, to go to the verge of nihilism, and perhaps beyond, in their search for a positive that is powerful enough to overcome the negative.

There are many who anticipate the eventual repression of the movement, or its exhaustion through the unrewarded burning out of its own energy and who, out of genuine concern for their students, wish desperately that there was some way to protect them from the ruthless exposure they subject themselves to when they desert the university and their pedigree and their security to venture into the South or the urban slum or some other area of the movement. But there is no protection that can be accepted. All that can be offered is whatever commitment those people can themselves make to building and interpreting the movement, and in keeping the society from crushing it and the people in it. The only shelter we have is in one another.

But the great majority of students in the movement will choose to stay in the university and maintain some bond or connection with the system. And these are the students who will be involved not only in counter-education but in challenging the universities directly and more and more aggressively about their basic premises. If I have little hope of full success, I nonetheless feel that a movement to reconstruct universities, as part of a movement to reconstruct society, will gain constant and more compelling strength.

You may be wondering why I have said so little about college administrators and college presidents. A few years ago, I certainly would have spent a much more substantial part of my time hurling invectives at the way you manage to run universities. Although I have hardly retracted those sentiments, I am less inclined today than I once was to view you as a group of very powerful men who have considerable latitude in determining the way your institutions are run. I do not believe that, even if you wanted to, you could change your universities into the kind of institutions I have described or, for that matter, move substantially in that direction, *e.g.*, demand that your board of control rule that, for every new research dollar that comes into the university, an equal amount be raised for educational experimentation, the experiments to be determined by a jointly elected body of students and faculty who would review applications made by an individual or group in the university.

If my feelings are correct about the direction of campus protest, you may for the time being be exempted from much of the direct pressure of student discontent. When and if there are organized groups of students and faculty who have demands to make about how the university should operate, or when classrooms begin to get disorderly, or when a number of teachers in a department refuse to turn in grades, or when students who have been crammed into crowded or inadequate classrooms and study space begin to appropriate research facilities for their own work and interest, you will have an opportunity to respond. But the time when just the administration and legal structure of the university were singled out for protest may be going. Still, it is an overly schematized version of what is happening to suggest that student protest will move consistently or in any one direction. Much of what happens is fortuitous—the administration or students unwittingly creating a confrontation in some area that comes to represent accumulated discontent and must be played to its conclusion. Nonetheless, the campus protest of the coming years is likely to be much less dependent on the response you make, *i.e.*, much more focused on the deeper issues, issues that cannot be circumvented by a sophisticated response. As official arbiters and squelchers of conflict, you are likely to be most unsuccessful.

Still it is important that you understand that new forces are at work on your campus, raising most profound questions about the kind of education students are receiving there. Something that no one can stop you from doing is to take these new forces seriously, learn to listen to them, begin to toy with the notion most people are so quick to dismiss, that maybe the students may be right and America may be wrong, that the course the nation has charted may be opposite to the one we should pursue, that now in the mid-twentieth century the time may have come to ponder the possibility of reconstructing our schools and our politics and our society in a new image—this time in the image of man.

Section V-4

The Dropout in Conflict with Society

LAWRENCE A. PERVIN *et. al.*

The matter of dropping out of college, with its widespread ramifications in the educational and social realms, transcends the merely personal psychology of the individual. It is a phenomenon that highlights the ancient struggle between the environment and the individual, each striving to modify the other in ways as complex as life itself, until a better balance is achieved. This book, by focusing in its first section on social or environmental factors related to dropping out and in its second on the inner life of the dropout himself, attempts to avoid an attitude that favors either society or the dropout, but seeks rather to invite study of the highly emotional interaction between the two. If examination of this interaction discloses elements of ignorance or extremism on both sides, more rooted in emotionalism than in calm objectivity, perhaps the dropout may be less widely included among the failures, delinquents, and other undesirables. The sensitivy of students to the value system of a society that condemns dropping out is hinted at, even if half-facetiously, in the remark of one student: "If you quit school after your bachelor's degree, you're a dropout."

DROPOUTS AND EDUCATIONAL ISSUES

The eighteen-year-old daughter of a utilities executive decides that college is incompatible with marriage and drops out in her freshman year....

The nineteen-year-old son of a middle-class businessman finds himself without a vocational goal and bored. He drops out in his sophomore year to enter military service....

From Lawrence A. Pervin, Louis E. Reik, and Willard Dalrymple, *The College Dropout and The Utilization of Talent*, Princeton University Press, 1966. Reprinted by permission of Princeton University Press, pp. 3–21.

The twenty-year-old son of a steelworker, a lad with an I.Q. of 152, suffers a schizophrenic illness in his junior year. He is able to return to college two years later, shifting from a major in mathematics to one in psychology. . . .

The nineteen-year-old daughter of an accountant who has wished since high school that she had had the courage to try a career of free-lance writing leaves a small liberal arts college to live in Greenwich Village and work seriously on a novel she has had in mind for three years. . . .

An eighteen-year-old National Merit Scholar is required to withdraw from an outstanding metropolitan university for plagiarism. . . .

A junior at a leading engineering college has always been known to be brilliant in mathematics and theoretical physics. He has never attained outstanding marks in college, nor has he sustained creative work of any kind; at the end of the junior year he fails. . . .

To these fictional but representative capsule narratives most readers can add their own examples. Though the strands are so dissimilar, American education binds them all together into the rope called "dropouts." What is the significance of these events to the individuals and their families, to the colleges, and to society and the nation? What complicated personal and institutional factors led up to them? What are the issues raised? The investigation of these questions forms the subject matter of this book.

Clearly the investigation must cover considerable ground, and the problems involved lead into many of the great contemporary issues of higher education. Indeed, the fact that there are great issues today which demand a central place in the public attention accounts for the rise in interest in the college dropout. With typical commitment, the American people are convinced both of the desirability of education and of its perfectibility. While their commitment does not carry over into agreement on specific issues or methods, it does lead to general impatience with whatever stands in the way of progress and perfection. If a college education is desirable, society asks, why should any young person not seek to attain it in the appointed time? Society's immediate reactions are that the dropout has sacrificed his own future, squandered his institution's resources, and indeed detracted from the national interest itself.

Are these reactions justified? This volume urges a dispassionate point of view, and though few definitive answers to broad problems will be offered herein, the reader will find many suggestions that cases and problems differ, and that dropping out of college is not necessarily undesirable or wasteful. For some, leaving college—usually temporarily, but on occasion permanently—may be more educational than staying.

In a majority of the examples given at the start of this introduction, it is possible that the student advanced more rapidly toward maturity, including educational maturity, by leaving college than if he had been required or enabled to continue. In many cases, the student's intellectual efficiency in learning has dissipated; he has "lost motivation"; he has "run out of gas"; he has suffered any of numerous emotional disturbances or distortions. The dean, the faculty adviser, the counselor, the psychiatrist know empirically that time away from college may help his efficiency.

And yet a nagging thought urges itself: if educators were more knowledgeable, more effective, better at preparing themselves and their students, could this event have been avoided? Here the trap may be the traditional inclination to think of education as preparation for life, although, as Dr. Kubie suggests, it may be equally true that life is a preparation for education.

"Education as preparation for life" regards education as the acquisition of tools and the skill to use them. Once accomplished, it provides the thoroughly educated young person with competence to deal with life's problems and to be a contributing member of society, earning a higher income in so doing. The faster, the better; so runs the theory. But "life as a preparation for education" regards a varied experience as valuable for learning. Not only does motivation often improve following a period of living away from the academic scene, but also comprehension, sense of proportion, and the ability to deal with content and methods meaningfully.

In this connection, there is a surprising and striking contrast between the concern of the older generation about college dropouts and the limited attention it pays to the desirability of submitting to recurring periods of formal education throughout life, particularly for those in professional fields where the rapid accumulation of new knowledge and change would suggest periodic reexamination of professional competency. Are there parallels here between the prolonged educational ordeal for the younger generation in the civilized world and the various initiation rites of primitive peoples? In both cases, once having passed through the ordeal and having been granted the privileges of adulthood, the initiated and the community are apt to assume that their education is complete.

But the issues raised by the dropout are much broader than the timing of education. As the colleges admit increasingly higher proportions of academically gifted students, both students and colleges are showing a growing preoccupation with matters having to do with the optimal utilization of talent. Is higher education's traditional insistence on disciplined conformity to a prescribed curriculum harmful to the creative few, though perhaps beneficial to the many? Are the students who wish to drop out because they believe that college stifles their creative impulses necessarily those with true creative potential? Or are they those who imagine, as many adolescents seem to do, that the informal life of Bohemia is a necessary condition and stimulus for creativity? How can students with a sustaining and sustained drive toward creativity be distinguished from those with a record of high academic achievement and occasional flashes of brilliance who are, nevertheless, basically hampered by inner conflict and so find it impossible to organize their energies in disciplined and creative ways?

And, then, what about the "match" between student and college? How often is dropping out the result of a mismatch? Should the aim be to evolve educational institutions of various kinds, each of which selects and admits only students with conforming expectations and needs? Or is there virtue in mixing the types of students and even the types of intellectual and sociological characteristics at any one institution?

Other issues raised by the dropout question are highly practical. What is the responsibility of society in training certain classes of professionals? The large supply of medical school applicants not only ensures enough manpower to fill available places in medical schools, but also means that selection is so rigorous and motivation so excellent that dropouts are relatively rare—less than 10 percent of any one class in recent years. The issue then becomes: who has the responsibility to provide the new facilities to educate the added doctors needed by the nation? At the other extreme is the plight of engineering education. There are too few young people interested in engineering, and of those who enter engineering schools far too many drop out before the completion of their course—over one-third in recent years. Whose responsibility is it to develop new methods to decrease the number of dropouts and to increase the number of applicants?

Some of these issues will be dealt with directly in this volume; others will be left to the reader to develop. The findings and hypotheses reported will all have relevance and significance beyond the immediate problems of the dropout, applying in addition to some of the fundamental questions facing our educational system.

DEFINITIONS AND ASSESSMENTS

In this volume, the term "college dropout" refers to any student who leaves college for any period of time, regardless of reason, and thus does not obtain his degree at the same time as the class with which he originally enrolled. The definition is perhaps excessively broad, in that it includes transfer students with non-transfer students and fails to distinguish between students dropping out for differing reasons, such as academic, health, personal, disciplinary, and other cases. At the same time, the definition may be too narrow, since it fails to indicate the limits of the general problem of society's failure to utilize all talent effectively—disregarding, for example, the talented individuals who never attend college at all as well as those who graduate on schedule but whose intellectual and psychological growth in college is far below their capacity.

At any rate, college dropouts as defined above actually outnumber non-dropouts. Only about 40 percent of the nation's students graduate at the date scheduled for the class of their matriculation. The table below shows the variation from college to college in those graduating on schedule:

University of Georgia	35%
University of Iowa	37%
University of Wisconsin	38%
Pennsylvania State University	43%
City University of New York	45%
Hollins College	53%
Princeton University	80%

Summerskill's review of the literature (1962) reports variation in these rates from 12 to 82 percent. Despite changes in colleges, students, curriculum, tuition fees, scholarship aid, and teaching methods, the national dropout rate appears to have been relatively constant since World War II.

Not only do the dropout rates vary from college to college, but also the year of withdrawal and the stated reasons for dropping out. Half of all withdrawals throughout the United States occur by the end of freshman year. At the University of Iowa, over 74 percent of the withdrawals take place before the beginning of the sophomore year. At some other colleges, such as Princeton and Harvard, dropouts are more evenly distributed over the four years.

To some extent, these differences in rates and patterns result from differences in selection and economic background. State institutions which must by law accept all or a majority of the state's high-school graduates on application usually have a high, early dropout rate. Moreover, many of these students do not have the financial reserves with which to meet personal or family reverses.

But there is reason to suspect that other factors, such as motivation, are of considerable importance, apart from the variables of selection and economic background of students. At another state institution, the University of California, for example, only the top 15 percent of high-school graduates are eligible for admission, yet 45 percent of the students withdraw before completing the requirements for a degree. At Pennsylvania State University in 1958, over 74 percent of the freshman class came from the top two-fifths of their high-school class, yet over 50 percent of the class did not graduate in four years, and in spite of a considerable increase in admission selectivity over the previous decade, the withdrawal rate showed little change. The most prestigious colleges nowadays admit only students believed capable of completing their college work; nevertheless, they continue to have dropouts. Even among such a select group as winners of Merit awards, from 10 to 15 percent become dropouts from college.[1]

These variations in patterns and rates of withdrawal, together with evidence of the importance of motivational factors, suggest the need for extensive, systematic research in this area. As Dr. Kubie suggests, the learning process and disruptions in it constitute a significant and complex area. Only research on all phases of the problem from a variety of points of view can hope to result in clarification of the relevant problems. This means that we need demographic studies, sociological studies of institutions, psychological studies of individual students to determine who drops out under what circumstances, and studies of individual students in interaction with different aspects of the college environment. The essays in this volume represent the findings of current research in this area and suggest avenues of research for the future.

THE DROPOUT AND SOCIETY'S VALUE SYSTEM

When a student leaves college before graduating, he evokes a variety of responses from the social milieu, from his college, from his parents, and from himself. These responses may to some degree be appropriate and reasonable, but they are often strongly colored by the kind of emotional excess that an individual's deviation from some widely accepted and institutionalized value system is apt to evoke. The danger is that there then follows a shift in emphasis away from the event of dropping out itself—the rationale for which remains unexamined because the act is judged in advance to be rebellious or perverse —to a tangential debate between those who uphold and those who seem to threaten conventional standards. Experience with dropouts themselves, the majority of whom seem immersed in a struggle to find solutions for private troubles and personal aspirations, suggests that they are far from soliciting such a debate, for it only compounds their difficulties.

In the state of present knowledge, it is of course difficult to demonstrate conclusively to what extent society, whether at the national level or otherwise, is guilty of premature judgments and emotionalism when it looks at the college dropout. There are, however, hints that the guilt is there. The dropout is often referred to as a drain on national resources. He is presumed to represent wasted talent, so that a dropout rate of 50 percent is taken to mean the loss to the national economy and welfare of 50 percent of the most talented population, which then becomes a cause for national concern.

As applied to engineering, this concern becomes particularly acute. The proportion of students completing their bachelor's degree to students matriculating in engineering is particularly small: 36 percent for state universities—as low as 20 percent in some—and 55 percent for private colleges. These figures led the members of a committee on engineering student attrition to conclude:

> We are living in an age of swiftly evolving technologies, as well as of rapidly rising scale of technological needs. Our burgeoning population, the growing emphasis upon research to unlock the new sciences and to develop the new technologies, the mounting needs of industry, and the astronomical needs of our defense and space technology programs are all geared to a much higher order of science and technology in the years ahead. The increasing sophistication of technology in itself is demanding not only a higher level of scientific and technological competence to bring about innovation, but also a much larger total engineering manpower pool to translate innovations into technological progress.
>
> Competition with Europe, Russia, and Japan will continue to mount at an accelerating pace, jeopardizing large sectors of American industry. A recent report of the Engineers Joint Council has made it abundantly evident that the diversion of scientific and engineering manpower resources to the military and space programs has seriously retarded technological growth in many areas vital to our industrial economy and public needs.
>
> Beyond our own needs, there is our growing moral commitment to the free world to assist newly emerging nations in their educational and technological growth.
>
> From a purely competitive point of view, it is a virtual certainty that within a decade, Russia will have an engineering manpower pool exceeding our own by a numerical amount equal to our engineering manpower pool today. During the next decade, Russia will graduate about 1,350,000 engineers, as against an estimated 435,000 in the United States. Today, both nations have approximately equal engineering manpower tools. With Russia able to deploy her technological manpower to suit her aggressive political ambitions, this could be

a decisive force in the struggle between Communism and the free world.

In the face of growing needs, the year-by-year decline in engineering enrollments and graduations poses a severe threat to our nation's wholesome industrial and economic growth, as well as to its influence as a stabilizing force in the free world.[2]

In this case, society concentrates on the need for specially trained manpower to meet certain needs, particularly in competition with foreign countries, and neglects the status of the individual in the educational system and even the possibility of other sources of such manpower.

The questions raised by this engineering report can be generalized as follows: Should the attitude expressed in it apply to fields of less critical national interest? Does the report realistically represent the problem? How does one measure the loss of talent either to the engineering profession or to society as a whole? Realistic answers to such questions can be given more confidently when more information is available about why these students drop out, what happens to them afterward, and what alternative means exist for increasing the supply of engineering manpower.

The engineering report stresses national concerns. What is the overall federal responsibility in the college dropout problem? What type of investment might the federal government be willing to make to deal with it?

Federal concern to date has focused primarily on the high school dropout. Even here, an eminent economist, Martin Weisbrod, after a benefit-cost analysis of an attempt to reduce the high-school dropout rate, concluded that the experimental attempt was successful in many ways but was not profitable on a purely economic basis. While the preventive program kept some students from dropping out of high school, few monetary returns could be proved. Furthermore, "the data suggests that waiting until students are 16 years old to cope with the dropout hazard may be too late. Prevention seems to be difficult at that stage, even when extensive counseling and work-study programs are tried; attitudes and motivations may be too solidified."[3]

These conclusions seem relevant to the college dropout problem as well as to the high-school dropout. At the very least, proposals for extensive programs to prevent dropping out need critical consideration and evaluation by pilot projects before adoption.

The United States is not alone in its concern about college dropouts. In Costa Rica, they are one of the major research interests of the colleges; and at the University of Costa Rica each person leaving the university is interviewed by a social worker.[4] In England, where only the intellectual cream has been admitted to the universities and 75 percent of the students are grant-aided, 20 percent leave college without a degree. Malleson notes the increasing interest in the college dropout at British universities as pressure upon university places increases. But the quotation that follows raises the question whether in England, also, the dropout is too readily consigned to the category of failure and waste, and whether the assumption is too easily made that whatever time he spends in the university is worthless if he does not go on to qualify for a degree: "Since they all stay at least one year at $1,200 per head, the cost of failure to the British community is about twenty million dollars a year."[5]

In the Philippines, the community's extremely liberal attitude toward admission to college is in sharp contrast to the severe selectivity that prevails in England, where only one out of 640 can be accepted. "To most [Philippine] parents, a high school diploma is a sure passport to the university, hence many students are actually enrolled in universities who have neither the inclination nor the aptitude for higher education. The solution appears to be simply one of selection and screening of students who enter the universities."[6] Contrast this proposal with Malleson's disillusionment regarding careful screening as a device to solve the dropout situation in England: "It is our view that improved selection, even if proven methods are available, could hardly make a very great difference .... In our view any substantial reductions in the failure rates must be brought about by modifications in university practice and by improved techniques of managing the difficulties, both academic and personal, that individual students will inevitably meet during their course. Further research in this field can lead in two directions, to the university on the one hand and the student on the other, for it is in their mutual interaction that failure is born."[7]

Next, what response does the dropout receive from his college? How does the problem which he embodies relate to the college's own value system?

At a recent conference on the college dropout sponsored by the United States Office of Education, a preeminent item of discussion was the philosophy of education relating to dropouts. The following questions were raised: What percentage of entering and transfer students "must" be failed? Is the first semester of a student's college career a "trial" period? Is the college dropout really viewed as a problem or a responsibility by a sizable percentage of faculty and administration? Knoell, in her review of the dropout literature, raised the questions: Can the college afford to admit students whose objectives can be met with less than a four-year program? Does the faculty feel that a certain percentage of dismissals or probationary cases is healthy? Does the college regard the freshman year as a screening device, at least in part?[8]

Just as the college dropout can be viewed nationally from an economic perspective, so can he be viewed by the college in terms of the economic implications for facilities, faculties, and students. Robert Iffert, a pioneer in research on the college dropout, has analyzed some of these implications. He notes that a reduced enrollment leads to inefficient use of dormitories, laboratories, libraries, and other facilities. "On the other hand, the practice of overloading facilities with first-time students on the assumption that dropouts will bring enrollment and capacity into line is educationally irresponsible. Admission of replacements in the academic year will help utilization indices, but may seriously complicate programming and scheduling in smaller institutions."[9]

Iffert further notes that the withdrawal rate has implications for college faculties. A high dropout rate must inevitably have an effect upon faculty morale, particularly in relation to teaching introductory freshman courses. It seems likely that there is a circular effect here, with freshman students becoming disenchanted with faculty members who have become disenchanted with the high proportion of student withdrawals. Finally, the student who attends college briefly and obtains little has lost the money used to support this period at school, plus the income he might otherwise have made. Iffert concludes that "no adequate cost figures are available with which to estimate the aggregate cost of unused higher education facilities resulting from student dropout. Responsible administration dictates that these costs be determined institution by institution and that they be related to the costs of preventive measures such as increased faculty salaries."[10]

If the college sees itself as a place where all high-school graduates have an opportunity to experiment with higher education, then a high dropout rate may not detract from its mission. If it sees itself as a place where values and ideals are formed, then the success of the college depends upon the assimilation of those values and ideals by the students, a process that may or may not be related to the dropout rate. If the college's goal is the training of students in certain vocational skills, particularly if these skills are considered equivalent to a bachelor's degree, then a high dropout rate would clearly mean that the college was not effectively attaining its objective.

Obviously, colleges differ in their missions. Therefore, while the dropout phenomenon has ramifications common to all colleges, its significance varies from college to college. Furthermore, the relative amount of approval or disapproval of dropping out also varies. One dean of a liberal arts college has said, "My particular interest in the college dropout problem is simply related to the fact that if you lose 6 or 7 percent of a highly selected group, you want to be very certain you lose them for good reasons." Many of the contributions to this volume will be devoted to what these "good reasons" are, judged on various levels of practical and psychological sophistication. Administratively, of course, each college must decide for itself what represents a reasonable dropout rate and what constitutes a good reason for dropping out. The data and arguments presented here can only be background material for such decisions. And, of course, beyond the educational philosophies at play, the college must analyze the effect of the dropout rate on its own efficiency. What is the effect on the utilization of its physical plant, on student and faculty morale, and on the ratio of lower-level to higher-level courses, for example?

The Parents' Point of View

While government and college administrations ponder dropout rates in general, parents react to individual dropouts. Rationality and objectivity become even more difficult to achieve. Not only are the parents' affection and concern for their child immediately involved, but his dropping out of college also touches upon their own aspirations and upon their own uncertainties as to their role as parents. If the parental conclusion is that dropping out is a failure, then it may lead to the further conclusion that the parents have failed as parents. If the departure from college is attributed to psychopathology, this may also imply failure to the parents—failure to give the child something he needed or failure to help him in time of need. On the other hand, if dropping out expresses courage to pursue one's own goals, then the parents may feel proud that they have helped to give their child certain strengths which allow for individuality.

As Levenson points out . . . , parents interpret dropping out according to their own life experiences. For many, the child's admission to college, particularly a select college, represents a fulfilled dream and the fruition of years of struggle and hope. Any interruption of the smooth course of this dream shatters the image of hope created during the worthwhile years of effort. For example, the parents of a freshman who was having psychotic delusions and hallucinations struggled to keep their son in college. When the university insisted that he withdraw to receive psychiatric help, the parents sought to take him home for a week, after which they hoped he would be able to return. Another student who had reached the decision to drop out told of the struggle with his parents. They called him names, interpreted his behavior as an expression of hostility toward them, and said: "This will cost you $150,000. You'll kick yourself in the pants ten years from now. You're lazy and a coward. Don't expect to be able to bury your head in the ground."

These reactions are extreme but consistent with the attitudes of a substantial group of parents of dropouts. But they are not the only attitude parents express toward dropping out. Some are indifferent. Some, viewing it as wise, encourage it. Others see it as the only choice, and many view it with mixed feelings. Some parental attitudes are helpful to the student; others are destructive. Some are realistic; others, unrealistic. One of the functions of this volume, . . . is to help parents and others have more realistic attitudes toward dropping out of college and to enable them to be more sophisticated and effective in their attempts to assist young people in their search for valid education goals.

The Attitude of the Student

Not the least important is the attitude of the dropout toward himself and his own action, which must take into account the reaction of society, college, and family toward what he does. Indeed, he may have many attitudes toward dropping out, both at any one time and at different times. Previous to becoming a dropout, he may feel quite differently than immediately afterward. His feelings a number of years later may change still further. Pervin's chapter on long-term follow-up studies of dropouts documents some of these changes in attitudes.

Students' attitudes toward withdrawal are rarely independent of parental feelings. The interaction between student and parental attitudes is complex, involving rebellion, passivity, identification, counter-identification, and other dynamic processes. . .

Not only the event of dropping out but also the expressed reasons may be influenced by factors of which the dropout is not fully aware. One student wanted to leave college but could not decide to take the positive step of doing so. His partly unconscious strategy was to perform so poorly in his academic work that he would be required to leave. Obviously, disciplinary withdrawals, particularly when out of character, may have strong unconscious determinants, as in the case of a student whose brother, with whom he had long been in rivalry, had recently attracted parental attention by leaving college to live a bohemian life. It was in this setting that the student stole an item from a college-owned store in obvious fashion.

The social setting and size of the dropout rate similarly may influence withdrawals. The student at a large state institution with a high dropout rate may find it possible to be relatively comfortable about dropping out. In sharp contrast is the student who is the first representative of his home town at a prestigious college. Dropping out may mean to him that he has let down not only himself but his family and home town in a particularly conspicuous manner.

Over the years, predominant conventional wisdom has frowned on dropping out. This negative attitude has been summarized by Reik as follows: "To the colleges, dropping out appears equivalent to a kind of death, if only an intellectual one. Dropouts are referred to in academic circles as 'casualties' or 'non-survivors.' The dropout rate is called the 'mortality' rate."[11] These negative attitudes have not only had the effect of placing the dropout under increased pressure but have also often determined policies, particularly those concerning readmission and even concerning transfer students.

As this volume indicates, the tide seems to be turning in this value system—turning, at least, to the point where there are beginning signs of realization that individual dropouts need from society the forbearance and understanding that can come from a careful hearing in an atmosphere as free as possible from prejudice. The pioneering long-term follow-up studies of the fate of dropouts referred to in this volume have led to the discovery that many of them are not permanent dropouts, and that leaving college for a period, voluntarily or even involuntarily, may be useful to individual and society. R. Sargent Shriver, former director of the Peace Corps, has aptly summarized this more hopeful attitude: "If the college sophomore wants to drop out of school, let him. Let the bored or the confused or the burned-out undergraduate have a short, meaningful interlude—a sojourn in reality—for a year or two years, so that he can come back revitalized, committed, concerned enough to finish both college and graduate work."[12]

CONFLICTING VALUES OF
SOCIETY AND THE DROPOUT CONCERNING
THE UTILIZATION OF TALENT

When a Merit Scholar or an apparently gifted student decides to leave college—an event that is less uncommon than many parents realize—society is apt to be puzzled and uncomprehending, if not alarmed. Its concern with the apparent failure to utilize talent leaves out of account, however, two considerations that seem very important from the dropout's point of view. First, many college dropouts challenge conventional standards of talent. And, second, many of these young people are struggling to free themselves from bonds and shackles preventing the free and effective use of their talents.

As the Harvard psychologists Bruner[13] and McClelland[14] point out, a new kind of meritocracy has developed with heavy emphasis on academic excellence as measured by grades, skill in taking examinations, and finding solutions to problems set by others. Yet, Holland and Astin[15] find that grades often have little relationship to such desirable attributes as leadership, vocational achievement, creativity in science and the arts. McClelland asks, "What of the little boy who doesn't make it academically? Is he a failure? Can he feel that he can contribute importantly to society if he does not make the academic grade? Overstressing academic merit can discourage young people with types of talent that are very important for our society and can create in them a discontent and sense of frustration that lasts a lifetime."[16]

Some of the dropouts seem to be rebelling against and challenging this meritocracy, and at the same time show certain of the attributes of creative people noted by MacKinnon: a lack of interest in small details and facts for their own sake, a freedom from conventional constraints and inhibitions, less inclination to strive for achievement in settings where conforming behavior is expected and rewarded, independence of thought and action leading to unwillingness to accept the interpretations and values of their teachers.[17]   In short, these students, as MacKinnon observes, are not always to their professors' liking.

It is interesting that many of the issues that are of concern to college students and which sometimes lead to their dropping out are relevant to characteristics of creative people.   Consider the following characteristics of such people as noted by MacKinnon and how frequently dropouts are seen to be struggling to define themselves in these terms: some signs of psychopathology but clear evidence of adequate control mechanisms; openness to feelings and emotions, including the feminine side of one's nature; ability to admit complexity and disorder without becoming anxious about the resulting chaos; flexibility and spontaneity; tolerance for the tension of holding opposing values; openness to ideals and freedom to explore them; freedom to rebel as opposed to fear of doing so or compulsive need to do so. In one way or another, dropouts not infrequently complain that their college environment is not assisting them in acquiring these characteristics, but that college may do so at some other place or at some future time.

The question of how students become blocked or freed to use their talents involves the study of intra-psychic conflict as well as conflict in the social sphere. Part II of this book deals at greater length with the problem of the utilization of talent—a subject that is, of course, closely bound up with dropping out and has important psychological facets. Admittedly, the two spheres, psychological and social, are mere abstractions, and no one can say where one begins and the other leaves off. But for practical purposes, particularly in the case of the gifted dropout where the interaction between society and the individual shows clear signs of needing improvement, it is well to examine this interaction with care in the hope that the way will open up for mutually beneficial new solutions. But these solutions will probably always have to take into account the unique needs of individual students, rather than rely on general formulae, however admirable in principle the latter may seem. Perhaps the only general proposition that society and the dropout can both accept—especially at a time when mass methods and sentiments have an increasingly powerful appeal—is one that seeks to preserve the individual and to prevent him from becoming lost in the crowd.

REFERENCES

1. A. W. Astin, "Personal and environmental factors associated with college dropouts among high aptitude students," *Journal of Educational Psychology*, 1964, 55, pp. 219–227.
2. "Engineering student attrition," New York: Engineering Manpower Commission, 1963.
3. B. A. Weisbrod, "Preventing high school Dropouts—a Benefit cost analysis," The Brookings Institution, November 1963.
4. M. L. Coronado, "Costa Rica," in D. Funkenstein (ed.), *The student and mental health*, New York: World Federation for Mental Health, 1959.
5. N. Malleson, "Great Britain," in *ibid.*, p. 48.
6. E. Aldaba-Lim, "Philippines," in *ibid.*, p. 59.
7. N. Malleson, "Student performance at University College, London, 1948–1951," *Universities Quarterly*, May 1958, pp. 288–319.
8. Dorothy Knoell, "Needed research on college dropouts," in J. R. Montgomery (ed.), *Proceedings of the research conference on college dropouts* (Cooperative Research Project No. F-065), Knoxville, Tenn.: University of Tennessee, 1964, pp. 54–83.
9. R. E. Iffert, "Institutional implications—facilities, faculties, students," paper presented at the Princeton University Conference, October 8, 1964.
10. *Ibid.* For a review of studies of institutional efforts to help college dropouts, see the appendix to this volume: "Programs and selected publications relating to college dropouts," by Montgomery and Hills.
11. L. E. Reik, "The dropout problem," *The Nation*, May 19, 1962, pp. 442–446.
12. R. S. Shriver, *Wesleyan University News*, 1964, 2, p. 1.
13. J. Bruner, *The process of education*, Cambridge: Harvard University Press, 1960.
14. D. C. McClelland, "Encouraging excellence," *Daedalus*, Fall 1961, pp. 711–724.
15. J. L. Holland and A. W. Astin, "The prediction of the academic, artistic, and social achievement of undergraduates of superior scholastic aptitude," *Journal of Educational Psychology*, 1962, 53, pp. 132–143.
16. McClelland, *op. cit.*, p. 714.
17. D. W. MacKinnon, "Nature and nurture of creative talent," *American Psychologist*, 1962, 17, pp. 484–495.

Needed: Another Seven to Eleven Billion Dollars

By ROGER FREEMAN

American colleges and universities are in trouble. Not that many of them are likely to become bankrupt or go out of business, though some of them probably will. But there is a clear danger that higher education may not be able to do the job which this nation expects it to do in the years ahead if it is to survive and maintain its leadership in the free world.

Our institutions of higher learning—to which I shall henceforth simply refer as I.H.L.—managed to more than double their student enrollment since the end of World War II, to multiply their research activities many times over, and to sharply expand their services to government, communities, industry and to the public in general. In the process, the role and stature of higher education has grown tremendously. Its position in the life of the nation and in the councils of government and business is beyond anything known to earlier generations.

This dramatic advance did not come easily. There never seemed to be enough manpower or facilities to do the things which were demanded of the institutions or which their own aspirations called for. Much had to be improvised, some ambitious plans deferred. As time went on, administrators, scholars, trustees, and alumni increasingly turned into money raisers. College presidents became accustomed to devoting much or most of their time not to academic pursuits or intramural problems but to lugging around a begging cup or to camping in legislative halls to lobby for higher appropriations.

We have come a long way but the crest of the hill is not nearly in sight. With each passing year the mountain ahead looks higher, the slope steeper, and a much needed respite farther away. Over the past

From *Crisis in College Finance*, by Roger A. Freeman, Institute for Social Science Research, Washington, D. C. Reprinted by permission of the Institute for Social Science Research, pp. 11–18.

twenty years I.H.L. have added almost four million students to their rolls. In the next five years they will be called upon to accommodate another one and a half million or more. Will they be able to do it? Clearly, the nation must, in this competitive and hostile world, offer *all* of its youth, regardless of color or economic background, an opportunity to develop its God-given talents to the utmost. It cannot retrench from this commitment. Nor can it afford to relax its research effort without running the risk of falling behind other countries bent on scientific advance.

The questions to which we must find answers are: Will the present effort of institutions, of governments, of donors, of students and their families be adequate to reach the essential goals or will they fall short? Will all those qualified and willing to acquire a higher education find adequate opportunity in the years ahead? Will our traditional methods of raising money and running colleges suffice or must we seek new ways of operating and financing them? What must we do *now* to forestall disaster in years to come?

Why Higher Education Needs More Money

Somehow, money has always seemed to run short in higher education. But several trends converge in the 1960's which give the old story a particularly ominous note. The low birth rates of the depression-1930's and of the war years resulted in a college-age population (eighteen to twenty-one years) which remained virtually stable at about nine million. In proportion to the rest of the population it declined. But the picture is changing. The "tidal wave" of post-war babies which swept through the elementary and secondary system is now concluding its twelve-year cycle in the lower schools and reaching college age. It began to pound on the doors of academe in the fall of 1964. By 1970 we shall have five million more eighteen to twenty-one year-olds than we had in 1960, a fifty per cent growth in ten years. In 1980 we shall have another two and a half million. The educational aspirations of our young people have been on the upgrade and pushed college enrollment from twenty-four per cent of the eighteen to twenty-one year group in the fall of 1951 to thirty-eight per cent in 1960. A few years ago the Office of Education projected the "enrollment percentage" in 1969/70 at forty per cent; as of now, forty-six per cent may be a more likely figure, forty-eight per cent a possibility.

Some observers feel that too many young people with inadequate ability, desire or tenacity are being pressured into college by ambitious parents and that admission standards ought to be tightened. But there is also evidence that many youngsters with sufficient intellectual capacity fail to enroll. Viewing the strong and persistent trend there can be little doubt that an increasing percentage of our young people will continue their formal education beyond high school graduation. By all appearances enrollment in I.H.L. will, during the 1960's, jump from three and a half million to between six and seven million. That calls for a huge expansion in manpower and plant facilities.

But numbers tell only part of the story. Knowledge and the need for it are expanding at an unprecedented pace, demanding ever greater specialization and the addition of more departments and increasingly costly laboratories and equipment. The prime factor, however, in all scientific advance is the ingenuity and technical competence of those who man the institutions. We need scholars who are able to penetrate more deeply into the mysteries of nature and of the human mind and human action, and we need more of them than we are now getting. And, whether we like it or not, there is a relationship between the level of compensation and the caliber of men and women whom we can attract into academic life.

Academic salaries have long lagged behind the advance in the general income level and behind the earnings in independent professions or industry. Pay scales must be substantially elevated if I.H.L. are to do justice by their major tasks: to train the natural intelligence of our young people, to do the research necessary for our national well-being and security and for the maintenance of American leadership in the free world, and to give governments and the public the services they have a right to expect.

All of those who have studied the needs of higher education agree that the job ahead calls for far larger sums than we are now allocating. To be sure, there are many other difficult questions to be resolved and I shall discuss some of them later on. But many observers agree with the panel on education of the Rockefeller Brothers Fund Midcentury Project, which concluded in 1958:

> All of the problems of the schools lead us back sooner or later to one basic problem—financing. It is a problem with which we cannot afford to cope half-heartedly. Education has always been essential to the achievement of our political and moral objectives. It has emerged as the necessary ingredient in our technological advancements. And now events have underscored its value in terms of sheer survival.[1]

The Rockefeller panel suggested that educational funds at least be doubled within ten years. Actually, education has been doing better than that for some years and several reports have suggested a speed-up in the rate of growth. So the question is, how much is enough?

How Big an I.H.L. Budget for 1970?

To project a budget for some years ahead is not simply a matter of applying the expected rate of enrollment growth to the current budget. There is much demand—and some hope—for increased efficiency (or "productivity" as industry calls it) and for savings from structural and technological improvements. On the other hand there is the matter of salaries which, as I mentioned before, must be substantially raised. And salaries are, of course, the biggest item in the educational budget.

To estimate a future educational budget takes much detailed study and above all a balanced judgment of institutional operations and of the country's fiscal and economic prospects. Several committees and individual researchers in recent years have selected 1970 as a convenient target year to project higher educational finances.[2]   Unfortunately, some of them excluded from their computations such items as for example organized research institutes or auxiliary enterprises (dormitories, dining halls, etc.) so that some adjustments are needed to make their figures comparable. But let us first review the historical record.

EXPENDITURES OF I.H.L. IN SELECTED YEARS 1940 TO 1964
(in billions of dollars)

Academic year	1939/40	1949/50	1959/60	1963/64
Current operations & student aid	$ 0.5	$ 1.8	$ 4.7	$ 7.7
Auxiliary enterprises	.1	.5	.9	1.5
Capital outlays	.1	.4	1.3	1.3
Total Expenditures	$ 0.7	$ 2.7	$ 6.9	$10.5

Between 1950 and 1960 total expenditures grew 159 per cent, and when adjusted for the shrinking value of the dollar, 110 per cent.   In the succeeding four years the pace accelerated.

President Eisenhower's Committee on Education Beyond the High School headed by Devereux Josephs concluded in 1957 that I.H.L. would need by 1970 $6.8 to $7.0 billion, not including auxiliary enterprises, student aid or organized research. Adding an estimate for those items and for price changes since 1957 we would arrive at a total of about $12 billion.[3]   In 1959 two of our best-known public finance experts, Harvard economics professor Seymour E. Harris and Brookings Institution president Robert D. Calkins, arrived at a total of $9.8 billion for 1969/70, excepting capital outlays and auxiliary facilities. Adjusted, the total would run to between $13 and $14 billion.[4] Alvin C. Eurich, vice president of the Fund for the Advancement of Education, and one of the country's most knowledgeable men in higher education prepared a comparable estimate.[5]

A later projection of the Office of Education, prepared by Selma J. Mushkin and W. Robert Bokelman, placed budgetary needs far higher. It suggested that instructional costs will triple and capital outlays double between 1958 and 1971; the 1962 report of the Department of Health, Education and Welfare placed operating costs of I.H.L. in 1970 at $15.5 billion and capital additions at $2.5 billion for a combined total of $18 billion.[6] In 1964 the Office of Education projected 1970 spending at only $13.8 billion.[7] But a sample survey whose results it released in August 1965 disclosed a 28 per cent growth in current income and expenditures between 1962 and 1964 which rate, if continued, would bring total spending of I.H.L. in 1970 to $18 billion or more. That may well be the most likely outcome, by present indications.

Several methods have been suggested for fuller and more effective use of the available manpower and facilities which could keep the rise in financial requirements to more moderate proportions. A number of institutions have introduced such methods and others are experimenting with them. But long-established practices change slowly in education and it is quite uncertain just how optimistic we can be in expecting a widespread or general adoption of cost-saving measures.

The various projections I quoted foresee a rise from an actual outlay of $6.8 billion in 1959/60 to a requirement between $12 and $18 billion in 1969/70. Trends during the 1950's and early 1960's suggest that expenditures of I.H.L. will multiply between two and two and a half times between 1960 and 1970 with a good chance for an increase of about 120 per cent. This means then that I.H.L. must find an additional $7 to $11 billion during the 1960's. Where are these vast amounts to come from?

How Can I.H.L. Raise an Additional $7 to $11 Billion?

The major sources of funds for I.H.L. are: state appropriations, student charges, gifts and endowment earnings, federal research grants and contracts. In 1963–64 I.H.L. derived their current income as indicated on the following page.

Can such established major sources of higher educational income as state appropriations, student fees, donations, research grants, be sufficiently expanded during the current decade to meet the requirements? Or should the federal government's share in the general support of I.H.L. which so far has been minor be substantially expanded?

So far, the traditional sources of higher educational support have certainly displayed a strong capacity for expansion and they continue to do so. Income of I.H.L. has on the average more than doubled

	All I.H.L.	Public	Private
State and local governments	25%	43%	2%
Student tuitions and fees	20	11	30
Auxiliary enterprises (mostly student room and board)	17	17	17
Endowment earnings and gifts	9	3	16
Federal research grants, contracts and services	18	14	25
Other federal funds	4	5	2
Other sources	7	7	8
	100%	100%	100%

Source: U.S. Office of Education, *Preliminary Report of Financial Statistics of Institutions of Higher Education, F.Y., 1964,* July 1965.

every ten years and has been rising at a faster rate than the country's economic resources, particularly in recent years. Current and plant fund receipts climbed from .9 per cent of the national income in 1930 to 1.3 per cent in 1950 and may be estimated to equal 2 per cent of the national income at the present time. This is a greater share than the Soviet Union devotes to higher education. To be sure, such comparisons are tenuous, to say the least, because of statistical uncertainties and differences in educational structure. But appropriations for higher educational institutions have been showing less than spectacular increases in the U.S.S.R. budget in recent years and barely equal one per cent of the national income.

It is exactly the sharp increases for American education in recent years which have caused some observers to believe that state governments, students' families and donors may have exhausted their capacity and cannot keep raising their contribution at the past rate. Secretary of Health, Education, and Welfare Arthur S. Flemming published a report in January 1961, on the day before he left office, in which he suggested that the traditional sources of revenue "will certainly be inadequate to meet increasing needs in full," and that the facts "point strongly toward federal assistance as a necessity."[8]

The American Council on Education declared simultaneously: "All the major studies show that after traditional sources of income including student tuition and fees, have been stretched to the limit, there will still be a large gap that can be filled only by greater support from the federal government."[9] The chairman of President Kennedy's Task Force on Education, President Frederick L. Hovde of Purdue University, testified in March 1961 before the United States House of Representatives Education Committee: "I don't think that the taxing power and the ability of the states is sufficient to meet this kind of growth in the next ten years." He specified "that the highest priority need of colleges and universities, both public and private, is for general operational support and particularly for faculty salaries."[10]

Reviewing ten recent books on the subject, J. Kenneth Little, former United States Deputy Commissioner of Education, found that the authors showed a surprising amount of agreement on the need for strongly increased federal financial support of higher education.[11]

Will the Federal Government Supply the Needed Funds?

What plans have been developed to have the federal government contribute a significant share of the $7 to $11 billion by which the revenues of our I.H.L. are to be increased during the 1960's? It will come as a surprise to many that there are no such plans on record. No national group in higher education has requested federal support of academic salaries—which as President Hovde in his above-quoted statement declared should have the highest priority—or for a substantial share of their other operational costs. Nor has any President of the United States ever recommended sizeable grants-in-aid either for current operations or for general construction at I.H.L. President Eisenhower's Committee on Education beyond the High School and President Kennedy's Task Force on Education advocated federal grants-in-aid for the construction of higher educational facilities, but neither President translated those recommendations into legislative proposals. In 1961 and again in 1963, President Kennedy proposed loans to I.H.L. for the construction of academic buildings. But such loans are, according to the testimony of most witnesses from higher education of little if any help to institutions, most of which can borrow at equally or more favorable terms from other sources. As a rule I.H.L. do not wish to finance their plant needs through bonds.

The failure to advance major programs of federal aid to higher education has been criticized, and President David D. Henry of the University of Illinois complained at the annual meeting of the American Council on Education in October 1962 that the concern of United States Presidents seemed to be mere lip service: "Presidents have made speeches on the general importance of higher education, but the administrative practices of their departments and the thrust of their own legislative recommendations have not reflected this approach or concern."[12]

The grant-in-aid programs for higher education which President Kennedy proposed in his 1963 Message on Education were of relatively small size. They aimed to assist teacher institutes, general university extension, student work-study programs, graduate schools, library construction and acquisitions, etc. and totaled about $250 million per annum. If enacted they would have provided no more than about two to three per cent of the prospective over-all budgets. To be sure Congress approved, and President Johnson signed, in December 1963, the Higher Education Facilities Act which provides $290 million in grants for science, engineering, and other specified types of college construction and $120 million in loans for academic buildings per annum. But those grants cannot be used for general classroom or administrative buildings nor, of course, for operating purposes and are thus quite limited in their application. They equal barely three per cent of the higher education budget. Congress authorized a substantial increase in the amount of construction grants in 1965 but retained the restriction on the use of the funds.

How can we explain this obvious discrepancy between the size of the budgetary requirements which, according to many students of the problem, cannot be met from the traditional sources, and the nature and magnitude of current and proposed federal programs? Are the proposals intended to be mere down payments for far larger programs yet to be advanced? Are the plans deliberately kept small so as to arouse less opposition? Should we then regard them as merely a "foot in the door?" Or are statements about the inadequacy of state and local revenues, student fees and donations not to be taken at face value? Is it then assumed that the sources which have traditionally supplied most of the educational funds for I.H.L. *are* capable and willing to continue providing them? Do differences of opinion within higher education cause the President and Congress to go easy on aid programs? Or are there other reasons for the apparent reluctance to advance a program of massive assistance to I.H.L.?

Obstacles to Federal Aid

At the annual meeting of the American Council on Education in 1962, at which President David Henry of the University of Illinois made the earlier-quoted critical remark about the inadequacy of presidential plans for aiding higher education, Clarence Scheps, vice president and controller of Tulane University, advanced his own explanation:

> Perhaps the most fundamental reason why there has been no major federal aid to higher education is the basic and instinctive objection felt deeply to many, including those in education, to the general proposition of federal support to higher education. There are a great

many sincere individuals who are concerned over any possibility of federal control over our schools and colleges.[13]

Only ten years earlier the Committee on Financing Higher Education sponsored by the Association of American Universities had strongly objected to an expansion of federal activities in education for that very reason.

Many of the participants in the debate over federal aid do not realize that the American tradition of education as a state-local and private responsibility is more deeply rooted than appears on the surface. They fail to understand the widespread aversion to giving the national government a major role in the field. Over the past quarter-century, federal spending for domestic public services jumped from less than $5 billion to $45 billion and grants-in-aid to the states from less than $1 billion to over $10 billion. But efforts to enact a program of general federal support for the operation or construction of schools or colleges have so far failed and face a doubtful future. Experience with federal aid programs in welfare, urban renewal, highways or agriculture, as well as sheer logic have convinced many that large-scale federal support would sooner or later lead to federal control of the institutions and their programs. This may be the basic reason why no broad popular support for major federal educational programs has developed, as members of Congress well know from their incoming mail and as observers of the national scene have regretfully acknowledged.

There is of course nothing new about federal moneys being channeled into education—now between $2 and $5 billion annually, depending on definition—with a major share going to I.H.L. Some of our largest universities have disclosed that almost half their revenues come from the federal treasury. But in most instances the federal agencies are not *aiding* higher education; they are *using* it for their own purposes. Most of the amounts which the Department of Defense, Atomic Energy Commission, or National Aeronautics and Space Administration pay to I.H.L. are compensations for services. They can no more be called "federal aid" than similar and far larger sums flowing into private industry. Those contracts benefit grantor and grantee equally, as may be expected of freely negotiated and fair contracts. Federal grants to I.H.L. for their instructional programs now amount to but a few million dollars and are insignificant in their budgets.

Advocates of federal aid tend to be impatient with the "federal control" argument which they deem insubstantiated, artificial, and a mere sham to cloak the true motives of the opponents. They point at the urgent need to multiply federal *general purpose* funds for I.H.L. and press for prompt action. But their demand has run into another and no less formidable roadblock—the church and state controversy.

Out of more than 2,000 I.H.L. in the United States, over 1,300 are under private auspices and 800 of them are church-connected. If the federal government were to aid only public institutions, as President Truman's Commission on Higher Education recommended in 1947, it would further tip a balance which in recent years has become increasingly lopsided. Until 1950 student enrollment was about evenly divided between public and private I.H.L. The sharply growing discrepancy between public and private tuitions was probably the main reason for the subsequent change. Of the 2.1 million enrollment increase between fall 1948 and 1964, 78 per cent went to public and merely 22 per cent to private I.H.L. So the private enrollment share dropped to 35.7 per cent. If this trend continues, it will dip to 33 per cent or less in 1970 and to 20 per cent later on, as a projection by the Fund for the Advancement of Education suggested.[14]

This is not at all unlikely, considering the relative size of tuitions and salaries. If large-scale federal support were made available to public institutions exclusively, hundreds of private colleges would within a measurable time have to close or turn public and only a limited number of prestige institutions would be able to survive. Such an event, many hold, would be a calamity. A free choice among a large number of diverse colleges and universities and a reasonable balance between public and private institutions are widely regarded as sources of strength of higher education and as essential parts of the American tradition which ought to be preserved. Few would favor a quasi-monopoly of public higher education for all but a few students from well-to-do families. It is thus understandable that Congress has always been careful to treat public and private I.H.L. alike and to make benefits available to both on an equal and nondiscriminatory basis.

But to appropriate federal funds for church-connected institutions raises some weighty problems, constitutional and otherwise. Convictions on this point run deep on both sides of the controversy and allow little leeway for compromise. Some will not vote for grants-in-aid if they include private institutions and some if they exclude them. Some object to proposed restrictions on the use of federal funds because they are too tight and some because they are not tight enough.

Some of our best brains have tried to devise a formula that can satisfy if not all then at least a majority in both Houses of Congress sufficient to pass a bill. For some years a construction aid program was kicked back and forth between the House and the Senate by apparent disagreement over technical points and terminology which revealed basic underlying conflicts. When a tenuous compromise was reached in December 1963 on a small construction program, it was concluded with many misgivings. Use of the funds was severely restricted. The difficulty of arriving at an agreement between the two Houses suggests that the drive for an expansion in coverage faces an uphill battle. That is why President Johnson, in an apparently correct appraisal of the political situation, refrained in his 1965 Education Message from suggesting anything approaching federal aid for general classroom construction or current operations at I.H.L. No compromise appears possible nor magic formula in sight for federal assistance to faculty salaries although they are the most critical item in the higher educational budget.

The record of the long drawn-out battle for federal aid to education is an ironic comment on a statement about the speed and magnitude of federal action by the Problems and Policies Committee of the American Council on Education in February, 1958: "The truth seems to be that the federal government is the only agency which can act with sufficient speed and on a scale large enough to enable schools, colleges and universities to accomplish their tasks."[15]

Only after many years of battle and after several defeats was a small program of federal grants for selected types of construction at I.H.L. enacted late in 1963. Even with an enlargement in 1965 there is hardly a chance that the federal government might supply a significant share of the $12 to $18 billion which our I.H.L. will, according to the cited projections, need by the end of this decade. Seymour E. Harris and Robert D. Calkins, whose projections I cited earlier, both of whom favor increased federal funds for higher education, projected only moderate increases by 1970. Harris showed federal operational support at $500 million, Calkins at $250 million, in addition to unspecified but obviously limited construction funds.

Does this sound too pessimistic? Then why has no President of the United States ever sent to Congress a program of federal grants-in-aid for the general operation or construction of our I.H.L.? Advisory committees which Presidents Franklin D. Roosevelt, Truman, Eisenhower and Kennedy appointed suggested such plans. But none of those Presidents saw fit to transmit them to the Congress. Surely nobody will assert that the past four Presidents—or their predecessors—lacked interest in higher education. Why have even small-scale and highly restricted proposals invariably run into trouble? Are we to believe that the members of Congress are prejudiced against education? Is it not more likely that basic ideological convictions run too deep to be easily compromised? If a hundred-year battle over federal aid to education has not been able to produce a program of general federal support, what reason do we have to believe that the philosophical conflicts will soon be resolved and the situation changed radically within the next few years?

A Case for Federal Aid?

All of this does not mean that the national government should not or cannot aid higher education. There is much support and, in fact, a good case for some type of federal action, and the platforms of both political parties subscribe to it. But it seems that an effective approach has not yet been used which can accomplish the objective while avoiding the obstacles which have defeated the drive for federal aid year after year.

Few will question that there is a strong national interest in education. Under a division of labor, such as was established by our federal system of government, each level of government has a vital interest in the activities and satisfactory performance at the other levels. The word "federal" itself implies an obligation of mutual aid when needed. There is little doubt but that the national government by imposing an exorbitant tax burden has made the financing of education more difficult. If states, communities, and institutions are unable to meet their educational responsibilities and the national government has the necessary means at its disposal, then it appears proper that it render assistance.

Some will of course question the proposition that the federal government has the necessary means at its disposal. The national treasury is experiencing a succession of vast budgetary deficits and is probably in no position to engage in large new commitments. But let us assume that through restraint upon other expenditures and with the help of increased revenues the budget is brought into closer balance—however hypothetical that case may be at this time. Could the national government aid higher education by indirect methods if, as it seems, the direct approach appears blocked by insurmountable obstacles? If it is the magnitude of the federal tax burden which restricts the capacity of states and individuals to pay for higher education, could not carefully designed tax remission remedy the situation?

Tax Relief—an Indirect Way of Aiding Higher Education

About ten years ago a new type of proposal was advanced by the Yale Alumni Board and later sponsored by the American Council on Education and numerous other educational organizations: income tax relief for students and their families. The plan aimed to enable institutions to levy higher tuitions and fees without placing the whole burden upon those paying them. Such an indirect method of helping I.H.L. would avoid the two major roadblocks: the argument over federal control and the church-state issue.

The first educational tax relief plan was introduced in the 83rd Congress in 1953, and every succeeding Congress saw a substantial increase in the number of such bills. Over 100 bills on educational tax benefits have been introduced in the 89th Congress. There is probably no single type of proposal pending in Congress on which so many bills have been submitted, in both Houses and by members of both political parties.

Despite this apparent popularity of educational tax relief plans in Congress, no such bill or amendment was ever reported out by a proper committee (House Ways and Means or Senate Finance) or received consideration on the floor of either House in the 1950's although innumerable speeches praising the idea were delivered in both Houses. By the end of the 1950's some of the organizations which used to pursue this type of legislation tired of their repeated failures and decided to devote their efforts to securing direct grants-in-aid.

Deficiencies of Educational Tax Relief Plans and Their Correction

How can we explain the apparent paradox of the consistent failure of a proposal which, judging by the number of bills and speeches, enjoys great popularity with members of Congress? The cause probably lies in technical deficiencies of the bills which, if enacted might defeat the purpose. With but few exceptions educational tax relief bills can be divided into three types:

a) Deductions: The cost of tuitions, fees, and also possibly books, supplies, travel and added living expenses would be deductible from adjusted gross income up to a specified upper limit.

b) Exemptions: A student or his family would be entitled to one or several additional personal exemptions of $600.

c) Credits: A specified flat percentage—most frequently 30 per cent—of the sum of tuitions, fees, and also certain other expenses attributable to attendance at an I.H.L. would be offset against the *tax liability*, rather than deducted from the income base as under (a) above.

The first two methods (a) and (b) above have been criticized for giving the greatest benefit—up to 91 per cent of the expenses involved (by the tax rates in effect until 1963)—to persons in high tax and income brackets and only 20 per cent to those of moderate income. A flat credit of 30 per cent or some similar percentage would reduce the amount of benefits going to the wealthy but would not provide enough relief to students from low- or middle-income families. None of the three methods would enable institutions to boost their tuitions and fees without burdening the student and his family with most of the increase, unless they happen to be in a high tax bracket. In other words, these proposals would help the least where help is needed the most. They would add little strength to the finances of I.H.L.

A 100 Per Cent Tax Credit or a Sliding Tax Credit Schedule?

More recently it was proposed to permit a 100 per cent offset against the federal income tax liability for tuition and fees, and for donations, instead of deductions from the tax base. That would offer substantial help both to institutions and to families with college students. Ceilings would have to be placed on such credits to avoid an incentive for exorbitant tuition charges and to limit the resulting revenue loss. Such a plan would be an effective and fair vehicle for carrying the tax relief idea into practice. But it has so far found little support in Congress. A low ceiling such as for example $100 would offer only limited aid. But as the ceiling is raised it becomes increasingly difficult to maintain a balance between low-tuition (public) and high-tuition (private) institutions.

As a compromise between conflicting interests and ideas a sliding tax-credit plan was developed in 1963 which would grant a 100 per cent tax offset (or close to 100 per cent) up to a low maximum (say, $100) and a series of declining percentages up to a liberal maximum of about $1,500. Another version would grant a 75 per cent credit for the first $200 of tuitions, fees, books, supplies and equipment, 25 per cent of the next $300 and 10 per cent of the next $100.

The sliding tax-credit plan avoids the shortcomings of some of the other proposals and soon gained the support of leaders in both political parties. It was debated in the Senate in February 1964 and narrowly defeated. Most observers agreed that a clear majority of the Senate favored the plan but that strong pressure by the President and the Treasury Department caused several of its original sponsors to vote against it when it appeared that the proposal was about to be adopted. However, the closeness of the final vote—45 to 48—and the evident strong popularity which the plan enjoys among the broad public encouraged its sponsors who announced that they intended to continue the fight to victory. The proposal was reintroduced in January 1965 with greatly broadened sponsorship.

Neither the tax-credit plan nor any other single measure offers a "solution" to the financial problem in higher education. But tax credits for educational expenses and donations can make a significant contribution toward helping higher education weather the tremendous increase which the institutions are facing in the second half of the 1960's, and assist many families to bear the heavy cost of sending their children to college.

To be sure, the cost of attending college has grown no faster than the general cost of living in the past twenty-five years and, in fact, it has risen proportionately less than average family income. That enrollment keeps climbing steeply is in itself proof that the colleges have not been pricing themselves out of the market. But that economic fact offers slim comfort to the moderate income family which is trying to put several children through college. More of our young people now enroll in higher education, which places a severe strain on parental budgets.

Institutions try to avoid boosting tuitions and fees in proportion to spiraling costs, and some have in recent years sought means of controlling expenditures more effectively by fuller use of the available physical and manpower resources. An increasing number of I.H.L. are changing to all-year operation which not only reduces the need for additional construction but also enables some faculty members to earn more and some students to complete their degree in fewer years. Some colleges are improving the utilization of their building space which has been traditionally poor on most campuses. The trend toward community colleges helps to keep down the outlays of students—who can then continue to live at home—as well as to reduce institutional needs for construction and operations.

A reversal of the long-range trend toward course proliferation and lower faculty-student ratios, the use of television and teaching machines, cooperation between neighboring colleges, independent study and other methods of placing greater responsibility upon the student, have a great potential for keeping costs from rising too fast. Some I.H.L. have adopted such methods, some are experimenting, and others are merely thinking about them as a distant possibility. Only the force of necessity is likely to cause the majority of educational institutions to adopt new methods which mean radical changes from cherished and long-established traditions. But support of the essential activities in higher education in the years ahead is unlikely to be adequate without a combination of these and similar courses of action. . . .

REFERENCES

1. *The Pursuit of Excellence*, Education and the Future of America, Panel Report V of the Special Studies Project, America at Midcentury Series, Rockefeller Brothers Fund, Inc. (Garden City, New York: Doubleday and Company, 1958), p. 33.
2. Office of Education, *Financial Statistics of Higher Education, 1959–60*, 1964; same, *Preliminary Report of Financial Statistics of Institutions of Higher Educ., F. Y. 1964*, July 1965.
3. The President's Committee on Education Beyond the High School, *Second Report to the President*, 1957, pp. 85 & 86.
4. Seymour E. Harris, "Broad Issues in Financing" and Robert D. Calkins, "The Role of Government Support," in: *Financing Higher Education, 1960–70*, ed. Dexter M. Keezer (New York: McGraw-Hill, 1959). Harris estimated that twenty per cent inflation during the 1960's would boost I.H.L. budgets proportionately.
5. Alvin C. Eurich, "Increasing Productivity in Higher Education" in: *Higher Education in the United States, The Economic Problems*, ed. Seymour E. Harris (Cambridge: Harvard University Press, 1960).
6. Selma J. Mushkin and W. Robert Bokelman, "Student Higher Education and Facilities of Colleges and Universities: Projections" in: *Economics of Higher Education*, ed. Selma J. Mushkin, Office of Education, 1962. U. S. Department of Health, Education and Welfare, *Annual Report, 1962*, p. 269.
7. Kenneth A. Simon and Marie G. Fullam, *Projections of Educational Statistics to 1973–74*, Office of Education, Circular 754, 1964, Tables 21 and 23.
8. *Ten-Year Objectives in Education, Higher Education Staffing and Physical Facilities, 1960–61 through 1969–70*, Dept. of Health, Education and Welfare, 1961 (proc.), p. 4.
9. *A Proposed Program of Federal Action to Strengthen Higher Education*, American Council on Education, January 1961, p. 1.
10. *Aid to Higher Education*, Hearings before the Subcommittee on Education, Comittee on Education and Labor, H.R., 87th Congress, 1st Session, 1961, pp. 166, 169.
11. J. Kenneth Little, "Higher Education and the Federal Government," *Higher Education*, October, 1963.
12. David D. Henry, "A Program of Action for Higher Education," *Higher Education and the Federal Government*, Programs and Problems, ed. Charles G. Dobbins (American Council on Education, 1963), p. 103.
13. Clarence Scheps, "Federal Programs of Loans and Grants for Capital Improvements" in: *Higher Education and the Federal Government*, p. 53.
14. Sidney G. Tickton, *Letter to a College President* (The Fund for the Advancement of Education, May 1963), Chart 4.
15. *Congressional Record*, April 3, 1958, p. 6190.

Equalizing Educational Opportunity for the Disadvantaged

By Lawrence E. Dennis

The year 1963 was the year of civil rights and the year of education, the year in which both turned a corner to become in new ways a part of the American consensus. For civil rights, there took place a nationwide protest of conscience aimed at bringing the Negro equality of opportunity on all fronts. For education, it was the year of sweeping national legislation affecting medical education, occupational education, and higher education—symbolic of a growing, widespread recognition that, in a democratic, technological society, education is the only wellspring.

Inevitably, 1964 is emerging as the year in which civil rights and education coalesced. Two great revolutions in our time are now as one: it will be primarily through education that the Negro enters the mainstream of American life. It is now the primary task of educators to bring the Negro into the mainstream of American education. Ten years after the Supreme Court decision on school integration, those who were once simply committed to the goal of equality of educational opportunity have finally become involved in the struggle to make it a reality.

At present the Negro is largely outside the mainstream of American education, particularly higher education. Measured against what must yet be done, only bare beginnings have been made in expanding postsecondary opportunities for Negroes. What is important, however, is that the start *has* been made; there *is* a consensus that much more can and must be done in higher education—and done immediately. What could not have been said even a year ago is now in fact a majority sentiment: higher education (Homer Babbidge has said) must "pierce

From *Current Issues in Higher Education*, 1964, Association for Higher Education. Reprinted by permission of the Association for Higher Education.

the veil of surface equity, and make some positive effort to provide not only 'equality of opportunity' but 'opportunity for equality' as well."

Without in any way deprecating the years of patient work on the part of many individuals and institutions concerned with Negro education, the momentum behind *present* efforts to expand opportunities for Negroes in higher education can be traced to events of 1963. At a White House meeting last June, President Kennedy urged over 200 leading educators to redouble their efforts to expand opportunities for Negroes at all levels of the educational system. Shortly thereafter, the American Council on Education informed the President of higher education's renewed pledge "to further the cause of equality of educational opportunity." This pledge was underscored with a unanimously adopted resolution at the 1963 ACE annual meeting in October.

On that occasion President Logan Wilson of the Council announced the appointment of an eight-member Committee on Equality of Educational Opportunity, under the chairmanship of President Elvis Stahr of Indiana University. That Committee was specifically charged to advise President Wilson on the Council's continuing role in advancing the cause of expanding opportunities for Negroes in higher education. One of its first recommendations was that the Council should establish a clearinghouse to provide leadership and coordination to the efforts of colleges and universities to equalize opportunities at both the faculty and student levels. This spring, the clearinghouse will begin operation with publication of a series of reports and case studies describing and interpreting steps being taken to expand postsecondary opportunities for the disadvantaged in various parts of the country.

Actually, there is no sure estimate of the total Negro enrollment in higher education, though a commonly cited "working figure" for the undergraduate level is 180,000. This represents a rate of college attendance markedly lower than that for whites. Nearly two-thirds of these 180,000 students are enrolled in some 116 predominantly Negro institutions, over one-third of them unaccredited, and all but six of which are in Southern or border states. The other one-third is scattered among hundreds of predominantly white colleges and universities throughout the United States.

There are several contrasts between the situation with respect to Negro education in the South and in the North and West, such that it is both convenient and logical to discuss these regions separately.

1. The South

The eighteen-state region stretching from Delaware to Texas at present embraces fifty-five percent of the nation's Negroes. Prior to World War II this figure stood at seventy-seven percent. Despite this percentage decrease, the total number of Negroes in the South increased by fifteen percent between 1940 and 1960. Negroes account for two-fifths of the population of the eleven Southern states, and about one-sixth of the population of the seven border states. One percent of Southern-state Negro children are enrolled in schools with white students; fifty-six percent of border-state Negro children are.

The predominantly white colleges and universities: There is no longer any state in the South where the right of a qualified Negro applicant to be admitted to his state university has not been specifically declared by the courts. Three states—Arkansas, North Carolina, and Tennessee—have in fact or policy opened all public colleges to qualified applicants of both races. Nearly half of the public and private predominantly white colleges and universities in the Southern states have now experienced desegregation; in the border states the percentage is higher. Nonetheless, total Negro undergraduate enrollment in predominantly white institutions is no more than a fraction of one percent.

Over-all, the traditionally white institutions in the South play only a relatively minor role in the education of Negro undergraduates. The gains over the past ten years in many cases represent important vindications of Constitutional rights, but they have had little practical effect in expanding opportunities for the great part of Negro youth. Even as the pace of integration in these institutions speeds up and as they approach a position of racial equity in their admissions policies, indications are that they will continue to provide only limited opportunities for Negroes. There are several factors that will make this so: (1) In the rising competition for college admission Negro youth from segregated and frequently inferior public schools will fare poorly against better-prepared white applicants. (2) With average Negro family income in the South only forty-eight percent of white family income, many white institutions, especially the private ones, will be financially beyond the reach of many talented, but disadvantaged Negro youth. (3) Many Negro students and parents wish to avoid the tensions and social limitations of an overwhelmingly white milieu.

As a matter of simple equity it is vitally important that all institutions of higher education in the United States open their doors to all qualified applicants. But the removal of procedural obstacles to equality of opportunity offers little expectation of that goal becoming a quick reality. Until such time as predominantly white colleges and universities in the South decide to offer "opportunity for equality," which would of necessity embrace the concept of "compensatory education," they will maintain their relatively minor role in the undergraduate education of Negroes, and the major burdens will continue to fall on the predominantly Negro college.

The predominantly Negro colleges: These have traditionally been the chief source of higher education for American Negroes, and they constitute the most obvious focal point for efforts to improve educational opportunities for Negroes.

It is as difficult to generalize about the predominantly Negro colleges as it is about any other group of colleges. About seventy of them are regionally accredited. The thirty-two private institutions in the United Negro College Fund and some twenty-seven state colleges and land-grant institutions form the core of the accredited schools. Considering this group of institutions only, it is still difficult to count them as being fully in the mainstream of American education. Their obstacles are legion.

The first and most obvious obstacle is monetary. The state-supported institutions are long used to making do with five or ten percent of their state's total appropriation for higher education. Among the private Negro colleges, the chief source of outside funds has been the United Negro College Fund, which has, up until this year, been able to distribute an average of only $70,000 a year per institution. Endowments are often negligible, as are alumni fund returns. A year's fund raising by a president typically might net his institution $20,000.

A second obstacle lies in the prior schooling of their students. Almost all come from segregated school systems, unequal by nearly any standard of educational measurement. Negro colleges admit freshmen that lag from one and a half to three years behind national achievement norms. They are thus forced to spend one to two years on what amounts to remedial work, leaving only two years for college work. To their great credit, most Negro colleges have faced this situation squarely and have done the best they could with what they had.

Beyond this, Negro colleges suffer from a host of ills common to many small colleges. Salaries are low, many faculties are uncommonly inbred, with many who were not educated at their present institution having been educated at another Negro college. Urgent expansion and improvement of physical facilities are needed. Opportunities for cultural enrichment are severely limited. Combined library resources for all Negro colleges are smaller than those of any one of a dozen state university libraries. Few have been touched by the recent ferment over goals and standards. Federal research grants are rare. Fellowships are uncommon.

Thus, the total picture of higher education opportunities for Negroes in the South is one marked by great disparities. In many areas fifty to seventy-five percent of Negro boys do not complete high school; since Negro family income averages only half of white family income, boys must leave school early to work. Two-thirds of the Negro high school graduates who do go on to college are girls. Education is by far the most common major, with various vocationally oriented curricula following in popularity; whole hosts of curricula normally found in large universities are not offered, simply because they relate to fields in which the Negro has traditionally not been welcome. The dropout rate in Negro colleges is about three times that in other institutions. Few Negro college graduates go on to graduate school. Only eleven of the 1,500 recent Woodrow Wilson Fellowship winners were graduates of one of the predominantly Negro colleges. In sum, opportunity is limited, the loss of talent great.

In the long run, the anachronism of the Negro college should disappear. For the present and foreseeable future, however, it will continue to play an important role in the education of Negro youth, especially in the South. The very factors that mitigate against any large Negro enrollment in the predominantly white institutions of the South will serve to keep the predominantly Negro institutions alive for many years to come. The Negro colleges constitute a higher education resource that neither can nor should be abandoned. They remain the only realistic opportunity for college success for the many graduates of segregated secondary schools who can profit from additional education but who would suffer in competition against better-prepared white students.

2. The North and the West

Almost all Northern and Western institutions of higher learning have long since taken on the trappings of nondiscrimination. Resolutions abound from the board of trustees down to the student council. Gifts marked by clauses are not accepted. Photographs have been eliminated from application forms. References to race and religion have been expunged from the registrar's office. Dormitory room assignments are on a first-come-first-served basis. Placement interviews are never arranged by race. The director of athletics insists on common accommodations for his teams on the road. Yet, relatively speaking, Northern schools have very few Negro students. In short, says Wisconsin President Fred Harvey Harrington, "Nondiscrimination has not brought us to the place where we want to be."

A precise count of Negroes on the Northern campus is virtually impossible. On the whole, it is thought that less than two percent of the Northern undergraduate student body is colored. A large part of these Negroes are found in low-tuition urban universities, though even in these institutions the Negro-white ratio is likely to be only a fraction of the city-wide ratio. In suburban and rural institutions, the number of Negroes is likely to be very small, often countable on the fingers of one hand. There are more than a few colleges in the North which at any given time are not likely to have a single Negro student, and an even larger number who escape this category only by virtue of the diligence of the department of athletics.

The reasons are several. One is the steady rise in tuition, which with sixty percent of Negro families earning less than $4,000 a year, has already priced many Negro youth out of the market. Although students in high-tuition schools are supposed to have larger scholarship sums available to them, in fact few schools have been able to increase scholarship monies at the rate of tuition increase. Similarly, loan funds are often of little help to those economically disadvantaged youth not able to run the risk of going several thousand dollars in debt. In many states, particularly those that maintain easily accessible, low-tuition public institutions, the problem is partly a combination of low Negro aspiration levels, ineffective elementary and secondary guidance and counseling programs, and poor or nonexistent articulation between colleges and the high schools. At the same time, under the twin pressures of the squeeze of numbers and the desire to pursue excellence, many public and private colleges have raised their entrance requirements quite dramatically in the last few years; in the process, urban disadvantaged youth have fallen further behind their counterparts in wealthier suburban schools in the competition for college admission. Finally, the college prospects of Negro youth have been limited to some degree by the ever-widening use of standard testing materials— materials which do not, it is generally hypothesized, recognize cultural difference. Whatever the precise effect of standard tests has been, one thing is clear: they have been effective devices for screening out Negroes, but not for finding Negro talent. Of the 1,100 merit scholars selected last year, only seven were Negroes.

At every rung of the educational ladder there is a high loss of Negro talent, an attrition that frequently shows little correlation to scholastic ability. The majority of Negro children in the North receive their elementary and secondary education in predominantly Negro schools and suffer educational and cultural handicaps for it. Dropout rates at many urban, predominantly Negro high schools commonly run between fifty and eighty percent, with lack of interest and financial distress outranking scholastic failure as a reason for leaving. Negroes who do graduate from high school run into the college admission barriers mentioned above, often with financial (or athletic) ability rather than scholastic potential the prime determinant of success. Once in a predominantly white college, the cumulative cultural, educational, and financial handicaps lead to high rates of dropout and discontinuous schooling. These handicaps, plus seeming employment barriers at the end of college, channel Negro college students primarily into prepro-fessional (law, medicine, and divinity) and public service (including teaching and social work) curricula, with relatively few continuing on to graduate school or preparing for careers in engineering, science, business, journalism, and a host of other fields. It is estimated that there are only 500 Negroes in doctoral programs at the present time, only 6,000 Negroes with doctorates (the great majority in education), and only 12,000 Negro engineers (the majority of whom were graduated in predominantly Negro colleges).

It is not particularly difficult to justify or rationalize the present situation at each educational level. School districts running *de facto* segregated schools can point to neighborhood composition. Primary grade reading instructors can point to cultural deficiencies in student backgrounds. High schools can point to inadequately developed verbal and computational skills in the students they receive. Predominantly white colleges can point to the inadequate number of "qualified" Negro high school graduates, just as graduate and professional schools can point to the lack of "qualified" Negro college graduates. Up to now the breaking of this circle of buck passing has been almost nobody's business. Thanks to the impetus of the civil rights revolution, however, some educational organizations and institutions are making it their business to expand opportunities for Negroes up and down the educa-tional ladder.

During the summer of 1963, major educational foundations were considering how they might effectively allocate resources to help equalize educational opportunities. Proposals seeking support for various projects designed to expand opportunities for Negroes were beginning to cross the desks of foundation officers at an increasing rate; and before intelligent decisions could be made as to which programs deserved foundation support on a long-term basis, it was apparent that four needs had to be met: (1) more extensive information about the predominantly Negro colleges and universities, in both quantitative and qualitative terms; (2) more precise information concerning the availability of opportunities for Negroes—at the faculty, student, and administrative levels—in the integrated institutions, especially those in the North and West; (3) guidelines and priorities to assist foundations in determining where and how their resources might most effectively be allocated; and (4) a clearinghouse, or some type of coordinating center through which information in the field of expanding opportunities could be channeled, evaluated, and reported, and to which institutions or organizations seeking support could turn.

Accordingly, at the suggestion of foundation officers, the American Council on Education convened a special conference in Washington on October 17–18, 1963. The roster of conference participants included the presidents of fourteen predominantly Negro colleges, several presidents of predominantly white universities, foundation officers, faculty representatives, federal officials, and Council staff members.

Certain propositions found widespread approval: (1) A national goal in higher education must be the removal of all discrimination because of race, creed, or color. Nonetheless, it is realistically impossible to foresee complete integration within at least another decade. (2) The geographic center of population in this country is shifting at a rate and in a manner that now makes equalizing educational opportunities a truly national problem, requiring top-priority attention in the North and West as well as in the South. (3) Leadership in solving problems relating to expanding opportunities for Negroes in higher education must come principally from within the college and university community itself. (4) Economic, social, and cultural handicaps being what they are, just letting "nature take its course" with respect to the enrollment or employment of Negroes in integrated colleges and universities is not enough; it should be the responsibility of administrative officers and faculties to work systematically to expand opportunities for Negroes in higher education, especially in the large urban population centers. (5) The emerging dialogue between the predominantly Negro institutions and the predominantly white universities (which President Kennedy had called for in June 1963) should be supported as a constructive step toward the improvement of all of higher education. (6) While an enormous amount of basic research in this whole field remains undone, action programs can no longer be delayed.

The Flight from Teaching

TRUSTEES OF THE CARNEGIE FOUNDATION
FOR THE ADVANCEMENT OF TEACHING

The years ahead will see a rapid rise in the college-age population. The age group from 18 to 21 years provides a useful index of this rise (though obviously it does not include all college students): its number will increase from 12 million in 1965 to 17 million in 1980.

And with each succeeding year a higher proportion of the age group will attend college. In 1965, 43 per cent of the 18- to 21-year-old population will enroll in college; in 1980, it is estimated that 60 per cent of the same age group will enroll.

The resulting rise in the number of full-time college students will be dramatic. In 1965 enrollments will run something over 5,200,000; in 1980 they will exceed 10,000,000.

The figures below tell the story.

Year	18- to 21-year-old population	Per cent in college	Estimated enrollment
1965	12,090,000	43	5,200,000
1970	14,244,000	49	6,900,000
1975	15,768,000	54	8,600,000
1980	17,051,000	60	10,200,000

MORE STUDENTS AND FEWER TEACHERS

To predict precisely the number of college and university teachers needed in the years ahead is difficult and involves numerous assumptions, but all experts agree that there will be serious shortages in most fields. For the year 1964–65 alone, colleges and universities have been searching for 31,900 new full-time teachers; in 1969–70 they estimate that they will need 35,700.

Report of Discussion of Board of Trustees, Carnegie Foundation for the Advancement of Teaching, 1964.

The prime source of teachers for higher education is the graduate schools, and the doctoral output of these schools is rising, as indicated in the two fairly conservative projections below.

Year	Office of Education Estimates	National Academy of Sciences Estimates (L. R. Harmon)
1965	13,600	15,364
1970	18,300	21,548
1975	24,600	30,222

If all of those who obtained such advanced degrees went into teaching, our problem would be considerably less difficult. Unfortunately for the colleges and universities, a substantial number are drawn into nonacademic careers. Here are the percentages of new doctor's degree recipients who entered (or stayed in) teaching in recent years.

Year	Per Cent
1954–55 and 1955–56	45.2
1956–57 and 1957–58	44.5
1958–59 and 1959–60	45.6
1960–61 and 1961–62	46.7

In other words, only about half of future doctor's degree recipients will find their way into teaching, and they will be no more than a fraction of the number needed.

The shortage will be more severe in some fields and more damaging at some levels of higher education than at others. The strong colleges and universities, whose prestige and dollars will attract whatever talent is available, will suffer least. It is in the less strong institutions that the harm will be done.

MORE RESEARCH, LESS TEACHING

The failure to produce enough teachers is only part of the problem. Other factors diminish the use we are getting of those who are now in the ranks of teachers. Most important, perhaps, has been the extraordinary rise in funds available for research. Federal expenditures for research and development increased over two hundred times between 1940 and 1964:

Year	Expenditure
1940	$ 74,000,000
1950	1,083,000,000
1960	7,738,000,000
1964	14,979,000,000

For professors, research dollars mean the freedom to pursue a significant intellectual interest. They also bring the status that is associated with research grants, make it possible for the faculty member to travel, buy him free time for reflection, and enable him to attract the best graduate students and bind them to him with golden stipends. And out of his research grants come publications and promotions. It is in the nature of things that research should bring certain kinds of rewards more predictably than does teaching. The able researcher, through publication, gains a national reputation. But the able teacher is rarely known, as a teacher, beyond his own college or university. Good teaching is not only a relatively private performance, but it resists measurement.

Another factor that has tended increasingly to divert time and energy from teaching is the rise in consulting opportunities with government and industry. Consulting assignments often enable the professor to perform an important service to society and their value should not be minimized. They also enable him to add variety to his life and dollars to his income. Indeed sometimes the financial returns from such work equal or exceed the professor's salary. Most colleges and universities have been liberal in permitting outside work on the theory —often accurate—that besides serving a worthy purpose and benefiting the faculty member financially, it enriches his teaching. But the trend toward consulting has become so marked that leading institutions are faced with the necessity of reappraising the rules under which it is permitted.

Still another factor contributing to our present difficulties is the reduction in teaching hours in many leading universities. Harold Orlans of the Brookings Institution offers the following figures:

Year	Institutions	Field	Teaching Hours
1930–31	57 mid-west colleges and universities	Sciences	19+
		Humanities	14
1960–61	12 liberal arts colleges	Sciences	12.7
		Humanities	11.2
1960–61	"eminent" universities	Sciences	6
		Humanities	8.3

Orlans reports that in three leading institutions science faculty members put in an average of only four to five classroom hours per week.

In interpreting these figures, the reader should bear three things in mind. First, the extremely small teaching loads are an attribute of the leading institutions. Second, it is by no means easy to calculate teaching loads in all cases, particularly for members of the graduate faculty who spend many unscheduled hours supervising dissertations or working in the laboratory with students. Third, the leading universities have a conception of the professor's role that requires a different calculation of his duties. These institutions believe that they are engaged in a kind of education that can only be offered by men and women who are themselves active scholars. They think of the professor as engaged one-half time in teaching and one-half time in scholarly work of his own choosing, the latter being as much a part of his duties as the former. So if a normal full-time load is considered to be twelve hours, then in these institutions the professor would be required to teach six hours.

It is not easy to say to what extent huge federal research funds have contributed to the reduction in teaching hours, but it is certain that the reduction is most marked in the "federally involved university." The competition for outstanding scholars is of course a factor. The man with a glittering reputation is often lured with the promise of minimum teaching duties. Indeed he may be given the promise that he will not have to teach at all.

REDUCING THE SHORTAGE: GRADUATE SCHOOL OUTPUT

The most obvious means of alleviating the college teacher shortage is to expand graduate school output, and few issues in higher education have received more intensive study in recent years. Expansion will occur, as indicated by the figures quoted earlier, but several factors will severely limit the rate at which it can take place. One is the teacher shortage itself: we do not have enough graduate school faculty to produce new teachers as fast as we might wish. Another is cost. The graduate student cannot be mass produced. Each student must have a supervised research experience, which in some fields requires expensive laboratory facilities or costly field trips. In all fields it calls for a heavy investment of faculty time.

The federal government is seeking to expand the number of strong centers of graduate training, and its efforts will have substantial consequences. We need additional centers of excellence. But federal appropriations and new buildings are not enough in themselves to create an excellent graduate school. It takes the patient and devoted efforts of good faculty members—and it takes time.

A frequent suggestion for increasing the output of graduate schools is to invent a new degree short of the Ph.D. Although there seems to be little likelihood that such a degree will come into being, the argument in favor of it grows increasingly cogent. A high proportion of teachers in higher education today do not hold a doctor's degree and it appears that in the years ahead an even smaller proportion will hold it. Furthermore, so the argument goes, large numbers of teachers are working at levels of higher education that do not really require that degree, but do require *some* well-conceived program of preparation involving both research and course work. According to the critics, the attitude of the graduate schools to these people is to pretend that they do not exist.

Most qualified observers agree that any sensible program for increasing the output of Ph.D.'s should include vigorous efforts to shorten the period between the A.B. and Ph.D. According to National Research Council data, this averages six years in the natural sciences, eight in the social sciences, and ten in the humanities. Prolonging this period is costly in every way. With each year that passes after the A.B., the graduate student is more likely to be married, burdened with dependents, and in need of substantial fellowship support. Financial pressures often force him to leave graduate work (temporarily and briefly, he tells himself) for full-time teaching, and there are no adequate inducements to encourage his return. It has been suggested that such individuals be provided with fellowships sufficiently generous to take account of their usually heavy family obligations.

ADDITIONAL SOURCES OF TALENT

GRADUATE STUDENTS AND EMERITI. One way of adding promptly to the supply of teachers would be to make greater use of graduate students in college and university instruction. We shall deal with that possibility later.

At the other end of the age scale, more effective use of retired professors is an obvious possibility. Most institutions have mandatory provisions for retirement at a specified age—generally between 65 and 68. Some have recommended that retirement be postponed to a later year, but the truth is that while some faculty members are capable of effective work well beyond 70, others have ceased to be effective long before 65. All the facts of differential performance in later years weigh against raising the mandatory retirement age. Rather, each institution should create flexible arrangements so that the mandatory provision can be waived in selected cases. A good many institutions now have such provisions.

If the faculty refuses to accept any retirement arrangements that are not equally and uniformly applicable, then the only alternative is to let even the most vigorous go and hope that other institutions will pick them up. This is happening with increasing frequency, and the trend will almost surely continue. But there are still not adequate arrangements for placing vigorous emeriti.

PH.D.'S OUTSIDE THE UNIVERSITY. As we said earlier, many young Ph.D.'s pass up teaching careers to enter industrial, governmental, and nonprofit research institutions. Any organization that harbors substantial members of highly qualified research personnel should find ways of making them available for teaching in collaboration with nearby universities. A number of major industrial and governmental laboratories (e.g. the Hanford Atomic Plant, Los Alamos Scientific Laboratory, and Monsanto Chemical Company) have already worked out such arrangements with their educational neighbors. Such collaboration not only makes new teaching talent available to students, but enables bright young people in the laboratories to continue their graduate work.

WOMEN. Women who have completed part or all of their graduate work but have interrupted their careers for family reasons are another rich source of talent. It is discouraging to note that the percentage of women doctorates has fallen off considerably over the past 40 years.

Percentage of all
doctorates awarded to women

1920–24	15.1
1925–29	15.3
1930–34	14.6
1935–39	14.8
1940–44	13.3
1945–49	13.4
1950–54	9.3
1955–59	10.5
1960–61	10.9

A number of experimental programs are now being developed to encourage talented women to continue their education beyond the A.B., and there is overwhelming evidence that both the talent and motivation are there. But frequently the opportunities are lacking. Often the chief obstacle is the rigidity of graduate school rules, e.g., rules against fellowship aid for part-time students.

OTHER SOURCES. Still other sources of teaching talent for higher education are highly qualified professional people in the community and exceptionally qualified high school teachers. The latter group is already moving into junior college teaching and will do so increasingly in the years ahead.

OTHER SOLUTIONS

ENLARGING THE TOTAL SUPPLY.   Industry, government, the academic world, and all of the professions are competing for the same limited supply of trained talent. So sooner or later we must go behind the obvious question "How can the universities get a larger share?" to the more basic question "How can the total supply be enlarged, so that *every* field can have a larger share?"

This forces us to face the fact that we have neglected the development of existing resources of talent in our society. We lose talent in the slums of our great cities through the economic and social deprivation that blights motivation and stunts intellectual growth. We lose it when we allow race prejudice to limit opportunity for some Americans. We lose it when we accept a notion of the role of women that denies them full opportunity to develop their gifts. We lose it when bright young people go from college directly into jobs that offer them no opportunity for further growth.

We are just beginning to understand what we might do to prevent such waste. It is too large a topic to be dealt with here, but it deserves mention as a fundamental aspect of the problem.

BETTER USE OF PRESENT FACULTY. Colleges and universities could make better use of the talent they already have. They could, for example, provide more supporting personnel—such as secretaries and teaching assistants—so that precious faculty time will not be siphoned off into clerical and subprofessional tasks. They could provide more imaginative arrangements for keeping veteran teachers refreshed and up to date. And they could seek ways in which students could be thrown on their own resources for more of their learning, while receiving ample individual attention at critical points. (In a recent test of Pennsylvania State University's "pyramid plan," a cluster of undergraduates, led by a senior and supervised by graduate students and faculty, taught themselves the course content as effectively as it was taught in conventional classrooms and produced disproportionately high numbers of majors in the subject.)

Television and programed instruction can be used to reach larger numbers under circumstances in which the new techniques threaten no impoverishment of the educational experience. And finally, we now know that it is possible to create collaborative arrangements between neighboring institutions so that they can share teaching talent and facilities in mutually beneficial ways.

MORE EFFECTIVE RECRUITMENT. One reason many able Ph.D.'s have been diverted from teaching careers is that the colleges and universities have never brought to bear their full energies and capabilities in recruiting. If they did, they might considerably diminish the loss of potential teachers to nonacademic callings.

OFF-CAMPUS EDUCATION.   Another approach to the problem is to ask how many of the vast numbers of students headed for college in the years ahead could be provided with adequate educational opportunities off-campus. If we could accomplish a major improvement in our off-campus educational ventures, we might serve large numbers of students without their ever having to crowd onto the college campus.

RESTORING THE STATUS OF TEACHING

Though all of these measures may be helpful, the college teacher shortage will never be solved without an intensive and thorough-going effort to re-establish the status of teaching.

In many small liberal arts colleges no such restoration is necessary because the status of teaching has not deteriorated, but in universities the problem is acute, particularly at the undergraduate level. As a rule the university administration is so busy struggling to maintain the strength of its huge graduate and professional schools that it neglects the undergraduate. And so does the faculty. Harold Orlans writes:

> A Brookings Institution survey of over 3,000 faculty members showed that in colleges as well as universities, small and large, in the humanities and social sciences as well as the natural sciences, faculty members at every rank, regardless of how little time they devoted to undergraduate teaching, wished to reduce that time still further, although all groups wished to increase the time devoted to graduate instruction and especially to research.*

Some graduate school professors believe that the teaching of undergraduates is such a different venture from graduate and professional education that it should be handled in a separate institution. But historically almost every effort to separate the two in this country has come to naught; most university people today believe that a single faculty should teach both undergraduates and graduates.

It would be folly to suppose that the status of college teaching can be restored without the active collaboration of the federal government. In some measure, at least, the problem stems from the enormous impact of federal grants on the academic world. Responsible university leaders agree that that impact has been on the whole highly beneficial. In the matter under discussion, however, there can be no doubt that federal grants have helped to create the problem we must now solve.

---

*Harold Orlans, "Federal Expenditures and the Quality of Education." *Science*, Dec. 27, 1963, (vol. 142, no. 3600), p. 1626.

And we shall not solve it until we bring about some changes in governmental attitude and practice. Putting the matter broadly, the federal government must understand how essential it is to maintain the vitality of our colleges and universities as teaching institutions. It must see that without that vitality, these institutions will ultimately be of little help to it in achieving its research and development goals.

If federal agencies ever see that point clearly, they will find ways to be helpful. Congress is reluctant to approve funds that go directly into teachers' salaries, but there are plenty of other steps that can be taken. Certainly the common practice in federal fellowships of forbidding the grantee to teach must be re-examined; it is quite possible to devise programs of federal grants for graduate students that combine research and teaching.

But more important than any possible action by the federal government is action by the universities themselves. One aspect of the problem as it exists today is a crisis in values. The seemingly limitless supply of research funds, consulting opportunities, easy promotions, and dazzling offers has been around for some time now. There is a whole generation of able young faculty members who never knew a time when affluence did not prevail. Thus it is hardly surprising that a few of them exhibit an opportunism that startles their elders. Some of these heavily-bid-for young people appear to have no sense of institutional loyalty whatever and simply follow the offers where they lead. They regard the agencies that provide the research grants as their real sources of nourishment. Whether they correspond with the National Science Foundation from Stanford, Michigan, or M.I.T. really doesn't matter very much. In their view students are just impediments in the headlong search for more and better grants, fatter fees, higher salaries, higher rank. Needless to say, such faculty members do not provide the healthiest models for graduate students thinking of teaching as a career.

Only a small percentage of the academic world is guilty of such opportunism. The large majority who do not share this approach to life should consider the possibility of formulating ethical standards to curb the crassest opportunism in grantsmanship, job hopping, and wheeling-dealing.

There are other things that faculty leaders, departmental chairmen, and university administrators could do to restore the status of undergraduate teaching. They could accord both economic and status benefits to those who do unusually effective work with undergraduates. At U.C.L.A. the administration holds certain reserve funds to be distributed to those departments that demonstrate that some importance has been given to undergraduate teaching. At M.I.T. recently the Visiting

Committee for Sponsored Research urged the university to be highly selective of new research projects in the future

> to ensure that the further growth of campus research makes not only its well-recognized contributions to graduate education, but also strengthens undergraduate instruction, providing the undergraduate with opportunities for participation which enrich his total educational experience.*

Leading universities might agree among themselves to exercise restraint in offering reduced teaching loads as an inducement to move. They might even agree that no new nonteaching faculty would be hired. (Some universities have already adopted the latter principle.)   One university president has said flatly, "No one should be added to the faculty who is not willing to communicate with freshmen," but this goes further than most faculties would accept.

Another step any university can take is to make fuller use of its graduate students as teachers.   Writing of Harvard's new five-year Ph.D. program in history, which includes two years of teaching experience, Franklin Ford, dean of the Faculty of Arts and Sciences, says:

> We simply cannot do many of the things we want to do for students in the College unless we find ways to make more use of the *best* graduate degree candidates.

But he hastens to add that the teaching is beneficial to the graduate students as well as to the College.

> We (at Harvard) are saying that, insofar as funds and classroom opportunities permit, teaching experience ought to be a part of training for the Ph.D., and that it ought to be undertaken by graduate students not as a chore imposed by financial need but as an invaluable part of their own education.**

One practical measure open to any university is to set higher stipends for teaching assistantships than research fellowships.   The reverse is usually true today, and the ablest students make a beeline for the fellowships.

In short, faculty and administration leaders should behave as though undergraduate teaching is important. They will be surprised how quickly young faculty members—and government officials—will get the message.

---

*Report of the President, Massachusetts Institute of Technology, 1963, p. 18.
**Franklin Ford, "Ph.D.'s and the College—a Quiet Revolution." Harvard Alumni Bulletin, Oct. 26, 1963, p. 113.

The Berkeley Student

THE SELECT COMMITTEE ON EDUCATION

A. AMBIGUOUS ATTITUDES

During the turmoil of the last academic year, ostensibly caused by a dispute over whether students should be allowed to engage freely in political activity on campus, some students publicly questioned the adequacy of this University as an educational institution. Since then many observers have interpreted the events of that year as evidence of widespread dissatisfaction among students with the way they were being taught. It may come as a surprise, therefore, that surveys taken while the events were still fresh show a large majority of the students to be reasonably content with the University. In April 1965, nine tenths of a sample of students carefully selected to be representative of the entire student body, graduate and undergraduate, agreed with this statement: "Taking everything into account, Cal is a good place to go to school." Four fifths said they were satisfied with courses, examinations, and professors.[1] In a survey conducted by the Committee in September 1965, three quarters of the undergraduate students felt that the amount of course work required of them was reasonable.[2]

---

[1] Kathleen E. Gales, "Berkeley Student Opinion, April 1965." Copy of typescript in Select Committee files. A random sample of 439 students was used and its characteristics carefully checked against the known features of the whole student body.

[2] Questionnaire Study of Returning Undergraduates conducted for the Select Committee on Education in September-October 1965 by Mervin B. Freedman and William L. Nichols II (hereafter referred to as "Select Committee Survey"). Questionnaires were distributed to one-quarter of the undergraduate students enrolled in the spring 1965 semester who returned to register in the fall 1965, in all schools and colleges at Berkeley except Forestry, Optometry, and Public Health. 2576 questionnaires were distributed and 2203 or 85.5% were returned. The high rate of return lends support to the study's conclusions, but it is somewhat offset by the fact that the procedure used did not permit contacting seniors who graduated in June 1965 and students who did not return, those most likely to be dissatisfied with the University's undergraduate program or less successful in coping with it.

From *Education at Berkeley,* a Report of the Select Committee on Education, Copyright 1966 by The Regents of the University of California. Reprinted by permission of The Regents of the University of California.

In the light of events, the results of these surveys are paradoxical. A vast majority of the students said they were happy with the University; yet at the same time a good part, perhaps half, of the same students had been willing to cut classes in order to demonstrate their opposition to the administration of the University.[3] The answer is not so simple as to say that the issues were political and not academic, or that the students were swept up in a wave of youthful exuberance or hysteria. The same surveys which showed apparent student approval of the University also revealed deep discontent with specific aspects of the education provided. A third of the students who were questioned complained that some of their classes were so big that they learned very little in them. Forty-two per cent stated that the grading system reflects "only slightly" the student's actual knowledge and understanding of the subjects studied, and another 5% believed it does "not at all." Forty-six per cent said professors spend too little time with their students, and 42% held that most professors are more interested in their research than in teaching. Half of them said students should have more control over educational policies, and half also wished they had more time for non-academic activities. Finally, nearly four fifths agreed with the popular cliche that the University operates as a factory.[4]

Obviously there is ambiguity in the attitudes of many Berkeley students toward the University. They both respect it and feel dissociated from it. This ambiguity suggests that the sources of their discontent go deeper than their specific criticisms of the University, though these criticisms are at times justified. If we can understand the basis and significance of the conflicting attitudes of the students, we shall know a great deal about their nature and needs.

B. THE MISSING COLLEGE COMMUNITY

In attacking the problem, it is well to begin by describing certain features of the student body.

Few American university campuses have a larger enrollment than Berkeley, and certainly none has a more diverse one. In the fall of 1965, there were 26,832 students, including 10,224 graduates, 9,952 in

[3] Eugene Bardach, Jack Citrin, *et al.,* "The Berkeley Free Speech Controversy (Preliminary Report) Prepared by a Fact-Finding Committee of Graduate Political Scientists," Dec. 13, 1964, mimeographed, p. 15.

[4] Select Committee Survey (grading and non-academic activities); Gales, "Berkeley Student Opinion" (professors and factory). The Gales survey found that only 49% of the students agreed with the statement: "Grades at this university are an adequate measure of ability." The agreement with the Select Committee Survey percentage is close.

upper division (juniors and seniors), and 6,656 in lower division (freshmen and sophomores). About two thirds of them were men. They came in varying numbers from every state in the union, six from Mississippi to 976 from New York, besides 19,684 from California itself. Two thousand and thirty-seven were from foreign countries.

These students were in fourteen schools and colleges, each with its own curriculum and degree requirements. Each college and school has its student group with its jargon, mores, and legends. The largest, the College of Letters and Science, with 12,384 undergraduate students majoring in such varied fields as physical and biological sciences, social science, and humanities, is in itself a diverse set of groups.

This much complexity is inherent in the organization and purpose of the University. The student body is further fragmented by the mobility of today's students. Under the traditional four-year college program, most of the class that entered as freshmen in September 1961 would have graduated in June 1965. In fact only 50% of them have graduated by January 1966 or are still on campus. The other half (54% of the women and 46% of the men) have left; many of them will later complete their education here or elsewhere. On the other hand, 38% of the class that did graduate from Letters and Science in 1965 (the only college for which figures are readily available) had done half or more of their work elsewhere.[5] That is to say that only half of our freshmen graduate here within five years, while about two fifths of the graduating class (in Letters and Science at least) consist of transfer students who were at Berkeley only as upper-division students. Then, as is to be desired, there is another large influx at the graduate level. In the fall of 1964, 36% of the graduate students were new, and of these, only one fifth came from Berkeley. In other words, there were in that semester among the graduate students 3,000 faces that were new to the campus.

When a new student arrives here, he does not find a tight-knit college community. In the survey conducted by the Committee, 30% of the undergraduates stated that they live more than ten-minutes walking distance from the campus, and it is safe to assume that this is true of a higher percentage of graduate students. Most of these undergraduates spend between two and six hours per week commuting to the University. Going to class represents for many of them somewhat the same pattern of life as going to a daily job.

---

[5]Mervin B. Freedman, "Dropouts at Berkeley," typescript in Select Committee files. Data supplied by Dr. Robert Suczek and Dr. Lise Alfert of the Department of Psychiatry, Cowell Hospital, University of California, Berkeley. Figures on graduates from the study of the graduating class of 1965 of the Letters and Science Committee on Academic Program.

In such a large student body with widely scattered residences and a high rate of turnover, it is hardly surprising that many students feel alone in a community of strangers. In the April 1965 survey, almost two thirds of the students felt the University to be an "impersonal institution," and one third agreed that they "often feel lonely walking on campus even though there are crowds of people around." Loneliness is one factor behind the decision of many freshmen and entering transfer students to drop out of Berkeley. The women who transfer to other campuses of the University of California give as their main reason for leaving Berkeley their feelings of isolation because of its large size and impersonality. Loneliness is, of course, a general problem of the individual in society and is very likely to assail young persons who are leaving their homes or local schools for the first time. A residential situation that provides close relations with other students reduces the rate of drop-outs. Students living at home (and therefore presumably commuting considerable distances) or in private rooms and boarding houses are much more prone to leaving than those who enter dormitories, co-op housing, fraternities, and sororities.[6]

A dearth of close student contacts has its effect on the informal intellectual life of the campus. The opportunities for active intellectual exchange among peers are far more restricted at Berkeley than at small private colleges. Many Berkeley students find their friendships limited to a few intimates. For many of those who remain at the University, solitude or social intercourse with a few associates, which began as a necessity, ends by becoming a way of life. There is a notable tendency for students after some time here to shift to private apartments, either alone or with a roommate or two. They move into converted private homes and old apartment buildings in the flats south and west of the campus, seeking quiet and privacy and the freedom to come and go as they please.

Many of these features of student life at Berkeley have a long history. Transfer students and apartment living have long existed. In the last decade, the replacement of former boarding houses with new high-rise dormitories has counteracted the scattering of student residences. Nevertheless, the fragmentation of the student body has been magnified, if only by the sheer increase in numbers and places of origin.

As a result, a unified college community cannot be found here, even among the undergraduates. When a student's year of graduation has little relation to his year of entrance, when almost half a graduating class has done most of its work elsewhere, when a third of the students

---

[6]Freedman, "Dropouts."

live outside the vicinity of the campus, the small-college loyalty to graduating class and even to college must wither. It is not surprising that in the usual student elections for class officers only about one tenth of the eligible students vote.[7] A large proportion of this tenth lives in fraternities, sororities, and certain dormitories—havens of tradition in which the world of college spirit still finds refuge. For the other students, Berkeley is first and foremost a place to get an education. Lacking the old-fashioned sense of college community, they fall back on smaller campus groupings and limited circles of friends. Their normal activities do not imbue "Berkeley" with the connotation of shared experience that exists at smaller institutions.

A feature of many colleges which adds to the student's sense of belonging is close contact with members of the faculty. A professor can assume the role of surrogate parent for the student newly departed from home or can provide personal adult recognition of his work in preparation for life in an adult world. These needs, more than dissatisfaction with the particular method of teaching, lie behind the frequent complaints about the large lecture course in the lower division. The same reasons account for much of the prevailing resentment expressed against undergraduate advising. Advisers spend little time with students and change all too frequently. "I can't remember the names of my advisers for the last three semesters" is a quotation that could come from countless students in many areas of the University. In the absence of a real adviser, a student will sometimes turn to one of his professors, but these too change, and as one student put it, "You never go back to see a professor after you're out of his course." These complaints are directed especially at certain parts of the College of Letters and Science. The professional schools and colleges are smaller and frequently do provide the desired intimacy with professors.

Under these conditions the popularity of the "factory" metaphor begins to be comprehensible. Incoming students contrast their experience at Berkeley with their lives in high school or junior college. The University does not fit the common concept of what a college should be, and in their disappointment, they find "factory" an apt description. Few students have actually worked in a factory, but they know that it is a place where identical articles are mass-produced and workers are treated impersonally.

---

[7]ASUC election, December 1965: All undergraduates eligible to vote: 16,610; Number of voters: 1,808; Per cent voting: 10.9%. In the spring of 1965, in the aftermath of the Free Speech Movement, and in the fall of 1965, for the special Constitutional Convention, all-time high records of students turned out to vote: approximately 6,000 students or about 35%. These elections were extraordinary; the 10% of December 1965 is more typical.

C. THE VARIETY OF STUDENTS

Another important reason for the fragmentation of the student body is the wide diversity among the students themselves. Variations that are common at all universities are magnified here, for Berkeley is at the same time both a community college and a world-renowned center of learning. Its students are unusually heterogeneous.

One of the most important variations is in academic potential. A comparison of the entering freshmen of 1960, for whom we have Scholastic Aptitude Test scores, with the entering classes of leading private universities and technical schools, reveals a much wider range of ability here. Although one should use aptitude tests with caution, the SAT verbal profile offers a rough indication of intellectual ability. At Harvard, Stanford, MIT, and Cal Tech, between 70 and 90 per cent of the entering freshmen had SAT verbal scores of over 600, and none of these colleges had more than two per cent of the class with scores of under 500. Berkeley had about a third with scores over 600 and the same fraction with scores under 500. Although Berkeley has a more selective admissions policy than most state universities, the mean verbal score here is still far below that at the leading private institutions. The dispersion is also much greater, and the number of students much larger. In absolute numbers, therefore, there are as many students of high academic potential here as at any of the four institutions mentioned. In 1960 Berkeley admitted 420 students with verbal scores over 650 and at the same time 500 students with scores under 450. Professor Martin Trow sums up the situation: "In other words, in this [SAT] or other measures of academic ability, we have in the same institution and within the same classrooms and lecture halls, groups that match the entering classes of some of our most distinguished colleges and universities side by side with replicas of entering classes of far more modest institutions."[8]

From 1947 to 1960 the Scholastic Aptitude scores of entering classes at Berkeley rose markedly.[9]   Although complete figures have

[8]Martin Trow, "Notes on Undergraduate Teaching at Large State Universities," mimeographed, 1966, pp. 18–19.

[9]Mean SAT Scores for Freshman Entering Berkeley:

	Verbal		Mathematical	
	1947	1960	1947	1960
Men	491	557	508	595
Women	483	543	411	518

The University of California, Office of Educational Relations, "A Review of CEEB Entrance Testing at the University of California, 1947–1963," mimeographed.

not been compiled since 1960, the state-wide admissions office reports that without question the quality of our entering students has continued to improve. The proportion of outstanding students is therefore higher today than in 1960. For these students to achieve their potential, they must have the opportunity to advance at a faster rate than the ordinary student. They need the opportunities provided by honors programs and responsible individual study, such as are common at selective private colleges. Only four per cent of our graduating class of 1965 had been in honors programs, and only eight per cent had received any individual instruction.

In determining varieties of students, sex is as important a distinction as academic ability, for it has a marked influence on the choice of field and the attitude toward academic work. There is a concentration of men in the sciences and professional schools (except Education), and a concentration of women in the humanities. There is only one woman to every hundred and fifty men in Engineering, one to every ten in the College of Chemistry and the College of Environmental Design, one to every seven in Business Administration. The sexes are evenly divided in the College of Letters and Science, but the men dominate the sciences (fourteen to one in Physics, three to one in Mathematics) while the women take over some of the humanities and social science majors (two to one in English, Sociology, and Anthropology). Others are evenly split (History and Psychology), and men still control the more abstract majors (Philosophy and Political Science are about two to one, Economics, seven to one). The ratio of men is also much higher in graduate school. There are three men to every two women undergraduates, but three men for every women among graduates.

A major reason for these different ratios is the purpose for which students come to Berkeley. When asked to pick from a list of reasons for going to college those that were most important for them, a higher percentage of men than women placed first the desire to obtain "vocational training." A more detailed analysis is revealing. It was the first choice of two thirds or more of the men in Engineering and the sciences, but of only half the men in social science and of a third in humanities. The most frequent first choice of men in the humanities (and of the women too) was to obtain "a basic general education." The women showed no such clear vocational orientation as did the majority of men. Only in Engineering and the physical sciences did more than half the women give vocational training as their most important reason for coming to college. This attitude helps explain the higher drop-out rate among women noted earlier.[10]

The marked differences between the sexes in choice of major and in attitudes toward their education show that a review of the educational needs of our students must consider the different orientations of men and women. The women who come to college highly oriented toward a career are in a minority both in the majors that women dominate and in the traditionally male fields. It is not surprising that the ratio of men to women is twice as high in graduate school as undergraduate, and the ratio of men to women in the faculties vastly greater. When we consider that the Scholastic Aptitude scores of the sexes are about equal, we must question a social and educational system that does not encourage more women to develop profitably their intellectual potential.

The students in the various fields have a tendency to be differentiated not only by their vocational orientation, but also their social and political attitudes as well. A test of the entering freshmen of 1959 showed a distinct correlation between their attitudes and their intended majors, especially among the men.[11] The men students who most frequently gave answers indicating their opposition to existing social and political conditions were those entering the humanities and fine arts. The group which found existing conditions most acceptable were the potential engineers. Women showed less clear trends. Those in the humanities were on the whole more non-conformist than others, but were far less so than the men in humanities. The group most consistently in opposition to existing conditions were the men majoring in humanities. Their very choice of major (for non-vocational reasons) already distinguished them from most men, as noted above.

---

[10]First Choice of 1959 Berkeley Freshmen among Goals for College Education (see p. 18):

I. To provide vocational training

	Engin.	Phys. S.	Biol. S.	Soc. S.**	Human.
Men	72%	64%	72%	52%	35%
Women	62%	53%	8%*	37%	26%

II. To provide a basic general education

	Engin.	Phys. S.	Biol. S.	Soc. S.**	Human.
Men	19%	26%	17%	35%	47%
Women	38%	28%	—*	40%	58%

*Fifty-one per cent of the women in Biological Sciences gave no answer.
**The survey placed Business Administration and the other professional schools under the Social Sciences, so that we do not have independent data for them or for the social science students in Letters and Science (Center for the Study of Higher Education).
[11]Ibid.

Differences in temperament are, in fact, related to the whole way of life of the student. They show up, for instance, in the choice of housing. According to a recent psychological survey of Berkeley students, those who live at home, particularly in their freshman year, tend to be less independent, less tolerant and more conventional than the average student. They have less "complex personalities" in psychological terms. In later years women of this kind who do not drop out are more likely to move into sororities than into other housing, the men into dormitories. At the other extreme, the more unconventional, forceful, and tolerant, that is, the more "complex" students, either start out in apartments or move into them by the time they are seniors. This type of student also moves most frequently during his years in college. High academic potential shows a similar correlation. Students with the highest *verbal* Scholastic Aptitude Test scores are most likely to be found in apartments, and those with the lowest at home or in fraternities and sororities. Dormitories occupy a middle ground.[12]

Comments by individual students interviewed by the Committee give life to these statistics. The atmosphere in fraternities is not conducive to hard study, according to students who have belonged to them.[13] Even when special places or hours are set aside for study, the group pressure is for cooperation in informal and formal activities— a basketball game that someone suddenly starts, a fourth at bridge, decorating the house for a dance or a football weekend. The serious student finds these living arrangements unsatisfactory and moves into an apartment. The women who move into apartments have much the same to say about dormitory life. Berkeley's high-rise dormitories represent to them lack of privacy and intellectual stimulus, and restrictions on their personal freedom. One young lady who had shifted to an apartment recalled the dormitory as "thirty screaming girls on one floor."

The large size of the student body, the number of schools and colleges, and the differences of intellectual ability, sex, and temperament all combine to produce vast diversity among the students at Berkeley. They need many kinds of academic programs and many kinds of teaching, especially at the undergraduate level.

---

[12] Mervin B. Freedman, "Some Considerations of Housing at Berkeley," typescript in Select Committee files.

[13] One of the major informants of the Committee was a candidate for the ASUC Senate from a fraternity who feels that the only hope of survival of the fraternities is to become more academic.

D. THE ACADEMICALLY ORIENTED STUDENTS

As we have seen, among these varieties of students there is a wide range of intellectual ability. Those in humanities are likely to be higher in verbal aptitude than in mathematical, those in science and engineering higher in mathematical aptitude; among both groups, but particularly in science, there are many who are intellectually the peers of any student group in the country. Most of these students, both at the undergraduate and graduate levels, have fixed upon careers and are seizing the opportunities offered by the University to educate themselves for a lifetime of work and advancement in their fields. They are the self-disciplined, serious students who appear in every survey.

The values of these academically-oriented students are aptly described by Professors Burton R. Clark and Martin Trow:

> The essence of this system of values is its identification with the intellectual concerns of the serious faculty members. The students involved work hard, get the best grades, talk about their course work outside of class, and let the world of ideas and knowledge reach them.... [They are] both identified with the college and involved in learning. For these students, their attachment to the college, which may be as strong as among the collegiate crowd, is to the institution which supports intellectual values and opportunities for learning; the emotional tie is through the faculty to the college, and through campus friends of similar mind and temper.... The products of this culture are typically aiming at graduate and professional schools; it is not surprising that they identify so strongly with the faculty, and internalize the scholarly and scientific habits of mind and work as part of their anticipatory socialization to future professional roles.[14]

Berkeley is fortunate in having a large number of these students. The University may be imperfect, like all human institutions, but these students are more apt to make the best of the opportunities it offers than to belabor its imperfections. In a word, they are more responsive to its virtues than to its flaws. In our present efforts to devise the best possible education for all students, those who are academically oriented compel less of our attention than do the others. But if they present fewer problems, we have no less an obligation to them, and their comfortable allegiance is no guarantee that we are meeting their needs as well as we could.

---

[14] Burton R. Clark and Martin Trow, "Determinants of College Student Subcultures," mimeographed, in Committee files.

E. THE DROP-OUT AND THE REBEL

Yet the needs of all students are not the same. This fact becomes clear when we observe their attitudes toward the University. Although discontent with certain aspects of the University is fairly widespread—even those who are most proud of it recognize that it has flaws—the majority of students express basic satisfaction with their experience here. Dissatisfaction is most prominent among the non-conformist students who are typically inclined toward the humanities and social sciences. It takes a form of alienation whose effects can be observed in certain drop-outs and in the students who demonstrated against the University during the Free Speech Movement.

The drop-out is the extreme case of the student whose education here has been unsuccessful. Some leave because of failing grades, but others do so without such a clear academic reason. That students are admitted who prove incapable of meeting our standards is a disturbing phenomenon and calls attention to the need for reviewing our admission procedures and our liaison with high school and junior college advisers. Not all the fault lies here, of course, for students may do poorly not because of inability but because they are emotionally upset. The difficulties faced by these students are often the same as those of the students who drop out with passing grades. These last offer the most direct challenge to our educational system, since they are young men and women who have demonstrated the capacity to continue at Berkeley and choose voluntarily not to do so. Their percentage in the total number of drop-outs increases with each year of college. Only one fifth of the freshmen who leave are in good academic standing, compared to two thirds at the upper-division level.[15]

There appears to be a significant relation between the probability that an academically capable student will drop out and the variety of student to which he belongs. Women are more likely to leave than men, partly, no doubt, because they lack as strong a vocational orientation. Students living in fraternities, sororities, and dormitories are more likely to remain than those in private residences. A recent study suggests also that drop-outs who have had satisfactory grades have

---

[15] Per cent of Undergraduate Drop-Outs of the Berkeley Entering Class of Fall 1961 who had passing grades:

	Men				Women			
Years	1	2	3	4	1	2	3	4
Per Cent	14	27	59	61	38	46	83	70

Freedman, "Dropouts at Berkeley."

more complex personalities and are more non-conformist than the average student. Continuing students are more conventional, show more self-discipline, and are most interested in social and religious activities.

Frequently the academically capable drop-outs have had difficulty in finding their place in the world. Many of them have experienced family conflicts and tend to be isolated from their peers, lonely, and unable to accept help from friends or counselors. Many women experience conflict in their roles as women and are more preoccupied with sex than are the continuing women. These students are more prone than the average to suffer from the loneliness of the campus, even though in their living habits they seek privacy—often at the price of loneliness.[16]

For such students the Counseling Center and the psychiatric division of the Student Health Service offer help. One bright woman in humanities told the Committee of the following experience. Although she entered a dormitory upon arrival, she disliked its life and received poor grades. She finally consulted a University psychiatrist, who analyzed her difficulty as arising from her belief that she should belong to a group. Once she could accept the desire for independence as a normal wish, she began to do the excellent work of which she was capable. Many potentially good students, unfortunately, are not motivated to seek this kind of help. When beset by serious academic or personal problems, they become drop-outs.

These students are by no means unique to Berkeley; they resemble, for instance, the alienated and uncommitted Harvard students recently described by Kenneth Keniston.[17] These young men, too, had difficulty adjusting to the world in which they lived. They sought to escape the past and ignore the future, preferring the emotional experience of the present. While they were children the fathers of many of them were absent from the home, or, if present, paid little attention to their families. To fill this void, mothers and sons drew close together. During adolescence these young men felt estranged from other boys, and they did not learn to be comfortable in the presence of girls. By the time they reached college, they had rejected social norms, yet were unable to use the freedom that they sought for any clear purpose. Their out-

---

[16] Freedman, "Dropouts at Berkeley;" and Keith Elmer Merrill, "The Relationship of Certain Non-intellective Factors to Lack of Persistence of Higher-Ability Students and Persistence of Lower-Ability Students at the University of California, Berkeley," Dissertation in Educational Administration, University of California, Berkeley, 1964.

[17] Kenneth Keniston, *The Uncommitted: Alienated Youth in American Society* (New York, 1965).

look included no social commitment, no desire to join with others to change the society that they disliked. Although they were unusually intelligent, their personalities prevented them from profiting fully from their education.

Such extreme alienation is the result of personal and cultural factors beyond the control of the University. Nevertheless, something can be done for students who may drop out for reasons of this kind. Advisers who have the time to talk seriously to them about their education, and instructors who get to know them in small classes or seminars, could offer personal help at critical moments, and, when it is called for, could encourage the use of campus facilities for professional counseling and treatment.

Most of the academically capable drop-outs continue their education elsewhere or eventually return to Berkeley. Many of those who return end up as superior students. They say that they needed a break in their education to "reevaluate things," to "think over what I am doing," to "see how I fit in the world," and the like. They were confronted with the dilemma of continuing their current academic programs or leaving the University entirely. Sometimes, a period of complete break with the University is the best possible move. Alternatively, some of these students could do educationally valuable work off-campus in various kinds of supervised field-study programs. This would save them from the trauma of interrupting their college careers and at the same time provide them with the opportunity of developing maturity and purposeful re-orientation.

Alienation from the University does not necessarily lead to dropping out. At Berkeley the uncommitted student, who has no meaningful goal for his life and who leaves college to find himself, has been less conspicuous than the student who discovers meaning in championing the downtrodden. Berkeley has a longstanding tradition of student political activity in support of radical and unpopular causes. One can recall speeches outside Sather Gate in the Thirties in support of the Popular Front, student participation in the loyalty-oath controversy of the early Fifties, the demonstrations in favor of Caryl Chessman and against the House Un-American Activities Committee in 1959-60, and civil rights activities in 1963-64. This tradition has attracted to the campus students seeking through political and social activities some kind of commitment for their lives.

These facts were brought home by the Free Speech Movement of the fall semester of 1964. Because the events of that period were traumatic for the entire University community, they gave rise to many studies of activist commitment among Berkeley students. The most obvious causes of student support of the movement were their desire to obtain freedom of political advocacy on campus and their outrage at what they viewed as foul play on the part of the University administration. But many less explicit motivations must have played a part: prior participation in civil rights causes, dislike of certain aspects of the University, an unsatisfied longing for the shared experience so lacking in the impersonality of Berkeley life, and dissatisfaction with their own unmotivated existence.

Students tend to fall into distinct categories as regards their support or opposition to the FSM. One can consider arrest for the Sproul Hall sit-in of the night of December 2–3, 1964, as a sign of strong commitment to the FSM. Among those arrested whose majors are known, humanities and social science students were most numerous. The major with the highest percentage of its students arrested was the Social Science Field Major (14%). The next five majors, all with more than 10% of their total graduate and undergraduate students arrested, were in the humanities.[18] The departments with the largest contingent of arrested students were English, History, and Political Science. At the other extreme, the majors with the lowest percentages of arrested students were mainly professional: Law, Electrical Engineering, and Education. Finally, there were some schools with sizable enrollments and with no students identified among those arrested: Agriculture, Forestry, Optometry, and Public Health.[19] The sciences fell in the middle, with the biological sciences having a higher proportion of arrested students than the physical sciences.

Supporters of the FSM not arrested in Sproul Hall had similar characteristics. All surveys agree that there was wide support among social science majors (three quarters of whom were favorable to the movement, according to one survey), with less support by humanities and science majors.[20] In contrast, over half the students in Business

---

[18] Dramatic Art, Philosophy, Humanities Field Major, Classics and Comparative Literature. The major with the highest percentage was actually Molecular Biology, with three students out of fourteen arrested, or 21%. The major is too small to be statistically significant.

[19] English: 78 students, 6.5% of undergraduate and graduate majors; History: 62 students, 5.6%; Political Science: 53 students, 5.5%; Law: 2 students, 0.2%; Electrical Engineering: 2 students, 0.2%; Education: 1 student, 0.1%. These figures are based on the self-identification of 501 of the 645 arrested students. Many of the remaining students were probably in the lower division and had not declared a major.

[20] Gales, "Berkeley Student Opinion"; and Paul Heist, "Representation of Respondents: Percentage of FSM Members and Students in Comparison Samples Distributed by Academic Year and Major Field of Specialization," mimeographed table in Select Committee files.

Administration and Engineering disapproved. Nearly three-quarters of the students living in apartments favored the FSM, whereas a similar ratio of those in fraternities and sororities disapproved of it.

The students arrested in Sproul Hall also included an unusual percentage of scholastically able young people. Their grades were significantly higher than those of the average student. Nearly half had grade-point averages higher than 3.0, whereas only 21% of the total student body had grades this high. Among the graduate students arrested, more than two thirds had averages above 3.5; only 55% of all graduates were at this level.[21] Many of the most promising students in the College of Letters and Science and in graduate school, especially in the humanities and social sciences, were strongly enough devoted to the cause of the FSM to face arrest in its behalf.

Moreover, if we explore the reactions of the student body at large, we find that there was considerable sympathy for the FSM, though its extent would be difficult to gauge accurately. Over four fifths of the students surveyed in April, 1965, said they agreed with the goals of the FSM, although only one half approved of its tactics. Moreover, three quarters believed the leaders of the movement to be idealistic and motivated by moral values.[22] On the whole, support was greater among those students with high scholastic records than among those with low records. According to the principal study available, 80% of the surveyed undergraduates who had grade-point averages over 3.5 (more A's than B's) approved of the FSM, but only 44% of those with less than 2.5 GPA (more C's than B's) did so. Among graduate students the figures were even more startling. Only one fifth of those with less than 3.0 (B) averages approved, but nearly three quarters of those with over 3.5 averages did so.[23] These surveys show that the spirit of the FSM touched more students than simple arrest figures indicate.

For reasons already observed, many students failed to find here a community spirit, and the FSM suddenly offered them a cause with which they could identify. For them the FSM imbued the name of

---

[21] Ibid.

[22] Eugene Bardach et al., "The Free Speech Controversy." The information came from 598 questionnaires completed by the persons arrested, of which 537 (80%) came from currently enrolled students. Eighteen per cent were graduate students, 46% upper-division students, 36% lower-division students. In the total student population of that semester, the graduates were 35%, upper-division students 36%, and lower-division 28%. Graduate students were underrepresented in Sproul Hall, but the ratio of upper-division to lower-division students was the same as in the total population (1.3 to 1).

[23] Gales, "Berkeley Student Opinion."

Berkeley with a meaning and an ethos, and gave them a feeling of belonging to an identifiable and worthwhile group.

As was seen, even during the excitement of last year, a large majority of the students expressed general satisfaction with the University. One can attribute the return of calm in the fall of 1965 in part to this spirit. Nevertheless, the experience of the FSM offers serious lessons. First of all, the ease with which a majority of students could find, however ephemerally, a commitment and a moral drive in opposing the University administration is evidence of a widespread, if latent, alienation which can be turned against the University. This alienation is different in degree, but probably not in kind, from that of the more active protestors.

Secondly, the high intellectual abilities of many strongly committed members of the FSM may mark them for positions of leadership in our society, particularly in cultural and political fields. The success of the movement demonstrated their capacity for leadership. Whatever judgment is made of their behavior, Berkeley can be proud of the presence of this kind of student. There is danger, however, that the effectiveness of their education may be lost through alienation and antagonism.

F. THE NON-CONFORMIST STUDENTS

To suggest that we should consider the needs of the discontented students is to evoke in many quarters the immediate reply that they are but a vocal minority, that we should concern ourselves with the majority of students who are satisfied with the education they receive. This reply oversimplifies the realities of the situation.

The Bay Area has become a leading cultural and scientific center of the United States, located in great natural beauty and favored with a pleasant climate. High among its attractions is the University at Berkeley. The magnetic force of such a community has attracted a diverse populace of unorthodox artists, writers, and thinkers, as well as self-appointed social reformers, seekers after excitement and notoriety, and irresponsible cranks. But it has also brought to our campus a remarkable group of intelligent and imaginative young men and women who both contribute and respond to the atmosphere of the local community.

At the same time, more restrictive admissions policies, forced upon us by the growing number of college-age youths, are reducing the number of students who keep alive the traditional college spirit. Evidence of this change is apparent in the recent marked decline in numbers of students belonging to fraternities.[24] Meanwhile, the commitment of the master plan for higher education in California, to reduce the size of the lower division at Berkeley while increasing the number of graduate students, will raise the age of our student body. Our students in the future will be more mature, more independent, and less attracted by the traditional collegiate culture.

Thus for various reasons, partly extrinsic, partly indigenous, the number of students who are susceptible to discontent with the University is likely to grow. It is, of course, impossible to know whether the number of alienated students will actually increase and what form alienation may take in the future. Much will probably depend on the attitude of the University. For the time being, however, we must recognize their presence, their feelings, and their influence. Even the large number of generally satisfied students cannot isolate themselves from non-conformist attitudes and ideas: they react positively or negatively. In the middle ground, there are many more students who share with the non-conformists their doubts about some aspects of the University. Educational changes that will affect the attitudes of the more intelligent and often more discontented minority will affect the attitudes of the entire student body toward the University. We need to understand the mentality of these intelligent non-conformist students.

The subject is one that calls for the illumination of time, and for a much more extensive study than the Committee has been able to make. Nevertheless, we feel that it is important enough to merit a provisional attempt now. Our description is more impressionistic than scientific and more simple than the description of a highly complex phenomenon should be. But we offer it in the belief that even in its broad outlines it may help to dispel some of the confusion and misunderstanding that has gathered about a group of our students.[25]

---

[24] Berkeley Campus Fraternity Membership (Actives and Pledges):

Fall Semesters

Year	Membership
1960	1,939
1961	1,901
1962	1,958
1963	1,859
1964	1,814
1965	1,646

[25] The following analysis of the non-conformist student is based on various types of information: current articles on the subject, interviews with undergraduate and graduate students, and study of the literature and music popular among students. Several of the research assistants of the Committee contributed by observing the culture of the non-conformist students, meeting in discussion sessions with members of the Committee, and writing their own reports on the subject.

The most obvious feature of their outlook, which every observer notes immediately, is their outright rejection of many aspects of present-day America. They find much to fear and condemn and, overtly at least, little to praise. Essentially, they see our society as controlled by a group which has abandoned the common welfare in its own self-interest and has resorted to many techniques to disguise its activities and to manipulate the general public. As these students see it, while the dominant group claims to champion freedom, religion, patriotism, and morality, it produces and condones slums, racial segregation, migrant farm laborers, false advertising, American economic imperialism, and the bomb. In private life, moreover, the students find as much immorality and injustice as in public life. They commonly explain it as the product of an all-pervasive hypocrisy.

To succeed in this society, they believe, you must mask your real feelings and become an organization man, wear what you're expected to wear, say what you're expected to say, and praise the product of your company when you know it has been built to wear out. It's all a game, playing a role; and these young people find that Americans in this other-directed age have been conditioned to accept without a thought or a murmur their own falsity. They accuse Americans of sacrificing conscience to the quest for status. In this society, they say, those who claim to be moral are really immoral and those who claim to be sane are truly insane.

All this these students condemn. What terrifies them is their conviction that the failure of the individual sense of responsibility, in combination with technology and cybernation, is producing a bureaucratized, machine-run society. They find themselves in danger of losing both their freedom and their humanity to IBM machines and to those who use them. They say that a man must fight hypocrisy to live in a moral world, but he will have to halt the computers if he is to remain a man at all. The fear of 1984, common in the Forties and Fifties, of the totalitarian state based on ubiquitous terror, has reverted among the present generation of radical students to a fear of the scientifically conditioned Brave New World. In the student mind, the dominant group takes the form of the "organized system" that Paul Goodman decries, or the "power structure" opposed by civil rights organizations, or simply "the establishment." "You can't trust anyone over thirty" expresses a vague but pervasive belief that their elders have been corrupted past salvation by the system. Commonly, the students, taking an existentialist position of belief in individual responsibility, seek individuals to blame for the evil actions of society—men who through fear, weak character, or dishonesty have abdicated their moral responsibility. Student radicals find, for example, McGeorge Bundy,

Robert McNamara, and ultimately President Johnson responsible for what they see as American aggression in Vietnam.

For a significant number of young people the older generation is represented most clearly by their parents, who have accepted the system and made their way in it. If the parents remain faithful to religious practices and teachings, the child may be further alienated, since he is likely to be religiously skeptical or atheistic. What most exasperates members of the new generation is their belief that their elders do not take them seriously. "How many roads must a man walk down before you call him a man?" the popular protest singer Bob Dylan asks in a song adopted by the FSM.

Ultimately the students find their society decadent and the dominant group intellectually sterile. For them, American art is created by folk singers, Negro musicians, and bohemian artists and writers. In their most pessimistic moments, America, and indeed the whole West, no longer appears to have any message for the world. Zen Buddhism offers more hope for humanity than does Christianity.

The revolt turns against the traditional ideals of America which the older generation holds up for admiration: the puritan ethic, individualism, and old-fashioned patriotism. Against the puritan ethic non-conformist students flaunt sexual and emotional freedom. They find individualism in the form of private property evil when it justifies exorbitant wealth, dishonest products, and segregated housing. The past history of America becomes for them a sordid tale of the exploitation of non-Anglo-Saxon cultures and races at home and of innocent countries abroad. They see patriotic appeals to the ideals of life, liberty, and pursuit of happiness as trappings to cover sham and hypocrisy.

Before 1960 the usual reaction of the few young people who held this view of our world was to withdraw from society, as did the uncommitted youths studied by Keniston at Harvard. They "went beat" and demonstrated their rejection of the system in their personal life and dress. Since then, this type of reaction has become much more widespread. Beards, long hair, and bare feet protest the conspicuous waste and conformity of the status-conscious society. Instead of the whiskey of their parents, many of these students prefer to use marijuana. Revolt also takes other forms which an outsider can view only as self-destructive; some students can explain laziness, procrastination, and irresponsibility as rejection of the puritan ethic of hard work. Thus many young people clothe in a quasi-moral garb the traditional student difficulty of buckling down to work. This attitude can lead brilliant students to fall behind and eventually drop out.

Another disturbing and ironic development of the new generation is its commitment to form. It has lost respect for the public-relations mentality of "the system," but it has its own admiration for style. In personal relations the highest mark of style is being "cool." Originally the praiseworthy quality of not losing one's head in a crisis, in the Fifties being cool came to mean not opening oneself up, not revealing one weaknesses, having love affairs without becoming emotionally involved. Keeping cool involves as much role-playing as does the hypocrisy the student finds in the scorned minion of the system.

The search for style is in fact a manifestation of the internal conflict and ambiguity that plagues many of these young men and women. Freed from traditional inhibitions, they find that their new role-playing, their "cool," deprives them of the satisfying personal relationships that more traditional patterns used to foster. Paradoxically, old-fashioned romantic love remains their ideal. Some attempt pathetically to simulate love at first sight. Through the exchange of intense confidences, they seek to "communicate" completely and to "build meaningful relationships." To little avail. Instant love proves exhausting and empty.

The search for genuine experience leads also to experimenting with non-addictive hallucinatory drugs. The student hopes through them to free his mind from the shackles of reason and logic, to apprehend the ineffable truths about himself and his surroundings, and to become truly creative. This desire for instant poetry, instant psychoanalysis, and instant mysticism is a further form of escape from hard work, a translation to intellectual and emotional spheres of the American cult of the labor-saving device. The belief that experience through drugs provides more insight than hard rational thought cannot but affect the attitude of young people toward formal education.

These ways of rejecting society in one's private life are outgrowths of the patterns of the earlier "beat" or non-committed generation. At Berkeley the non-conformist has always had another avenue of protest against society: in preference to ironic withdrawal, some have chosen alienated commitment. Since 1960 the radical students of Berkeley have been at the forefront of a wave of student activism that has spread throughout the country.

The activists often reject formal ideologies as a suspect heritage from their elders and attack instead specific policies that they find evil: atomic testing, racial segregation, and, lately, American involvement in Vietnam. Admitting their admiration for anarchism and existentialism, these students assert that the individual must oppose evil directly no matter how strong the system that protects it; for to condemn without acting, as did the Germans who submitted to Hitler, is to share in the guild. Yet they seldom act as individuals; instead they form groups to organize public acts of protest—petitions, marches, vigils, and, ultimately, sit-ins and civil disobedience. Besides giving strength to their voices, organizations with a high purpose can serve to compensate for a lack of rewarding relationships in their private lives. To join a cause is part of the anxious search for a new "sense of viable community" that makes this generation seem hardly less other-directed than its elders.

There is a similar ambiguity in their expectations. On the surface they display a quiet determination and optimism: "we shall overcome." At times, they seem to believe that a solution to society's ills is at hand if only their demands are met: "Freedom now!" Except in moments of exhilaration, however, as during the height of the Free Speech Movement, this confident appearance masks an underlying pessimism. They are not very hopeful of achieving instant freedom and instant reform. Their acts of defiance are often also acts of despair.

When one turns from description of student non-conformity to an explanation of its source, one enters more unsure territory. A thorough explanation of their alienation and their desires awaits a careful study, but some insights can be offered.

In some ways the current student protests have different origins from those of previous decades. Since the Second World War, a generation has grown up and entered college in a society of unparalleled affluence. They have been unimpressed by the possibilities opened up by wealth, but at the same time they take a certain amount of economic well-being for granted. Hence, they do not feel a pressure ro achieve the traditional forms of success in business or the professions.

They have grown up under the dread, not of poverty, but of annihilation. Their childhood and youth were filled with stories of the dangers of atomic testing, of poisoned milk, rain, and air. Behind their existentialism and their pessimism lies a long awareness of the possibility of sudden death should an irresponsible adult push the wrong button. It is hard to document such a fear, but it is a recurring theme in the songs and literature that appeal to this generation of students.

This much is new. What is old is the very concept of social protest in America. Behind these students lie the examples of Thoreau and the Pilgrims. The twentieth century has seen a long and painful revolt against the established groups which have run the United States since its birth. In the end the "organized system" or "power structure" of the students is largely the traditional American Protestant society. Forces and traditions far older than today's students are behind the revolution that continues to stir America, but the students are keenly attuned to it and view it as their very own. Youths of traditional background who belong to this student culture find themselves cut off from their parents not only by the conflict of generations but also by their rejection of the traditions their parents revere. Their break is difficult, their position frequently ambiguous. They often seek to prove their liberation by forming relationships with members of other racial and religious groups.

There is much youthful impatience in the search for instantaneous remedies to public and private ills. The unconventional student is inordinately sure that his own picture of the world is the correct one. He lacks the perspective necessary for self-criticism and for an appreciation of his opponent's position. Of course, there are also some who enjoy the notoriety and power offered by leadership of protest movements.

Members of the older generation are more willing to tolerate the evils of the world, believing they can be reduced but never entirely eliminated. They may find these students immature and impatient; the students retort that to be willing to tolerate and explain is a sign of middle-aged compromise. There is a need to create a dialogue between these two points of view.

Understanding cannot be demanded only on the students' side. While their reaction is often emotional, their picture of the world has a rational structure and is not entirely a mirage. Too many highly intelligent and sincere young people are among the non-conformists for their protests to be dismissed out of hand. Perhaps one of their troubles is that they have taken seriously their school lessons on the high aims of America.

G. THE STUDENTS AND THE UNIVERSITY

This analysis has made students, conformist and non-conformist, appear more stereotyped and less individual than they are. Unavoidably, it may have suggested an artificial polarity between the concerns of the "conformist" and the "non-conformist." This polarity is indeed believed in by many radical students and their adversaries, but we regard it as a stereotype to be challenged. We would rather say that any student with enough motivation to "make it" at this campus is in fact committed to some aspect of our common and rather tolerant heritage, whether he would admit it or not.

Of course, no single student, however non-conformist, accepts the above picture of society in its entirety or engages in all the above forms of protest. Some of those whom the description fits most nearly have close associations with other young people who are no longer in college or graduate school but who remain near the University because of the excitement and social acceptance they find in Berkeley. Non-conformist students and alienated drop-outs of similar outlook produce much of the flavor of Telegraph Avenue. Although these students are a definite minority, their view of the world in attenuated form extends very widely through the rest of the student body. Their attitudes cannot but affect profoundly the relation of the students to the University.

The University takes pride in its devotion to finding and teaching truth and knowledge.   Accepting it on these terms, the potentially alienated students expects to find within its walls idealism silencing cant and hypocrisy. Disillusioned with his elders, he comes to the faculty seeking a "prophet" or a "wise man" (the terms are quoted from students). Here he expects to fill his need for a community in which he can participate, find satisfactory communication with adults, and enlist their support in his struggle to right the wrongs of society. With such high, if unformulated, expectations, this kind of student is bound to be disappointed. Communication with the older generation often fails to materialize in large lecture courses. Few if any of his teachers even know his name. He comes to believe that his worth is measured in answers to mass examinations, not in personal assessment of his work and ideas. He learns to play a game within the University, to select his courses according to the grade he is likely to receive, to write ritual papers, and to second-guess the instructor. He decides that the University is too busy conforming to the needs of the establishment to produce men capable of opposing its evils.

In the critical student's eyes, the professors turn out to have their own system and play their own game. He sees their research as a means for their own advancement rather than as a search for truth. They turn out to be neither prophets nor wise men, only specialists in one area with all their prejudices in other areas intact.

We have seen that students who have this outlook on life are more likely to be in the humanities and social sciences than in the natural sciences or professional schools. Some of these students soon become convinced that even in the humanities and social sciences the professor's command of his specialty and fame through publication count for more than teaching the elements of a subject to beginning students. They decide that the only refuge may be outside. But while they prefer creativity in art and literature to its exegesis, the reforming of society to its analysis, most realize that they must still work to live, and in their disillusion end up playing the game.

In sum, the dissatisfied student finds the University to be just another part of the established order. His alienation from society turns into an alienation from his University. His distrust of the older genera-

tion makes it difficult for him to appreciate traditional methods of instruction or the faculty's idea of a good education, especially when
some professors do in fact display insouciance in their teaching. The
student's view of the University is molded to a large extent by the same
unwillingness to accept human imperfection that molds his general
views of our social system.

This explanation of the attitudes of alienated students collapses
into simple logical sequence what is in fact a complex evolution. The
potentially alienated freshman or transfer student comes with no clear
idea of what to expect in the University, and with inchoate, largely
traditional views of society. His images of American society and of the
ideal university take shape simultaneously as a result of what he sees
and hears after he arrives.

To say that the students reject the University because they regard it
as an extension of the organized system is hardly a novel insight; it is a
charge that has often been repeated by student leaders. There is a further, less obvious connection between the students' general outlook and
their reaction to the University. Those who believe that there can be
short cuts to social reform, mysticism, and love cannot conceive that
there are no short cuts to learning. Difficult courses that make them
pore over facts and theorems can seem a tedious waste of time con-
cocted by unimaginative professors. There must be instant knowledge
— if only the faculty would become attuned to the modern world. To
overcome this attitude the University must discover how to impart once
more the truth that there is no royal road to mathematics.

The anti-rational aspects of student thought contribute to this attitude. Students who hold unreflectingly the belief that feeling is a surer
guide to truth than is reason, cannot readily appreciate the University's
commitment to rational investigation. If they believe that Western
culture is decadent, they cannot appreciate the University's devotion to
its preservation and transmission.

Commitment to social action also prevents students from accepting as valuable an autonomous world of ideas. They find it hard to
conceive that the purpose of the University can be to seek and preserve
pure knowledge. They feel that impartiality cannot exist in the social
sciences, or for that matter in any subject that deals with man and his
culture. Instead of praising the impartiality of the teacher who does
not relate his lessons to immediate problems, they accuse him of moral
irresponsibility.

There is a contradiction in this criticism that betrays the anti-intellectual stance of the non-conformist students. They condemn the University because it is a factory that turns out the products demanded by

society and trains students in the rules of the game; yet they want their education to be related to present-day life and to their personal needs, not to the abstract concerns of the humanities and sciences. They see the University as an agent of the power structure, and they want it to become instead an agent of their moral revolution. A major task of the University is to convince the students of the value of free and independent inquiry, of the need of the University for autonomy from all quarters if it is properly to serve society.

H. CONCLUSION

This brief look at the ferment among our students has attempted to make clearer some of the reasons for the ambiguity of their attitude toward the University that was observed at the outset. There are many varieties of students. Those who by and large approve of American society as it is, those who enjoy the culture of fraternities and dormitories, and those who come here specifically to prepare for a profession are on the whole satisfied, or at least not inclined to demonstrate their discontent by breaking with the University. Those who have more complex personalities or who are upset, those who choose to study humanities and social sciences, those whose individualism makes them prefer living alone, and those who reject important aspects of American society are more likely to react against their education, dropping out or protesting against the University. These attitudes are not mutually exclusive and the different mixture of them in different students can account for the same person's voicing expressions of both criticism and admiration. The fact that their attitudes toward the University are as much influenced by their outlook on society as by the actual nature of the education they receive makes it unlikely that any set of reforms can satisfy all of their complaints.

Responsibility for their attitudes lies in part with an older generation whose members do not try to understand them, and who go about their own lives and their teaching in the ways they learned when they were brought up. A majority of our students agree with most of these ways, and few of the dissatisfied can think of reasonable reform. It is up to the faculty, with its greater experience, to listen seriously to the students, to analyze the problems of our present system of education, and propose new directions.

We cannot think of education here in terms of a traditional four-year college at the center of the University, and a graduate school and two or three professional schools juxtaposed to it. We have at all levels a constant movement of students, with the result that many find themselves with only vaguely collegiate loyalties. To some "Berkeley" may mean a department or a professor, but for most it connotes an atmosphere of culture, and a way of life in which personal freedom counts for much.

For students to take a real interest in their education, they must feel that the educator is also interested in them as individuals, not just as an amorphous student body. In the end we must try to build bridges across that gulf between generations that separates students from their teachers and from their own past. Personal contact with professors will tend to dispel the legends that circulate about the achievement orientation of the faculty and will make the students more likely to develop respect for hard intellectual work. If students exchange views directly with teachers who accept and embody the values of our civilization, they will be more ready to respect these values than if Western culture and the American past are handed to them from above as something to memorize and regurgitate in examinations. In the process of achieving these objectives, professors may themselves re-discover the youthful spirit. We hope that a number of the proposals that follow will help accomplish these aims.*

---

*Prof. Peter Scott wishes to add the following comment: "I find something oblique and misdirected about the foregoing references to the problems of our society, as mirrored in the alleged 'outlook' of 'the new generation'. Not only do I question many of the judgments which ensue, I doubt the initial value of focusing on the mirror. Disillusion with this world is and always has been the beginning of heightened self-awareness; but one will learn little more from a catalogue of its outward manifestations, which may be either constructive or escapist. Nor am I happy at the tranquillizing prospect of 'teachers who accept and embody the values of our civilization'. Both students and teachers have, I think, a more vital job: not to accept values, but to make them new.

"On a more practical level, the students will only come to identify with the University when a richer, more active student culture develops, as at Harvard or Oxford. It is not so much that we do too little to educate students, as that they need to do more for themselves. 'The popular cliche that the University operates as a factory' will not be dispelled simply by a smoother program of Student-Faculty (or Administration) Relations. Facilities are not yet adequate to encourage active, self-directed student learning; they are still too efficiently linked to the preparation of a desired vocational product."

Section V-9

Classrooms

By MEL ELTIN

A major new university is rising from the rubble of a massive slum clearance project on Chicago's South Side. There, at the intersection of two of the nation's busiest expressways, the University of Illinois is building a new, $150 million city campus. The new university, sched-· ules to open sometime in 1964, eventually will be the academic home for 20,000 students. And it may become an architectural prototype for urban universities of the future. Its significance as a model is symbolized by a "Great Court" that will be at the heart of the tight, 106-acre metropolitan campus.

The court, like the agoras of ancient Greece and the piazzas of Renaissance Italy, will serve as a great public square for the University's community of scholars. Set one story above ground and free of vehicular traffic, the court will become a center of busy, bustling human traffic. With its four huge exedras (circular concrete benches) and 2,500-seat Greek amphitheater, the court also will be a natural meeting and resting place for students and faculty. As architect Walter A. Netsch, Jr., of the Chicago office of Skidmore, Owings and Merrill, put it:

"It should be a perfect spot for student rallies, for jam sessions, for meeting dates, and for just sitting in the sun and feeling young—or at least trying to."

The court represents an imaginative attempt at creating a feeling of community on a big city campus. However, its most significant feature is not what will take place on it, but under it. Actually, the court is something of an illusion: in reality it is the paved and landscaped roof of a one-story lecture center.

With 20,000 students on its rolls, the new campus will require an

From *Bricks and Mortar Boards*, Educational Facilities Laboratories, Inc., 1964. Reprinted by permission of Educational Facilities Laboratories, Inc.

assortment of facilities for large-scale instruction. Rather than scattering these facilities across the campus, architect Netsch has grouped them in a single building. The resulting plan calls for a lecture center including nine auditoriums seating 250 students; six seating 75; three seating 150; one seating 500; and two, 250-seat halls equipped for scientific and other "wet" demonstrations.

The need for such a variety of large-scale teaching spaces for a single university illustrates one of the paramount problems troubling college authorities everywhere: the campus is becoming crowded with more and more students. Unhappily, the supply of teachers is not growing as fast as the supply of students. This means that the college professor of tomorrow will have to teach and reach far more students than his colleague of today. New campus facilities like the Chicago lecture center must therefore be designed to help the professor instruct large groups of students as efficiently as possible.

At the same time, tomorrow's professor will have to cover more ground in the same period of time. The body of knowledge is expanding even faster than the body of students. Clearly, if coming generations of college students are to keep pace with a world of accelerating change, the learning process itself will have to undergo accelerating change.

Fortunately, modern technology offers higher education a deskful of valuable aids with which, hopefully, it can promote more efficient instruction. Films, television, tape recorders, slide projectors, computers, and test-scoring machines are all tools both teacher and student may employ to cope with the educational demands of the future. The significant fact is not that this equipment exists, but that hitherto it has been so little used by institutions probing the frontiers of human knowledge. Hubert Wilke, educational director of the Teleprompter Corporation (which was a pioneer in the application of technology to pedagogy) said: "Almost every field of human endeavor is assisted by the tools of modern technology. There is no reason why the teaching profession should not be so assisted."

PROBING INNER SPACE

What do all these changes and potential changes mean for the college planning new instructional facilities?

For one thing, new classroom buildings and lecture halls must enable a relatively smaller number of teachers to instruct a relatively larger number of students. This can be achieved only in large teaching areas or in small areas which are linked electronically. On the other hand, new classroom buildings must also accommodate and encourage independent study as students are thrown more and more on their own. This requires an entirely different kind of space, one emphasizing privacy and individuality. And the campus also must include spaces for the traditional, and invaluable, small group and seminar instruction.

Some colleges, of course, are big enough or affluent enough to afford a variety of spaces for a variety of educational purposes. However, since most institutions operate on severely limited budgets, they frequently must make the same spaces do double and even triple duty. Their new classroom buildings must be designed to be both flexible in size and adaptable in function. A college may have no immediate plans for using any of the new electronic classroom aids. Nevertheless, new buildings should be designed to allow for their possible introduction later on without great additional expense. Thus, the necessary cables, electrical outlets, and utilities should be installed when a building is constructed, not after it is open and in operation. As architectural afterthoughts, electronic aids can be prohibitively expensive.

Walter Netsch was very much aware of the problems of technological obsolescence when he designed the University of Illinois campus in Chicago. All the major instructional areas on the campus, including six low-rise classroom buildings, will be equipped with conduits and cables that will permit the institution to keep up with future electronic developments. Mr. Netsch also hedged his technological bets in planning the audio-visual facilities in the lecture center. He has designed several auditoriums for both front and rear projection (to be discussed at length later on). "These buildings," says the architect, "represent the best gamble we could make, considering that educational technology is not a fixed art."

The Chicago plan also represents, in the most concrete fashion, a burgeoning trend in campus design—the grouping of spaces according to function rather than academic discipline. On more and more campuses, chemistry and physics buildings are emerging as laboratory and science centers. History and mathematics buildings are giving way to unlabeled classroom and lecture centers. For example, no fewer than 10 lecture centers similar to the one at Chicago are on the drawing boards or under construction at various units of the widely scattered State University of New York. The centers, based on a design concept developed by Morton C. Gassman and Alan C. Green, two bright young members of the School of Architecture faculty at Rensselaer Polytechnic Institute, vary greatly in size.

On some of the smaller campuses, the centers will include as few as eight auditoriums ranging in size from 40 to 120 seats. In contrast, the elegant campus planned for the new State University Center at Albany by Edward Durell Stone, will boast one huge building housing 20 auditoriums, ranging all the way from six double classrooms seating 60 each to a theater-sized hall seating 500 students. As at Chicago, the New York lecture centers will lie at the physical as well as the pedagogical heart of their respective campuses.

"We've probably gone overboard on providing large spaces, particularly at Albany," said Elwin Stevens, director of planning and development for the State University. "However, at the rate with which our enrollments are increasing, there is a good possibility that our projections for the future may be too low. If that happens, the facilities for large group instruction may be even more important."

With a larger proportion of the student's time devoted to lectures, the seminar room and study desk will assume a new and critical importance. If the material offered in the lecture hall is to be explained, amplified, and questioned—if real teaching, rather than the simple transmission of facts is to occur—maximum effectiveness must be built into seminar rooms, classrooms, and individual study facilities.

The new, $2.75 million James W. Wood Learning Center at Stephens College in Columbia, Missouri, reflects an awareness of that need. The red brick and glass complex, now under construction, houses a 300-seat teaching auditorium, a 135-seat theater-lecture hall, and an assortment of classrooms seating between 25 and 80 students. But the center, built at a cost of about $22 per square foot, also includes 67 faculty offices, each one planned to do double duty as a small seminar room seating six to eight students.

Behind the plan is the intent to maintain a long-cherished tradition, shared by Stephens (enrollment: less than 1,800) with many institutions of similar size—informality and close student-faculty relations. The office-seminar spaces offer not only an economy, but the opportunity for frequent, direct contact between teachers and students.

A comparable experiment will be tried at the new university to be opened by the State of Florida in Boca Raton, on its southeast coast. Called Florida Atlantic University, the new institution will be the first, if not the only, university in the nation dedicated solely to the junior and senior years and graduate level education.

"This," says Dr. Kenneth Williams, president of the university-to-be, "means that we will have more mature students who will be more highly motivated and know considerably more about the direction in which they are headed than the average student at other institutions. Consequently, our facilities will have to promote a greater intimacy between the student and the instructor, a feature of graduate education at most universities, and one that we will now have to bring down to the undergraduate level." To accomplish this, Florida Atlantic plans to put faculty and students in close proximity.

The university will create something new in academic facilities—offices for commuting students. The student offices will be adjacent to faculty offices, a location the administration hopes will foster friendly, two-way traffic. The solution was arrived at partly because of the relative maturity of the prospective student body and partly because two-thirds of the students (estimated 1970 enrollment: 10,000) are expected to be commuters drawn from the sprawling megalopolis on Florida's southeast coastal strip. The student offices will be comparable to resident students' dormitory rooms in every respect, except that bed, bureau, and other appurtenances of living will not be included. But the offices, to be rented by the commuter on a semester-to-semester basis, will be convertible into dormitory space (and vice versa), should there be a change in the commuter-resident "mix."

The growing importance of the commuting student on the American campus is equally evident at Chicago Teachers College-North, a two-year-old institution operated by the Chicago Board of Education on a 33-acre, parklike site on Chicago's North Side. Architect Philip Brotherton of Perkins and Will has designed a cluster of buildings which is handsome, functional, and suited to the needs of a small (fewer than 2,000 students) urban college devoted to training its commuting students as teachers.

For about $5.6 million, Chicago has acquired a 256,000-square-foot complex, including lecture halls seating 253 and 673 students, large classrooms for as many as 90 students, smaller spaces for seminar groups of up to 15 students, and spaces for individual and semi-individual study. The private study areas have been almost a Perkins and Will trademark since partners C. William Brubaker and Larry Perkins invented the term "Q (for Quest) Space" to describe their function. Others refer to them as student study stations or as carrels (after an ancient French word for a monk's cell). Two hundred of these Q-Spaces or carrels line the window-walls of several wide corridors at the college. The carrels, furnished with lockers, lamps, chairs, and formica-topped desks, cost about $175 each. Unfortunately, they have so far been the scene of far less questing than the Teachers College administration had anticipated.

One Midwest architect attributed their low utilization to the carrels' location. "Who wants to study in a corridor?" he asked. In reply, designer Brotherton insisted that the academic and extracurricular programs should be so planned that the Q-Spaces would become natural and regular study centers. However, one pretty young sophomore questioned the whole idea. "This is a commuters' college," she explained, "and no matter how interesting the after-school program and no matter how comfortable the facilities, it's usually easier to study at home. Besides, many of the girls are married or have boy friends, and they don't want to hang around school a moment longer than necessary. So when their classes are through, they go home."

THE WANDERING WALLS

The college's administrators are confident that, through time and changes in the educational program, the individual study areas ultimately will be fully utilized, commuting students or not. Meanwhile, the college has been much more successful in obtaining a high rate of utilization in other instructional areas. Its buildings, which cost about $19 a square foot to construct, receive the intensive use called for in an urban institution, where the high cost of land and construction must be taken into account. The secret: flexibility.

Each of the college's 13 instructional areas, for example, can be subdivided into smaller areas by means of immediately movable, operable walls. The operable wall is hardly new. Sliding, folding or accordion-type partitions have been with us for many years. What is new about the new operable wall is its effectiveness as a sound barrier. The old operable partition was about as soundproof as a sieve. But the push-button models installed at Teachers College lack that acoustical disadvantage. Noise transmission between class areas has been reduced to the point that activities in one room rarely distract classes on the other side of the partition. The architects had to go a step further, however, in solving the problem of noise from motion-picture sound tracks, normally not contained even by the most efficient operable partition. The solution was to replace the single loudspeaker normally used to cover an entire class area with a series of low-volume speakers mounted in the ceiling.

The operable walls at Teachers College cost about $52,000, or roughly five times the cost of permanent walls. But their installation has made possible an increase in the utilization rate of classroom space from an estimated 65 per cent to about 85 percent. "As it works out in practice," Mr. Brotherton said, "the operable walls give Teachers College the equivalent of six additional classrooms." At the going rate for construction in Chicago, that is an unqualified bargain.

Columbia University has had equal success with the operable walls built into its new Law School on Morningside Heights in New York City. One of these walls, 15 inches thick and 17½ feet tall, divides a classroom seating 380 into two rooms seating 190 each. The same versatility was designed into the Law School's moot courtroom by architect Max Abramovitz of Harrison and Abramovitz. When the courtroom is not needed for the dispensation of mock justice, an operable wall slides in front of the judge's bench and witness chair and, *ipso facto*, the Law School has another useful classroom.

Justifiably or not, the acoustics at Mr. Abramovitz's newest Manhattan project—Lincoln Center's Philharmonic Hall—have been subjected to noisy criticism. But no similar complaints have been voiced about Columbia's Law School. "The acoustics are so good," says Professor Jack Weinstein, "that even with a large class of more than 100 you can conduct a Socratic discussion in a conversational voice and have everyone in the room hear what's going on." The sliding walls are no problem to the teachers or students.

They are, however, a problem to the Columbia maintenance staff, which has complained that the panels take too long to move into place and that they frequently slide off their tracks. The staff also has reported that it takes more time (and therefore more money) to keep the nine-story Law School neat and clean than other campus buildings. The building, incidentally, cost more than $8 million, or between $26 and $27 per square foot, including air conditioning.

The operable wall is not the only means of producing convertible space on the campus. Consider the extraordinarily versatile area that architects Joseph D. Murphy and Eugene Mackey of St. Louis have designed for the Wood Learning Center at Stephens. Seating arrangements and lighting (and an operable wall), give the center a chameleon-like capacity for change: it can serve as an auditorium seating 150; as two 60-seat classrooms; as a small theater-in-the-round; or as an actor's lounge and rehearsal room for another theater down the corridor. Stephens also regards the lobby outside its 300-seat teaching auditorium, which doubles as an art exhibition hall, and the landscaping outside the learning center, used as a "living botanical library," as learning facilities.

Convertibility, flexibility, and versatility probably have been carried to their ultimate in higher education in the twin "concourses" at Delta College, a two-year-old institution in Saginaw, Michigan. To the startled outsider, the concourses may seem about as conducive to learning as a busy corridor in the Pentagon. But, Delta officials insist, "it works."

Set on the east and west sides of a glassed-in interior court, the 265 × 28-foot concourses function as walkways, lecture halls, art display halls, lounges, and small seminar areas. Fully carpeted (cost:

$21,000), these combination classroom-corridors can simultaneously house groups of students clustered around one or more of 18 closed-circuit television monitors; groups of students relaxing on sofas or settees; or scattered individuals strolling through to the cafeteria. "It may sound confused in theory," says Franklin Bouwsma, assistant to the president of Delta, "but in practice there's no problem."

FUNCTION VS. DISCIPLINE

Delta College (principally designed by Alden Dow of Midland, Michigan) is an excellent example of the movement away from monumentality in the design of college campuses. Built as a simple, one-story rectangle, Delta bears little resemblance to the structures which have traditionally dominated the American campus. Architect Charles Brubaker of Perkins and Will explains that, through the nineteenth and most of the twentieth centuries, universities erected rigid, single-function buildings which were as unchanging and unchangeable as Greek temples. "These were buildings," observes Mr. Brubaker, "that seemed to say to the individual: 'You are nothing; the organization is what matters.'"

On the contemporary campus, Mr. Brubaker senses that rigidity and monumentality are yielding to a new concept of free-flowing space, an architecture that does not seek to dwarf the individual but to serve him. Except in rare cases, such as a military institution like the Air Force Academy, Mr. Brubaker believes that monumentality is as out of place on the campus as a quarterback at the University of Chicago.

Walter Netsch, who designed the Air Force Academy, does not completely agree with Mr. Brubaker. He earnestly holds that too much flexibility and too many functions can rob a space of character. "There are many environmental advantages to committed space," says Mr. Netsch. "The feeling of permanence is just one. I myself would not like to go to school in a world in which everything might disappear the next day."

At the University of Illinois Chicago campus, Mr. Netsch shunned large scale convertibility, but managed to commit his space gracefully. He was able to do so largely because of the sheer size of the institution. With 20,000 students and a construction budget of $150 million, Mr. Netsch could program any number of different sizes and kinds of lecture halls, classrooms, laboratories, and offices. Smaller and less affluent universities lack the advantage of size and may have to resort to operable walls and convertibility.

Is there a middle ground between Mr. Netsch's committed and Mr. Brubaker's convertible space?

Architect Gyo Obata of the St. Louis firm of Hellmuth, Obata and Kassabaum seems to have found that middle ground in his shrewd design for the new branch of Southern Illinois University at Edwardsville. Mr. Obata found that there would be few occasions when instantaneous convertibility of space would be required. But some flexibility might be required on a campus scheduled to grow from 5,000 students in 1964 to 20,000 by 1970. To Mr. Obata this meant a requirement for change measured not in seconds or minutes, but in days and weeks. What he had in mind was the sort of alteration that might be accomplished between semesters or during school vacations. His solution was a design that keeps the main instructional areas free of any permanently fixed elements that might hinder the taking down and putting up of semi-permanent—or movable—partitions.

In his highly functional plan for the first classroom structures at Edwardsville, Mr. Obata has placed all the service elements—plumbing, stairs, elevators, etc.—in separate towers on the periphery of each building. Thus the entire 40 × 60-foot interior span of the buildings can be divided and re-divided as required. If desired, whole floor areas can serve as single large spaces; or, as most often will be the case, the areas can be partitioned off into classrooms seating 12, 24, 48, or 72 students.

Light, heat, air conditioning, and cables for closed-circuit television are brought into the individual classrooms through a three-foot dropped ceiling (the gross floor to ceiling height: 12 feet). At five-foot intervals, Mr. Obata has provided aluminum "T's" to facilitate the erection of movable, soundproof partitions. Each classroom will have its own movable chalkboards and tackboards. The architect estimates that the concrete, brick, and glass classroom buildings will cost about $23 to $24 per square foot. "Of course," says Mr. Obata, "the flexibility we have designed costs more, but the difference is not that great. In the long run, the flexibility will more than pay for itself."

A similar solution was reached by Mr. Brubaker in his design for Southern Illinois' new science and technology center on the main campus at Carbondale. He has planned a series of buildings connected by service towers. Given the continually changing nature of science teaching and research, it was necessary to provide as much interior flexibility as possible. The answer was to construct buildings in an architectural "chain" that permits expansion in any direction, with the service towers as connecting links. As Mr. Brubaker put it: "The plans allow the center to grow in a natural, agreeable manner and at a minimum of expense."

THE SHAPE OF EDUCATION

The debate over committed versus convertible space reflects a lively architectural interest in the design of the classroom itself. Unfortunately, there has been far less concern over what to put inside the classroom once it has been designed. Of the existing studies on the subject, one of the most useful and extensive was put together in 1961 by R. P. I.'s Morton Gassman, Alan Green, Harold Hauf, and Wayne F. Koppes. The study, called *New Spaces for Learning*, had one major shortcoming: most of the design principles were based on theory, not practice.

It was to test the principles outlined in *New Spaces* that the R.P.I. team constructed and furnished an experimental classroom on the Troy campus (aided, as in the case of the original study, by an EFL grant). The classroom mock-up is located in one of the newest and most unusual spaces for learning on any American campus—the crossing of a deconsecrated Roman Catholic Church.

The classroom-in-a-church is shaped, lighted, painted, and furnished in accordance with the tenets of *New Spaces*. The 100-student facility is equipped with several chalk and tackboards; a complete panoply of audiovisual projection equipment; raised seating and instruction platforms; continuous formica writing surfaces instead of individual desks; and an excellent sound system. The acoustics, in fact, proved to be a little too good. "When the classroom first opened," recalls Morton Gassman, "the sound of shuffling papers could be heard so clearly that we built a little acoustical 'perfume' (ambient sound) into the air-conditioning system to correct the condition."

In addition to a course in architectural history, the experimental classroom has been used for classes in economics, engineering, biology, and for a summer refresher course for high school science teachers. A poll of these teachers is to date the only significant attempt at evaluating the effectiveness of the classroom and its furnishings. The complaints were minor. For example, there was some criticism that the white writing surfaces were too "glary." Others teachers recommended that the edge of the surface be beveled, since it cut into their arms. But the over-all environment delighted most of the respondents. The reaction was summed up by one teacher, who wrote: "I wish I had one to teach in, in my school back home."

On a much more limited scale, the University of Indiana is experimenting with a new space for learning in the design for its new $5 million School of Business. Indiana plans what it calls the "10 by 10 classroom," in which swivel seats are arranged in 10 rows of 10 chairs each. This will permit the future executives to swivel through 360 degrees to view the chalkboards, tackboards, and projection screens arrayed along three walls of the classroom, as well as to follow the instructor and his assistant as they move around a three-sided platform. Students will be almost completely surrounded by learning stimuli, a situation that prompted Dean Arthur Weimer to remark facetiously: "It will be awfully hard for a kid to go to sleep in this classroom."

Wakefulness probably will be a by-product of another innovation being tried in the teaching auditorium of the University of Texas' new, $4.75 million academic center. Three stages and screens will be set in the shape of a "U" at the front of the lecture hall. The eyes of Texas students thus will be confronted by a variety of images. The students will have a choice among three varieties of seating: 116 fixed seats on a raised platform in the rear, 110 swivel chairs in the center, and 58 movable chairs in the front section.

Other features: microphones will be placed at every tenth seat to facilitate student discussion, and audio outlets for simultaneous translations will be installed at every chair. The translation capability will make it possible for the university to call upon many of the Spanish-speaking scholars who live in or visit Austin. The University of Miami, located in the center of a growing Spanish-speaking population, plans a similar installation.

Versatility of another sort is planned for a new Physical Sciences Lecture Hall at the University of California at Berkeley. The $600,000 hall will boast a revolving stage, the purpose of which will be educational, not theatrical. The design concept was explained in the April, 1960, issue of the *American Journal of Physics* by Berkeley's Professor Harvey White. Professor White proposed that the center section of the front wall of the auditorium—the chalkboards, and most of the long demonstration table and lecture platform—be built in triplicate. The three platforms would be arranged to form a triangle and then mounted on a large revolving platform. Utilities, such as electricity, gas, and compressed air needed for scientific purposes, would be brought in from a ring mounted above the center of the platform. Waste would be removed from below.

Thus, while one demonstration table and set of chalkboards were in use, laboratory assistants behind the scenes would be setting up physics and chemistry demonstrations for classes to follow. "Between periods," wrote Dr. White, "the push of a button will bring either of the prepared lecture fronts into the lecture room."

The White scheme attacks one of the major obstacles to better utilization of science teaching facilities—the great length of time normally required to set up classroom experiments. Sometimes a large lecture hall must remain empty for at least one period while apparatus from the previous class is removed and a new demonstration prepared. Even when only a few minutes are involved, they usually are subtracted from instructional time at the beginning of a class. Dr. White points out that some schools use roll-in demonstration tables, but that the very act of rolling-in consumes classroom time. Furthermore, the portable tables limit the size and type of demonstration apparatus which can be used. Professors sometimes prefer to skip an experiment rather than perform it with inadequate apparatus. The revolving stage is one answer.

ENTER THE ELECTRONIC AGE

Another answer, discovered by Professor White when he taught physics on a network television series, involves the problem of sight. No matter how efficiently a classroom experiment is handled, it is of little use to the student unless he can see it. To the student, an experiment in physics sometimes seems more like an exercise in eyestrain, particularly if he is at the rear of a large lecture hall. Some instructors have tried to overcome this deficiency by using oversized apparatus. But there is a point where giant equipment becomes more trouble than it is worth. And, some demonstrations simply cannot be enlarged. Professor White's solution: the television camera.

In his *American Journal of Physics* article, Professor White suggested that two or three television cameras be mounted above the demonstration tables to pick up the experiments. The images then would be transmitted on a closed circuit to monitors suspended from the ceiling of the auditorium. Even those students in the rear of the auditorium would have a close-up view of the demonstrations. Dr. White listed other advantages to the use of closed-circuit television in the lecture hall:

"Because television cameras can move in for close-up views, apparatus can be physically small. This means that most new devices are less expensive to make, require far less space for storage and are easily and quickly transported and set up in the lecture room .... Since the camera is focused on the exact area to be viewed, the students see exactly what the instructor wants them to see. As a result, the students are not distracted by things of little consequence."

Professor White's article focused attention on the second great change affecting the design of classroom buildings on the nation's campuses: the electronic revolution. Television, the motion-picture projector, the tape recorder, and similar devices are an old and by now familiar story on the campus. But until recently, television and the other audio-visual gadgetry have been used largely as occasional supplements for learning. Only in rare instances has a college or university harnessed the full pedagogical potential of the electron tube.

Now, however, a number of institutions have found that modern technology offers teaching aids of incalculable value. The result is that some architects are designing buildings as electronic machines as well as human shelter. In these cases, television, movie projectors, and the like no longer are installed in campus buildings as an afterthought. In a sense, the buildings are being designed around the machines, as was the case at the revolutionary University College at the University of Miami.

Opened in 1961, University College was conceived, designed, and engineered for the primary purpose of instructing large groups of students through the medium of closed-circuit television. Six of the eight pie-shaped wedges which make up the octagonal building are air-conditioned, windowless, 300-seat lecture halls. The other wedges are temporarily broken up into small classrooms. In the front of each lecture hall looms a 10-foot square viewing screen. Through these screens, televised instruction in the humanities and natural and social sciences is projected to most of Miami's 4,500 freshmen and sophomores. The televised lectures are supplemented by seminars and laboratories, but the video tube remains the sparkplug of underclass education on the Coral Gables campus.

The Miami octagon, which cost about $672,000—or $15.26 per square foot, including air conditioning—is a model of educational efficiency. In it, the University's finest lecturers sit in a television studio and address 1,800 students simultaneously. With the aid of video tape these same professors can reach another 1,800 students gathered in the same lecture halls later that same day. Theoretically, a single professor can lecture to a "class" of 3,600—more students than some teachers confront in decades of teaching.

The heart of the Miami operation lies in the projection core in the center of the octagon. From this core, films, film strips, slides, and television images are projected onto the screens at the front of each lecture hall. Because the projection equipment is behind the screen, students are not distracted or disturbed by mechanical operations.

Through the middle of the octagon runs a service "spine" housing a television studio, storage areas, facilities for the projection of visual aids, and offices for the 22-man staff of producer-directors, technicians, clerks, and artists who provide back-up services for the teaching staff. (Similar spines run along the sides of rectangular lecture centers on the campuses of the State University of New York.)

For "live" classes, instructors use lecterns on the stages of each auditorium. Each lectern gives the teacher push-button control over lighting and sound levels in the classroom as well as over the projectors and tape recorders behind the screen. In addition, one auditorium has been outfitted with utilities and waste outlets to facilitate science demonstrations.

As might be expected in a pioneering structure, the Miami octagon is not without its critics. Some faculty members are less than enthusiastic about television teaching, while others who favor it complain of conflicts with the technical staff. Still others grumble about the lighting, the size of the seats, and shaky tablet arms (which since have been re-engineered). One local technical journal criticized the building as "heavy-handed" and aesthetically unattractive. Architect Robert Fitch Smith of Miami wishes he could have "done more" with the outside of the building, but explains that the stringencies of the budget did not allow for more.

Nevertheless, University College gets high grades from most of the Miamians who teach and learn there. "This building has yielded some unexpected educational dividends," said social science professor Robert Munson, one of the faculty's star performers. "With those walls sharply tapering down to the big screen, all eyes naturally focus on the image of the teacher. The effect is like on of those 'Uncle Sam Wants You' posters. You can't get that in the ordinary classroom."

For Professor Munson, one of the major advantages in teaching at University College is that each of his lectures is given a re-run in the afternoon. "I like to watch the tape showing," he confessed. "It lets me look for weak spots in my lecture. I can also watch the reaction of the kids. I don't think the medium bothers them. This is a generation raised on television."

By and large, the students seem to agree. Typically, Barbara Thompson, a junior from Coral Gables, asked, "In a large university with large classes, what difference does it make whether the teacher is there in person or on television? I don't think anyone minds one way or the other."

University College, not surprisingly, has become a pedagogical mecca for educators and technicians concerned with the effectiveness of television as a teaching tool. In its use of television, the new Miami installation is unique. But in its equipment it is just one of many examples of what is called the "systems" approach to audio-visual engineering. Several other institutions have linked up an assortment of electronic devices for use in the classroom and lecture hall. At Teachers College-North, for instance, the Teleprompter Corporation hooked together a $40,000 system in a 673-seat auditorium. Dubbed "Telemation" by the designers, the system provides for completely integrated and automated rear screen projection of images and sound from an array of motion-picture, slide, and film-strip projectors; stereophonic tape recorders; and closed-circuit television.

The Telemation system makes the instructor the master rather than the confused servant of the equipment. Using a remote control or "automated" lectern, the professor can activate appropriate audio-visual devices at moments of his choosing, merely by pressing a button. In more sophisticated applications, the instructor doesn't even have to be present. By placing cue strips on a pre-recorded taping of the lecture, the required audio-visual equipment can be brought into play automatically without the aid of either the professor or a behind-the-scenes technician.

Telemation employs three screens for the simultaneous projection of visual images. The triple images are supposed to reinforce the learning process by enabling a student to quickly compare and contrast different views of the same subject or object. Some audio-visual experts consider the multiple screens as one of the exciting innovations of recent years. However, Professor C. R. Carpenter of Pennsylvania State University, cautions against placing too much emphasis on the sheer number of images and screens.

"It is quite possible," says Professor Carpenter, director of the Division of Academic Research and Services at Penn State, "that the additional screens and display surfaces are more distracting than helpful to the student. There is, I feel, a limit to the amount of information a student should be required to absorb in a limited period of time." The new, $3 million circular lecture center to be built at Penn State will have only two screens in each of its four auditoriums. Moreover, Penn State refuses to commit itself completely to the increasingly popular rear screen projection method. "We'll use the rear screen system," Professor Carpenter said, "but we've made provision for front screen as well. It is a much better means for showing color films frequently used in the art school."

THE ELECTRONIC TUTOR

The electronic tube also has had an impact on individual study, which since the invention of the printing press has been largely limited to books, a student, and a source of light. At Teachers College-North, for example, electronics will be used to lure students to the Q-Spaces. By March, 1964, the college hopes to have eight carrels experimentally outfitted with a set of earphones, a tape recorder, a small television monitor, and a telephone-type dial. By dialing a number, students will be able to hook into a master random-access system of tape-recorded instructional materials. They will also be able to tune in one of several closed-circuit television channels featuring a variety of supplementary instructional programs. If the experiment succeeds, both educationally and electronically, all the carrels eventually will be fitted out in the same way.

Florida Atlantic University plans to equip each of the 200 carrels in its learning resources laboratory (a combination classroom and study center) with its own writing surface, tape deck, earphones, television monitor, and either a telephone dial or set of pushbuttons. The idea, explained Len Singer, director of Learning Resources, "is that somewhere on campus we will post a daily calendar or menu of what will be available on the 'Quest Channels' at a particular time. Then, a student enrolled in a humanities course can come to the lab, be assigned to a station, press a button or operate a dial, and listen in comfort and privacy to a Shakespearean sonnet on his earphones. Or, if he is in a social science course, he can listen to a Churchill speech or a foreign policy debate. We also anticipate leaving an open channel, so that a student can request the playing of any tape which is catalogued and filed in the library. In this way, if a student wants to come in and hear something like the Mormon Tabernacle Choir, he can do that, too." Mr. Singer expects that Florida Atlantic will handle its television programing in similar fashion. As many as six closed-circuit channels will be in operation once the video system is established.

Florida Atlantic University will not build a traditional language laboratory as such. The fact that Mr. Singer can refer to such a recent innovation as the language lab as "traditional" may be one measure of the rapidity of change in educational technology. The learning resources laboratory will double as a language lab. "Whenever we need a language lab," Mr. Singer explained, "all we will do will be to bring down an operable wall and section off 50 to 75 of the 200 stations in the learning lab. We don't intend to put expensive electronic facilities into a language classroom and then see them lie idle half the day."

Ultimately, Florida Atlantic's Q-Spaces will be equipped with a system through which students will respond to questions preprogramed into the audio and visual tapes. Such a system has already been developed by Corrigan and Associates of San Mateo, California. In the Corrigan system, when the student presses the correct button to respond to a question, a green light flashes on a plate attached to the television monitor. A wrong answer produces a red light. The student continues to press buttons until he finally gets the green light. However, each time he presses a button, a hole is punched in an IBM card. When the telecast is over, the professor (or studio technician) presses a button, releasing the cards for machine grading.

Less elaborate and less automated response systems are being installed in the new lecture halls at Miami, Texas, Teachers College-North, and Penn State, where Ray Carpenter built the forerunner of all such systems in 1948. In the live teaching situation, the response systems can be used both for grading purposes and to help the instructor determine how well his lecture is being received. Several commercial response systems feed student answers into a box or meter on the instructor's lectern. If a large number of students press the wrong button, in response to a simple verbal or visual question about the lecture, the instructor will see the result on his lectern. Then, theoretically, he can pause, go back over his material, and ask the same question a second time.

"In the old days," said one professor, "students were asked to raise their hands if they were unable to follow what the teacher was saying. That was a little like asking a group of women at a party to raise their hands if they felt they were not as well dressed as the other women there. You never got much of a response. The electronic system should make the problem of determining who has gotten what out of a lecture a little less embarrassing to the student and a little less frustrating to the teacher."

Response systems may help universities to determine the precise educational value of the expensive audio-visual systems they are installing in their classrooms and lecture halls. Just such an evaluation is under way at the University of Wisconsin's School of Education, where a Telemation system has been in use since 1961 in a 277-seat auditorium. During the spring of 1962, Dr. Michael Petrovich presented an automated and pre-recorded course in Russian history. The tape carried not only Dr. Petrovich's voice, but appropriate background music such as Tchaikovsky's "1812 Overture." On the triple screens, students viewed an integrated succession of maps, pictures, charts, diagrams, names, and dates designed to reinforce the verbal presentation. Queried at the end of the semester, 69 of the 73 students indicated that, given a choice, they would prefer a Telemated presentation to a simple lecture.

Not that the system at Wisconsin is perfect; far from it. The visuals are somewhat crude and frequently irrelevant. Many of them, particularly those thrown on the smaller screens are not legible from the rear of the not-too-large auditorium. But Dr. John Guy Fowlkes, the moving spirit behind the program, explained: "We're not wedded to any one screen size, method of projection, lighting, or type of auditorium. This is a multi-media laboratory in human learning. We want to find out what effect visual and audio aids have on learning. We want to know, among other things, what kind of aids should be used, how many should be used during each class session, and how long they should be kept on the screen."

Similarly, Chicago Teachers College-North has not been without problems in making proper use of its Telemated auditorium. During the first year of operation the system rarely was used as it should have been. The reason was simple: no one had time to give it much thought. Instead of exploring the potentials of the automated system and multiple visual images, most of the lectures in the auditorium were presented in rather traditional fashion. "What we should have done," said Dr. Jerry Sachs, dean of the academic program, "was to have found out what we needed and wanted in a large auditorium and then gone ahead and built it. We're pleased with what we have, but we now have to adapt our programs to the auditorium, instead of the other way around."

But progress is being made. Already, one English course has been fully programed to take advantage of the system. Other courses will be adapted in the future as Robert Walker, the industrious young speech teacher who directs the auditorium operations, orients the faculty in its functions. Mr. Walker feels that, once this happens and once the auditorium is equipped with a response system, it will begin to fulfill its purpose: involving the student directly and actively in the learning process. "When the student is brought into the lecture with the response system and when we use the multiple screens to produce a panorama of sensory experiences rather than to illustrate a verbal point," he said, "then we will have begun to exploit the potential of Telemation."

Obviously the electronic teaching facility requires an expertise generally not found among most college faculties. For a system such as Telemation to function as it should, a technical staff must work in close conjunction with the faculty. Adrian TerLouw, educational consultant at Eastman Kodak, believes that, even in the smallest college, a minimum staff of three would be needed to provide proper back-up service for the faculty.

The technicians, in the ideal arrangement, should do more than run the machines and produce the audio-visuals. They must, in Mr. TerLouw's view, be prepared to work with the faculty in the time-consuming and sometimes painful task of reorganizing a course for audio-visual presentation. All too frequently, there has been only token integration of audio-visuals in lectures. Mr. TerLouw, who has worked directly with several universities in revamping courses for audio-visual presentation, insists that the instructor must sit down with the technical specialist and learn to look at his course material from the student's point of view. This, he says, takes a good deal of the professor's time and a large measure of professional and intellectual adjustment. "The criteria of a good lecture is not what happens to the professor's ego, but what happens to the student's mind," said Mr. Ter-Louw. "The teacher must learn that he is just one part of the learning process. He must, in other words, learn to keep his mouth shut."

THE RELUCTANT PROFESSORS

In many hallowed halls of ivy, this prospect is about as inviting as a fellowship to the South Pole. The truth is that many scholars have a highly un-communal feeling about television and other audio-visual devices. They view the new gadgetry with a combination of discomfort, disdain, and distrust. The ever growing shortage of teachers renders groundless the professional fear of technological unemployment. But it doesn't alter the professional attitude toward the machine. Elwin Stevens of the State University of New York commented: "We can build all kinds of new spaces for learning, but getting the professors to teach in them is another, and thus far unsolved, problem."

Doubtless, the cold war between the scholar and the machine will intensify as the electronic revolution accelerates on the campus. It will be difficult to disabuse some faculty of the notion that an audio-visual system consists of a hare-brained student lugging a half-broken projector into a dimly lit room to show a scratchy old film that is as academically pertinent as a "Three Stooges" short. But the state of educational technology has come a long way from this doleful image, and it will travel considerably further in the years to come. Just beyond the frontier of learning lies an educational tool that has barely been explored by the colleges and universities: the computer.

Data processing machines are making up payrolls, writing checks, and handling other administrative chores in higher education. But few institutions have explored the computer's possibilities as a teaching device. Philip Lewis, director of the Bureau of Instructional Materials for the Chicago Board of Education, says the day is not far off when "closed-circuit television and the computer will be employed along with scientific programing to determine important ways in which instruction can be individualized for each student—the teacher modifying sequences based upon regular checks of progress, and the computer itself modifying presentations automatically as a result of the success or failure of student responses."

There is promise that in the near future the computer will be in use in a good many college classrooms across the country. But there is reason to question whether equipment and programing costs ever will be reduced enough to put the computer within the reach of all colleges or the most advanced computer technology within reach of any of them.

One story making the rounds of faculty dining rooms, concerns the bright young instructor of 25 years hence who becomes appalled at the cost of equipping each student with an electronic carrel, each classroom with automated audio-visual systems, and each building with computers and color television receivers and transmitters. One evening, adding up all the costs and dividing them by the number of students at the college, a startling idea strikes the young teacher. The next morning he rushes in to see his dean and announces: "Look, instead of spending all this money on operable walls, revolving stages, and coaxial cables, why don't we just divide up the student body into groups of 25 or 30 and put each group into a small room with a live Ph.D.? I don't know how the faculty will like the idea, but it's worth trying."

The story has a simple moral—there still is much to be said for the old-fashioned classroom and the old-fashioned "live" teacher. Any student who has ever sat within a few feet of a really great teacher—a Samuel Eliot Morison at Harvard, a Frederick Pottle at Yale—knows that there is an indefinable magic in the human presence that no electronic tube can ever duplicate. If the human presence made no difference, the legitimate theater would have disappeared during the nickelodeon era. Clearly, many professors are reluctant to introduce technology into their classrooms not because they fear for their jobs or their status or because they do not understand the machine. They fear something else entirely—the dehumanizing of one of the most human of all experiences—learning.

There seems to be a need, therefore, to plan the new, "automated" instructional facility with man—or boy and girl—uppermost in mind. The coldly perfect building doesn't seem to fit into the environment of learning. The University of Miami discovered this in its highly efficient and functional University College. The problem was that, if the televised lectures in the auditorium became too slick and too perfect, student attention tended to wane. The solution was to program small but obvious errors into the scripts to keep the audiences mentally alert.

Practice had made Miami instructors too perfect. The deliberate "slips" somehow made them more human and more believable.

The experience of the University of Miami has also proved the wisdom, in an era of large group instruction, of following up mass lectures with frequent face-to-face contacts between student and teacher. The "University College auditorium," explained Dean Paul Vonk, "has enabled us to expose more students to our best teachers and at lower cost than would be possible by traditional methods. But it would be of little educational value if we did not supplement the televised lectures with smaller seminars and laboratories and frequent student-faculty conferences."

What emerges from the present ferment in teaching practices, and consequently in facilities, is not a simple answer to tomorrow's problems. A drive for increased efficiency, both in teaching and learning, the utilization of more educational tools, and at the same time a growing concern for the individual and for amenity, seem to offer a series of basically conflicting factors. One of the great challenges to education, and to architecture, will be to reconcile these factors in a new synthesis over the remaining years of this century. To develop a new balance in education between the human and economic factors, in the face of the pressures created by enrollment growth and faculty shortages, is the key issue.

Ultimately, each college or university must develop its own educational programs and, from them, determine what form its buildings will take and how they will be equipped. The most successful instructional facilities are more than bricks and mortar. When they are appropriate to the individual college, they can become teaching tools in themselves.

The Culturally Different, Deprived or Economically Marginal Student: A Challenge to Education

By Edmund W. Gordon

Over the last two decades a number of economic, political and social factors have combined to bring to the forefront of our attention the condition of under-development among human beings in all parts of the world. But though we have become increasingly aware of the economic and social disparities which exist everywhere, nowhere are the handicaps imposed by deliberate and accidental underdevelopment of human resources a greater source of embarrassment and concern than in the United States in the second half of the 20th Century. Faced with an embarrassing situation we have done as we are prone to do; we have looked for a scapegoat, and no one in this situation has seemed more available to bear the blame than the professional educator. The choice is not without justification. Granted that the school has not created the conditions that make for social disadvantage and economic deprivation, it is quite clear that neither have professional educators done much to help significantly the children who are products of those conditions—this in spite of the fact that there have been tremendous gains in educational technology and educational resources.

The Panel of Education Research and Development has reported:

"By all known criteria, the majority of urban and rural slum schools are failures. In neighborhood after neighborhood across the country, more than half of each age group fails to complete high school, and 5% or fewer go on to some form of higher education. In many schools the average IQ is under 85, and it drops steadily as the children grow older. Adolescents depart from these schools ill-prepared to lead a satisfying, useful life or to participate successfully in the community." (Zacharias, 1964)

From a speech given in June 1966 at Stanford University.

Who are the children so poorly served by this, the most affluent nation in history?

The term socially disadvantaged refers to a group of populations which differ from each other in a number of ways but have in common such characteristics as low economic status, low social status, low educational achievement, tenuous or no employment, limited participation in community organizations and limited ready potential for upward mobility. Variously referred to as the "culturally deprived," the "socio-economically deprived," the "socially and culturally disadvantaged," the "chronically poor," the "poverty-stricken," the "culturally alienated," and so on, these are people who are handicapped by depressed social and economic status and, in too many instances, by ethnic and cultural *caste* status as well. For a number of interrelated reasons more and more of these families are coming to be concentrated in the decaying hearts of our great metropolitan centers. Predominantly Negro, Puerto Rican, Mexican and southern rural or mountain whites, these people are the bearers of cultural attitudes alien to those dominant in the communities they now inhabit, and their children come to the schools disadvantaged to the degree that their culture has failed to provide them with the experience "normal" to the kinds of children the schools are used to teaching.

Consequently, in the schools, the children of these families show disproportionally high rates of social maladjustment, behavioral disturbance, physical disability, academic retardation and mental subnormality. Such problems are acute wherever they are found, but they have been exacerbated and brought to the center of our attention by the recent increasing concentration of this population in our center city areas.

Now, the fact is, that the presence in our schools of children whose background of experience and whose readiness for traditional school demands differ from those of white, middle-class U.S. nationals is not a new phenomenon. We have had large numbers of such children in the past, particularly during the period of great migrations to this country, and history reveals that the schools were challenged at that time just as they are today. It is also clear that they failed in their attempt at providing for the educational needs of many of these children. But the schools' failure in previous years had far less serious consequences for the children and for society than do our failures today.

Unlike the industrializing economy of the 19th and early 20th centuries, our automating economy has little need for the talents which the uneducated have to offer: manual strength and manual skill, the products of strong backs and clever hands. We have instead, a growing need for trained minds, educated judgments and conceptual skills. We have arrived at a period in human history in which man is increasingly required to manage vast categories of knowledge, to identify and solve highly complicated interdisciplinary problems and to arrive at infinitely complex conceptualizations and judgments in order to maintain, control and advance the technological and social organization by which we live. The quality of intellect, the adequacy of conceptual competence, and the depth of human understanding and compassion required of those who must man that organization are not routinely produced in today's schools. In fact, we school people are constantly embarrassed by the large numbers of young people whom we have failed to prepare for much less complex intellectual, academic, vocational and social functioning. We are also under attack, from a number of quarters, for our failure to give adequate preparation even to many of those who seem to succeed in our system. Witness the large number of high school and college graduates who have difficulty recognizing a concept and are practically incapable of producing a clear one. Professional education has a long history and is not without its successes, but its failures are many and in its present state it is hardly ready to meet the demands of the latter half of the Twentieth Century—this time of crisis in the management of knowledge and technology.

Our nation has faced crises before. Following the great depression of the early thirties we were confronted with the incongruities caused by high level industrial potential existing side by side with low level social-economic organization. Organizing workers by challenging the status quo, led our nation into new avenues of governmental responsibility for the promotion of the general welfare. New concepts, new techniques, new approaches to political, social, and economic organization were introduced and ultimately accepted as *social necessity* in a modern industrialized society. It was these innovations which in large measure enabled this nation to meet the domestic and international challenge of midcentury.

Now another social revolution has emerged, one not unrelated to the growing crisis in intellectual resources and the management of knowledge. This time the fight is being waged by Negroes—and their allies, soon, no doubt, by the poverty stricken as well—in the name of civil, or more properly, human rights. What they are demanding is total and meaningful integration into the mainstream of our society, with an opportunity to share in the wealth of our nation. As a means to that end, equality of educational achievement is viewed as crucial, and herein lies the challenge to the school. For there is little doubt that the revolution will succeed, but just as the social revolution of the thirties challenged our society to move to a higher level of social-economic organization, so the civil or human rights revolution, the accelerating technological development and the explosion in knowledge will force some changes for society in general and for education in particular. The schools can no longer postpone meeting the challenges, the responsibilities and the opportunities of this new situation. And they are not. In many parts of the country school systems and responsible agencies have begun to invest both talent and concern in developing special programs to educate disadvantaged children. Such programs have come to be designated as compensatory because they attempt in a variety of ways to compensate for the cultural handicaps with which these children come to schools.

It is quite evident, though it has not always been acted upon, that as an initial step in providing equality of education for disadvantaged children we must first determine the exact nature of their disadvantage —that is, we must investigate, describe and evaluate the ways in which they differ from those children with whom our traditional education system has been successful. For though the fact of academic deficiency among a high percentage of this population is well documented, the specific nature of the deficiency is not. Psycho-educational appraisal has been directed more often at the fact and quantity of deficit than at its quality and nature. In attempting to define the conditions of disadvantage, California's Advisory Committee on Compensatory Education concluded that such children could generally be identified among those who were "below average in school achievement as measured by standardized tests" and who, in addition, have some combination of one or more of the following problems:

1. economic deprivation attributable to an absent, nonproducing, or marginally producing breadwinner;
2. social alienation caused by racial or ethnic discrimination with all its accompanying deprivations in housing, employment and education, or by membership in a different and/or non-English speaking sub-cultural group; and
3. geographic isolation because they are transient or live in an area far removed from adequate educational facilities.

If such are the social factors which correlate most highly with disadvantage, what are the qualities common to children who are the products of such socially handicapping backgrounds. The California report suggests:

"They tend to lack in the social experience which our curricula assume to be common to all students. This is to say that their experiences in the society are marked by sharp differences from the 'normal' or 'regular' pattern assumed by the middle-class oriented school."

"Their motivation may be inappropriate to normal school achievement or success. That is, they may display sense of failure or lack of drive."

"They often have been subject to value and expectations which tend to generate conflict between themselves and the school."

Valuable as this classification of traits may be in identifying children who should be included in specially designed educational programs, it can hardly serve as an adequate theoretical basis for structuring such programs. To say that a disadvantaged child lacks readiness, motivation and a learning-oriented value structure is not so much a description of what a disadvantaged child is as it is a description of the way he appears to be when he is faced with a traditional school environment. In order to determine whether or not the disadvantaged child is, indeed, what he appears to be, a number of researchers have attempted to define much more specifically the factors in disadvantaged or deprived backgrounds which produce disability in these children as well as the specific qualities of which this disability consists.

Available research data permit the identification of several categories of behavior which are encountered with great frequency among socially disadvantaged youth. First there are several studies which suggest that children from disadvantaged backgrounds in comparison with middle class children are less able to make use of conventional verbal symbols in representing and interpreting their feelings, their experience, and the objects in their environment. It is important to note that the apparent deficiency is in the use of such conventional verbal symbols—there is no definitive evidence that such children suffer from an underlying deficiency in symbolic representation.

Available evidence suggests that depressed language function can be the result of a variety of circumstances which make for disadvantaged status. Kellner, Pringle and Tanner (1958) found in a group of youth of comparable economic level, age, sex, and I.Q. differences on all quantitative measures of language function, differences which consistently favored children raised in their own homes as opposed to children raised in institutions. The authors suggested that youth raised in the institutions studied were disadvantaged by an insufficient language stimulation resulting in restricted capacity for language development. Other investigators have been concerned with language development in different economic groups. Davis (1937) found a considerably higher percentage of youth with good articulation among upper occupational groups than among lower. Beckey (1942) reported finding significantly more children with retarded speech among lower socio-economic groups. Templin (1953) found a significant difference between children of upper and lower economic groups on tests of articulation, the difference being in favor of the higher economic group. Her data indicate that children of the lower socio-economic group take about a year longer to reach essentially mature articulation than do those of the upper group. Irwin (1948) reported that children after the age of one-and-one-half showed significant differences in their mastery of speech sounds according to their father's occupational status—with the advantage in the direction of the higher occupational groups.

Anastasi (1952) compared Negro and Caucasian children and found among the Caucasians a greater frequency of mature sentence types, more complex construction and better elaborated concept. Hilliard (1957) approaching the questions inferentially, found that children with rich information backgrounds were better equipped for reading than were pupils whose previous experience had been meager. In studies by Thomas (1963) and Templin (1957) in which the variable studied was number of words used per remark, Thomas' subjects drawn from a low socioeconomic group showed a mean of 5.6 words used, while Templin's subjects drawn from a middle class population showed a mean of 6.9 words per remark.

In what is probably the most careful, though limited, study of linguistic behavior in lower and middle class subjects, Bernstein (1961) reported that the language of lower class youth tends to be "restricted" in form. He characterized this language as serving to communicate signals and direction and to confine thinking to a relatively low level of repetitiveness. On the other hand, he described the language of the middle and upper classes as "elaborated" and serving to communicate ideas, relationships, feelings and subjective states. These works suggest that symbolic representation is present in both classes, but also that important qualitative differences exist in the form and utilization of the symbol or language systems. These differences may have important implications for learning. However, since these studies have not included analysis of learning facility or lack of it in terms of language forms and vernacular peculiar to the population, the data do not enable us to determine accurately the specific nature of the learning disabilities involved.

But the inferential conclusions drawn from these studies, relating school failure to differences in language development in disadvantaged children, gain some support from studies of concept development in this population. Reissman (1962) has described concept formation among the disadvantaged as content centered rather than form centered, their reasoning as inductive rather than deductive. Such a conceptual style has been viewed as limiting the child's ability to make accurate generalizations and to transfer knowledge utilizing previously learned concepts (Gordon, 1963).

Deutsch (1963) and Hillard (1957) have noted that increasing age amplifies the difference in the quality of language usage between classes; and Deutsch has suggested that if the acquisition of language is a prerequisite of concept formation and problem solving, then these evidences of relative increasing language deficiency would indicate a tremendous lower class deficit in conceptual function. Deutsch (1963) found that his subjects, drawn from a disadvantaged population, were relatively proficient on motor tasks, on tasks which required a short time span, and on tasks which could be most easily related to concrete objects and services; but, as he later reported (1964) he found lower class children generally inferior in abstract conceptualization and in the categorizing of visual stimuli. Ausubel (1963) concluded that when there was a delay in the acquisition of certain formal language forms, there was a resultant difficulty in making the transition from concrete to abstract modes of thought.

In a cross cultural inventory of the arithmetic concepts of kindergarteners, Montague (1964) found significant differences between social classes in favor of the higher SES group; but Deutsch (1960) found that arithmetic scores were higher than reading scores among a population of lower class children, even though both were depressed below national norms. In interpreting this finding, the investigator suggested that the difference might be accounted for by an hypothesis that reading involves motivations ariving from specific value systems not shared by the disadvantaged society, while arithmetic may involve concrete acts, such as marketing, which are common to the society. In the work of the author (Gordon, 1965) in Prince Edward County, Virginia, arithmetic scores were similarly found to be less depressed than reading scores in the 7 to 10 year age groups. These children who had been deprived of formal education for four years are thought to have developed simple arithmetic skills in their everyday chore experiences, which experiences did not, however, provide a basis for the casual or incidental acquisition of reading skills.

If these assumptions about the experience-based distinctions between acquisition of reading and arithmetic skills are correct, then the Montague, Deutsch, and Gordon data would seem to support the observation that disadvantaged children tend to depend more on concrete than symbolic experience in dealing with concepts. In a study by Siller (1957), however, this view is subjected to closer examination.

Studying 181 white sixth graders, he found that higher status children (a) scored higher than lower status children on all tests of conceptual ability; (b) showed a significantly greater tendency toward abstraction in making choices between types of definitions than lower status children; and (c) when matched with lower status subjects on non-verbal tests, scored higher than their counterparts on tests of verbal concepts. Had Siller stopped there, his findings would confirm the impressions of others. When, however, the groups were matched on the basis of I.Q. scores, none of the above differences remained. The investigator suggests that this is due to an elimination of the lower extreme of the low status group which in turn suggests that differences with respect to conceptual style may be a result of generally lower levels of intellectual function (as measured on intelligence tests) among lower status children. Thus, while there is a considerable body of evidence to support the statement that lower status children tend to show preference for concrete as opposed to abstract frames of reference in concept formation, the origin and nature of this style dominance and its relationship to intelligence and the teaching-learning process are yet to be established.

Among other disadvantageous characteristics, disadvantaged children have been noted by several investigators and observers to demonstrate perceptual styles and perceptual habits which are either inadequate or irrelevant to the demands of academic efficiency. Although high levels of perceptual sensitization and discrimination are often present, these skills tend to be better developed in physical than in visual behavior and in visual than in aural behavior (Reissman, 1962). Probably the most significant characteristic in this area is the extent to which these children fail to develop a high degree of dependence on the verbal and written language forms of academicians for learning cues. Many of the children simply have not adopted the modes of reception and expression which are traditional to and necessary for success in school.

The extent to which styles of perception and expression differ among children of different backgrounds is well documented. In his study of retarded, average and gifted children, Jensen (1964) concluded that many children viewed as retarded have merely failed to learn the verbal mediators which facilitate school learning. Earlier Carson (1960) found white children superior to Negroes and northern Negroes superior to southern Negroes when it came to understanding the meanings of words used in communication. In a study of children's use of time in their own stories, Leshan (1952) found that time orientation varies with social class and that middle and upper class children told stories involving a more prolonged period of time than those of lower class children. Reissman (1962) includes slowness as a feature of the cognitive functioning of disadvantaged youngsters, a conclusion arrived at by Davidson some ten years earlier (1950) on finding differences in speed of response to be primarily responsible for racial differences in I.Q. estimated by timed performance tests.   Deutsch (1964) found lower class children relatively poorer in auditory discrimination, in recognizing perceptual similarities, and in the syntactical manipulation of language.   Earlier (1960) he had found them inferior to a control group on tasks requiring concentration and persistence.

In fact, many of the children with whom we are concerned show a marked lack of involvement with, attention to, and concentration on the content of their academic experiences.   There are few academic tasks which commit them to deep involvement.   Their work habits are frequently insufficiently developed.   Because of the high interest demands of non-academic experiences and the relatively low-interest demands of academic experiences, they are limited in their ability to inhibit responses to those stimuli which are extraneous to academic learning and to disinhibit responses which are pertinent to academic learning.   Deutsch (1960) reported that lower class children tend to ignore difficult problems with a "so what" attitude and that as a result over a period of time their learning is decreased proportionally.   Ausubel (1963) found that lower class children depend more on external as opposed to internal control than do children from the middle class.

Moreover, socially disadvantaged children have been determined by several investigators to be less highly motivated and to have lower aspiration for academic and vocational achievement than do their middle and upper class school peers.   The degree of motivation and the direction which it takes among many of these children are often inconsistent with both the demands and the goals of formal education. But although the quality of aspiration is often depressed, it is usually consistent with the child's perceptions of the opportunities and rewards available to him.   Symbolic rewards and postponements of gratification appear to have little value as positive motivators of achievement. For these children goals tend to be self-centered, immediate and utilitarian, as are the goals of the dominant culture.   However, children growing up under more privileged circumstances have available many sources of immediate satisfaction and immediate feed back as well as many more evidences of the utilitarian value of academic effort.   The differences between the privileged and the disadvantaged in this area are not so much differences in values as differences in the circumstances under which the values are called into play.   Although the values from which motivation is derived in the disadvantaged child seem to reflect the dominant-culture concern with status, material possessions, in-group morality, Judeo-Christian Ethics, competition, etc., there is usually lacking a concern with the aesthetics of knowledge, symboliza-tion as an art form, introspection and competition with one's self. In other words, dominant societal goals and value are operative, but their direction and context may not be complementary to academic achieve-ment.

Rosen (1956) observing a relationship between high motivation and high grades postulated that middle-class children are more likely to be taught the motives and values which make achievement possible. Similarly, in Gould's study (1941) only sons who internalized their parent's values of aspiration were sufficiently motivated to overcome obstacles which faced them in school. Bernstein (1960) found achieve-ment strivings arising from parental demands for success to be a more central motivational factor among middle-class than among lower-class children.

Closely related to these motivational factors are attitudinal factors, and these too are often a source of problems in educational planning for disadvantaged children. Hieronymus (1951) found that higher socio-economic status was correlated with a level of aspiration and positive attitudes toward school while negative attitudes toward school and lower levels of aspiration were more frequently encountered in lower socio-economic status groups. Sewell's (1957) finding that edu-cational aspirations tend to be greatly influenced by class values in a manner favoring the middle and upper classes is consistent with the earlier work. Among other characteristics which have been referred to in this population are utilitarian attitudes toward knowledge and nega-tive attitudes toward the pure pursuit of knowledge. Many of these children and their parents view education primarily in terms of its job market value and their orientation is toward achieving the mini-mum level of education commensurate with employability. Carrol (1945) sees the lower class ideal self as characterized by personal beauty and fame, not the moral and intellectual qualities which characterize the ideal self of middle class children.

As important as these attitudes toward school and learning may be, it is in the area of attitude toward self and others that the crucial determinants of achievement and upward mobility may lie, and it is in these areas that our data are least clear. It has been observed by some that disadvantaged children show affinity for ingroup members and demonstrate a sense of distance from or even hostility toward repre-sentatives of out-groups, whether in peer or non-peer relationships.

Contrastingly, other observers have noted the high degree of respect and awe in which these children hold selected out-group status persons or idealized models. Tendencies toward self-depreciation and depressed self-concepts have been noted by several observers (Dreger, 1960; Keller, 1963; Silverman, 1963). Good (1954) found that lower class children have more feelings of inadequacy in school than do children from the middle class. On the other hand, some recent findings (Gordon, 1965) suggest that depressed self-concept is not so prevalent a condition, and that even where present it may have little negative bearing on achievement. In fact, it is entirely possible that positive or negative feeling of self-worth may operate respectively to depress or accelerate achievement. Furthermore, it is in this area that the rapidly changing national and world situations involving underdeveloped peoples are likely to be most influential, and it is difficult to predict the ultimate effect of these altered situations on self-perception and behavioral change. Our knowledge and even our researchable hunches are as yet limited. But it is around these changing situations that the school may yet find a fulcrum on which to lever up motivation, aspiration and involvement. There is growing empirical evidence to support the view that young people actively associated with current civil rights struggle draw from their involvement in that effort a new source of motivation and an enhanced view of themselves (Coles, 1963). The impression is gained that such experiences are reflected in greater application of effort to and greater achievement in academic endeavors. The evidence for such improvement is less clear, yet there can be little doubt that attitudes toward self and toward the environment in relation to self are crucial variables in academic as well as in social and emotional learning situations.

It is noteworthy that much of the work done on characteristics of disadvantaged children has focused on their weaknesses, deficits or limitations. With the notable exception of Reissman (1962) attempts at identification of positives or strengths in this population are hard to find. However, even in Reissman's treatment there is a tendency to romanticize these characteristics which may be a more serious error than to ignore them. Among the several positives which may be identified are those behaviors and conditions which can be utilized upon for the purposes of educational improvement. It is extremely important to recognize that *selective* motivation, creativity and proficiency are present in this population, and, as Reissman has consistently stressed, if we look for these characteristics in their traditional form and along traditionally academic dimensions, we shall merely insure that they not be found. These children, like others, *are* motivated by *some* factors in the field. They show creativity in *some* situations. They are proficient at *some* tasks and under *some* conditions.

Reference has earlier been made to problems in language development and use. In contrast to the colloquially accepted concept that language is inadequate in this population is the proposition that there exist in disadvantaged populations quite complex languages. The form in which the language is expressed may not be verbal nor may the specific symbols be consistent with those normative to the dominant culture. But the presence of a language system or a system of symbolic representation adequate to the needs of the culture in which it has developed should not be ignored. The important question then becomes not whether language exists, but to what extent a given language system may be utilized in understanding and managing advanced conceptual problems. If the facts and integrative relationships of science, or the conceptual explorations of philosophy cannot be expressed in symbols capable of incorporation into the language system in question, then that language, though it may be adequate for the culture in which it exists, is inadequate to the demands of contemporary educational processes. To date, investigations into the utilitarian dimensions of divergent language patterns have not been conducted. Our research has established the fact of language differences (Deutsch, 1963, 1964; Jensen, 1963; John, 1965), and in addition we know something of the nature of these differences. The Bernstein work (1961, 1962) referred to earlier characterized lower class language as restricted and middle class language as elaborated. Strodbeck (1964) has described a mechanism by which such language system may develop and be perpetuated. He identifies this mechanism in the context of intrafamilial decision theory where the elaborative characteristic of middle-class language is a product of parity (and thus conflict) in the decision making process in the middle class home. Restricted language on the other hand develops as a product of unilateral decision making in the lower class home. In a situation involving equality and conflict of ideas the learner (child) early develops sensitivity to language as a vehicle for the elaboration of ideas. Where the opposite situation obtains, the child early develops sensitivity to language as a vehicle for the communication of signals or directions. Some findings of C. Deutsch (1963), that there are significant class differences in the time spent in parent-child communication, are not unrelated. Her data indicate that the length of such communication is considerably shorter for lower class than for middle class subjects. This difference has been viewed as a handicap, but it may be that given a different instructional method this proclivity for brief verbal communicative contact could be an advantage to the learner.

Much of our knowledge concerning children from socially disadvantaged backgrounds has been drawn by inference from the wide literature on juvenile delinquency. Sensitive analysis of this literature leads to an awareness of several other characteristics of this population. One can not study the literature on boys' gangs or juvenile offenders without coming to the conclusion that these youngsters show ingeniousness and resourcefulness in pursuing self-selected goals and in coping with very difficult and complex conditions of life. Such coping behavior reflects accuracy of perception and generalization around a variety of social, psychological and physical phenomena. It is at once obvious that these children are capable of meaningful and loyal personal relationships and operate with an in-group morality that surpasses that of some more privileged segments of society. In many situations where the problems flow from the experiences and are important for self-selected goal, such operations as memory, recall, computation and representation have been demonstrated to be functionally adequate.

The second area to which research attention has been directed is the environment. Studies referrable to environmental concern have consisted largely of a cataloguing of the factors in homes and communities from which disadvantaged children come which may interfere with normal school achievement. Such studies have often been conducted with the ultimate aim of incorporating knowledge obtained from them in the training of school personnel so that they may "understand" the culture and values of their pupils. The concurrence between certain conditions of life, certain population characteristics and poor school adjustment has been interpreted as indicating a causal relationship, though the evidence supports only the conclusion that these phenomena are correlated. Such studies, while they may have social-anthropological value, are of questionable use in planning educational programs for these children. It is probably true that adverse conditions of life do not facilitate academic achievement in most children, but we have no firm evidence that such conditions preclude academic success. In fact, there are sufficient cases of success despite adverse conditions to make untenable the conclusion that difficult life circumstances prevent success in school. Insufficient attention has been given to the fact that many "normal" and well-functioning individuals have such adverse circumstances in their lives. There are many good reasons for improving the living conditions of the disadvantaged, and there is certainly no good excuse for an affluent society to fail to do so, but a concern on the part of the school for changing poor conditions of life should not substitute for a primary concern with the improvement of the teaching-learning process.

As one who is actively identified with the civil rights movement in this country, I was troubled two years ago when the struggle to achieve employment for Negroes focussed on the building trades. Of course I believe that the crafts unions should be open to Negro workers as members. There is no question but that employment opportunities in the construction industry must be available to all segments of our citizenry. However, it was tragic that the effort to change the lily-white character of that industry and its unions came at a time when the established skilled workers in this field were in excess of demand and the unions were under tremendous pressure to spread that available work through the shortened week and other devices to increase the demand for manual labor. The civil rights effort in this field should have come 20 or 30 years earlier. The goals being sought by the Negro workers were more appropriate to an earlier period.

Lest we make the same mistake in the projection of goals for disadvantaged youth, let us examine the direction in which our society is moving and identify some of the implicit educational goals to which we must be sensitive.

The educational tasks faced by the United States in the next three or four decades have been enlarged and complicated by three revolutionary developments. The first of these is an explosion in the quantity of knowledge available to man. It has been traditional to consider that the body of knowledge doubles every fifteen years—that today's information is, at worst, outdated tomorrow. However, in the light of the pace with which new discoveries are emerging, and in the light of the advances in technology which permit rapid processing and integrating of both new and old information at higher levels, this morning's information may well be outdated before noon. It is no longer possible for any individual to be master of the knowledge available in any basic discipline. Moreover, as knowledge expands, the distinctions between disciplines break down, thus extending the breadth of knowledge required to solve problems in any one of them. Meanwhile, there is every indication that the information pool will continue to grow, not only by arithmetic, but by geometric progression.

The second aspect of the triple revolution involves the massive increments in technological competence. The industrial revolution combined the power of the machine with the skill of man. But today we are embarked upon a new era—the cybernetic era—in which the skill of the machine is added to the power of the machine. Its principles of organization and its implications are as different from those of the industrial era as those of the industrial era were from those of the agricultural era. The union between the computer and the automated self-regulating machine can result in a system of almost unlimited productive capacity which, in contrast to the mechanical system which preceded it, requires progressively less, not more, human labor. Cybernation will force the reorganization of our economic and social structure to meet its own needs.

The third aspect of this triple revolution consists of the significant changes of the realm of political, social and economic relations which have taken place over the last two decades—the civil rights-human rights revolution at home, the rise of underdeveloped nations abroad, and the new forms of military weaponry which have eliminated war as a method of resolving international conflicts.

These revolutionary developments have serious implications for education. To enable our educational efforts to match the demands of this changed and rapidly changing situation, we must focus attention on remodeling the concepts and structure of education so that the schools of the future will not only be more appropriately aligned with the needs of that future society but will also be a positive force in facilitating societal transition.

Probably the most significant change—or at least the one with the most serious implications for education—will be that which requires the schools to shift away from an emphasis on simply rewarding the successful student. The emphasis will have to fall instead on the school's responsibility for insuring success in academic, emotional and social learning for all students save a very few who are truly mentally defective. The future will also demand of us that we abandon our focus on more and more content mastery and substitute for it a primary focus on learning to learn as a continuous process throughout life. The vast amount of knowledge available to man, together with the demands of the advanced technology by which our society moves will require of our student-future-citizens skill in the management of knowledge; just as changes in the politico-social sphere will make more necessary than ever before competence and skill in intrapersonal and interpersonal management.·

A society which approaches education with these concerns might appropriately give attention to five specific educational goals. The first of these is a renewed commitment to effective teaching—sufficiently effective to provide for all students mastery of *basic communication skills*. A real commitment to the goal of developing universal competence in speech, in reading and writing, and in arithmetic computation has crucial implications for education and for society. For education it will mean the development of such materials, methods and conditions for learning as are appropriate to the different experiential backgrounds and learning styles of children other than those for whom most of our educational practices have been designed. These practices have not even succeeded with all the pupils for whom they were designed, and they have failed completely to meet the needs of most of the children who have been designated socially disadvantaged. Consequently, a genuine determination on the part of the schools to assure universal mastery of basic communication skills would constitute a self-imposed challenge of some magnitude. The school has no choice about taking on such a challenge. In the agricultural and industrial eras, physical strength and manual skills were sufficient tools for man's survival, but it is increasingly clear that the survival tools of the cybernetic era are communication skills. If the schools cannot universally provide these tools, they will be institutionally dysfunctional in modern society.

For those lacking courage to meet the challenge, let me remind you that our concepts of educability have consistently followed society's demand for educated persons. At one time it was only the religious and political nobility from which educable persons were thought to come. When the Reformation and emerging industrial revolution required that more people be educated, we learned that educability existed in broader categories of human kind. Gradually in the West, there came a general acceptance of the notion that all white people were at least potentially educable, and in this country it was only the Negro who could not be taught. When, at last, out of humanitarian concern and societal need we began to discover that Negroes could learn, we came to accept a tacit responsibility for the education of all people. But though we have accepted the theory of universal educability, we have not attained universal education—at best we have learned how to teach that majority who meet certain rather stereotyped criteria. However, educability is a function of societal definition and societal need; and I submit that in the latter quarter of the 20th century educability will be defined in the broadest and most inclusive terms. It is in those terms that the school will be challenged to produce.

A second goal of education, only somewhat less crucial than the mastery of basic skills, involves providing students with an attitude of readiness toward, and an increasing capacity for, continued learning. We must teach people to think of the acquisition of knowledge of a lifetime undertaking, not as a pastime for youth, for the accelerating technological innovations are effecting profound changes in our job structure. Occupations are rapidly altering. We are seeing a developing stratification of people on the basis of intellectual function and technological skills. Over the last ten years the proportion of white to blue collar workers has altered radically. Now for the first time white collar workers outnumber the blue, and the trend is not likely to reverse itself. We already have the capacity to install a productive system based primarily on machine power and machine skills. The coming replacement of man by the machine will destroy many more existing jobs and render useless the work contributions of vast numbers now employed. When that time comes, and it is coming rapidly, obtaining employment in one of the new fields will depend largely upon the level of adaptive skill and the quality of education of the applicant. Unemployment rates compiled in 1959 for those with seven years of schooling or less reached 10%, compared with just over 3% for those with 13 to 15 years of schooling, and just over 1% for those with 16 years or more. A willingness to learn, and continued practice in learning will stand in good stead those who would be employed in such a marketplace.

But motivation for learning is not, of itself, enough. In any given field or group of related fields, available and necessary knowledge has already outstripped any single individual's capacity to master content. Only the student who by practice, by utilization of techniques of selection, discrimination and evaluation—has honed techniques which will allow him to sort out the worthwhile from the worthless and the significant from the insignificant—can escape being inundated in a sea of paper. Those who would succeed tomorrow, must learn not only how to acquire, but how to manage knowledge.

And this is the third of the tools with which educators should consider themselves obligated to equip tomorrow's students—the techniques of managing knowledge. Successful functioning on an intellectual level consists not in having a headful of facts, but in problem-solving, in knowing how to conceptualize problems and how to pursue the information which will provide solutions. The intellectual leaders today are those who have mastered the techniques of conceptual analysis and synthesis; and, increasingly, those who would succeed must gain competence in these skills—in the identification and analysis of principles and in their subsequent reassembling around new data to produce newer or more advanced concepts. These are the skills necessary to the successful functioning of today's intellectual elite. Tomorrow in a highly technical society, they may be necessary for most of us, not only to enable us to do productive work, but also to provide us with armor against the ravages of idle leisure.

For leisure may well be the most important industrial by-product of our coming generation. As an outgrowth of a computerized age in which 2% of the population will be able to produce all the goods and food that the other 98% can possibly consume, leisure will replace work as man's most time-consuming activity. At a meeting in 1964 of leading political and social scientists, the president of the American Academy of Political and Social Science recommended such revolutionary measures as the establishment of departments of leisure in the 50 states and the compulsory teaching of leisure skills in the public schools. He was immediately challenged from the floor as being hopelessly conservative in his approach. An economist at the meeting claimed that we face such an explosive increase in leisure that within a mere ten years we may have to keep the unemployed portion of our population under sedation unless we can quickly figure out something better for them to do. Unemployment will be concentrated among the older workers and the youngsters entering the labor force, and, according to Theobald (1963), "no conceivable rate of economic growth will avoid this result." Of the 26 million people who will enter the job market during this decade, 9.8 million will have less than a complete high school education. Many, if not all of these people, will face a lifetime without market supported work.

How these people are to be kept solvent is a problem which we educators are not immediately asked to deal with. How they are to occupy themselves is at the heart of our concern. Even now America is a land of golfers, travellers, bowlers, amateur painters. After finding free time for all the marginal chores of living—mowing the lawn, taking a fishing trip, driving the kids to the library, what will a man do to fill his extra leisure hours? Americans are ill-equipped to absorb leisure in any but the smallest doses. Our education, our informal training, our mores, our Horatio Alger kind of tradition, our Puritanical mythology honoring the no-play-hard-work-equal-success tradition, have made us a people who feel guilty about "wasting time."

It must, then, become the fourth goal of our new educational system to teach our students just how creative and how elevating the wise use of leisure can be. Such a change may well be among the most difficult asked of us. Our public school system has always been a training ground for its students to "get ahead." It has consistently expounded the principle that only hard work and study will prevent failure after graduation. But it has rarely equated hard work with pleasure or self-satisfaction. It has more enthusiastically taught English as the language of business letters than as the language of Shakespeare, Shelley, and DuBois. Our schools will have to start teaching a drastically new philosophy, one appropriate to our new age of abundance— the new educational standards will have to reflect, as well as encourage, a basic alteration in our cultural standards. The pursuit of pleasure will have to be accepted as a virtue. But at the same time pleasure will have to cease being equated with non-doing and idleness and come to be associated with self-management, with self-imposed and self-chosen activity. To a people freed from the need to work we shall have to teach the skills of leisure as if our lives depended on it—and indeed they may.

For now, in the latter half of the 20th century, we have reached a point where the abundance of knowledge and technology available to this country would allow us to create a society based on humanist rather than survival values. In earlier generations, when the hard realities of life seemed on every hand to run counter to copybook maxims about justice, equality and humanity, the school necessarily based its teaching of these values on exhortation and fabricated example. Now the school could well take as its fifth goal the education of citizens whose competencies in self-management and human relations render them capable of an appropriate creative response to the fact that we now possess the material potential to create a society truly respectful of human rights, a society where respect for one's fellowman no longer conflicts with his need to provide for his family and himself. The challenge of the new condition is to match the formal learning experience to this new reality and to meet the new opportunity of a freer social system with a new approach to educational methodology and to societal organization. The great danger is to pretend that there has been no fundamental change and to go on using a methodology which was not maximally useful even in the old condition, thus missing an opportunity to advance learning and behavior when such advance is not only possible but desperately needed. The failure of man to create a humane social order under the new conditions will carry with it the threat of societal suicide. For the same conditions of scientific advance and material plenty which make it possible for man to now be truly human also make it possible for him to be definitively and conclusively anti-human.

Section V-11

Liberal Learning in a Changing World

THE COLLEGE AND WORLD AFFAIRS

The change that has swept the world in our century has altered the lives of nearly every person in it, or will soon do so. Unfortunately, it has not yet produced anywhere in corresponding magnitude the necessary adaptations in education. There has come into being a fateful lag between the circumstances of life in which men and women must live and their inner preparation to do so wisely and effectively.

The most painful consequences of that lag may lie in store for the United States, whose 190,000,000 people have been thrust by events into the vortex of world affairs. So great are the changes in perspective and the increases in knowledge required of us, that new approaches to learning are essential at every level from the elementary school to the continuing education of adults.

A NEW STRATEGY OF LIBERAL LEARNING

We regard an intelligent understanding of our changing world as the basic ingredient of liberal learning today. We do not regard liberal learning as the exclusive possession of formal education, let alone of the liberal arts college. On the contrary, it holds a central place within the wide range of institutions which offer advanced education to the great majority of our youth. Although we tend to take for granted the meaning of liberal education, the need to restate its purposes and methods has never been greater. At the same time, the task of prying the essence of liberal learning out of academic verbiage and jungle-like curricular growth has never been more difficult. The central aim of liberal learning is to free and enlarge the mind and spirit of man. It helps the individual to break through the crust of preconception and customary inhibition in which he may have been reared, to choose in freedom his values and goals, to liberate himself from the meanness and meagerness

384 HIGHER EDUCATION IN THE REVOLUTIONARY DECADES

of mere existence. It enables him to rediscover in himself a nobler and larger aspect, a process to which George Washington referred when he used the epithet "liberal" as the ultimate compliment for his finest officers. As perhaps its greatest gift, liberal education bestows upon a person the "power to multiply and explore choices so that the world ceases to be a little place trimmed to the dimensions of one's private experience...."[1]

The basic philosophy of liberal education thus provides the point of departure for new strategies of learning indispensable in today's world. It expands a man's horizons by freeing his intellect. It removes the blinders of parochialism and leads the emancipated person toward an affinity for all that is human. In doing this, it forces him to look deeply into his own society, to see it whole, and to see it in relation to all of human endeavor. Viewed thus, liberal learning is a dynamic that animates the intellectual community in its entirety. It is not something that a man can inherit or accept passively as the gift of a free society. It is a creative and sometimes painful process that must take place within the individual. It is continuously and actively liberating. It endures because those whom it has enlightened and inspired arouse these qualities anew in each succeeding generation.

To state the purposes of liberal education thus is to indicate what can be and what should be rather than what is. The actual state of liberal learning has too often fallen far short of these enlightening aims. Its central purposes have been lost sight of under the impact of unsympathetic philosophies and religions, or certain economic and political forces. They have suffered attrition during periods of deep schism in educational or political principle. Beyond this, many colleges and universities that profess liberality in education have made difficult the attainment of its purposes by emasculating or cheapening the curriculum, or by permitting the course structure and the college community itself to become weedy with modes of living and learning antithetical to liberality of mind and spirit

When the purposes and processes of liberal learning are reassessed in terms of the changing world, the need for new concepts and a new emphasis becomes self-evident. If liberal education is to meet the requirements of a new kind of world, it must undergo one of those fundamental overhauls that have kept it alive for centuries. There is need for more than adding a course here and there, more than repackaging of old courses. There must be a reformulation of purpose. The great humanistic philosophy in liberal learning must be translated into twentieth-century terms.

---

[1] Van Doren, Mark, *Liberal Education* (New York, 1943), p. 66.

THE CHANGING WORLD

The changes that liberal learning must encompass touch every aspect of man's activity and have occurred in every geographic region of the globe. They are revolutionary in scope and have transformed the world in the past half century. Technological innovation has spread into areas that have, until recently, known only limited technical growth. Improved roads and airstrips link towns and villages and metropolitan centers. Jet planes reach the most remote capitals in less than 48 hours. Communication with any part of the world requires only minutes, or at most hours.

A wave of modernization has swept through societies that previously had clung to ancient or primitive ways. Their economic capacities have been improved. The aspirations of peoples at all levels of economic development have been raised. New social and political patterns have arisen within nations. Some new states, as well as old ones, have moved toward liberal and democratic political systems. Some, caught up in the revolution that has spread from the Soviet Union since 1945, have communist regimes. Others are in the throes of the struggle between communist and anti-communist forces. New world configurations have taken form in trade, in the movement of ideas and persons, in ideological affinities, in the distribution of power, and in the expression of political will.

Three major historical thrusts have been selected to demonstrate the new dimensions and strategies of learning that will be required within our educational system. They are (1) the shift in relationships that has moved the United States, along with very few other nations, into the center of world affairs, (2) the emergence of new nations and the vast increase in the world importance of their cultures, and (3) the new complexities as well as the new opportunities that have been introduced into the process of interaction among cultures and nation-states by the growing participation of peoples as well as officials in this process.

THE NEW ROLE OF THE UNITED STATES

It would be difficult to overestimate the far-reaching implications of the shift in the locus of world power and responsibility that has thrust the United States into the thinly populated center of world affairs. It is a change that has brought within the grasp of this nation, for better or for worse, the capacity to influence decisively our own future and that of humanity.

It is trite to observe, two decades after the beginnings of this shift, that both power and responsibility came to the United States before either the government or the people were prepared for it. They had neither the knowledge, the outlook, the skills, nor the understanding required. Unfortunately, this condition still persists even after twenty years. It is this continuing lack of preparation for world leadership that poses a serious challenge to education.

This lack of preparation exists in part because the world has become infinitely more complex in recent years, requiring higher levels of understanding. It exists in part because the American people have been shielded from the raw impact of world affairs by generally high levels of national prosperity, and have been preoccupied with developments inside the nation. And it exists in part because the people of this nation, although growing in their capacity to respond to world tensions with a greater measure of wisdom and patience, have not yet perceived clearly the great forces of change that lie beneath those tensions. With their traditional concern about domestic problems, neither the people nor all elements of their government have fully discerned how intricately intertwined are domestic affairs and world affairs. Nor have they learned how to use the complicated and sometimes cumbersome mechanism of democracy in such a manner that it will serve efficiently both American national needs and the needs of the rest of the world.

This situation imposes unmistakable obligations upon liberal learning in the United States. A liberal education must be the means for bringing into balance an intelligent understanding of forces at work both inside and outside the nation. An adequate understanding of the United States must include insight into both the structure and function of its society and government. There must be an intelligent appreciation of this nation in its current and historical manifestations. The relationship of its culture to other cultures must be perceived, as well as the changing place of the United States in the world. Attention must be given to the intricate processes by which the nation reaches its decisions and asserts its leadership both at home and abroad. Domestic change must be viewed in a world dimension and world change in its domestic implications. This new approach to liberal education must produce a generation of young Americans equipped to discharge with wisdom the grave responsibilities that rest upon their country.

THE EMERGENCE OF NEW NATIONS AND CULTURES

The upsurge of new nations and the consequent increasing world importance of their cultures places a special obligation upon liberal learning.

National independence in recent years has been coupled with high aspirations for international status, economic advancement, and better education. It has included also a justifiable pride in indigenous languages and cultures. The newly independent peoples wish these respected and understood by other nations, no matter how many cultural importations from Europe and the United States they may choose to adopt.

A liberal education must impart an understanding of both new states and old states that have achieved new world status. To accomplish this, a new strategy must be devised to divest learning of its present provincialism, or more properly of its historical and current preoccupation with the heritage of Western civilization. The new strategy must extend liberal learning to include the great teachings of other world cultures and thus fulfill its purpose of embracing life in all its diverse human forms. It must lead the student to understand these cultures in the same manner as he does those of the West—as growing and dynamic, with a past, a present, and a future.

The change is coming slowly. Before 1945 it would have been difficult to find programs of liberal education in undergraduate colleges that had escaped from the historical confines of Western culture. Individual courses were available in some colleges. Language training programs were introduced into some universities after 1941 as the United States responded to a war of world dimensions. There was little change, however, in the general concept of the liberal arts. As late as 1943 Mark Van Doren could write a book on liberal education that neither took into consideration its application to cultures other than those of the West, nor sought new meanings in those cultures. Alfred North Whitehead also confined himself to the traditional West when he wrote on education in 1929 (although he did mention Chinese as a language preferred for study), even as he discussed in the same volume the educational implications of "Space, Time, and Relativity."

The cultures that have been neglected are those of the Asian and African countries, of Russia and of Latin America. The culture of Russia draws, of course, upon the cultures of both Europe and Asia. The historical blending of Orient and Occident in Russia has been overlaid by still a third culture, that of communism. The cultures of Latin America have strong roots in the Western heritage. They need to be better understood because, despite their European roots, they have a content and style different from those of North America and Europe. The Western heritage in Latin America has been modified in varying degree by contact with indigenous cultures.

All of these cultures have been subjected to profound study by experts in the United States and Europe, but only very recently have they aroused popular interest. It took the rise of new nations from the ashes of colonialism after the Second World War to focus attention upon the importance of cultures other than those of the West. Almost overnight the cultures of Asia and Africa, and in succeeding years, those of Latin America, began to assume a new significance. For the first time, the United States began to acknowledge the intrinsic importance of cultures beyond the Western periphery and to speak, at first softly, of the "provincialism" of its undergraduate education.

Realizing that a wide public understanding of foreign cultures was now essential, educational critics turned to the schools, colleges, and universities and found them wanting. The undergraduate curriculum of higher education had not kept pace with the new dimensions of world involvement. Liberal learning, conceived in the civilization of the West, remained parochial. As the new need became apparent, a few undergraduate programs were modified. They drew stimulation from events and from the graduate programs of the universities. Too few institutions, however, in the nineteen years since the war ended, have taken vigorous action to educate our youth to meet the requirements of a changing world. We have perceived the need for a new strategy of liberal learning but, as a nation, we have realized it only in small measure. Today the need has acquired a note of urgency.

THE PROCESS OF INTERACTION

The undergraduate, in the course of acquiring a liberal education, must achieve yet another dimension of understanding. In addition to a deeper perception of his own society and its world role, in addition to a comprehension of cultures within and beyond the West, he must achieve insight into the continuous process of interaction among peoples and cultures. Continual interaction, accelerated by the changes of the past half century, is the context within which both states and individuals must live and conduct their affairs. It is an intricately tangled network of social, economic, and political forces acting and reacting upon one another, both within the borders of states and among states. This complicated process can be understood only when it is perceived as having roots deep within each of the cultures involved.

Interaction is of many kinds and on every scale. It may consist of the simple cross-cultural contacts of two human beings. It may involve organized private ventures of economic or social character. It involves the continuous interchange of thought and knowledge. Only when this is understood, is it possible to discern undercurrents of meaning in the formal conduct of political relationships among states. Together the many different kinds and levels of socio-cultural interaction form a powerful and turbulent stream. Liberal education must make it possible for young men and women to understand and occasionally to withstand the powerful currents which make up that stream, with intellectual certitude, with poise and with a clear sense of the direction in which they are moving.

There has been a striking popularization of relationships among peoples and states in the past fifty years. Although the process of interaction has never been wholly the business of governments and technical experts, today the role of the individual citizen and of private cultural enterprises has been greatly expanded. It has become a normal dimension of life for many persons. It has become the prevailing milieu for persons who share in civic judgment and exercise any measure of leadership. The young man or woman who does not gain some understanding of the dynamics of interaction and change will in that measure remain uneducated.

THE LIBERALLY EDUCATED STUDENT

The new strategy of liberal learning can best be described in terms of the qualities a liberally educated student should possess. Not every student will possess all of these qualities, but taken together they suggest the ways in which liberal learning must be modified to meet current world needs.

The student enlightened by liberal learning must be aware of the revolutionary scale of the changes wrought in the world during this century. He must perceive clearly the major forces at work, both at home and abroad. He must have a feeling for history and a capacity to project present trends into the future. He must know how to use his historical knowledge to test his projections. With such intellectual skills he will be equipped to understand the technological revolution that has swept the world, the wave of modernization, the new configurations of ideology, the economic relationships and political affinities. He will be prepared to understand and assess the effects of the communist revolution.

To understand a culture other than his own, whether in the West or beyond, the student must first acquire a clear perception of the meaning of culture. He must learn to compare his culture with another, to seek out what they may have in common, where they differ in structure, content and dynamic. He must discover how the peoples in his and in other cultures go about solving the same kinds of problems. He must penetrate as deeply as possible into the history and living forces of the culture he seeks to compare with his own.

The requirements for understanding a culture outside the Western tradition vary widely according to the source of judgment. Many specialists on Asia, the Middle East, Africa, and the Soviet Union insist that only an adequate knowledge of the indigenous languages will provide meaningful insights. This reasoning is familiar to those steeped in the tradition of liberal learning, where the knowledge of a language, classical or modern, has always been regarded as an essential key to the literature, thought, and customs of a people. Others believe that, valuable as the language may be, it is not always indispensable. They hold that by using European languages, students can reach an adequate level of understanding, especially now that good translations of works from non-European cultures are becoming available. For the undergraduate a good translation may be a better vehicle for understanding than a poor knowledge of the language.

The extension of liberal learning to foreign cultures will involve the student in adventures with unfamiliar philosophies and religions, traditions and values. The liberal tradition in our education is essentially a product of the West. It was born of Hellenic thought, strengthened by the Roman and Judeo-Christian heritage, rediscovered in the high Middle Ages, and reemphasized by the humanistic revival of the Renaissance. It stresses the individual human being, the liberation of his intellect and talents, and their realization in the society of which he is a part.

The experience of those who have worked intensively with foreign cultures demonstrates that by learning to know the institutions, practices, and beliefs of another society, the student is forced to re-examine those of his own. Inevitably he acquires greater knowledge and understanding of both. He emerges with respect for the traditional values of the second culture, and also with a deeper and more conscious respect for those of his own. This must be regarded as an essential characteristic of the liberally educated student.

By means of the comparative approach, furthermore, he will learn to see cultural traits in perspective and to judge them with some objectivity. He will discover some of the likenesses and differences among cultures. He will see the relationships among them, and begin to appreciate the value of diversity as against standardization in the world. The liberally educated student will grow in stature to the extent that his mind is stretched to encompass the ways of life, the thought and the creative expression of other cultures. Out of this experience, which hopefully will be shared in their own way by young men and women reared in other cultures, there should emerge not only clearer perspectives but also the kinds of borrowing, adaptation and synthesis that have led historically to new bursts of creative effort.

Not only must the student learn about other cultures, he must also be made aware of the continuous interaction among peoples, cultures and states, of which he is a part. When he understands the dynamics of interaction, history will become more meaningful, and he will gain new insight into how his world came into being. He will discover how Asian art forms moved to Europe and there influenced the development of European art. He will discover how modernization moved, piecemeal and by fits and starts, from Europe and the United States to Russia, to Asian and African countries and to those of Latin America. He will discover how the hunger of a developing nation for modernization has sometimes produced disturbance and conflict. He will see how the attributes of the modern world are absorbed by some ancient cultures, changing them; how they continue to lay upon others like a veneer and do not penetrate to the deep roots of custom and history.

He will begin to comprehend the ingredients of economic growth, and the anomalies to which it gives rise. He will discover how sensitive are the economies of some older, still developing countries, to the synthetic products poured into the streams of world commerce from the laboratories of the West. He will see how the more progressive of them parry threats to their economies with programs of diversification which they have learned from the West. He will be able to grasp and evaluate the economic and political forces that have brought about the revival of strength in Europe. He will perceive the drives and mechanisms that have given cohesion to the Common Market and have bestowed upon Europe a new world influence. He will be equipped to understand the communist revolution, and the ways in which it bends or is bent by the cultures and histories of the countries it has affected. He will be prepared to discover how Russia and mainland China seek to maintain or enlarge their respective communist domains by a combination of overt and covert instrumentalities. He will discern vividly the role of change when he contemplates how a confluence of forces in the period since the Second World War has made possible almost twenty years of vitality and prestige in the manifold endeavors of the United Nations, whereas the forces at work in the 1930's started to bring about the disintegration of the League of Nations within twelve years after its birth.

Besides such specific insights, the student who learns the processes of interaction will acquire understanding of certain broad patterns of relationship. He will become aware of the complexities of communication. He will become alert to differences in the shades of words by which truth can be confused, either deliberately or inadvertently. He will begin to discover what drives men apart and what brings them together. He will learn how force is used in combination with ideas and political alignment to achieve international goals, many of which may be entirely peaceful. He will see how little, or how much, the ties

HIGHER EDUCATION IN THE REVOLUTIONARY DECADES

of history bind peoples in friendship and how human are the reactions of a people to the possession by another group of great power or great wealth.

These insights, and others essential to the fulfilled individual and the intelligent citizen, will develop in every life where awareness and curiosity have been aroused, broadened and deepened by liberal learning. Let there be no misunderstanding about the realism of these educational aims and aspirations. We know from our own lives and from our daily work how thinly and how imperfectly these things are learned by any student, even under the most favorable circumstances. But we know also that the readiness and taste of an adult for that "education which begins when your formal education is over" is mostly determined, so far as liberal learning is concerned, by what happens in the undergraduate years. The resources and opportunities available to an American adult today for a lifetime of liberal learning are far greater in both scope and quality than most college graduates are prepared to exploit. In this respect today's college is not making a solid educational connection with the modern world.

TO REALIZE THE NEW STRATEGY

If a strategy of liberal learning commensurate with the changing world is to be realized, a clear-cut program of action will be required of colleges and universities. Above all, they must be imbued with a strong sense of institutional commitment to the reconceived educational program. The commitment must be so unequivocal that there develops within the institutions an articulated sense of mission. Basically this commitment and sense of mission must reside in the faculty who will transmit it to the students. But members of the faculty will be able to sustain their dedication and extend it only in the measure that they are supported by the institutions of which they are a part. The achievement of such institutional commitment will depend, in turn, upon the levels of conviction among trustees, alumni, and officers.

With commitment present, the college or university can move to meet the second requirement: development and use of its resources to achieve a program of learning that will meet the requirements of the changing world. There will be difficult but not insoluble problems to be overcome. Any effort to add a new dimension to liberal learning will have to be carried forward at the same time that the college is being asked to cope with great increases of knowledge in all fields, with larger numbers of students, with conflicting pressures from specialized education and with crushing financial burdens. Learning about other cultures and about the processes of interaction must go forward without weakening instruction about the United States, or displacing our traditional concern with Europe and related cultural areas. The task is a formidable one, but many institutions have demonstrated that it is not beyond our capacity.

The specific means by which a new world outlook can be achieved will vary. Each college or university will have to discover for itself which changes in its educational program will come closest to meeting its requirements. The need cannot be met by half measures. Through liberal learning the aim is to achieve the capacity to see one's own actions and those of one's society in their broadest human implications. For this reason any mere patching up of existing curricula will not suffice.

Because of the multiplication of knowledge today, the new liberal learning cannot aspire to all-inclusiveness. It must be limited to selected examples. The student must discover how to adduce from such examples the principles involved, and learn to think in terms of those principles, seeking additional information to verify or modify them as he can. He may engage in the comparative study of cultures by focusing upon one or at most two cultures other than his own. He may be able to study in depth only two or three aspects of interaction among cultures and states, before reaching some conclusions about the general process which he will go on testing as he is able to expand his knowledge.

For all these purposes, the college or university may find it advisable to modify its present courses in government, literature, or art, for example. They may become comparative courses, drawing their examples from other cultures. The traditional course in international relations may become one in inter-cultural relations, or specifically in the process of interaction. Where it does not now exist, the college or university may find it appropriate to introduce a course in the economics of developing nations. Some institutions are already experimenting with a course that aims to provide the student with the means for analyzing and evaluating any culture other than his own.

Even with sincere commitment and the best of intentions, the college or university may not always be able to undertake entirely on its own the implementation of a new strategy of liberal learning. It may need to draw upon other institutions for guidance and resources. Where geographic proximity permits, the college may be able to augment its efforts by cooperation with other colleges or universities and thus overcome its limitations. In addition, there must be more systematic diffusion of educational experience on a nation-wide basis. This will involve the preparation of more college-level teachers who perceive the advantages and requirements of an expanded liberal learning. It will mean the development of better teaching materials and library guides, and the mobilization of badly needed cultural resources.

Many of these necessities may be available to the college within the framework of the large and expanding university. Although the independent liberal arts college may have less immediate access to this kind of help, it is possessed of certain compensating advantages. Because of its character and normally smaller size, it is more susceptible of change and can convey with some ease to its students, faculty, and other constituencies its sense of institutional commitment. It is under less pressure from specialized schools; research usually serves, but does not dominate, its teaching.

These are details—real, stubborn, and essential—and they must never be overlooked. But they must not obscure the central fact that the reorientation of liberal learning to encompass the great revolution in world relationships calls for nothing less than a major change of purpose and the application of a new strategy. The necessary adaptation of courses and programs and resources will follow. The ultimate result must reflect a comprehensive rethinking, not a mere reshuffling of premises, concepts and content. The same is true for the apparatus of undergraduate liberal learning. There must be a careful fitting of means to purposes, and no mere juggling of arrangements without regard to the central purposes of the new strategy.

If we are to bring into being the new strategy of liberal learning, we must inevitably run some risks of being less than profound. We can reduce these risks by recognizing that area knowledge, language competence, and a sophisticated sense of how the world works, will be required of those who build the world component into liberal learning. Of the teacher-scholars who perform this task, we must require the tolerant recognition that the man of liberal learning is better off with an intelligent layman's awareness of what the scholar knows in professional detail, than he is with no awareness at all. Awareness need never remain superficial in an educated man, whereas any unawareness is certain to be ignorance, probably compounded by arrogance.

Section VI

THE SHORE DIMLY SEEN

The responses which American higher education makes to the revolutionary challenges it faces will determine its future form. Although some believe that the present is still so revolutionary that it is impossible to predict the future, others see at least the period to the year 2000 as essentially evolutionary. These four essays recapitulate many of the arguments already advanced and attempt to look into the future.

Section VI-1

American Higher Education in 1980
Some Basic Issues

By JOHN W. NASON

1 SIZE AND DIVERSITY

No projection of the course of American higher education over the next
fifteen years can avoid the problem of numbers. The 1964–65 enrollment in colleges and universities was 5,320,000, approximately double
the enrollment in 1955. There is no evidence of any slowing down, and
forecasters such as Sidney Tickton have projected a college and university student population by 1980 of 10,000,000.

This incredibly rapid growth is one of the brute facts of academic
life at the present time, and its impact on higher education is in many
respects brutal. There was little disposition at the conference to spend
time bemoaning the situation. The participants were too well aware of
the forces at work: popular belief in the monetary value of post-high
school education, the affluence of our society, the Berkner thesis in *The
Scientific Age* regarding the ever increasing need for scientists and tech-
nologists in order to keep society affluent, the increasing professionalism in general of our society. We cannot imitate King Canute's
attempt to order back the onrushing tide.

The increase leads inevitably to the dominance on the educational
scene of the public, i.e. tax-supported, university. Up to 1950 more
than half of all college and university students in the United States
attended private institutions. Today only 34% do so, and by 1980 they
will constitute only 25%. This shift in the center of gravity is creating a
variety of stresses and strains of seismological character, but those who
are inclined to view the shift with foreboding can find comfort in two
considerations. One is a national commitment to a wide diversity of

From *American Higher Education in 1980—Some Basic Issues* by John W. Nason,
Paper No. 1, 1966, Aspen Institute for Humanistic Studies.

institutions; the other is the increasing support of privately controlled education from public funds. The latter raises problems of autonomy which will be discussed anon. Nevertheless, it may well be that the survival of privately controlled institutions, in this country as in the United Kingdom, will ultimately depend on the successful partnership of private and public philanthropy. Whatever the future may bring in that regard, there is no doubt that as a nation we are committed to educational pluralism and that we view diversity in control, in size, in source of support, in areas of instruction, and even in quality as a source of enormous educational strength.

If the conference spent little time wringing its hands over the avalanche of students—the metaphor is not inappropriate to Aspen—it should not be assumed that the participants ignored a variety of consequent problems. Many of these will appear in later sections. Here I propose to indicate the framework within which much of the discussion occurred by drawing together various observations on one of the major problems of American higher education today. This problem, largely though not entirely created by increase in size, is: how do we develop and maintain a sense of community?

It is easy to argue the case for size. The cost of education—meaning by cost faculty salaries, administrative supervision, building maintenance, supporting peripheral activities—is less per student in a large university than in a small college and in a larger university than in a smaller one. This assumes comparable quality. There may come a point where the economy of large-scale operation reverses itself, but no one has yet demonstrated whether there is such a point or where it is. Equally important is the influence of size on quality. The diversity of a large university, the quality of the people it can attract, the excellence of its various programs, all these are advantages which the smaller institution often does not share.

There remains, however, the problem of the academic community. We hear a great deal these days about the depersonalization and dehumanization of education, particularly undergraduate education. Clark Kerr talks about it in his book, *The Uses of the University*. The Berkeley students used the IBM card as the symbol of their loss of academic and human identity. Whether it is a question of the place of the students in their academic context or of the role of the faculty in institutional policy or of the relations of students, faculty, and administrative officers to one another, the factor of sheer size is relevant.

The academic world tends to view community in much the same way the Greeks once viewed the city-state. One of the strongest arguments for the small college is its alleged capacity to maintain a sense of community, and one of the most frequent criticisms of the large university, particularly the large state university, is its alleged factory quality. I say "alleged" in both cases because it is by no means clear that all small colleges retain a genuine sense of community and because large universities are experimenting with ways to carve out communities within their total mass. Harvard and Yale have subdivided into colleges or houses. The University of California is experimenting with a cluster of small units on its new Santa Cruz campus. The University of Michigan and Wayne State University are creating wheels within wheels. How successful these new experiments will be remains to be seen. At least they are attempts to cope with a real and recognized problem.

Size, however, is by no means the only relevant variable. Students and faculty in many small colleges bemoan the absence of community. In the following section I shall explore some of the reasons for the accusation and some of the suggested remedies. As might be expected, the members of the conference came to no agreement on the course which higher education should take. We could, however, recognize that the inevitable growth in student population, a variety of changes in the social and intellectual climate of our generation, and the consequent dislocation of long accepted academic practices combined to create an uncomfortable and unstable situation which will take our best efforts over an indefinite period to improve.

2   IS THERE AN ACADEMIC COMMUNITY?

Until fairly recently educators would not have wasted much time or thought in giving an affirmative answer to the question which constitutes the heading of this section. Today we are not so sure. A college or university ought to be a community. But is it, and if it is, what kind of a community is it? How can we preserve or re-create it in the face of trends in our society in the years ahead? The participants in the conference returned again and again to these pervasive questions.

An academic community may be a community of scholars (e.g., All Souls College, Oxford, or the Institute for Advanced Study in Princeton) or a community of teachers and learners. From the time of Plato's Academy the latter has been the conventional pattern for the Western world, though medieval monasteries, Renaissance Royal Academies, and recent scientific task forces suggest variations on the traditional pattern. What are the minimal conditions necessary for a community in either sense?

Sociologists offer a variety of characteristics of a true community. For our purposes we can reduce these to four.

(1) A community must be infused with a common purpose or with common purposes which are consistent with one another. I shall have

something to say on this point in the next section. Its immediate application to colleges and universities needs little further elaboration.

(2) The members of a community must be prepared to accept the values and functions which reflect or realize the common purpose. Their motivation must be consistent with the ends of the community. Students who go to college for a good time or to postpone employment tend to destroy or to impair an academic community centered on learning. Faculty members who live for research and view students as necessary evils reduce the effectiveness of an academic community where teaching is central to its existence.

(3) Each member of the community must have his place and function. He has his worth as an individual and must be recognized as a member of the community. The application of this criterion to colleges and universities is obvious and leads directly to the last characteristic.

(4) There must be some kind of personal communication among the members of the community. We cannot expect all members to communicate with all others, but there must be some machinery by which each member can identify his place and know that others recognize his function. We know from experience that a small rural town where everyone knows everyone else, or nearly so, is more of a community than a city; that a board of directors of 15 is far more closely knit and responsible than one of 60; that a college of 500 has enormous advantages in terms of community over one of 5,000.

Can the modern multiversity be a community? It is a congeries of scholars and students, teachers and learners. Has it reached the point where, like the dinosaur, its own unwieldy size dooms it to destruction? No single answer will be obtained from present-day educators. Whether we like it or not, we live in a period of large-scale operations. The aggregations of individuals in academic institutions will grow larger, not smaller. There is the rumble of thunder on the academic horizon, however, and Berkeley may be the portent of storms to come. There is substantial agreement among students, faculty, and administrators that the nature of the learning process requires that students be treated as persons and not as numbers. It is sometimes said—of small colleges as well as of large universities—that the students are the forgotten men. Insofar as this is true, it may be in part the reflection of an attitude of faculty members and in part the consequence of too rapid growth.

Could it be that our struggle for the efficiency and economy of size will inevitably defeat our purpose, or will do so unless we take heroic measures? I have already suggested in Section 1 some of the experiments designed to reconcile large-scale operations with individual attention. It is a complex issue with many subtle nuances. A community of teachers and students will depend in part on physical arrangements which encourage personal communication, in part on institutional policy which promotes such exchange, in part on the exigencies of personal need. A college which is geographically isolated has certain advantages over a large university in the middle of a great city. One member of the conference suggested the paradox that a small faculty of limited quality may provide more incentive to faculty cultivation of the brighter students than a first-rate faculty of reasonable size where faculty members find more intellectual communication among themselves.

To what extent do our modern aggregations of scholars constitute a community? I am thinking here not of the Rand Corporation or the Institute for Advanced Study, but of the great university faculties of a thousand or more members. What communication is there among them? What sense of commun purpose or bond? The proliferation of knowledge has reached the point where scientists who claim the same generic field can no longer talk intelligibly to one another. The most common complaint on college as well as university campuses is the lack of time to talk to one's colleagues. When we add to this the current mobility of scholars, it is small wonder that colleges as well as universities are suffering from the lack of any sense of common purpose and common commitment. And if scholars cannot form a genuine community, what chance is there for one composed—to borrow the happy language of British universities—of junior as well as senior members?

The years between now and 1980 will be crucial for this aspect of higher education. The situation may well get worse before it gets better, though some pessimists would question whether it could be worse than it is at present. Experiments are being tried, and growing concern is being expressed. We know we have a problem and that it stems from the very nature of the educational process. There is no reason to believe that we cannot resolve the dilemma of community and size, but the solution may demand some drastic reappraisals of the organization of higher education and of the units costs.

3 CLARIFICATION OF PURPOSE

For Americans education is a form of salvation. It is the high road for social mobility, financial success, greater realization of individual capacity. Few nations have tried to carry so high a percentage of their young through secondary education as in this country, and no nation has approached the United States in the percentage enrolled in institutions going beyond the high school level. These institutions, as already pointed out, are many and varied. And in the years immediately ahead they will become more so. Junior colleges, community colleges, new varieties of trade schools and technical institutes are taking their place alongside the conventional colleges and universities with all their traditional diversity of attributes—public and private, church-related and independent, undergraduate and graduate, broadly liberal and professionally limited.

There are dangers as well as strengths in this national attitude. The faith in education is frequently naive and sometimes blind. The hallmark of the degree becomes primarily valued even if stamped on shoddy or spurious content. The growing multiveristy, to use Clark Kerr's term, provides instruction in almost every conceivable field. There is a dangerous tendency to expect each institution to be all things to all people. The alumnus of the small college wants his alma mater to grow in quality and prestige and yet keep its doors open for his children regardless of ability; to remain small and selective and at the same time find places for the children of his friends, neighbors, and business associates. The taxpayer opposes increases in appropriations to state universities, yet expects the institution to accept all children of citizens and to provide both better education and more successful football teams. It is not surprising that there is confusion in the public mind over the nature and purpose of higher education.

Is the ultimate justification of our educational system the development of the individual or the preservation of society? It is quite possible on pragmatic grounds to reconcile these two goals, but there remain important and at times uncomfortable differences of emphasis dependent upon the end of the argument from which one begins.

In biological terms the species seeks to perpetuate the conditions essential to its survival. Translated into a sociological context this means that any given society normally educates its young people in those skills, arts, attitudes, and beliefs which the older members deem important for the preservation of the culture. A state university is presumably an instrument by which the taxpaying citizens of the state accomplish certain objectives thought to be socially desirable—the improvement of agriculture, an increase in the number of engineers or lawyers, discoveries which will improve health or attract new industry or add to national security, the enlargement of human understanding and enjoyment through liberal education. It must be responsive to the needs, or at least to the demands, of the citizens if it is to flourish. For the private institution the principle is the same although the practical pressures may be different. The private college or university can survive only so long as society is prepared to support it through gifts and tax-exemption and patronage, and presumably that support depends upon the conviction that the college or university is serving a socially useful and desirable purpose.

On the other hand, the spiritual forces which have shaped the Western world have gradually evolved from the Greco-Roman world and the Judeo-Christian religion, and in both cases the value and importance of the individual have been central, or have emerged as central. The religious tradition, the moral philosophy, and the political structure of the modern Western world have focused on the primacy of the individual. The state as well as the Sabbath were made for man. In spiritual and human terms the individual is the ultimate reality and the locus of all we consider of value. Therefore, the ultimate end of education must be the greatest possible development of the individual.

I have already suggested that these two views can be reconciled. The fullest realization of individual potentiality lies within a social setting. Hobbes' famous description of the life of man in a state of nature as "solitary, poore, nasty, brutish, and short" drives home the point that the greatest freedom for the individual exists only within an ordered society. Conversely the preservation of society may well depend upon its correction and this in turn upon the production of individuals who are free to change as well as to support the social order. Indeed, it can be argued that the greatest contribution a university can make to its society is to turn out the kind of sensitive and critical individuals who will challenge traditional values and institutions in the name of a better moral and social order. And yet, when the opposite ends of the argument have been bent to come together in a complete circle, there remains a difference of emphasis and direction, and higher education will continue to oscillate between the two.

Another dimension in any discussion of educational purpose is the relative emphasis on discovery and dissemination of knowledge. Proponents of one side or the other sometimes give the impression that the issue is one of teaching vs. research. In any absolute sense this confuses the situation. Very few individuals would seriously argue for one activity to the exclusion of the other. The issue is one of relative emphasis in a context where both are important, and in a group as mixed as the Aspen Conference it would be surprising if there had not been strong differences of opinion.

The fact that the issue is familiar does not lessen its importance in trying to define the goals of particular institutions. It is a little too simple to suggest that large universities have a responsiblity for the pursuit of new knowledge as well as for the transmission of what is already known, while small colleges have a primary obligation to teach. The effectiveness of teaching will depend on the cutting edge of a man's mind, and that, with very rare exceptions, will depend upon its constant application to the discovery of new knowledge or new insights or new syntheses of what has been antecedently discovered.

The problem is further complicated by the pressure on the smaller institutions by the larger universities to emphasize the kind of graduate the graduate school professor likes. This pressure is reflected not only in a creeping emphasis on more and more specialization at the undergraduate level, but also in the ideal held before the undergraduate seeking to determine his ultimate career. Our educational system will need more teachers. Is the scholarly world, however, in danger of putting too much emphasis on the duplication of its own kind?

If there was any one point on which the members of the conference were in strongest agreement, it was on the necessity of institutional integrity. Too often colleges and universities are unclear about their purpose, and the beginning of educational wisdom is to decide what end a given institution intends to serve. The second step is to make this clear to the general public in every possible way. It will necessitate constant reiteration. Every university faces a wide variety of publics. It must interpret its goals in different languages to different constituencies; but while the language is judiciously tempered to the audience, the purpose of the university must come through loud and clear. This will take courage on the part of the chief spokesmen, for it will involve saying no to certain demands and will run the risk of alienating certain potential friends. It requires the avoidance of what might be termed slick approaches to the public. In the long run, clarity of purpose and honesty of presentation are the best guaranty of institutional integrity as well as of the public's support.

4 MODERNIZING THE CURRICULUM

The expansion of knowledge and the growing professionalism of modern society are making enormous additions to the content of education. The curriculum of the large university is already reflecting these additions, and by 1980 the range will be even greater. No doubt, there will be confusion over what a university ought properly to teach, and subjects will find their way into the program which ought to be left to technical or trade schools. There is no way, however, of avoiding the multiplication of schools or divisions or courses as the fields of knowledge continue to subdivide.

The critical area is undergraduate education, and the next fifteen years may determine whether liberal education in any significant sense will survive. Recent improvements in secondary education make early specialization much more possible. From the other end come the demands of the graduate and professional schools to which an increasing number of undergraduates are going—demands for greater specialization at the undergraduate level. The conflict is not between liberal and professional, for professional subjects can be taught in a liberal way. The conflict is between liberal and specialized, between breadth of general understanding on the one side and a narrow competence on the other. Not only the forces of our society but the pattern of higher education are threatening the former, and the danger is all the greater because it comes at a time when the rapidity of intellectual change makes an understanding of basic principles more important than quickly obsolescent practical applications.

Undergraduate education, if it is to be liberal and significant, must speak to the condition of the students. They are concerned with the ultimate meaning and end of human existence. They want to understand general concepts in relation to the operating conditions of their own immediate environment. How does learning relate to their sense or need for involvement and commitment? These requirements point to the breadth of view inherent in general ideas and to the kind of understanding which results from an awareness of the interrelations of different manifestations of human activity and experience. They point also to the fact that learning goes on outside the classroom as well as within it, and that the gradual development of individual capacities is a total process involving emotions as well as mind, value judgments as well as intellectual analysis, motivation as well as intellectual ability.

One of the perennial debates of the academic world centers on the proper progression of ideas. Should we begin with the individual and proceed from his interests toward a more comprehensive view of the world, or should be begin with the pervasive ideas of human experience and then allow the individual to find his special interests within the larger frame? In the *Mission of the University* Ortega y Gasset argues that "culture is the *vital* system of ideas of a period" and that the transmission of this vital system is *the* mission of the university. Those who see the university as predominantly reflecting the needs of its society are likely to find this interpretation attractive. Those, however, who emphasize the function of individual realization will be more inclined to favor freedom for individual choice in selecting courses. The plea is to let the individual educate himself. Put the responsibility on him to get his education.

The greater the number of high school graduates who go on to college and university, the more important becomes some degree of direction or control. We have already seen that students go to college or university for a variety of reasons. Not all of them by any means understand what higher education is all about. Not all of them have any great motivation for further learning and readiness to impose some discipline on themselves. If our colleges and universities are to be educational institutions and not merely large-scale housing projects, some requirements in terms of subject matter and quality of performance must be made. This is the argument for the distribution requirements of liberal education. Some subjects are intrinsically more important than others. Some provide greater breadth of view than others. Is a person liberally educated who does not understand why many people are religious or how two societies can differ in their value systems? One might elaborate at length on the possible content of required programs—on the value of including more attention to the cultures of the non-Western world, on the greater role of the creative arts, on the central position of history and philosophy. But different institutions will end up with different formulae, and it is the spirit rather than the particular pattern which is all-important.

The abler the student, the more freedom he can use. It may well be that in our more selective institutions with students of high ability and high motivation, much more latitude for individual choice would make sense. Experimental colleges such as Sarah Lawrence have tried it. Others have moved at least partially in this direction. There is clearly room for much more experimentation.

Three conclusions are clear.

(1) There is not, nor should there be, a uniform pattern of liberal education.

(2) One of the challenges to higher education is to teach less, not more. Our danger is one of over-teaching, and we need not only to discipline our own enthusiasm, but to find ways to encourage students to educate themselves.

(3) A college or university should be a place where ideas are exciting. No paraphernalia of courses or requirements or equipment will take the place of an atmosphere where the excitement of learning is electric and contagious.

One further observation is relevant, for the methods of instruction are related to the content. The next fifteen years will undoubtedly see many new devices used, some of which we know about already. Many of these will be dictated by the need to cope with sheer numbers—closed television, video tapes, telephonic communication. But others may prove valuable for other reasons—e.g., language laboratories and programmed learning. These are technological aids to teaching and learning. Perhaps we should also take a more careful look at the traditional methods of lecturing, discussion, tutorials, and independent study. The academic world is one of tradition, and it gives up traditional methods with reluctance. The surplus of students and the shortage of teachers may force the reappraisal which a decent concern for the nature of the learning process might have prompted.

The important idea is innovation. The academic world is as loath to change its familiar ways as any other occupation. But the acids of modernity, to borrow Walter Lippmann's powerful phrase, will not leave the academic edifice unscathed. The old content must find new forms, just as spiritual truth is forever seeking a new temporal embodiment. The ancient methods must give way to modern improvements in communication. If there is value in the cumulative wisdom of the ages, one can derive assurance regarding its survival in modern guise from the old French proverb, "Plus ca change, plus c'est la même chose."

5   PROBLEMS RELATED TO FACULTY

Again and again throughout our discussions questions related to faculty came up. After all, the role and relations of faculty are central to the educational enterprise. In general, two types of concern received chief attention—the perennial issue of teaching versus scholarship and the role of the faculty member in policy determination.

The relative importance to be placed on teaching and research is a crucial issue for most faculty members. It is an issue compounded of personal preference, social need, and the prospect of professional advancement. No sentimental evocation of the good old academic days will suffice. We are living in an age of computers.

Some intellectual historian has estimated that 90% of all the scientists who ever lived are alive today. They are all at work grinding out new information about the physical world with new tools which enormously increase their productivity. Their colleagues in the social sciences are now emulating their example. The economic stability and growth of the industrialized West depend on constant scientific innovation adapted to the social and economic needs of complex and affluent societies. Nothing short of some planetary catastrophe will stop the accelerating proliferation of knowledge.

The discoverers of new truth are for the most part scholars. The greatest congregations of scholars are to be found in our colleges and universities. Therefore, our academic institutions have a direct responsibility for increasing the sum total of human information, and this means that their members must be concerned with research. It was pointed out in an earlier section that we have always had and are now developing anew groups of scholars who operate outside a pedagogical context. Let us hope that this pattern will not dominate the scene, for it would be disastrous to higher education. If all the creative and re-search-minded individuals were to be siphoned off from colleges and universities into "think tanks" of one kind or another, teaching insti-tutions would suffer irreparable loss.

On the other hand, colleges and universities began as places for the education of the young; and the dissemination of knowledge, the trans-mission of culture, the inducement to understanding have historically been their central and primary functions. Teachers as scholars have always been interested in the discovery as well as the propagation of truth. During most of the history of mankind the investigation of the unknown has been a leisure-time activity, making relatively slight de-mands on time and energy. It is the scientific explosion of our century which has created the dilemma. Research is today an activity which is taking the center of the academic stage—with the encouragement of society which sees in the results of research its only salvation. What, then, happens to the original function? One is reminded of the child-ren's story about Algy who met a bear and found him bulgy. The bulge was Algy.

The dilemma is complex, but not insoluble. The solution must begin, as suggested in Section 3, at the institutional level and in the clarification of purpose. Most universities would see their purposes as both the discovery of truth and the education of students. Their prob-lem is to determine the proper ratio between the two. How should a given faculty member's time and energy be divided, or should some faculty members spend all their time in teaching while others devote themselves entirely to research? Any number of combinations and permutations are possible, and in the end the controlling factor will be the relative allocation of financial resources. The record suggests that American universities have not faced the options clearly and made in-telligent and defensible choices. On the contrary, there is no little evidence that they have blundered along in the path of least resistance, accumulating research programs because of prestige and available funds, encouraging faculty members to believe that published research is the one highroad to professional success, and shortchanging the stu-dent body in the process. None of these negative consequences is in-evitable.

For the small college and especially for the teacher in the under-graduate college the problem is complicated by pressures from the uni-versities. The small college, predominantly undergraduate, is a teach-ing institution, and its faculty is appointed for the primary purpose of providing instruction. The best education goes on where there is an element of intellectual vitality—a quality or atmosphere more readily felt than defined. This is normally present where faculty members are scholars actively engaged in exploring unknown frontiers of their fields or in producing new syntheses of what is already known. There was no disposition among the participants in the Aspen Conference to challenge the proposition that, with very rare exceptions if any, the good teacher is in some sense also a scholar. This, however, raises the questions: how much of a scholar and what kind of a scholar? On both issues the prestige of the universities with their graduate and professional schools has had an unfortunate influence on the college with its primarily undergraduate teaching responsibility.

I shall take the second question first. Modern scholarsnip is dominated by science and understandably so, for "the scientific edifice of the physical world ... in its intellectual depth, complexity, and articulation," is, as C. P. Snow points out in *The Two Cultures,* "the most beautiful and wonderful collective work of the mind of man." The consequences of this dominance have been unfortunate, for scholarship has too often been narrowed to the kind of research which is most profitable and appropriate to the scientific field. The scientific edifice has been built by constant increments of new knowledge. The scientific world lends itself to further and further exploration as does a new continent or planet. The same processes of investigation are applicable, but with more limited returns, to the social sciences. Their extension to the humanities produces little more than trivial results. There are more ways of reaching truth than just the scientific method, and the sad fact is that the prestige of science has seduced scholars outside the natural sciences into too great preoccupation with the scientific approach to truth. The religious mystic, the poet, the artist, the musician may also discover truth. We do not normally brand them as scholars, but their contribution to the understanding and enjoyment of our world suggests that science has no monopoly of insight and that there may be many forms of intellectual activity.

Scholarship, research—call it what you will—tends to reflect the scientific style. It must be primarliy analytical. It must make order out of a mass of initially disorganized material. Furthermore, it must constitute a new piece of knowledge, i.e., it must lead to some new set of propositions never before recognized (or at least published) by man. Plato thought the purpose of philosophy was to see things *sub specie aeternitatis.* Is that not scholarship? Has the student not climbed a mountain even though others have climbed it before him? And if he climbs it by his own efforts, is he not thereby as much a scholar as the first man? In short, a broader concept of scholarship would ease the pressure on the teacher whose scholarly concerns fall outside the scientific straitjacket of our day.

How much of a scholar should the teacher be? How much of his time should be devoted to scholarship as distinct from teaching? This will obviously vary with the interest of the individual and with the type of institution where he teaches. I have already suggested that universities need to make a conscious and articulate answer. Can small colleges do the same? In one sense, yes. The college can affirm that its primary obligation is teaching and that scholarship or research is essential to good teaching. This justifies the small college in granting leaves of absence, in providing research funds and facilities, and in setting teaching loads that presumably allow time for research. The difficulty lies in the fact that there are honest differences of opinion on how much time should be allocated for research—50%, 25%, 10%, or how much? How much of a doctor's time should be spent in keeping abreast of new medical knowledge?

Just as the example of the large university influences the kind of scholarship which is pursued at the small college, so it affects the amount of time devoted to scholarly pursuits. Where are the rewards in the academic life? In terms of prestige, power, and income they lie in university appointments. What are the criteria by which university appointments and promotions are made? Published research! There are faculty members who prefer to teach. They may prefer the amenities of the small college to the advantages of the large university. Nevertheless, they have their careers ahead of them. They must stay in the main stream and avoid the back eddies of their profession. With a shortage of teachers and mobility consequently high, they know that advancement comes through offers from elsewhere. They know, or suspect, they will be judged less on their teaching performance than on their books and papers. The moral is obvious—and bids fair to be disastrous.

There is only one solution, and the mounting pressures of discontent and dissatisfaction may help us to apply it. That is to elevate good teaching once again to the position of prestige it once held in the academic world. This in turn means recognition for effective teaching in terms of promotion, salary, influence in the academic community. Small college presidents have talked this line for a long time. It is not entirely their fault that they have not been heard. But sometimes their talk has been louder than their actions. We have now reached the point at which action must support the conviction that good teaching is an end in itself. A broader interpretation of scholarship, as suggested above, will help. It might even lead to the recognition that we do not need the kind of Ph.D. so long considered essential and substitute some other preparation for the life of teaching—a conclusion which the increasing shortage of traditional Ph.D.'s may help us to reach!

We can agree that the faculty member should be both teacher and scholar. To what extent should he also be policy maker? It was interesting to note among the conference participants the degree of unanimity that faculty should participate in the major policy decisions of their institutions and the extent of the concern that faculty members were abdicating this function.

If colleges and universities are to be genuine academic communities, the members must participate in a common enterprise. It is difficult to see how this can be achieved unless the senior members share in setting the goals. Put negatively, administration and trustees may propose or legislate general policy, but the way that policy goes into effect depends upon the faculty. In Europe and the United Kingdom the various faculties of the university are in clear control. The rector or vice chancellor is not only one of them, but elected by them—frequently for a limited term of office. In this country a pattern of joint responsibility with trustees or regents has evolved, with the president occupying a more independent and therefore more powerful position between the two groups. Nevertheless, the governance of colleges and universities has been *shared* in a way which distinguishes them from the business corporation on the one hand and a political unit on the other.

Why, then, the present trend toward separation of faculty and administration, or more properly of the function of the teacher-scholar and the determination of long-range policy? Preoccupation with teaching and research, especially research, is one factor. There is not enough time for everything, so one puts one's energy where one's heart is. Support for research comes chiefly from outside agencies to which the academic scholar readily becomes more responsive and in which he becomes more involved than the university at which he temporarily resides. The short supply of teachers, the growth of institutions, the general affluence of our society, the availability of grants from government and from foundations have made the faculty member far more mobile and independent of his institution than ever before. The university becomes a temporary and convenient base of operations, not a community into which one proposes permanently to mesh one's life and career.

Furthermore, the business of administering a college or university is becoming steadily more complicated and technical. If this is true of the college where decisions regarding changes in the curriculum or relationship to a founding church or the terms on which government monies will be acceptable involve seemingly endless discussion, consider the complexities of the large university with its multi-million dollar budget. The management of this type of enterprise is a full-time job for a large corps of experienced people. The situation will become more, not less, complex over the next fifteen years, and there is danger that faculty and administration will separate even further into professionally distinct divisions. Some think this result not only inevitable, but desirable. I share with other members of the conference a feeling of alarm over such a denouement.

The solution, if there is one, lies in a double distinction. The first is the distinction between the determination of policy and its administration. This is relatively easy to make in theory, but much less easy to put into effect. In small colleges and to some extent in large universities the traditional pattern has permitted or required faculty members to carry a certain amount of administrative responsibility. Economy of operation plus a more leisurely academic pace have dictated such an arrangement. In the interest of more effective operation this combination of duties no longer makes sense. The scholar-teacher is far too busy with his proper activities, and the administrative chores have become too technical and complicated.

The second is the distinction between policy which the faculty should have a voice in determining and policy which transcends its proper concern. I am not suggesting that the decisions to multiply in size or to add new professional schools or to increase fees or to develop some aspects of the university more rapidly than others are of no concern to faculty; but only that they involve considerations which exceed the normal interest and professional competence of teachers and scholars. They would have to allocate a disproportionate amount of valuable time to becoming sufficiently familiar with all relevant factors to be able to contribute useful judgments. The smaller the institution or the smaller the unit within the large university, the more relevant and important become the judgments of individual faculty members. Policy with respect to the curriculum, conditions of teaching, the values represented by the institution are a proper concern of faculty. It is important to remember that in the long run colleges and universities are cooperative ventures, and that mutual understanding and cooperation among faculty, trustees, and administrative officers are essential to the strength and balance of all educational institutions.

6 ROLE OF THE PRESIDENT

The role of the American college or university president is unique. He holds his office at the pleasure of the trustees who have the power to make his life easy or difficult and who expect him to "run" the institution, telling them what they should support and do. He must lead through persuasion a faculty whose cooperation is essential and whose members hold their appointments largely independent of the president. He must interpret the purposes of the institution to its many publics—alumni, parents, donors, taxpayers, legislators, foundations—many of whom have conflicting interests in the institution and all of whom provide support, financial or otherwise, essential to its growth and continued health. More than any one person he represents the spirit of the institution and embodies its values, setting standards and ideals for students as well as the general public.

Douglas Knight once said of his job as president of Lawrence University that he was the only man who had an allegiance to the whole institution. Everyone else had responsibility for some part of the total. This suggests the diversity of assignment which the president is expected to fulfill. Above all, he must embody and make articulate an educational philosophy. To realize that philosophy he must make certain that the institution has the right kind of faculty, the right kind of students, proper facilities for carrying on the work of education, and an environment of genuine enthusiasm for learning. Some men are better in one area than in another. At different periods in its institutional life a college or university will need presidents with different strengths, but in one way or another the three basic requirements of any president are educational leadership, intellectual distinction, and administrative ability.

The participants in the Aspen Conference, being college and university presidents, were not much inclined to spend time exploring their alleged virtues. The problems of the position were of greater interest. One of those is the growing tendency to view "the administration" with suspicion if not outright hostility. Is there a growing separation between faculty and administrative officers? What accounts for recent student manifestoes to the effect that the proper role of administration is to sweep the sidewalks and police the parking lots?

The latter can be interpreted as one manifestation of the "Berkeley syndrome" and may prove to be a passing phase or fad. Antagonism to and contempt for administrative authority are natural reactions to what students consider the source of their frustration, whether that be denial of their demand for personal freedom of conduct or the apparent imposition of an impersonal bureaucracy. In certain student manuals of tactics the university should be governed by a coalition of students and faculty with administration serving the function of clerks and janitors. The arguments are silly rather than significant.

Most administrative officers are drawn from the faculty. Why, then, are they viewed by faculty with coolness and suspicion? An obvious reason is that they have power—power in particular over the careers of members of the faculty. The fact that some college and university presidents have been chosen from outside the scholarly world on the basis of their primarily administrative competence has lent some credence to the prevailing myth that administrators are a breed apart. There is a current trend toward special training for young and budding administrators, and this perhaps reinforces the impression of a distinction between the administrator and the teacher. There are those who deplore this trend, in part because it can be divisive and because it is naively believed that the college president should spring full grown from the brow of some academic Jove. With the increasing complexity of university operation, however, it is doubtful whether we can afford this kind of amateur approach. Too many college and university presidents become dropouts. Just as it is untrue that college professors are born, not made, and that any instruction in their profession is unnecessary, so it is false that good academic administrators come automatically and instinctively into being. University administration is now and will increasingly become a complex art for which some preparation and training are desirable. This should not in itself involve alienation of affections, but if it does, we shall have to make the best of it.

Another source of misunderstanding and friction lies in the difference in viewpoint of faculty member and administrator. I return to Douglas Knight's dictum about the responsibility of the president for the whole institution. It is his task to deal with *all* the publics of the college or university; he has a responsibility not just to students or to his intellectual discipline, but to harmonize conflicting claims and pressures. Professor X is properly concerned with his subject and his students. Why should he worry over changes in society which may bring to the fore new areas of research and instruction or which may inevitably decrease his following and force additions elsewhere? But these are precisely the problems which the president must face, however painful they prove to be to individual members of the academic community.

Or take the matter of timing. There is a time for everything, as Ecclesiastes reminds us, and much of the secret of successful administration is timing. It is sometimes hard for those who are not balancing conflicting forces to understand why one cannot always take forthright

action or why it may be better to postpone a battle in order to win it
than to fight instanter and lose. There is room for more breadth and
charity of judgment on the part of members of the faculty. On the
president's side the job calls for the art of constant compromise, but it
also calls for moments of courage and conviction. It is essential for the
well-being of higher education not to let the trivia of the daily routine
smother the vision and high purpose of the calling.

It has been suggested that three types of men are held in high regard in American society and therefore have great influence—the
captain of industry, the elected political representative, and the university president. There is no question that the general public accords
the university president great prestige. He is invited to serve on all
manner of boards and commissions. His opinions are sought on international crises, political issues, economic and social developments. He
is expected to have something relevant and wise and hopefully witty to
say on almost any conceivable topic. To what extent and on what
issues should the president take a stand?

An issue is by definition divisive. It would not be an issue if there
were not conflicting views or interpretations. The president, however,
is a symbol of the entire university. He represents all its members. The
most acute problem is probably that of a political campaign. Should
the president campaign for one party or the other or for one candidate
as against his opponents? The answer which most presidents would
give is no. It is a hard answer, for presidents have their convictions
along with everyone else, and sometimes those convictions are very
strongly held. I am not suggesting that college and university presidents should be less than normal citizens or should conceal their political affiliations. In this area as in others they must set examples to
their fellows. Prudence, however, suggests that they would be wise to
refrain from active politicking in areas where the taking of sides would
introduce distinctions or divisions irrelevant to the purposes of the
institution.

On issues affecting education or their own institution the situation
is quite different. A bill which would hamper the growth or effective
operation of the state university must be opposed, regardless of the
sponsoring party, and it may be necessary to oppose it by a deliberate
campaign throughout the state. Questions of federal aid to education
are the proper concern of the academic world, and presidents should
be prepared to stand up and be counted. Too often they duck behind
the academic sofa at a time when a little more courage is in order.

Between these two types of issue stretches a wide range of difficult
problems and decisions. Where should the univeristy president stand,

for example, on the great moral issue of our day—civil rights? Piously in favor, to be sure! What about the tough operating choices of such a stand? How could the president of a southern Negro college do other than defend students who have engaged in certain kinds of civil disobedience? Can the presidents of northern white colleges do less?

These questions lead into an even more complex problem. To what extent should a college or university as an institution engage in social action? The University of Chicago recently initiated a major urban redevelopment program on the South side of Chicago. Presumably its primary purpose was to safeguard the environment of the University. The result was also a major contribution to the city of Chicago and its people. Universities in other urban centers are facing the same kind of problem. Many universities have become involved in AID programs around the world. At a time when academic talent is in short supply at home, we are exporting a prodigious amount of brain power to improve the social, economic, political, and scientific conditions of peoples in underdeveloped countries.

Ought university resources to be used for such goals? The conference members were troubled and divided. There was little disposition to challenge American education's responsibility to contribute to improved living and educational standards in less fortunate parts of the world. But what is its responsibility to the Great Society at home? To what extent will direct action and direct involvement supplement or defeat its basic purpose to contribute to the betterment of society by the development of the individual? The trend is in the direction of involvement, one more indication that the ivory tower and ivied walls of academic legend have gone the way of the horse and buggy. The decision comes back in large part to the president and his role in society. One hopes that college and university presidents are good men. Perhaps we should remember Edmund Burke's dictum: "All that is required for the triumph of evil is that good men remain silent and do nothing."

On one aspect of the president's function there was complete agreement at the conference. He must be an innovator. The changes through which higher education is going require new techniques and new solutions. Its health depends on the capacity to innovate. Imaginative ideas are appearing all over the academic landscape—some brilliant, some useful, some worth trying, and some absurd. How do these ideas get translated into academic practice?

The truth is that colleges and universities are ponderous institutions. Tradition, size, diffusion of authority, and natural inertia make them slow to change. It is human to find the well-known methods easier to live with than the experimental. Legitimate differences among faculty tend to neutralize one another, as any attempt at curricular change illustrates. Occasionally a brilliant or hyperthyroid member of a faculty can bring about a major change. Normally the catalytic agent is the dean or the president. Once again I refer to the president's unique responsibility for understanding his institution in its entirety. It is that understanding and concern that enable him to select the best ideas of others and to press for their adoption. Perhaps his greatest contribution to his institution in the years ahead will be his capacity for innovation.

7 AUTONOMY OF THE UNIVERSITY

Any discussion of the purposes and problems of higher education is bound to bump up against the danger of threats to institutional freedom. Again and again the conversation at the Aspen Conference touched on questions of university autonomy. Such answers as one can find bring us back to the point where we began: what is the purpose of the university and to what extent it is a genuine community?

In certain important respects colleges and universities are creatures of their society, established to serve certain desirable social ends. It would seem to follow that society has the right to determine what educational institutions shall do and how they shall do it. I see no escape from this conclusion. The important questions are: what groups within society exercise society's right of influence, and in what ways do they do it? Six major groups can be identified.

(1) The legal control of colleges and universities rests with trustees or regents. They are the repository and agent of society's concern. At their worst, individual members of these governing boards have used their position to promote personal convictions and to stifle freedom of thought and expression. At their best they have interpreted the changing patterns and needs of society to academic communities which tend to be insulated in their own professional preoccupations. We can agree that the first kind of interference is wrong and the second kind of intrusion is salutary, but it is not easy to find a simple rationale for the distinction. Freedom of thought is being limited in both cases, for even in the second the institution is under pressure to abandon familiar and convenient intellectual paths for newer and more strenuous activities.

(2) Alumni have been both sources of great strength and influences of evil for American colleges and universities. Their loyalty and financial support have been enormously important, particularly to the private institutions. They have sometimes used their influence in undesirable ways—overemphasis on athletics, attacks on liberal pro-

fessors, interference with admission policy or internal student discipline. If we believe in freedom of thought and expression, we can hardly deny to alumni the right to express their views, and if we accept their support, we can hardly refuse to listen to them. Where is the line to be drawn between legitimate influence and improper interference?

(3) It is humanly awkward but institutionally not too difficult to resist the efforts of parents to interfere with the operations of the college. Deans are familiar with and hardened to the parental demands for special rules or dispensations for Johnny or Susie. In a larger sense, however, parents have considerable influence, for their patronage of an institution has an effect on its survival.

(4) To some extent this is equally true of donors, whether individuals, corporations, or foundations. Without their support a college is unlikely to increase in strength and quality; and not to grow in this day and age usually means to decline and wither. The horror stories of dictation by donors are too numerous to allow us to ignore this sort of interference, but it should be pointed out that gifts can be and sometimes are declined.

(5) The citizens of a state are in a position to exercise some control over their state-supported instutions, and the presidents of state universities are only too familiar with the constant threat to their autonomy. Both through appropriations and through restrictive legislation state legislatures can reduce the freedom and direct the course of state institutions. Few would deny them the right in principle. Where does it make sense to draw the line in practice?

(6) More recently considerable apprehension has been felt in many quarters regarding the influence of the federal government. The increasing availability of federal funds has been one of the dominant phenomena since World War II, and it seems clear that in one form or another federal money will continue to be available for a wide variety of educational programs. Does federal support entail federal dictation or direction, with consequent loss of autonomy?

The issue which has agitated and divided educators most sharply in recent years has been the support of scientific and technological programs. Is the federal government through the grants and contracts made available through the National Science Foundation, the Defense Department, National Institute of Mental Health, and many other agencies distorting the proper course of higher education? Are institutions becoming dependent on the continuation of government grants and contracts? Are the sciences being fattened while the humanities are left to starve? It is interesting to note that with the advent of federal support for the social sciences, the humanities, and the arts, new voices of alarm are being raised. Science and technology are, it is alleged, neutral; the humanities can never be. Therefore, government support of the humanities inevitably leads to government control of the thinking of the country.

Granted the tendency of some people to see burglars under the bed, there remain genuine problems of cooperation in ways that minimize the dangers of undue influence. It must be recognized that whatever programs the government supports—science, humanities, scholarships, loans, buildings—the very availability of funds tends to push the institution in that direction. Autonomy may well depend upon a high degree of self-denial.

Lest the picture be distorted, it should be added that federal funds may make possible advances in quality and performance that would otherwise be out of the question. Indeed, federal support may make the difference between the survival and disappearance of many private institutions. The emphasis in this nation has been on autonomy, and hence questions of control or interference immediately arose. There is another side to the picture, a much more encouraging one. The evidence to date does not justify many of the fears which have been expressed. On the contrary, the evidence suggests that federal support wisely handled is a godsend rather than a millstone.

When we consider what would normally be recognized as strong or outstanding institutions, we invariably find a high degree of independence. Universities will be judged in the long run by their contribution to society. The more independent of pressures from segments of that society, the more significant and enduring their contribution is likely to be. The history of human discovery in science makes clear that the greatest advances are made at times when men's imagination and curiosity are allowed to roam freely without too close an application to practical uses. The function of the university as the discoverer and developer of creative individuals depends upon freedom to encourage the unworldly, the maverick, even the apparently antisocial. The role of the university as critic of society would be impossible without a high degree of autonomy.

Society will always be impinging upon its educational institutions. It takes great understanding on the part of their constituency and great courage and conviction on the part of faculty, administration, and trustees to defend the university against these pressures. For the health of society it must be done. And yet, the college and university can never be completely free from outside pressure, nor should they be. Complete autonomy would mean sterility. It is the constant struggle and tension between the requirement to be free to follow one's independent vision and the necessity of justifying one's existence in terms of the total social good that keep institutions alive and productive. Nor is there any doctrinaire fence behind which autonomy can be shielded. In the end the test is a pragmatic one. Where institutions are directed by the imaginative, the intelligent, and the concerned, they can serve best if left free to serve in their own way.

8   THE STUDENT ENIGMA

Wherever educators gather these days, the topic of student behavior soon appears in the discussion. The Aspen Conference was no exception, though less time and attention were devoted to current student phenomena than might have been expected from the current play in the public press.

It has already been suggested that students are flocking to college for a variety of reasons. The more serious among them would answer the question which heads this section with the statement that they want the best possible education. An increasing number of them would go on to say that they want an education which is relevant to the social and human concerns of their generation. College and university students are not afraid of hard work. They are ready for any amount of it so long as it has meaning and relevance to the issues which really concern them.

Let us make no mistake about the present generation of students. Rebellious, recalcitrant, or unbuttoned—all these some students are, and they make life difficult for themselves as well as for their elders. At the same time they are idealists with a passion which has not had its equal since the missionary days of the late nineteenth century. There is little religious motivation for most, or at least religion in a conventional sense. The church and formal religious commitment are not popular. But the passion for social justice burns hot and leads to extreme acts of personal commitment—civil rights work in the South, the Peace Corps and VISTA, summer programs in urban slum areas, protests over the war in Vietnam or the draft, demonstrations in defense of free speech. Somehow, the quiet progress of a conventional curriculum seems in contrast both unexciting and irrelevant. Rightly or wrongly students are complaining that they do not find in their studies material that provides them with significant answers and a meaningful education.

Mixed with this idealism is a demand for personal liberty which to the students is a natural corollary to social justice and to their elders looks like license. What has produced this extraordinary situation? One can point to the consequences of thirty years of moral relativism in the social sciences or of an extreme doctrine of permissiveness in bringing up children. Without question, the philosophy of existentialism in one form or another has profoundly influenced the thinking of the younger generation. If nothing is right or good for me unless I see it as such, then the rules and conventions of society no longer have any authority. If the society is permeated with social injustice, then my concern for a better world demands contempt for the hypocrisy of the society which surrounds me. I can be true to myself only be condemning and rebelling against an immoral society.

The situation calls for delicate management, for it is easy to overemphasize one side or the other. One school of thought would ride with the demand for individual freedom. Students want to be taken seriously. They respond best when treated as mature adults. Give them their head, and they are wise enough and good enough to arrive ultimately at the right answer. The other school emphasizes the requirements of civilized society, namely the necessity for law and order and the willingness of the individual to subordinate his desires to the value structure of his culture. We all must live within a system, and there is no reason why college students should be exempt from that requirement. The recognition of authority in its rightful place is part of life. Indeed, the highest freedom for the individual is dependent not on anarchy, but on a society ordered and controlled by law.

There are no inalienable rights of students to dictate the nature of their academic community. They have the right to expect of their society some kind of education. They have a right to the best education which the institution they attend can provide—within the terms by which the institution exists. An atheist has no right to demand nonreligious instruction from a Catholic college. A student planning on medicine cannot demand medical instruction from a university without a medical school. Freedom of thought is integral to liberal education; freedom of personal behavior is not. The ground rules of every institution are constantly undergoing change due to the erosive interplay between student ingenuity and administrative authority. It does not follow from this fact that ground rules have no place, any more than it is true that an academic community consists only of its student members.

I return to the note on which this section started. Students are seeking for meaning. They are struggling on the one hand to discover who and what they are, on the other to develop significant connections with a tolerable, i.e., a moral, world. The more our education can contribute to these discoveries, the more relevant and important it will be. The more vital, the less the temptation to rebel and destroy. Relevance and meaning must be interpreted in personal terms. As colleges and universities grow in size, the intimate personal relations of a smaller and simpler society disappear. The pattern is no different from that in other institutions or communities. But the process of adjustment is always painful, and we would ease the situation for the students if we understand the problem and seek ways, as suggested in the first section, to perpetuate a genuine academic community.

9 A MORAL ENTERPRISE

As I reach the conclusion of this report, I am disturbed by the number of important issues and comments which I have passed silently over, and it is tempting to bring them all together in one final section. I shall content myself with emphasizing one motif which permeated the fortnight's discussion.

It is perhaps best expressed in Lord James' sentence near the end of his summing up: "For at their best, places of higher education are, in the modern world, a world where religion has lost its universal authority, the chief custodians and interpreters of value in society." No one at the Aspen Conference was ever in doubt that colleges and universities are the places par excellence where values are conserved, created, and transmitted in our society.

As one participant stated it, the university is a value-affirming institution for strengthening and elevating our society, and is thus a *moral* enterprise. It is an agency for the discovery and transmission of knowledge, and is thus an *intellectual* enterprise. It is a community of teachers and learners, people engaged in the two enterprises, just mentioned, and is thus a *human* enterprise.

As one thinks back over the course of the discussion, one can see why this is so. Whether public or private, the university must both preserve the culture with all its values and provide a constant critique of that culture. Whether the emphasis is on the development of the individual or the transmission of the ethos of the society, the recognition and adoption or absorption of values are central. We think it improper to impose a rigid and preconceived moral system on students, but we insist that they discover and develop their own value system. We hope to reconcile the legitimate claims of society, however imperfect, with the value of individual freedom. From beginning to end the educational enterprise is a moral as well as intellectual struggle, and to add its human dimension is merely to underscore that truth.

Automation and Technology in Education

By Norman D. Kurland

THE NEW TECHNOLOGY

Surveyor I is sending back thousands of pictures of the moon, but its most important message is about life here on Earth. It reminds us that it has been less than nine short years since Sputnik I. Children who were in kindergarten then will just be entering high school this fall. How much the world has changed while they have been in school! How much more will it change during the next nine years which will still see many of those same youngsters in school and college? And how much more change will there be in the fifty years beyond that which will be the life expectancy of these youngsters—years for which present schooling is supposed to be preparing them?

To pose the question in this way is to suggest a major dimension of the problems the school face, and why it is appropriate for a committee of Congress to ask how technology—the same technology that placed Surveyor I on the moon—can help increase the effectiveness of our schools. For I would hope that the question is asked not because our schools have been ineffective—the men responsible for Surveyor are, after all, a product of those schools—but because of the recognition that the schools need help to remain as effective in the future as they have been in the past.

Rapid technological change and the explosion of knowledge are only parts of the pressures to which the schools must respond. The civil rights revolution has posed a challenge to the schools to be as effective for all as they have been for some, and a growing prosperity and rising aspirations have extended the number of years of schooling expected by all. In the face of these pressures, were the schools to proceed along even the best of paths laid out in the past, a decline in effectiveness would be inevitable. Given the fact that the best was far

From *Automation and Technology in Education* by Norman D. Kurland. Reprinted by permission of Norman D. Kurland.

from universal, it is easy to see why there is a concern for effectiveness now and for the future.

How, then, can technology, which is part of the problem, contribute to the solution? Here exciting possibilities open before us, exciting as the possibilities thay lie beyond Surveyor. Let me try to suggest some of these be describing some of the innovations that I have seen as I have gone around the country.

INNOVATIONS IN EDUCATION

I have seen computers that present lessons to students in such a way that each student receives a lesson uniquely tailored to his needs. He controls the speed at which he moves through the lesson and his performance determines what the lesson will be. Where he has difficulty he gets help immediately, where he shows mastery he is moved ahead to more challenging materials. The presentation can be in written form, it can be by voice, it can be by pictures, moving or still, or any combination of these. The student makes his responses on a typewriter keyboard, by pressing buttons, or by pointing a light pen at a tube.

The computer can provide the student with a printed record of his own progress in each lesson, or over any span of lessons. The teacher can get a similar record of progress or a record of an entire class or any group within the class. She can get an analysis of the lesson itself to find out which parts are causing difficulty to which students. Changes can be made where difficulties are identified, and, as readily, new material can be added when called for.

I have seen other computers on which children go through exercises that simulate real situations—running a government, doing a chemical analysis or choosing a career. Development of problem-solving and decision-making abilities are the special aims of such programs.

I have seen a student dial into a central learning resources center and call up the lesson of his choice—a lecture on tape, a film, language instruction, music—anything indeed that can be stored photographically or electronically and transmitted electronically.

I have seen "talking typewriters" that help teach children and adults to read by creating a situation for learning to read that approximates that which makes learning to speak such a seemingly effortless experience for most children.

I have seen beautifully prepared instructional materials—books, slides, transparencies, produced so inexpensively that there is no excuse for not supplying them to every classroom and child who needs them.

I have seen copying machines used in ways such as to provide virtually instant textbooks—today's Congressional *Record* can be tomorrow's classroom text for a class of ten or a thousand.

I have seen classes taught by television, and children discussing the latest exploits in space seen live on television in class or at home. I have seen students and student-teachers complete an activity and immediately see and analyze themselves on videotape. I have seen exhibits under a microscope or too small for a class to see enlarged via television so that every student can see what the instructor is describing.

I have seen students select film cartridges, insert them in individual projectors and watch a frog embryo develop, see a reenactment of a civil war battle, or learn about a career.

I have seen classes talk via amplified telephone with an expert in the field of their current interest, debate an issue with their Congressman in Washington, or exchange experiences with children in another land.

I have seen a student engage in a dialogue with a computer to select his courses for the next year, and guidance counselors call up in an instant the full record of the student as well as relevant data comparing him with others of similar interests, abilities and experience.

I have seen the administrative and record-keeping chores of schools taken over by data processing equipment, thus freeing administration and teachers for more important tasks.

I have seen libraries automating their processes to provide more effective service and to keep pace with the explosion of knowledge.

I have seen school buildings using the latest materials and construction techniques to provide an exciting environment for learning at a cost that any community can afford.

THE SCHOOL OF THE FUTURE

Now imagine if you will all of these pieces put together into a single system. We can then look forward to a time of universal, individualized education when every person will be educated and no two will be educated alike. Teachers deeply committed to the art of teaching and thoroughly versed in the science of learning will have at their disposal a full panoply of learning materials to which they will direct each individual student in accordance with his needs, abilities and interests.

There will be no lockstep and indeed no common schedule. Each student will proceed at his own pace through a curriculum uniquely adjusted to his needs. He will have, through many media, access to the best teaching and the best information on each subject along his way.

Intrinsic motivation will largely replace extrinsic as the student early discovers the power of knowledge and the joy of learning and has opportunity to grow in directions which attract him. He will move smoothly and early from directed, highly structured learning situations to self-directed, unprestructured activities where the learner plays an active role in learning.

If one seeks a current model of this school of the future it is best seen in the public library. To the library each user comes with his own demands, and each is more or less successfully accommodated, though no two persons are served quite alike. There are almost no age or grade divisions—adult and child may work sided by side and even at times use the same materials. Each proceeds at his own pace toward his own goals. Moreover, the library never presumes that it must supply all the users' needs for information. It does what it can do best and leaves to other agencies in the community portions of the task appropriate to them.

I should remind you that what I have projected is based largely on electronic, computer and communications technologies in combination with new understandings derived from the behaviorial sciences. Present activity in biology in the studies of the brain and its functioning and in genetics may have even more profound implications for education.

INDIVIDUALIZATION AND EFFICIENCY

The central thrust of this application of technology to education is, as I see it, twofold: on one hand, to achieve for the first time truly individualized conditions of *learning* for each student and, on the other, to affect the efficiencies of *instruction* that can be achieved by mass education. With the new technology what is done well once can be multiplied a thousand-fold. The economies so realized can release resources to do for every child what once could be done only for a few. Thus education can become more effective even as it becomes more available. We can have *both* quantity and quality, though the latter will be much harder to achieve than the former. To the public school official this prospect of holding the costs of education to a reasonable rate of growth even as quality and quantity increase is extremely attractive. For each year we see school budgets rise and we now know that by traditional methods we shall never keep pace with the demand.

(In New York State expenditures for public elementary and secondary schools rose nearly three-fold from 1955 to 1965 to a level of $2.5 billion and are expected to rise another billion by 1970, an increase of 40%. During the same 1955 to 1965 decade public school enrollments went up 30% and are likely to go up another 10% by 1970 to a total of nearly 3 ½ million students.

In higher education, enrollments are expected to go from 5,600,000 in 1965 to 7,750,000 in 1970, an increase of nearly 40% while costs may nearly double.)

We also know that effective education is a key factor in economic growth. If educational expenditures are an investment, as many economists now argue, how much more so are the funds expended on the improvement of education.

One word of caution is in order at this point. I will yield to no one in my enthusiasm for the potentialities of the new educational technology. At the same time I rcognize that it will not perform miracles. Yet because of the success of technology in other fields and the exciting vistas it does open up in education, there will be a tendency to turn to it for solutions to the tough problems that confront us in education. The task of leadership in the years ahead will be to restrain those who would seek all answers in technology while ignoring those who believe no answers are to be found there.

HOW DO WE GET THERE FROM HERE

Let me stress that the above is but one limited vision of the possibilities inherent in our present technology. Others may have other visions more or less rosy. But to go from present reality to anyone's vision will require major effort, much wisdom, careful planning, and not a little luck. For the potential for evil in any technology is equal to that for good—as witness nuclear energy or the internal combustion engine. It is men who determine whether anything produced by man shall enrich or debase humanity.

Everything I have described is being done today at least experimentally. The hardware necessary for large-scale adoption is available or can be readily developed once the need is identified. Even the cost factors are such as to make this a relatively minor consideration in the decision to move to such a system. What is lacking are two essential ingredients—the software and the system to transform our present schools into those of the future.

By software is meant all of the program content, all the concepts of learning and instruction, all of the decisions about what *should* be taught to whom and when, without which the machines are useless. These elements have always been the heart and soul of education and nothing about the new educational technology changes this one iota.

And these are the costliest, most difficult portions of the system to produce. I don't know what the ratio of software to hardware costs is, but it is certainly high. Yet it is often so much easier to get funds for the hardware than the software, just as in the past it was easier to get funds for buildings than for teachers' salaries. I should like to urge that in any funding of the new technology by Congress, full recognition be given to this point.

Secondly, if the potentialities of electronic and related communication technologies are to be realized, they must be matched in ingenuity and creativeness by a new educational systems technology that matches machine and communications capabilities to human goals, needs, and capacities. To accomplish this task well will require the best minds of our society and the combined resources of the schools and private industry.

PUBLIC SCHOOLS AND PRIVATE INDUSTRY— A NEW PARTNERSHIP

Private industry has the technical capability, it has great flexibility to move in new ways on new problems, and it has the profit motive to make it seek the most efficient use of resources. I suspect that there will be great temptation for some of the new education-oriented industries to feel that they can do the school's job so much better that they will grow impatient with the schools.

But aside from the claims of tradition—a not insignificant claim— the schools have a vital role to play. They bring to education other values besides efficiency. For one thing they, particularly the public schools, are responsible for all children, not just those that can be most readily reached. They are concerned with basic goals of education that are not amenable to efficiency measures or susceptible to realization through technologically mediated means. And it is primarily through the schools and other public agencies that the public funds will be channeled for education.

SOME PROBLEMS

But before the new partnership between the schools and industry can become fully effective, problems such as the following will have to be faced and answered:

1. Because the investment required in the new educational technology will be very great, initially most of the funds will have to come from the public sector. How can an effective mix of public funds and private enterprise be achieved in education? Can public education agencies enter into working partnerships

with private businesses without being subject to the charge of favoring one company over another?

Can a company work openly with a public agency without jeopardizing its competitive advantage? Are changes in law needed to facilitate effective working arrangements between public and private agencies?

2. As the complexity of new educational systems increases, it will become increasingly difficult even for a knowledgeable administrator or teacher to evaluate them. How can the schools and the public be assured that the new educational systems are sound? Should the states or the Federal government provide some system for assessment of the products of the educational technology? If there is assessment, how can the values of diversity and freedom be protected?

3. Are existing copywright laws and rules regarding use of materials produced with public funds adequate both to protect the interests of the public and the producers and to provide incentives to private enterprise to undertake the risks of development?

4. There is likely to be a tendency for private industry to look to the Federal government as the primary partner in this new activity, both because it has greater funds and because it is easier to deal with one jurisdiction no matter how complex than with 50 or 25,000. What will this do to the traditional role of the states and localities? How can they be brought into viable involvement in the partnership? I would particularly urge the importance of the role of the states as the level of government primarily responsible for education and, in many cases, in the best position to provide the direction and coordination needed if the new is to blend smoothly with the old.

There are questions deserving of careful study by this committee or some other agency. The answers can greatly influence the speed of developments and the nature of the outcome.

There are also the larger questions raised by the new educational technology to which all who are concerned with the quality of human life must address themselves. Will the new technology transform man into a mere extension of the machine—mindful of the things necessary to keep the social machine operating, mindless of the things that make men human? Or will it enable each to become all that he is capable of and desires to become?

These questions need answers because our choice is not *whether* we shall apply technology to education but only how, by whom, and under what conditions.

The New Social-Industrial Complex

LYLE M. SPENCER

Little more than five years ago, Dwight Eisenhower, in his last message as President, warned of the growth of a military-industrial complex that could endanger American freedoms. It was an important warning. Commentators now and then honor it by repetition, but no one has yet suggested what to do about it.

Tonight I would like to strike a more optimistic note. I want to describe the early growth of a new complex in which industry and government also are intertwined, but towards a far different end. It might be called a "social-industrial complex." With the government acting as broker, a number of large American corporations are organizing some of the nation's best-trained and original minds in the fields of social reform, education and management to equalize the spread of opportunity in American life. Social causes which in the thirties, were the domain of college professors, labor unions and student demonstrations, are today becoming also the new business of business.

To describe this new concern of American business, I wish I could find a better word than "opportunity." It is an ambiguous word that calls up much of the double-talk of an earlier day when business was strictly business and "economic royalists" blockaded social reform. "Opportunity" was the watch-word of early industrialists who often apologized for child labor by saying that any juvenile might grow up to be President, or better still, a millionaire. It was the word of Willie Loman's brother, Ben, who believed that anyone could strike it rich among the black flies of Alaska and the veld of darkest Africa.

I am not talking about that kind of opportunity. I mean the simple opportunity of doing a week's work for a decent paycheck, of living in

From *The New Social Industrial Complex* by Lyle M. Spencer. An unpublished address. Reprinted by permission of the author.

a house one can afford on a street of one's choice, and, if you please, the opportunity of aspiring to live in a better house on a better street if one chooses. More than all these, I am speaking of the opportunity to acquire chunks of the accumulated knowledge which man leaves as a legacy to his children on printed pages and even in ordinary speech.

A few months ago, instead of "opportunity," I would have reached for the simpler and more specific word "education." I would have said that business is getting deeply involved in the problems of education, and left it at that. But my business competitors and I are rapidly learning that one cannot get involved in the difficult problems of education without also getting involved in the much more difficult problems of the organization of society itself. We talk about computer-assisted instruction, but we also talk about illiteracy and the so-called culturally deprived. If you overhear an IBM man talk about building an image, there's now a good chance he doesn't mean the corporate image. He may be talking about the citizens of New Bedford, a conservative old whaling town in Massachusetts, and the image they have of five hundred school dropouts in a Job Corps center at the edge of town. It happens that the Job Corps Center—known as Rodman—is operated by my company, Science Research Associates, a subsidiary of IBM. We have signed a contract with the people of the United States, in which we promise to deliver a product of social and educational reform.

If one swallow doesn't make a summer, neither does one contract make a social-industrial complex. But look at what is happening all around us. A list of the contractors for the Job Corps looks like a digest of trading on the New York Stock Exchange: Litton Industries, Xerox, RCA, Burroughs Business Machines, G.E., Packard-Bell Northern Natural Gas, and others.

We have all read of an epidemic of mergers and partnerships between electronics manufacturers and publishers of the printed word. When General Electric recently joined with Time, Inc., to form a new company called General Learning Corp., who did they install as the head of it? They hired Francis Keppel, the most forceful U. S. Commissioner of Education we have ever had. Mr. Keppel, whom many of you recall as dean of the Harvard Graduate School of Education, is not about to forget that his main work as Commissioner was to advance education by breaking down segregation, by establishing a network of educational research centers in universities all over America, and by supervising the passage of a billion dollars in Federal aid to education, chiefly to equalize the learning opportunities of the poor.

His company, my company, companies like Xerox and all the rest, expect to find themselves each day locked in ever-deeper competition.

Competition for what? Merely to sell textbooks by the carload and teaching machines by the dozen? Hardly. We are in a competition to ask questions and find answers which recently engaged a relatively small group of academics cloistered in research libraries of teachers' colleges. We are looking beyond the pages of a textbook and into the mind of a child. Instead of asking "What should he be taught?" we are asking "What makes him learn?" Aware that a child seems to get eighty percent of his education *outside* of school, we are trying to formulate some hard, practical questions. We want to find out—and intend to find out—how a classroom can become a more effective organizer of a child's experience.

Recently, Mount Vernon, New York, School Superintendent John Henry Martin told a congressional committee that "the center of gravity for educational change is moving from the teachers' college and the superintendent's office to the corporation executive suite." That may be overstating it, but we do hope to find out more about how a child learns, not only in classes of twenty-five, but in classes of one hundred, in discussion groups of perhaps five and six, and what he can best learn sitting all alone at a study carrel.

We plan to find out more—because we must find out more—about what is specifically meant when we say that pre-school children of the ghetto become educationally disabled for lack of certain sensory stimulations and language experience. We plan to find out because at some early date American industry—the companies engaged in the new social-industrial complex—will be competing to design, produce and market learning materials for children of the ghetto. I don't know whether these materials will be sold to the Federal government, to local public schools, local community action programs, or whether newly-enlightened ghetto parents will buy them at the five-and-ten. But I do know that our country is at last committed to equalizing the educational opportunity of every young American and that many large business firms are involved in that commitment.

We hope to find out more—because we must find out more—about what is specifically meant when we say that every school-child learns but in his own way at his own rate of speed. We—and other companies—are experimenting with high-speed computers as aids in teaching children. Possibilities growing out of the new electronic-curriculum mix are without number. Whether tomorrow's machines will be mechanical tutors, television sets, do-it-yourself kits, or simply words printed on file cards, or combinations of all these, we don't yet know. But we are deeply engaged, in collaboration with the Federal government and local schools, in finding out.

We hope to find out more—because we must find out more—

about what is specifically meant when we say that school dropouts can have the direction of their lives reversed. By what specific means do we change them to school "*drop-ins*" and persuade them to believe in themselves as rightful claimants to productive, secure, good-paying jobs? These high-minded problems require practical, hard-nosed questions. Just how handicapped is an 18-year-old who has learned the habit of consistent failure in ten or twelve years of schooling? Must he learn everything in the curriculum that he failed to learn before, or can he base a new, useful education on certain selected building blocks, such as reading and arithmetic? To what degree can he base a useful education on things he's really interested in, such as the mechanics of a hot rod, the social science of neighborhood gangs, the English of Popular Mechanics magazine, and the arithmetic of a paycheck in a work-study program?

We don't yet have many answers, but we are getting some new leads about where more of the answers lie. They lie not only in published materials and educational gadgetry, but in human relationships. We are finding out at the Rodman Job Corps Center some differences between conventional school teachers and what we choose to call tutor-counselors. We are finding out that school dropouts who never wrote a good school composition on "My Vacation Last Summer"—perhaps because they never had one—can turn out an electrifying issue of the *Rodman News,* the student newspaper at Rodman. They can write poems of surging anger and burning aspiration. Imagine one Rodman boy, John Castlebury, a failure in English and rejecter of school, who found within himself this short poem for the *Rodman News*:

> "I am a sky without a heaven or stars.
> Sugar and no sweetness
> Man without love."

Are we to say that this boy is beyond education?

I know that most of these questions are not new to most of you. But I believe it is somewhat new to find yourselves lectured about them by a businessman, speaking in his capacity as a businessman. Why are companies like IBM, Xerox, and RCA getting their well-manicured hands dirty in the problems of poverty? Perhaps if we used our brains, electronic or otherwise, we at SRA would stick to our old business of designing precise tests for middle-class teachers to give to bright-eyed youngsters. Economically speaking, it's a much more reliable activity.

Let me say at the outset that we believe the problems of education can eventually turn into a sensible business, too. Right now, they add up to far more cost than profit. So did color television.

But direct gain is not our only incentive. Every business is also part of the American economy. To see clearly one of our incentives in improving the social and economic health of the poverty ghetto, one need look no further than at the generation of our parents, many of whom were impoverished immigrants. Millions of them came to America sheerly by the drive of their ambition. They came undereducated and unskilled. Some acquired learning and skill and, indeed, found prosperity around the corner. But most of them drearily labored their lives away to guarantee educational opportunity for their children.

This is the story that accounts for many of you sitting in this great university hall tonight. In a sense, it is also the story that accounts for the growth of a corporation like IBM. The computer has created 250,000 new jobs and at least a dozen new professions. In a generation, this country has changed from a nation whose preponderate number of citizens worked at dull, repetitive, unskilled jobs in factories to one of automated manufacture. Each year a greater proportion of our people sit at desks manipulating pencils, around conference tables figuring out questions for electronic brains to solve. Modern, prosperous America is the product of our parents' unquenchable worship of education. Every educated man makes his country richer and, if you please, makes the institution with which he works more prosperous. If you will allow me one more word in this vulgarity of attaching dollar signs to the spreading of widsom, let me say that it's to the interest of busines that every down-trodden, socially-disoriented member of the ghetto becomes an economic contributor—or to use Lyndon Johnson's earthy phrase, to become "taxpayers instead of tax-eaters."

Purposely, I have cast this argument in the shape of profits because that is what you expect a businessman to do. As Tex Thornton, chairman of Litton Industries recently said, "There are those who characterize the businessman as something less than patriotic and compassionate.... The word seems to have gotten around that the business man is *for* poverty—*not* against it." While businessmen are against poverty in principle, too many of us have been indifferent to it in practice. We don't ask enough hard questions about its causes. We have not become sufficiently involved as businessmen with the national business of attacking poverty. We at IBM, and our competitors, are now beginning to do such thinking because it has become our business to do so.

This is a healthy development. The basic form of organization in American life is the organization of human beings into private enterprises. All other forms of great organization—government, labor unions, trade associations, even major sections of our schools—have grown in response to the demands of our basic form of organization. True enough, the degree of engagement by business in this attack on poverty is still quite small. But it will grow.

Both business and social reform stand to gain by a growing partnership. Until recently, agencies of social concern, chiefly government and education, stood at the short end of competition for our most vigorous minds. Business could easily win the competition. They offered the reward most valued in our culture—money. Academic skills and managerial talents that might well have been allocated to improving government and education have flocked into the manufacture of cars, into advertising of breakfast cereal and sale of insurance business. That's where the money is. Only in times of deepest national need—I am thinking of World War II—did it become popular among our most able people to devote their best energies to public need.

Recently, however, there are signs of great change in what our culture values as high reward. Some months ago, a story on the first page of *The Wall Street Journal* created as much concerned conversation among top businessmen as any I can remember. That story reported that students in our leading universities, by and large, don't want to enter business. Beyond earning a good living, making money is not their consuming goal. What they seem to want is to feel they are part of social change. Many are joining the Peace Corps, VISTA, and volunteering to help us with the Job Corps.

On the other hand, men who have committed their lives to public concerns are today moving from public agencies into private enterprises without changing their commitment. Frank Keppel is one example. In our own company, Burke Marshall, the former assistant attorney general for civil rights is now the general counsel of IBM, and he has just accepted the chairmanship of a Presidential committee to re-evaluate the draft.

A new vice-president of our corporation, Eugene Fubini, came to us from government, where he was Assistant Secretary of Defense. Another kind of example involves a University of Chicago graduate many of you may personally know. Some years ago, here in Chicago, Jerome M. Ziegler headed a group called the American Foundation for Political Education. Something like the Great Books Foundation but with more specialized subject material, his organization was devoted to promoting discussion groups and publishing reading materials on the complexities of international affairs and public administration. Later, Mr. Ziegler was twice a candidate for Congress in the western suburbs. Today, employed by SRA and IBM, he is an active agent of social change as director of the Rodman Job Corps Center.

   Let me turn now from these general ideas to specific ones we have had to cope with as a partner with government in operating a job corps center. When the first group of young men showed up at Rodman last August, what did Mr. Ziegler and his associates find? The typical Job Corpsman had quit school at the seventh grade. He couldn't pass a fifth-grade reading test. He was seven pounds underweight. Four out of five had never been to a physician or a dentist. Two-thirds are from a family whose head is unemployed. The family of one out of two is on relief. Almost one out of two come from broken homes. Out of this background, these boys build their self-concepts and are supposed to develop what we of middle-class values call aspiration. Is it any wonder that only one out of ten Corpsmen has ever held a job?

   About half of these Corpsmen are of an eligible age for military service. Traditionally, such young men are attracted to the military life. As Richard Rovere recently wrote, "The military is to a large degree the Negro's high school and his Harvard." The same might be said of the Appalachian white. But like Harvard, the military has an academic barrier at its gate. Of Job Corpsmen who are otherwise eligible for military service, forty-seven percent fail their entrance examination—seventeen percent for physical reasons, thirty percent because of a relatively simple educational test.

   With such a group of prospective students, who have cast school out of their lives and whom society has all but cast out of its life, you can readily see why SRA and our colleague corporations hesitated before undertaking Job Corps contracts. Were we ready to say that we could succeed where other public and private institutions have largely failed? Of all the various battle areas in the War on Poverty, only one section of the Economic Opportunity Act, the one establishing the Job Corps, allowed for participation by private contractors. Our alternatives were this engagement in the War on Poverty or the role of watching from the sidelines. We chose to get in.

   Our task at Rodman is to equip 750 Corpsmen, deficient in reading, writing and arithmetic and non-believers in themselves, to be, of all things, operators of sophisticated office machines, competent in office procedures, and, wherever there is hope of success, computer operators and programmers.

   Because so little is learned in classrooms, we have taken a total environmental approach—24 hours-a-day, seven days-a-week. One thing we learned almost immediately was that we were expecting too little from them. We had planned to take between 14 and 24 months to graduate them into on-the-job training. But the staff soon learned that the students' lack of education is not the equivalent of stupidity.

While few of the boys could read beyond the fifth grade, their test scores in other abilities almost equaled those of a high-school senior class. The staff decided to aim at getting the average boy ready for on-the-job training in ten months, many in six. Very shortly, we will know whether that staff estimate is sound.

The Corpsmen are taught in small groups of five or six. They study alone or with buddies, or in small groups, progressing at their own pace with a variety of learning materials, including workbooks and self-instruction materials. We have observed an eagerness among these young men for what we call "hands-on" training. If they hate arithmetic books, they may love adding machines. One of our most successful experiments has been asking each student as soon as he arrives to write a letter home on an electric typewriter. Most students have never seen such a machine before, and they tackle their new tasks with enthusiasm.

We have learned never to call their teachers "teachers." That term only stirs up the Corpsmen's deep negativism toward schools. Instead, we call them "tutor-counselors," and that is what they really are. Tutor-counselors are young and knowledgable about the backgrounds of students. They are accessible models of success with whom the boys can identify, and often the first friends they ever had in the outer world of the middle class.

If this description of what we do sounds as though we have found all the right keys, don't let me mislead you. We are only beginning to learn. We are not sure of where our education will lead us any more than we are sure of where theirs will lead them. But as one Job Corpsman wrote, "I truly think that it was the best mistake I have made—joining, that is."

One mistake we made at the outset was in thinking that running a Job Corps center was chiefly an educational task. We soon found out that our main adversary was hostility, not ignorance. The hostility of these young men is directed not only at school but at nearly every other established segment of our middle-class society, from which they feel excluded. At the same time, we have learned to be impressed at their determination to make the most of their Job Corps experience, which they openly describe as perhaps their last chance.

The boys seem to be torn by continuing struggle between their hostility and their positive determination. This struggle recently erupted in what citizens of New Bedford, Massachusetts, call a riot, although it was no such thing. Last May 21, word spread through the center that some local boys had attacked a number of Corpsmen in town. The Rodman Center and New Bedford had not always been comfortable with each other during their several months of living together. The Corpsmen felt the residents of this old New England town were cold and unfriendly. The townspeople had the impression that most Corpsmen had police records and were rowdies. Understandably, teenage boys of New Bedford were less than delighted at the import of hundreds of competitors for the attentions of their girl friends. In fact, one morning the sun rose to light a freshly-painted message on the side of an old brick building. It said, "War On The Job Corps."

This mutual mistrust, however, lay dormant until the rumor of May 21 swept through the camp. At 11:15 that night, about forty Rodman students, some with passes and some unauthorized, marched out of the center, down Rodney French Boulevard toward the center of town. Immediately, about twenty-five staff members left the center and overtook them. There in the middle of the boulevard, the staff members urged and cajoled the students to consider the consequences of their loss of temper. Meanwhile, alarmed residents along the boulevard called the police who cordoned off the area. The staff members, aided by a number of thoughtful students, persuaded the group to return to Rodman. The incident was over.

But today, weeks later, it is still talked about as the "Rodman riot." Soon afterward, a member of the city council, sensed an emotional local issue and introduced a resolution asking President Johnson to remove the Job Corps from Rodman. Although we knew that many councilmen had serious misgivings, we were not wholly prepared for the result: the resolution passed unanimously. From the beginning, we greatly underestimated the importance of good community relations in running a successful Job Corps center.

Of course the Job Corps Center has not been closed, we trust it will not be, and we are hard at work to help the camp and the town understand each other better. It is not an easy task, but it surely is an educational one. Believe me, it takes a fearful amount of management time, and we are learning things about public relations with which few public relations men at IBM ever expected to find themselves concerned.

Perhaps one solution to this local problem in the War on Poverty is as predictable as one national solution I cited a few minutes ago. Perhaps the city fathers of New Bedford, including its leading businessmen, will understand their relationship to Rodman to the degree that we find ways of involving them in its problems.

Scratch almost any New Bedford critic of Rodman and you'll probably hear him say what national critics of the Job Corps almost always say. The cost of trying to save a member of the Job Corps from failure comes too high. Indeed, it is high. Estimates of the cost of training a Job Corpsman for employment run up to $11,250 for a full two-year stint. The Job Corps says it is trying to reduce that average cost to $7,765. Even at that, the government would be spending more than the estimated budget for an undergraduate's first two years here at the University of Chicago. That's quite a bill for teaching a kid who may still be learning his ABC's.

Well, there are some standard, obvious replies. An alternative cost for many a boy may be to maintain him in jail, after he is fully convinced that society and its laws leave no place for him. That cost is $2,450 a year, for Heaven knows how many years. Another possible alternative is public welfare. This cost skyrockets in proportion to the young man's virility, and then what does society do about *his* children?

On the other hand, the cost of keeping a Job Corpsman includes certain overdue obligations that society has never met. It includes the price of physical neglect. More than one-third of Corpsmen are fitted with eye glasses they should have had long ago. It includes the cost of an average of six dental fillings per youngster. And it includes the cost of heaping upon them a quantity of food that has produced an average gain in weight of ten pounds per youngster. It includes all the costs of maintaining these Corpsmen 24-hours-a-day, seven-days-a-week.

For those who like all their answers in dollars and cents, there is the promise that a successful Job Corpsman will eventually repay his government's investment through income taxes. Someone has figured out that if a Corpsman graduates into a job at the extremely modest pay of $1.68 an hour—*and never gets a raise in pay for the rest of his career*—he will repay the $11,000 investment by the taxes he pays during his working life.

If these fiscal arguments don't excite you, I must admit that I don't find them the most persuasive ones myself. As one interested citizen, I am more interested in finding ways to end this problem forever than in what it costs to enlarge the tax-paying potential of the 500 students in our center. I am more interested in finding and cultivating the roots of human potential than in a cost-accounting approach to misery. For all the talk of saddling future generations with today's public debt, my concerns lie with saving future generations from the continuing price of social neglect, human as well as fiscal, perpetuated by previous generations, including my own.

There is yet another thing that concerns me. As an educational publisher, I have observed that new approaches to education for a changing world do not come easily to the mammoth establishment of our middle-class-dominated educational world.   The pressure for change usually comes from somewhere out in left field, and the location of left field keeps changing.   Right now, left field is the War on Poverty. The so-called culturally deprived child sits in the eye of a hurricane that is shaking the foundations of education.   For example, Project Headstart has already shaken loose an old, largely, unquestioned, but indefensible notion that six years old is the earliest age at which formal learning should begin.   For many years hence, nursery schools for middle-class children will undergo change in reaction to new research among nursery-age children who happen to live in the ghetto.

Similarly, if we, involved in the Job Corps, can indeed construct a method of successful education for teenagers with whom established methods have failed, we will have helped make a fundamental contribution with implications far beyond the Job Corps.   The eventual beneficiaries of our experience may be the sons and daughters of the middle class far more than of the poor.   We will have learned something important about what makes youngsters want to learn.   That will be a contribution in which I, for one, will be proud to have taken part, not only as one trained as a social scientist, and one who has lived his professional life on the rim of public education, but as a businessman.

It seems to me also that such a contribution to improving the quality of American life is a fit one for a corporation which may be sustained by the making of profit, but whose motives should and do include an obligation to earn its place as one of America's basic institutions.

Section VI-4

A Twenty-first Century Look At Higher Education

ALVIN C. EURICH

Striking as the increase in college enrollments has been up to the present, we are now poised on the brink of an expansion far, far greater than that of the past forty years. If we were to continue operating our colleges along conventional lines, we would need to construct more college facilities in the next fifteen years than we have built in all our history. Take Kansas as an example: from 1950–60 the number of college-age youth actually decreased. But during this period college and university enrollments increased about fifty percent. By 1980, on the basis of birth records, the number of youngsters will not decline; on the contrary, it will almost double. Thus college enrollments are likely to soar, conservatively speaking, from 250 to 300 percent.

Such explosive growth plagues us with a variety of critical problems. We obviously cannot accommodate such numbers within the conventional framework of our educational system. We are virtually forced to consider how we can use available resources more effectively and efficiently.

All our plans, moreover, must be made with the awareness that students entering college now will be in the prime of their lives when we move into the twenty-first century. The world will then be quite a different place. The changes of the next forty years, we are told, will equal in significance those of the last 400. They will affect higher education profoundly. We must be prepared to meet them intelligently.

Let us assume that the next thirty-seven years have become history. It is now 2000 A.D. From this vantage point, let us cast a glance at the development of higher education in the United States during the twentieth century.

From *Current Issues in Higher Education*, 1963, the Association for Higher Education. Reprinted by permission of the Association for Higher Education.

I am happy to report that we were able to avoid a Third World War during the twentieth century. Several times in the 1960's we came precariously close to a nuclear holocaust which could have wiped out all mankind. Russia and the United States were then the two major world powers. At one point, it is true, an atomic bomb was accidentally detonated, but fortunately the explosion occurred in the uninhabited Alaskan polar region. The crater it formed is now a major tourist attraction, and heavily laden helicopters hover over the many miles of its base, showing sightseers the geological wonders of the area.

Our population has expanded far beyond the estimates of forty years ago, when we numbered only 186 million souls. Today we are approaching 350 million and our posthigh school enrollment in institutions of learning is almost twenty-five million.

During the first half of the twentieth century, we established universal elementary and secondary education. During the second half we made higher education universal through the junior college. In the process we restructured our educational system. Many of our former liberal arts colleges were unable, for one reason or another, to solve their financial problems. Since their facilities were still urgently needed, local communities transformed them into junior colleges. The result is that a junior college is now available for every young man and woman within commuting distance from home.

During the quarter century following World War II, teachers colleges disappeared completely from the American scene. Their place has been taken by multipurpose institutions which, together with the strong liberal arts colleges and the universities, have discontinued the first two years, since these now come almost wholly within the province of the junior colleges. The transition took place with surprising smoothness. Once football, basketball, and other sports became completely professionalized and the social fraternities and sororities vanished from the scene, the need for the first two years of college abruptly ceased.

These new institutions now admit qualified graduates from the junior colleges and offer three-year programs culminating in the master's degree. During the last quarter of the century, there were heated debates at meetings of the Association of American Colleges on the question of whether the baccalaureate degree should be granted at the end of junior college work. The traditionalists won; the junior colleges continued to award the associate of arts or associate of science degree, while the baccalaureate of arts or science fell into disuse because students going beyond junior college pursued a program leading directly to the master's degree or a professional degree.

The largest universities, with their clusters of professional and graduate schools and research institutions, have now become virtually self-contained cities. Some, like New York University, enroll more than 200,000 students. We continue to wonder whether these institutions are getting too big.

During the past half century, the content of education at all levels was profoundly strengthened in two ways: (1) we became much clearer about the objectives of education, and (2) leading university scholars from various disciplines became sufficiently alarmed about our soft education that they were forced to produce, in cooperation with school teachers and administrators, new curricula extending from the kindergarten through the graduate and professional schools.

On the matter of objectives, our economy of abundance and our better system of distributing goods have made us less concerned with the strictly professional or vocational aims of education. We have overcome the temptation, prevalent during the 1950's and 60's, to judge the value of a college degree by the additional earning power it confers. We now minimize the time spent on acquiring practical skills and factual knowledge. We no longer seek to produce the person crammed full of knowledge. We now place much more emphasis on developing wisdom, on leading our young people to higher levels of maturity in dealing with the ideas that have made a difference in the progress of civilization. We also concentrate on instilling such ideals as those that help to make leisure time more satisfying than in the early days of the affluent society, when men were consumed to the point of boredom with strictly materialistic pleasures. We now recognize the truth expressed by Mark Van Doren fifty years ago: "Freedom to use the mind is the greatest happiness."

As part of this change, we have seen the resurgence of philosophy as a key academic discipline. Like other subjects in the curriculum it has had its ups and downs. During the early part of the last century it lost its vitality and degenerated into a study of philosophical systems and the microscopic analysis of language. After several decades, however, antiquarianism and logical positivism seemed equally sterile. No great philosophers emerged; the sciences dominated the college and university campuses.

Those were the days when physicists, chemists, biologists, and aeronautical engineers with a bent for research could get almost any amount of money to advance their projects. As a result, we added to our knowledge so rapidly that the accumulation shocked us into a realization that we were entirely aimless in our endeavors. For example, our geneticists and biochemists gave us the necessary knowledge and techniques to mold human beings to our specifications. We can now direct the evolution of mankind; it need no longer be left to chance.

With the genetic possibilities available, however, we found that we were completely devoid of ideas concerning the kinds of men we wanted to create and the nature of the society we aspired to build. Our desire for two automobiles, a boat on a trailer, a helicopter, and a twenty-hour work week had long ago been satisfied. We had come to the point where we recognized the urgency of freeing some outstanding scholars to help shape new directions for mankind. Some of our ablest minds were encouraged with fellowships and grants to follow up promising leads. The consequence is that exciting ideas are beginning to emerge from our explorations, and at least a dozen brilliant young philosophers are cutting across subject matter disciplines and showing signs of developing a new synthesis of knowledge.

The most prominent difference between today's colleges and those fifty years ago, however, is not in the curriculum, but in the use of learning resources. We have introduced devices and techniques which were not even thought of prior to the mid-twentieth century. Curriculum has always been the subject of educational debate and reform. But the learning resources which our students now take for granted were developed for the first time in the 1950's and 60's. These enabled us to fulfill the psychologists' dreams of making the best teaching available to all students, and of truly adapting instruction to individual rates of learning.

Take television, for example. Its use as an educational medium in colleges developed steadily after it was introduced in the 1950's. But educators were typically slow to see that this revolutionary device, which in a decade had transformed the living habits of a nation, would inevitably have just as great an impact upon our schools and colleges. It was only in the 1960's that the use of television soared, as demonstration after demonstration rammed home the fact that televised instruction was educationally effective and economically feasible. As early as 1962, 30,000 courses were being given over television in the United States. But not until recently have colleges recognized that television has made the standard lecture obsolete and the conventional laboratory demonstration inadequate and costly.

One of the reasons that television made slow progress at first was the fear that the availability of outstanding lecturers on television would somehow displace the classroom teacher and make the individual college obsolete. In this regard, the objections were essentially the same as those raised at Oxford and Cambridge in the latter part of the nineteenth century. When the "university lectures" were proposed, the Oxbridge dons predicted that the innovation would reduce the separate colleges to mere appendages. What actually happened was that the individual colleges became more important when they were relieved of the responsibility for lecturing. They could devote themselves to probing the student's mind and spirit individually or in small groups. And the students benefited from the opportunity to hear the very best lecturers in each field.

Television has had a similar effect. The first glimmer of this came in 1958–59 when a basic college physics course was offered over a national network under the direction of Professor Harvey B. White of the University of California. During the year, seven Nobel prize winners and other distinguished scientists helped to teach the course. They represented an array of talent that no single university could possibly have offered its students. Other courses in chemistry, biology, government, economics, and the humanities followed in rapid succession, first on national networks and then, with the success of Telstar, across national boundaries.

Now, fortunately, exemplary lectures by some of the greatest scholars of the world on the basic substance of their fields are available on electronic tapes. Because it was not until the middle of the 1960's that we began systematically to record the leading scholars of the world, we missed many great men who were alive in this period. Think how effective our teaching could be today if we had available taped lectures by such figures as Socrates, Leonardo da Vinci, William Harvey, Sir Francis Bacon, Sir Thomas More, John Milton, and Johann Wolfgang von Goethe.

The television courses that are now available are used on virtually every campus in the country. Students everywhere are privileged to listen to the great men who advanced our culture in every field of learning. We have made incalculable progress since the days when our youngest college students were taught almost entirely by academic novices.

After the students have mastered the basic materials through these taped lectures, they can meet with senior faculty members who, having been spared the drudgery of repeating over and over the basic substance of their fields, are eager to work with students on advanced topics. Moreover, the students themselves feel that they have a firmer grasp of the subject matter, because they have studied the taped lectures at their own rate, reviewing them on kinescopes as needed. In addition, the superb organization and planning which has gone into each lesson has had its effect, and the consequence is better teaching and easier learning.

Television has, in short, provided us with the technology we needed to build a genuine system of mass education—one in which each student has an equal opportunity to learn, no matter where his college is located or what its resources are.

But we have also made enormous strides at the other end of the spectrum, in teaching individual students. Here the most exciting developments have been in independent study, honors work, programed learning, and language laboratories. Independent study has had a curious history. Although we adopted the English college and the German university, we failed to import a basic ingredient of both, namely, their emphasis on independent work in higher education. Instead, we projected into the colleges and universities the elementary and secondary school notions of compulsory class attendance. It took us an unconscionably long time to recognize that independent study was essential to a maturing mind.

Programed learning, so common today, was hardly known fifty years ago. This scheme of instruction has developed into one of the most effective resources for adjusting instruction to the individual student's rate of learning. Yet as early as 1962, after experiments at Harvard, Hamilton College, and numerous secondary schools throughout the nation, it was clearly demonstrated that students consistently learned about twice as fast with programed materials as they did from conventional texts and lectures.

Here the resistance was different from that which confronted television. Educators knew what television was, but they refused to grasp its pedagogical implications. In the case of programed learning, on the other hand, most college teachers and administrators didn't even know what the new technique was—except that, largely because of its unfortunate linkage with teaching machines, they didn't like it.

As we can now see so clearly, television and programed learning, both introduced into education in the 1950's, defined the limits of a spectrum of instructional resources. Television provided the medium for mass instruction; programed learning provided the utlimate in individualized instruction. Between these two, and other devices and procedures such as language laboratories and independent study, a new diversity was added to the educator's repertoire. Together, these techniques enabled us to break through the ancient framework which used to bind college education into a rigid pattern. No longer do we have to divide the day into fixed fifty-minute periods, no longer do we measure a student's progress by the number of credit hours he has "banked," no longer do we march all students along through the same series of lectures and classes.

Today, flexibility and adjustment to individual differences are axiomatic. Each student progresses at his own rate. He studies much of the time on his own, or with fellow students, but always with instant access to the complete range of learning resources: taped lectures, programed course materials, language tapes, bibliographies, and original documents on microfilm.

As a result of this independent work by the students, a professor nowadays rarely lectures to a group of thirty or forty students, as he used to half a century ago. Rather, the professor meets with students individually or in small groups after they have mastered a given block of knowledge through the use of diverse learning resources. We now insist upon complete mastery rather than partial learning of the basic substance in a field. In other words, all students learn the same quantum of a subject; they vary only in the time it takes them to acquire it.

Our professors now do only what no text or other learning resource can ever accomplish: they develop the mind of the individual students through intimate give and take based on sound knowledge and understanding. Under this system the three-year colleges, far from becoming obsolete, have rediscovered their primary function in education. Instead of pretending to be microcosms of all human knowledge, the individual colleges now lean heavily on the use of learning resources to provide the base of their instructional programs. But this firm foundation enables them to build real understanding and creativity in their students through their achievements in the higher reaches of teaching. Never before have they had such an opportunity.

Even more drastic are the changes in our libraries. As a result of research carried on, not only in the United States but also in Japan, India, Belgium, Holland, France, and England, we have revolutionized the techniques of storing and transmitting information. Most of our actual documents are now reduced to pin-point size and stored on film in a miniature library. If we had not developed such procedures, some of our libraries would now be trying to store 100 million or more volumes. Instead, we have developed the National Research Library which, as John D. Kemeny of the Dartmouth Mathematics Department predicted some years ago, has reached more than 300 million volumes in miniaturized form. The information in these volumes is retrievable by computer systems through a multichannel cable. We can instantly transmit information from these volumes to reading units on campuses throughout the country. The space which was previously used for storing books has been freed by our new information retrieval system for faculty study, reading rooms, and independent study.

Even the architecture of our campuses reflects the innovations in teaching techniques. For the lectures over television, students listen to portable television sets in their own dormitory rooms. These lectures are generally followed by small group and individual discussions. The programed learning laboratories are open twenty-four hours every day, and the student may study whenever he desires to do so.

Along with the clarification of objectives, the upgrading and updating of the curriculum, the use of a variety of devices and procedures for learning, and our new library system, we have also vastly improved the process by which students are admitted to the institution, and the way in which they progress through the course of study. It is amusing now to read the hundreds of conference reports issued during the middle decades of the twentieth century dealing with the required courses in four years of liberal education. Like medieval theologians debating the number of souls which could be conveniently packed into a given corner of hell, educators of the 1950's seemed to have discussed endlessly the question of whether this or that course, in this or that order, should be included in the four-year program. They put things in, they took things out, they substituted one course for another.

Little progress was made, however, until educators began asking more fundamental questions. Why must the liberal arts curriculum fit into exactly four years? If students learn at different rates of speed, couldn't some of them achieve the goal in three years or two, while others worked at it for five or six? Would it not be wise to tell the student what is expected of him, what the end result of his liberal education should be—what kind of mastery he needs to earn his degree—and then let the student decide, in the light of his own personality, interests, and abilities, how he can best make use of the university's resources to achieve that mastery? To do this, of course, the colleges had to define more precisely the goals they were striving for in the liberal education of students. Whereas formerly the administration could lean heavily on the accumulation of credit hours as evidence that the student was acquiring an education, the new system required the colleges to specify what they were aiming for and then to devise measures or adequate observations of achievement.

The result, however, was exhilarating for students and faculty alike. They were freed from the four-year plague of course credits. Since the federal government increasingly financed the education of needy students, colleges no longer had to keep bright, young people on the campus for four years, just to collect the tuition.

The system which emerged was pioneered in California. Virtually all California students went from high school to a junior college. After an average of two years at such an institution, the top one-third of the students, plus some who entered advanced vocational programs, went on to college. From college, approximately the top twelve percent advanced to the university—though even at this rate, university enrollments grew enormously.

The important point was that students progressed through this system with complete flexibility. The principles of early admission, and admission with advanced standing, which did so much to facilitate the transition from high school to college fifty years ago, were applied to the transition from college to graduate work. Standard measures of achievement in each basic subject were worked out. But students could meet these standards at their own rate of learning, and in a variety of ways. Thus it was the criteria of achievement, rather than the students, which were standardized.

Fifty years ago educators spent their time trying to determine how all students could be given basically the same course of instruction in the same amount of time. The results were disappointing: students emerged from the standard program with very different levels of competence and mastery. Now we have a more fruitful approach. We have concentrated on defining with some precision what we want students to know and to be able to do at the end of their liberal education. Then we have provided as many different paths to that goal as the diverse talents and interests of the students demand. The results have been extraordinary. Today it is unusual for any two students to take the same sequence of courses with the same balance of lecture, small group discussion, and independent study. The "mix" is determined for each student on the basis of his needs and capacities. But at the end of the road, we can ascertain with some accuracy that each student has indeed achieved a comparable degree of true liberal learning.

As we look back over the progress of higher education in recent decades, we may wonder exactly when the major changes began to develop. Colleges and universities in the mid-twentieth century, we may recall, were run pretty much the way they had been run for the past hundred years. As Professor Jerrold R. Zacharias of the Massachusetts Institute of Technology expressed it in the 1950's, only about two percent of the total educational expenditures in those days was used for books, films, laboratory equipment, and other means of communicating "substance that did not come directly through the teacher's larynx."

When did the great transformation begin? When did our colleges and universities begin catching up with the technological revolution which had transformed the world but left the campus untouched? When did the colleges begin to use the new techniques of communication and organization, to which they had contributed so much, to improve their own operations?

It is difficult to fix an exact date for the beginning of this movement. But I believe an unquestionable turning point occurred in the mid-fifties and sixties. First, after 1957, we were spurred by Sputnik. Then in the years 1964–66 the colleges felt most sharply the upsurge in the demand for higher education. Educators had known quite well that the college population was likely to double, and perhaps treble, during the sixties. In fact, due to demographic factors, the most acute increases came in the mid-sixties.

It was this event, I think, which galvanized the leading colleges into action. They could see that the conventional methods of collegiate instruction were inadequate to meet the enormous challenge. The students were ready, willing, and able to absorb the best education the colleges could offer. It would have been disgraceful for the institutions of higher education to refuse to find a way to meet their needs.

Of course, many institutions failed to rise at once to the challenge. Some of the most prominent universities simply announced that they could not handle more students than they already had enrolled, and refused to consider ways of increasing their student bodies. This attitude could not last, of course. It collapsed when other institutions, more sensitive to their own responsibilities and the nation's needs, pioneered in designing improved instructional methods which could provide a first-rate education for more students. Through such relatively simple reforms as year-round operation, control over proliferating courses, and better use of independent study, many colleges found they could enroll up to one-third more students without any significant increase in instructional costs.

But these reforms are merely the beginning. Changes will come more rapidly and more sweepingly—of necessity—in the early decades of the twenty-first century; changes so great, so fantastic, that the imagination can barely keep pace.

So we have come to the end of our fantasy. We are back in the year 1963. Whether we are now in the wagon wheel, the steam engine, or the automobile phase of higher education, I am not sure. But I am sure that we will need to progress through the airplane, jet, and satellite stages.

Each of us can make his own projections—they will differ widely, of course—but the point is, we must make them. The old ideas will no longer do.

The address of Mr. Eurich was given at the annual meeting of the Association of American Colleges held in January 1963. AHE acknowledges with thanks the cooperation of AAC.

POSTLOGUE

Postlogue

Campus Conflict and Confluence

LEWIS B. MAYHEW
Stanford University

A sampling of newspaper articles reflects the present American college situation and indicates some answers that higher education has made to questions of change.

> The use of marijuana on college campuses is causing grave concern . . .
>
> The University of Oregon faculty refused to accept a legislative offer of $1000 awards for excellent teaching on the ground that the awards constituted legislative interference with academic affairs.
>
> Students in many colleges carried signs reading "I am a human being; do not fold, bend or mutilate."
>
> Yale students have created a magazine called *Political* which aims to present "the most important national issues each month by the men who make them."
>
> The Rutgers faculty supported the right of one its members to welcome a Viet Cong victory. This was in the face of demands from political candidates that the professor should be fired.
>
> At Yale some students will be allowed to help judge faculty members when such matters as tenure and promotion are at stake.
>
> The University of Chicago has mounted a three year campaign to acquire $160,000,000 in gifts.
>
> The University of California expects to have an enrollment of 300,000 students by the year 2000.
>
> Research has actually harmed university education in the sciences by draining off teachers into full-time research activities.
>
> In California, possessor of perhaps the largest and most complex system of education in the country, only three percent of the age group 20–24 received the bachelor's degree as compared with $3\frac{1}{2}$ percent for the rest of the country.
>
> Nine Negro students are suing the institution which expelled them.

457

Students at Berkeley have attempted to form a union which can engage in collective bargaining with the university.

University professors have become mercenaries in quest of research dollars thus shifting the focus of loyalty from the campus to the funding agency.

John Gardner criticizes "the crassest opportunism, job hopping, and wheeling and dealing among young college faculty members."

The University of Pittsburgh almost went under in a valiant quest for excellence.

These crosscurrents, conflicts, and tensions have been inherent in the nature of higher education and are of several kinds. First are those inherent in the nature of the university in western civilization or in the nature of man himself. Faculty and administration are in continuous conflict over financial support, governance of the institution, curriculums, and academic freedom. This is nothing new. Although actual controversy between administrators and professors in medieval universities was rare, it was chiefly because the idea of authority was so well accepted. When professors did exercise freedom, as when Abelard defied authority to use logic in studying theology, the same charges and countercharges were made as were heard in the struggle between faculty and administration at St. John's University. In the 1840's Charles Kraitser remarked that "The Board of Visitors . . . were gentlemen whom it was hard to please. They had kicked Dr. Blaetterman out because he had whipped his wife, and they have kicked me out because I have been whipped by my wife. What did they really want?"[1]

Faculty members are preoccupied with their own subjects, often to the exclusion of family problems, social amenities, even their own personal well-being, and are in a very real sense conservative, for they value most highly the small segment of culture which they have mastered. Although individual professors may exhibit either liberal or conservative tendencies in social, political, economic, or even personal conduct, on educational matters they are inclined to the status quo. Faculty views about academic innovation are reflected in the final speech of the retiring professor who remarked that he had seen many changes in his forty years as teacher and had been against all of them. W. H. Cowley identifies thirteen significant decisions regarding higher education in America and finds clear faculty initiative in one, and com-

---

[1]Frederick Rudolph, *The American College and University*, (New York: Alfred A. Knopf, 1962), page 157.

bined faculty-student initiative in another; eleven were engineered by administration, outside groups, or students, or were sheer accidents.[2]

Compared to faculty, administrators are both liberal and dynamic. General education as a reform movement is most closely associated with Hutchins, Carman, McGrath, Hanna, and Woods—all administrators. The trimester seems to have been sparked by Litchfield at Pittsburgh, cooperative work-study by a dean of engineering and a president, and tutorial study by a president at Swarthmore. It is the president and his staff who constantly search for fresh ideas and innovations. It is the president who challenges the faculty to make time-consuming self-studies, who imports the educational consultant, who circulates conference reports emphasizing educational reform, and who suggests that faculty financial well-being and educational reform are interrelated. Thus a conservative faculty and a dynamic administration exist in a perpetual state of tension, very likely conflict.

Then there are further tensions which stem from the many subcultures which share a broader, but ill-defined, academic culture. Martin Trow suggests that there are at least four student subcultures, each with discrete values and aspirations. The *academic* group values courses, ideas, and scholarship. The *vocational* group exchanges effort for specific job preparation and job placement. The *play* subculture views life in college as a pleasant interlude before adulthood. The *Bohemians* use the college setting to protest prevailing social values. To these must be added the ingredients of several faculty subcultures. Burton Clark has elaborated the concept of locals and cosmopolitans to include four different types. The locals include the teacher who is committed to students, the campus, and general education, and the demonstrator who is perhaps a local physician or dentist, and who is frequently in demand by local groups as a speaker. The cosmopolitans include the scholar-researcher who cares little for the local scene and gains his satisfaction from his discipline, and the consultant who has and values a broad national reputation and high mobility.[3]

These eight subcultures exist to some extent on all campuses and present almost limitless possibilities for conflict. For example, consider the tensions which would arise on campus where the teacher subculture predominates on the faculty, with a student body well represented by

---

[2]W. H. Cowley, "Critical Decisions in American Higher Education," G. K. Smith, *Current Issues in Higher Education 1963*, (Washington: Association for Higher Education, 1963), page 13.

[3]Burton R. Clark, *"Faculty Culture," The Study of Campus Culture* (Boulder: Western Interstate Commission for Higher Education, 1963).

Bohemians. John Bushnell has likened student subcultures to groups of American residents in foreign lands whose members will sample the local food and market places, but will regain their security by returning to the enclave at night. Students similarly may sample the wares of the faculty and purchase a few of their ideas, but in the end return to the more comfortable values of other students. Only a few go native and become the future graduate students and professors.[4]

The question whether the purpose of higher education is cultural or utilitarian is another long-time dilemma. In medieval universities the issue apparently was whether to prepare officials for the growing centralized, secular states or to pursue knowledge for its own sake through classical Greek education. Within the American tradition the issue has been faced and resolved in different ways at different times. In the late 19th century the utilitarian-research point of view seemed to be dominant in the concept of land-grant colleges and in the German-inspired research universities; but it was challenged by colleges and college professors, particularly along the eastern seaboard. Hugo Munsterberg reflects this reaction that the university technique misses the liberalizing culture which was the leading trait of Oxford and Cambridge.[5]

The dilemma continues. Is the liberal arts college dead or dying? Should the junior college emphasize technical-vocational or liberal education? Should undergraduate work be closely aligned with graduate and professional specialization? What should be the nature of graduate studies? The conflict is also reflected in the running dispute between the faculties of the arts and sciences and those of education. Russell Kirk represents the cultural point of view when he argues, "The study of literature . . . is the primary instrument of college education."[6] Those who suggest that junior colleges should offer courses in whatever a community wants represent the counterargument.

There is tension between town and gown. Medieval townspeople probably found university students as disturbing to their tranquiliity as do today's citizens. Some midwestern colleges still restrict student behavior, e.g., parietal rights, because interresidence visitation might offend the sensibilities of townspeople as well as parents. One can speculate that most of the cases involving academic freedom have arisen

---

[4]Marjorie Carpenter, ed., *The Larger Learning* (Dubuque: W. C. Brown & Co., 1962).

[5]Hugo Munsterberg, *American Patriotism and Other Social Studies*.

[6]Russell Kirk, *The Intemperate Professor* (Baton Rouge: Louisiana State University Press, 1966), page 52.

over the difference between lay and academic conceptions about the proper nature and function of the university.

And finally there is the generation gap. Older and younger people on the college campus exist in a somewhat artificial suspension and obviously do not always mix happily. The warning to trust no one over thirty involves the same element as in the story of a French youth and his father. In anger one day the young man knocked his father down and dragged him into the orchard. Finally the father cried, "Stop! I only dragged *my* father as far as that tree." Warfare and conflict between generations is thus nothing new.

But now there are new conflicts which compound the traditional conflicts. Chief among them is the student protest movement in its several manifestations. The intensity of the conflict is illustrated in the polemics of the student radicals and the counterstatements of college administrators. Perhaps a more thoughtful analysis is provided by one of the students at a 1964 joint faculty-student conference:

> Our position has grown paradoxically out of a new commitment to traditional liberal values. The traditional liberal accorded the individual the highest status in society; the individual is the end toward which all else was merely a means. But in serving this ideal, the traditional liberal invented the seeping bureaucracies he thought necessary to reach systematically every citizen. The problem of how to maintain the identity of the individual in this process, however, has become our inheritance.
>
> The civil rights movement has most clearly pointed up this problem. The American Negro represented one of the most passive elements in our society. One of the reasons for his plight was "organized America," which kept him in his place by the sheer weight of its structures. It became the task of the civil rights worker to convince Negroes that by standing up and asserting their individual identities, they could have some impact on their communities.
>
> On the campus, a student who understands this is outraged by the industrial values that have been applied to the educational process and by the bureaucratic models that the university follows in its organizational patterns. We find these things anathema to the realization of our objective, i.e., the resurrection of the individual. The structural-functional approach is itself irrelevant or, worse, destructive. It's this reliance on bureaucracy, the manipulation of structures, and the analysis of functions that makes some of us say, "Don't trust anyone over 30."
>
> Our solution is to inject into the system more human qualities, the most obvious of which is emotion. Perhaps the combination of the McCarthy era and the departmental approach to knowledge have sterilized the academic process. It has certainly made it irrelevant to

activist students because they have seen what a commitment to ideals can do for a group of people if it is fearlessly defended in front of the cameras of human conscience. No wonder the educational experience bugs us with its shallowness when professors aren't willing to lay their competence on the line publicly. Why load us with principles and ideals that obviously are less important than a $14,000.00 a year job and tenure?

The educational experience must be made relevant through a new solution. Just another new structure won't liberate the thinking of the student and open him up to the real learning experience—the one that goes on inside when we really try to examine ourselves. We need relationships with teachers who will help us face the big tough hang-ups: Am I a moral pacifist or a coward? Is abortion a humane answer to the problems of unwed motherhood, and what has the pill got to do with my answer? Who am I, where am I headed, and do I really want to go there? Is an academic career any less sterile than one in business? What are the things that make a society really worth fighting for?

No structure will ever open up the professor and the student to problems like these. Instead, we have to reshape the educational experience so the professor is more than a mechanism for dispensing information that enables the student to get the *symbols* of success.[7]

The militance of faculty demands for higher salaries, a greater voice in governance, and for more personal and professional autonomy is another new factor. For example in California, junior and state college faculties are pressing for the creation of academic senates to gain a direct voice in academic policy. At St. John's and Georgetown, the faculty openly revolted against the administration; some St. John's faculty, aided by the faculties of public institutions, justify and encourage strikes in the best trade-union tradition. Faculties seem to be saying that for too long they have been controlled by presidents and boards of trustees. For too long they have occupied a position of genteel poverty, trained to enjoy a rich cultural life but too poor to afford it. And they are now in a position to press their demands because of a relative shortage of teachers. The idea is growing that faculty members should control the curriculum, their own membership, conditions of student entrance and exit, and educational policy.

Historically American colleges have been located in small towns, partly because of the rural nature of society and partly through design, to keep youth near the farms as a family work force and to insulate

[7]Edward Joseph Shoben, Jr., *Students, Stress, and the College Experience* (Washington: National Student Association, 1966).

young people from cosmopolitan influences. But most colleges and universities are now large, complex institutions, located in equally complex urban areas. The spirit of the city has invaded the college. Why shouldn't college men and women live together when nonstudents of their age group do? How can the idea of the academic community survive when faculty members commute long distances? How can a church-related college cope with the pluralistic value systems of the city?

The tremendous emphasis upon research, starting with the World War II experience, poses another new problem for American higher education. The institutions capable of intensive research have become what might be called research universities, similar to the German model. Successful research brings more and more lucrative contracts and grants with attendant status. Young professors plot their careers to land in the research institutions. Liberal arts colleges try to approximate the research university in order to attract faculty. The criteria for professional advance, even in the hundreds of colleges where they were inappropriate, have become the doing and the publication of research, or at least the publication of something. The test of value for the professor has become the number of inches his bibliography contains, just as the worth of the student is his SAT score. This emphasis has caused two major distortions. It has tempted universities to orient their efforts in the directions dictated by available support, and it has fostered a reversal of priorities in America's colleges and universities, which after all must still attend to the education of college students.

By the end of the century the average American college will likely have twenty thousand students, and size itself is a problem. In this respect our colleges mirror the problems of our society. Size demands different and more impersonal forms of organization which often evoke a negative response in students and faculty alike.

> The salient characteristic of the multiversity is massive production of specialized excellence. The multiversity is actually not an educational center but a highly efficient industry engaged in producing skilled individuals to meet the immediate needs of business or government.[8]

To these currents and crosscurrents could be added many more: changing parental expectations, the notion of life-long education, shifts in curricular balance of power, and changing doctrines regarding

[8]Seymour M. Lipset & Sheldon S. Wolin, ed., *The Berkeley Student Revolt* (New York: Doubleday & Co., Inc., 1965).

student power. But further elaboration of the problems only belabors the obvious. All such problems are derivative from fundamental changes in society, and it is these changes which we must seek to understand.

Perhaps the first and most important of these is the existence of what Kenneth Boulding has called a developed society.[9] Although there is malfunctioning, our society has reached realization of many of its material goals. It is affluent, with a productive enterprise no longer needing the work energies of most of its citizens. Indeed, were it not for the dislocation of war and the defense spending occasioned by the national paranoia about Communism, unemployment would likely be at an all-time high. It is also a surfeited society in the sense that needs must be continually created to use the products of increasing automation. And it is a self-indulged society. The present college generation comes from families which tried to provide the incentives and conditions for healthy growth. This point is made by one of Berkeley's militant students:

> We grew up . . . believing that we lived in a great nation which had harnessed itself to the will of its people, providing them with education, the highest standard of living in the world, equality of opportunity, democracy, and the great middle class. We believed ours a humble nation that awkwardly and reluctantly shouldered the responsibilities a much more corrupt world forced upon her, but dispatched those responsibilities, once shouldered, with integrity, honor and the most peaceful intentions.
>
> We were, in short, the first post-depression, post-war generation to emerge into the world with all the assists of the mildly permissive (in some cases almost progressive) family culture of upper middle class America. If our parents sometimes despaired at our inability to understand the austerity and struggle that made possible their achievements, they were nonetheless pleased with the generally enthusiastic and alert products of their work.[10]

A vital implication of the developed society for education is the changed survival values which society must inculcate. In the past these have involved the various work skills. Now however, the old skills are becoming obsolete and the creative use of leisure and the ability to communicate are coming to the fore. And this is difficult for a generation

[9]Kenneth Boulding, *The Impact of the Social Sciences* (New Brunswick: Rutgers University Press, 1966).

[10]Paul Potter, "Student Discontent and Campus Reform," *Order and Freedom on the Campus* (Boulder: Western Interstate Commission for Higher Education, 1966).

that still venerates work. Complicating this is the sheer rate of change. This has received much comment, none more discerning than Charles Frankel's:

> We come at this point to perhaps the profoundest consequence of the present revolution in human affairs. It is the simple change in the tempo of change. For nothing cuts more quickly or deeply into a society's way of doing things than changes in its technology.
>
> This quickened tempo represents an unprecedented challenge to the human ability to adjust to social change. It took man roughly 475,000 years to come to the Industrial Revolution. We have arrived at the "Space Age" in a hundred and fifty years—and while we do not know where we go from here, we can be sure that we shall go there fast. Our expectations of change, and the ability of our nervous systems or our social systems to withstand the shock of change, have been formed in the long experience of the race. And this experience, even in the nineteenth century, has not prepared us for the pace of events that lie ahead.
>
> Such an extraordinary change in the basic tempo of human history means that new and deliberate efforts will be needed to control the processes of social change. As the last hundred years of Western history demonstrate, men can learn to change at a much quicker pace than before. But as these same years also suggest, there are limits, and it is difficult to imagine a day when it will not take time for men to adjust to new conditions, to learn new skills and habits, and to get over the nostalgia and resentments that come when old and familiar things are destroyed. There is a conservative in every man and, in the world into which we are moving, he is going to get a harder workout than ever before.
>
> Accordingly, if the things we cherish from the past are not going to be carelessly destroyed, and if the best possibilities of the future are going to be realized, it seems probable that we shall have to have institutions that have been deliberately set up to exercise long-range social forethought. A steady process of technological innovation, for example, can mean recurrent crises of technological unemployment. If this is not to happen, institutions will have to exist to envisage the new skills that will be needed, to undertake the continuing task of retraining workers, and to control the pace at which new techniques are introduced so that we can make a sensible adjustment to them. Given the pace and magnitude of the technical changes that are in prospect, we cannot count on the market place and the price system to do this job alone. Technological innovation means social changes; and there is no more reason to introduce such innovations, letting the chips fall where they may, than there is to introduce a new and powerful drug on

the market without first making it meet the test of medical examination and control.[11]

In any list of fundamental changes in society, the revolution in religious and moral values cannot be omitted. It is still too early to arrive at conclusions, but it is obvious that, in matters of morals, sexual standards, and basic beliefs, organized religion as we have known it is markedly less influential. Morality is becoming not religiously prescribed but humanly perceived.

We have examined the many changes, problems, and responses of higher education in the revolutionary decades since the Second World War. These will perplex the academy for a long time to come. The revolution in society is real. The conflicts on the campus are real. And in a sense the general directions which higher education must take are real and are perceived. But the actual future choices remain to be made and, as in all social insitutions, they must be made by men. Thus the future of higher education, like its past, lies in the moral and ethical nature of man. One hopes that we are fit for the task.

---

[11]Charles Frankel, "Third Great Revolution of Mankind," *Educational Issues in a Changing Society* (Detroit: Wayne State University Press, 1964).